Teacher learning in
language teaching

CAMBRIDGE LANGUAGE TEACHING LIBRARY
A series covering central issues in language teaching and learning, by authors
who have expert knowledge in their field.

Teacher Learning in Language Teaching

Edited by

*Donald Freeman and
Jack C. Richards*

CAMBRIDGE
UNIVERSITY PRESS

PUBLISHED BY THE PRESS SYNDICATE OF THE UNIVERSITY OF CAMBRIDGE
The Pitt Building, Trumpington Street, Cambridge, United Kingdom

CAMBRIDGE UNIVERSITY PRESS
The Edinburgh Building, Cambridge CB2 2RU, UK
40 West 20th Street, New York, NY 10011–4211, USA
10 Stamford Road, Oakleigh, VIC 3166, Australia
Ruiz de Alarcón 13, 28014 Madrid, Spain
Dock House, The Waterfront, Cape Town 8001, South Africa

http://www.cambridge.org

© Cambridge University Press 1996

First published 1996
3rd printing 2001

Printed in the United States of America

Typeset in Sabon

Library of Congress Cataloging-in-Publication Data

Teacher learning in language teaching / edited by Donald A. Freeman,
Jack C. Richards.
p. cm.
Includes index.
ISBN 0-521-551218. – ISBN 0-521-55907-3 (pbk.)
1. Language and languages – Study and teaching. 2. Language
teachers – Training of. I. Freeman, Donald A. II. Richards, Jack C.
P53.85.T4 1996
418'.007 – dc20   95–16773
                                                          CIP

A catalog record for this book is available from the British Library

ISBN 0 521 55121 8 Hardback
ISBN 0 521 55907 3 Paperback

Contents

Contents

Contributors

Francis Bailey, University of Massachusetts at Amherst, Massachusetts
Kathleen M. Bailey, Monterey Institute of International Studies, Monterey, California
Bret Bergthold, Monterey Institute of International Studies, Monterey, California
Belinda Braunstein, Monterey Institute of International Studies, Monterey, California
Anne Burns, Macquarie University, Sydney, Australia
Natasha Jagodzinski Fleischman, Monterey Institute of International Studies, Monterey, California
Donald Freeman, School for International Training, Brattleboro, Vermont
Karen Giblin, The British Council, Hong Kong
Gloria Gutiérrez Almarza, University of Salamanca, Avila, Spain
Belinda Ho, City University of Hong Kong, Hong Kong
Matthew P. Holbrook, Monterey Institute of International Studies, Monterey, California
Karen E. Johnson, The Pennsylvania State University, Pennsylvania
Anné Knezevic, School for International Training, Brattleboro, Vermont
Ora Kwo, University of Hong Kong, Hong Kong
Patrick R. Moran, School for International Training, Brattleboro, Vermont
Martha C. Pennington, City University of Hong Kong, Hong Kong
Jack C. Richards, University of Auckland, Auckland, New Zealand
Mary Scholl, School for International Training, Brattleboro, Vermont
Deborah Binnie Smith, Douglas College, British Columbia, Canada
Amy B. M. Tsui, University of Hong Kong, Hong Kong
Jennifer Tuman, Monterey Institute of International Studies, Monterey, California
Polly Ulichny, Boston College, Boston, Massachusetts
Ximena Waissbluth, Monterey Institute of International Studies, Monterey, California
Michael Wallace, Heriot-Watt University, Riccarton, Edinburgh, Scotland
Leslie J. Zambo, Monterey Institute of International Studies, Monterey, California

Preface

This book began as a conversation by the fireplace in the game room of the Ca D'Oro Hotel in São Paulo. It was July 1991 – midwinter in Brazil – and we were both speaking at the biannual convention of Brazil-TESOL. In our conversation, we recognized that the field of language teacher education had begun to change in important and dramatic ways. A shift was taking place in its rationale, as well as in the sources of theory, understanding, and justification on which the various practices of language teacher training and teacher development are based. People were beginning to ask questions about what language teachers know in order to do their work. How is language teaching learned? And what is the basis in experience and knowledge from which language teaching proceeds?

To a certain extent, these questions were – and are – the professional equivalent of asking about the emperor's new clothes. As we discuss in the Prologue, language teacher education is outgrowing the "unexamined stories" that have been the basis of its operation. It has been based either on plain assertion – "This works, believe me!" – or on disciplinary knowledge from beyond the realm of language teaching itself. In fact, as we talked, we began to identify a small and emerging community of researchers and practitioners who were working to understand teacher learning in language teaching as a phenomenon in its own right.

Thus this book came about. It is the first formal collection of research on teacher learning in the field of language teaching. The work of colleagues in Hong Kong, Australia, Canada, Spain, the United Kingdom, and the United States assembled here – all of it original research – establishes an initial knowledge base for this endeavor. Drawing from the broad traditions of qualitative, hermeneutic research, and the past three decades of work in teacher cognition, this volume is meant to start a conversation. We believe that the field of language teaching will be considerably enriched by deeper and closer examinations of how language teachers come to know what they know and do what they do in their work. The research in this book is an important and worthwhile step toward that end.

We would like to thank our fellow researchers from around the world who contributed to this effort, as well as our colleagues and graduate students at our respective institutions – the School for International Training and the City University of Hong Kong – for their support in bringing this project to fruition. The editorial staff at Cambridge University Press, in particular Mary Vaughn and Olive Collen, played an integral part in the project, and we thank them for their professionalism and support.

However, the real measure of a project like this one is the degree to which it fosters further inquiry, debate, and discussions, like the one at the Hotel Ca D'Oro that launched it. We trust that this book will provide a point of departure for interaction and dialogue among practitioners, researchers, and teacher educators around the world who share an interest in and a concern for the issues of teacher learning in language teaching and the need to better understand how language teachers do their work.

Donald Freeman
Jack C. Richards

Prologue: A look at uncritical stories

This book examines the process of learning to teach a second or foreign language, through descriptive accounts of the experiences of teachers. It contains sixteen original chapters which present different perspectives on how teachers and student teachers respond to teaching and to the experiences that are provided as part of their professional development. The book thus illuminates the nature of learning to teach second or foreign languages through research-based accounts of how teacher education programs and the experience of teaching shape the knowledge, thinking, and practice of language teachers. We do not limit "second language" to English, since we believe that learning to teach any language shares certain fundamental characteristics.

Like most work of this nature, this book makes an argument. Our point is a basic one, namely, that in order to better understand language teaching, we need to know more about language teachers: what they do, how they think, what they know, and how they learn. Specifically, we need to understand more about how language teachers conceive of what they do: what they know about language teaching, how they think about their classroom practice, and how that knowledge and those thinking processes are learned through formal teacher education and informal experience on the job. Although it should be common sense to examine the teacher as pivotal in the enterprise of teaching and learning, to date questions such as these have been largely overlooked both in general educational research and in the field of language teaching. Thus the argument we make is set against a backdrop that takes a great deal for granted in language teaching – about teachers, their learning, and the cognitive side of teaching.

Although people have been learning to teach languages for a long time, very little attention has been paid to understanding how those learning processes actually unfold or the knowledge and experience that underlie them. Most of what is done in language teaching and in language teacher education is based on conventions that define disciplinary knowledge from linguistics, psychology, and various other fields as the foundation for what language teachers should know and therefore what they should do in their classrooms (see Freeman 1994). These academic traditions spring more from the need to articulate a professional identity for language teachers than from any solid, inquiry-derived understand-

1

ing of what people need to know in order to teach languages or how they learn to do what they do as language teachers in classrooms.

The metaphor of uncritical stories

To cast this argument in terms of a metaphor, the professional literature of language teaching is stocked with stories of classroom methodologies, of good curricula, of effective practices, of worthwhile programs, and so on. While these stories provide informative and sometimes entertaining accounts of language teaching, they typically offer little examination of the characters or settings in which they transpire, or even a careful examination of how the accounts themselves are put together. Thus we operate in our various roles – as teachers, teacher educators, researchers, curriculum developers, policy makers, and so on – in a landscape of uncritical assumptions and myths about language teaching and language teachers. Although there have been calls to establish a research base in language teaching and language teacher education [Freeman (1989); Freeman and Richards (1993); Richards and Nunan (1990)], there has been little progress until the work reported here. The fifteen research studies that make up this book inaugurate a domain of educational inquiry into how people learn to teach languages. The outcomes of such research will serve several purposes. They can provide a more rational foundation for language teacher education and can help to shape more effective practices. Most important, however, these studies, and the others that will no doubt follow in this domain of research, can enlighten our understanding of language teachers' mental lives and how they conceive their classroom teaching.

An overview of the volume

In planning this book, we invited the contributors to provide research-based accounts of the phenomenon of teacher education, focusing on the process from the viewpoint of the teacher or student teacher rather than that of the teacher educator. We asked for chapters which captured, in as much detail as possible, the thinking processes, learning, problem solving, and theorizing in which people engage as they learn to teach, and which we believe are at the heart of the process of teacher education. In so doing, the contributors have provided multiple perspectives on the process of becoming second language teachers using a variety of data sources and approaches to data gathering and analysis (see Chapter 16). Teacher development is studied in a variety of contexts and locations—both pre-service and in-service and in second language as well as foreign language settings—and at different levels, using teachers' written or verbal accounts of their thinking, interviews, stimulated-recall, autobiographies, narratives, case studies, and observational data.

The chapters are grouped into three sections. In Section I, five chapters describe the beginning stages of teacher learning. In the first chapter, Kathleen Bailey and her colleagues describe their use of language learning autobiographies as a medium for examining their own professional development. They show how writing about past experiences of teaching and learning can serve as a powerful stimulus for further learning, revealing implicit assumptions and beliefs about the nature of teaching. In the second chapter, Karen Johnson examines the experience of a student teacher during a teaching practicum, and shows how this experience shapes the teacher's understanding of herself as a teacher, of second language teaching, and of the practicum itself. The gap between her vision of teaching and the practical realities of the classroom create a tension which interferes with her perception of what her students were learning. Gloria Gutiérrez Almarza, in Chapter 3, focuses on the relationship between student teachers' background knowledge and the knowledge they receive in teacher education courses, and explores how these sources of knowledge interact during teaching practice. Anné Knezevic and Mary Scholl describe their experience of collaborative teaching in a graduate Spanish course, and show how collaborative learning, teaching, and reflection shaped their understanding both of themselves and of teaching. In the last chapter in Section I, Amy Tsui provides a case study of how a teacher tried to introduce a process-based approach to the teaching of writing in her secondary school class. Tsui describes the problems created for the teacher and the decisions she made to resolve them, and shows how the teacher's understanding of the writing process itself changed as she took her students through a process-writing curriculum.

In Section II we focus on the practice of teaching itself, and on the cognitive processes that teachers engage in as they develop expertise in teaching. Patrick Moran examines the role that models of teaching can play in a self-directed process of learning to teach, and suggests that they serve as temporary learning strategies as teachers create their own personal teaching paradigms. Anne Burns examines six experienced Australian teachers who were confronted with a new teaching situation: teaching beginning adult learners. She examines how their preexisting beliefs affected their classroom practices and how subsequent changes in their beliefs occurred. She describes the interactions among institutionally derived beliefs, personal beliefs and thinking, and the process of instruction itself, and shows how top-down and bottom-up processes interact in a process she refers to as "intercontextuality." The third chapter in Section II, by Polly Ulichny, examines a segment of a lesson to clarify the contribution of context and personal interpretation in the teacher's resolution of a teaching incident. Her chapter shows how analysis of the discourse of teaching can provide insight into the teacher's cognitive processes. In the final chapter in this section, Deborah Binnie Smith examines a group of secondary ESL teachers in Canada, the instructional decisions they make, and the factors that influence those decisions, showing that teacher decisions are not isolated or arbitrary but part of a complex, interrelated process which is informed by beliefs, perceptions, experience, and context.

The chapters in the third section of the book examine the relationships between teacher education and teacher learning. In Chapter 10, Donald Freeman describes how a group of teachers in an in-service master's program integrate new ideas into their thinking about classroom practices. His analysis traces the ways in which the teachers reconstruct their classroom practice, using professional discourse to rename their experiences and thus to assign new or different meanings to their actions. In Chapter 11, Jack Richards, Belinda Ho, and Karen Giblin describe a group of teachers in an initial training course, and show how their individual conceptions of teaching lead to different concerns within lessons as well as to different perceptions of what makes those lessons more or less successful. They also demonstrate that what trainees learn from a program is not simply a mirror image of the program's content. In Chapter 12, Francis Bailey describes a collaborative approach to the methods class in a graduate teacher education program. He analyzes discourse sequences from interactions within small group discussions, which reveal how the instructor capitalizes on the heterogeneity of the group to achieve shared dialog among the participants. In the next chapter Michael Wallace examines the role of the professional project within teacher education and, by following the use of such projects in a B.Ed. program, raises questions concerning the nature of action research and its appropriateness within certain types of teacher education programs. Ora Kwo, in Chapter 14, describes how student teachers reflect on their learning in a methods course, and how they develop as teachers during their teaching practice. She attributes differences in the teachers' responses to the program to differences in cognitive styles. In the final chapter of this section, Martha Pennington describes a collaborative action research project for secondary school teachers, and focuses on how they respond to innovation in the teaching of writing, documenting the different responses of individual teachers to the program and exploring barriers to the acceptance of innovation.

In the closing chapter of the book, Donald Freeman reviews the field of teacher cognition and teacher learning within which the research in learning to teach second languages is emerging. He places this work in the context of general educational research, tracing its antecedents both in current educational research and in research in second language teaching. He then examines the central conceptual issues facing such work and the kinds of research methodologies exemplified in the studies reported in this book. The chapter provides both a review of the issues explored in the individual chapters as well as a framework for this new area of research.

Next steps

The chapters in this book thus represent a variety of perspectives on second and foreign language teacher development and education, and reflect different theoretical assumptions and research methodologies. However, they share a common point of view, namely, that understanding teachers' conceptualizations of teaching, their beliefs, thinking, and decision making can help us better understand the nature of language teacher education and hence better prepare us for our roles as teacher educators. Further, this collection contributes to a small but expanding research base in second language teacher learning, education, and professional development. The contributions exemplify not only the range of issues but also the useful variety of approaches to data collection in such research.

Seen as a whole, then, this book shows how second language teachers incorporate and make use of the theoretical ideas and theories as well as the pedagogical principles they acquire during professional education. This process of reconstruction, access, and use is not haphazard but is shaped by experience, previous knowledge, personal beliefs, and responses to both macro- and micro-level contextual factors in their classrooms, schools, and communities. Among the conclusions which emerge from material presented here are the following:

- In order to understand the nature of second language teacher education, we need to work with teachers to understand how they conceptualize and make use of their experiences, both in formal professional education and in their classrooms.
- The models of teaching and teaching methods we provide to teachers may be useful as heuristics, but they can serve only as temporary guideposts as teachers evolve their own goals and self-awareness.
- The professional discourse of second language teaching provides particular schemata and metaphors which influence how teachers describe and interpret their teaching experiences. This, in turn, shapes what they do.
- Learning to teach involves the development of theories and interpretive skills which enable teachers to resolve specific teaching incidents, creating their own working theories of teaching in the process.

– Teachers' previous learning, knowledge, and beliefs about teaching serve as a powerful determinant of teachers' perceptions and practices, and are often resistant to change.
– Individual teachers follow particular routes in the development of their pedagogical knowledge and skills, depending on their individual views of language, teaching, learning, and their changing understanding of themselves, their learners, their subject matter, and the nature of second language instructional tasks.

The research reported in this book marks a departure from the norm of uncritical stories. It provides a means by which to think more carefully and insightfully about language teaching and language teachers by taking the first steps to establish a research base for language teaching and language teacher education. As this research progresses, undoubtedly some of the conventions and stories that we live by in language teaching will be confirmed, while others will be challenged and some may be dethroned. Regardless, the new critical stance that is brought to bear by research that generates inquiry-derived understandings of teacher learning in language teaching will serve to strengthen both teaching and professional education in our field. It therefore stands to reason that teachers, and most importantly classroom language teachers, will ultimately benefit.

References

Freeman, D. 1989. Teacher training, development, and decision making: A model of teaching and related strategies for language teacher education. *TESOL Quarterly* 23(1): 27–45.

1994. Educational linguistics and the education of second language teachers. In J. Alatis (ed.), *Proceedings of the 1994 Georgetown University Roundtable on Languages and Linguistics*. Washington, D.C.: Georgetown University Press, pp. 180–196.

Freeman, D., and J. C. Richards. 1993. Conceptions of teaching and the education of second language teachers. *TESOL Quarterly* 17(2): 193–216.

Richards, J. C., and D. Nunan (eds.). 1990. *Second Language Teacher Education*. New York: Cambridge University Press.

Section I   Beginnings: Starting out in language teaching

The five chapters in this first section examine the beginning stages of teacher learning. Grouped under the rubric "starting out in teaching," these studies probe various dimensions of the initial experience of language teaching: how background and experience, teaching context, social relationships, and teaching methods all shape what and how teachers learn. The first three chapters address issues of pre-service teachers directly, while the last two examine experienced teachers who are starting out in new ways of teaching. Each chapter is about a beginning of some kind, and how that particular beginning contributes to shaping what and how teachers learn to teach languages.

The chapter by Kathleen Bailey and her colleagues looks at Dan Lortie's concept of the "apprenticeship of observation" and how the 13,000 hours spent as a student from grades 1 to 12 can influence new teachers' perceptions of teaching (Lortie 1975). In a collaborative research project that grew out of course work at the Monterey Institute of International Studies, Bailey and her students, who were starting out as language teachers, investigated how their apprenticeships of observation as language learners might contribute in shaping their ideas about classroom language teaching and learning. In view of the findings in general teacher education which Bailey cites in her introduction, that "teachers acquire seemingly indelible imprints of teaching from their own experiences as students and these imprints are tremendously difficult to shake" (Kennedy 1991: 7), Bailey's work is very important, both from a research standpoint and as a potential intervention in teacher education.

Karen Johnson's chapter reports on a study of a beginning teacher in her in-school practicum. Through Maja we can see the specific contextual demands and tensions faced by one teacher who is entering the classroom and school as a professional workplace. As Johnson observes, given the emphasis that is placed on teaching practice in schools as a key part of professional preparation, such closely textured examinations from the new teacher's perspective of what is learned – and unlearned – are crucial. The next chapter, by Gloria Gutiérrez Almarza, offers an excellent companion piece to Johnson's study. Gutiérrez Almarza reports on research she did with four novice teachers who were preparing to teach secondary school Spanish in London. Many similar themes emerge in both studies as these new teachers encounter the complex socio-cognitive demands of context: of managing students, creating pedagogy, putting subject matter into action, and participating in the life of their schools. Together these studies show us the raw interpretive nature of teachers' knowledge, as the initial intensity of context looms large in these first experiences of new teachers. Even as language teacher education puts its faith in the practicum to convey the "realities" of the classroom, we realize how little we know about the actual understandings that new teachers glean from such first experiences in front of the class.

In the chapter by Knezevic and Scholl, we see teachers' knowledge in action from a different perspective, that of the collaborative social relationship of team teaching. As graduate students with some previous teaching experience, Anné Knezevic and Mary Scholl chose to co-teach an adult conversational Spanish class. Their collaboration in effect forced them to make public to one another their individual thinking and experiences teaching the class. As they planned together, taught together, and evaluated their work together, and subsequently as they wrote about the process, they were pushed to articulate their own perceptions at every step along the way. It is relatively rare to find such a candid account of collaborative work, one which sheds light on the thinking and learning of the participants and thus highlights, by contrast, the extremes of isolation and autonomy in which most teachers work.

In the last chapter in this section, Amy Tsui writes about a study she did of one teacher's experience in introducing the new pedagogy of process writing to her secondary school classroom in Hong Kong. Tsui's research takes us into the complexities of initiating change in classroom practice. We see that any change in teaching must fit within an already crowded and complex web of meanings and values in a given classroom and school setting. Through the experience of the teacher, Julie, we revisit many of the issues raised in the preceding chapters in this section: how experience as a student, the demands of schools as social contexts, and the relative lack of support for new ventures complicate starting out in teaching.

Together the five chapters in the section lay out many of the key parameters in starting out in teaching. Issues of how expectations of content shape the initial experience of schools as social-cognitive contexts, the presence or absence of sustained interaction with like-minded colleagues, and the relative "fit" of teaching methods each contribute to shaping teacher learning.

Suggestions for further reading

The following books and articles are suggested as further reading on the key topics in this section.

On the apprenticeship of observation
Kennedy, M. 1991. *An Agenda for Research on Teacher Learning.* East Lansing, Mich.: National Center for Research on Teacher Learning.
Lortie, D. 1975. *Schoolteacher: A Sociological Study.* Chicago: University of Chicago Press.
National Center for Research on Teacher Learning [NCRTL]. 1992. *Findings on Learning to Teach.* East Lansing, Mich.: NCRTL.

On the teaching practicum
Britzman, D. 1991. *Practice Makes Practice: A Critical Study of Learning to Teach.* New York: The Press of the State University of New York.

On schools as contexts for teacher learning
Kleinsasser, R., and S. Sauvignon. 1992. Linguistics, language pedagogy, and teachers' technical cultures. In J. Alatis (ed)., *Linguistics and Language Pedagogy: The State of the Art.* Washington D.C.: Georgetown University Press, pp. 289–301.
Rosenholtz, S. 1989. *Teachers' Workplace: The Social Organization of Schools.* New York: Longman.

On teachers learning from one another
Feiman-Nemser, S., and M. Parker. 1992. Mentoring in context: a comparison of two U.S. programs for beginning teachers. East Lansing, Mich.: National Center for Research on Teacher Learning.
Levine, S. 1990. *Promoting Adult Growth in Schools.* Boston: Allyn & Bacon.

On teaching methodology and change
Richardson, V. 1994. *A Theory of Teacher Change and Practice of Staff Development.* New York: Teachers College Press.
Sarason, S. 1982. *The Culture of the School and the Problem of Change,* 2nd ed. Boston: Allyn & Bacon.

1 The language learner's autobiography: Examining the "apprenticeship of observation"

*Kathleen M. Bailey, Bret Bergthold, Belinda Braunstein,
Natasha Jagodzinski Fleischman, Matthew P. Holbrook,
Jennifer Tuman, Ximena Waissbluth,
and Leslie J. Zambo*

Introduction

If it is true that "we teach as we have been taught," rather than as we have been trained to teach, then it would appear that we are bound to perpetuate the models we have learned in our own teaching. How can we go about breaking that cycle? One way to begin is to bring our past experience to the level of conscious awareness.

Many teacher educators have commented on the power exerted by the implicit models in a future teacher's own lifelong education. Lortie (1975) has referred to this phenomenon as the "13,000-hour apprenticeship of observation." This lengthy history consists of the many thousands of hours we have spent watching teachers since primary school. During this period, we internalized many of our own teachers' behaviors. As Kennedy (1990: 17) puts it: "Teachers acquire seemingly indelible imprints from their own experiences as students and these imprints are tremendously difficult to shake." She further notes (1990: 4):

> By the time we receive our bachelor's degree, we have observed teachers
> and participated in their work for up to 3,060 days. In contrast, teacher
> preparation programs usually require (about) 75 days of classroom
> experience. What could possibly happen during these 75 days to signifi-
> cantly alter the practices learned during the preceding 3,060 days?

In terms of language teacher preparation, Freeman reports on a longitudinal study in which teachers recalled their own language learning experiences. He concludes that "the memories of instruction gained through their 'apprenticeship of observation' function as de facto guides for teachers as they approach what they do in the classroom" (1992: 3). Freeman further notes that "the urge to change and the pull to do what is familiar create a central tension in teachers' thinking about their practice" (1992: 4).

Context of the study

This chapter is a collaborative effort on the part of one teacher educator and seven teacher-learners to examine the "apprenticeship of observation." The purpose of the present chapter is twofold. First, we will describe the language learning autobiography, a simple procedure for helping teachers-in-training examine their own experiences as language learners for their potential impact on each individual's teaching philosophy and practice. Second, we will document what happened when one group of teachers-in-training wrote, analyzed, and discussed their own language learning autobiographies. This collaboration arose from interactions in a graduate seminar designed to prepare M.A. candidates for their roles as language teacher educators and supervisors. Thus, the chapter serves more broadly as an example of collaborative research (see, e.g., Freeman 1992; Murray 1992; Schechter and Ramirez 1992).

The study draws on work related to "reflective teaching" (Bartlett 1990), principle-based teacher education (Macdonald 1993; Priller 1992), and the concept of ownership (Kierstead 1985). In theoretical terms, it explores one small component of the education-versus-training dilemma (Larsen-Freeman 1983; Richards 1987) – specifically that of awareness raising (Ellis 1986; Freeman 1989; Larsen-Freeman 1983). By examining the "instructional conversation" (Tharp and Gallimore 1988: 111) among these teachers-in-training and the professor, we will describe both the product and process outcomes of the autobiography task. We will also discuss the power of the autobiography in terms of our involvement and sense of ownership in our own professional development. The chapter concludes with a discussion of two principles we derived from analyzing our own autobiographies collaboratively.

Autobiographies and journal entries: Our database

The learner's autobiography assignment in our seminar was not originally meant to develop into a collaborative research project. Instead, the intent was to get us to investigate critically the role of our personal "apprenticeships" in shaping our teaching philosophies and practices. A portion of the assignment was to write a prose summary of our language learning history, answering the following questions:

1. What language learning experiences have you had and how successful have they been? What are your criteria for judging success?
2. If you were clearly representative of all language learners, what would we have learned about language learning from reading your autobiography? What can be learned about effective (and ineffective) teaching by reading your autobiography?

3. How has your experience as a language learner influenced you as a language teacher?

By writing our autobiographies, including timelines of our learning and teaching histories, we identified trends, critical incidents, and salient factors influencing our development as teachers.

Our database also included journal entries written by the professor and the teacher-learners. When the seminar participants submitted their papers, some expressed a desire to discuss with their peers what they had learned from the process. The resulting two-hour discussion revealed the powerful reactions these teachers-in-training had to the autobiography assignment, prompting the professor to write a journal entry about what she was learning in the seminar and elsewhere. Several students responded by writing journal entries of their own. Some of these comments are also included in our analysis of the experience. From this exchange, there emerged a group that voluntarily formed a research and writing team, whose goal was to analyze their autobiographies.

In summary, the primary database for this chapter consists of (1) autobiographies written by the teachers-in-training, and (2) subsequent journal entries by them and the professor regarding this process. The autobiographies by the seven M.A. candidates who opted to co-author this chapter were read by everyone on the team and then analyzed for salient events and recurring themes within and across the documents. The collaborative writing process we followed has been described by Murray (1992: 103):

Collaborative writing was essentially a social process through which writers looked for areas of shared understanding. To research such an understanding, participants functioned according to several social and interactional rules: they set a common goal; they had differential knowledge; they interacted as a group; and they distanced themselves from the text.

In the following analysis, both the M.A. candidates' and the professor's points of view will be discussed. However, we will continue to write in the first-person plural (except in cases of explicit comparisons of the teacher educator's and the teacher-learners' voices), since the professor considers herself to be part of the professional development process under investigation. Throughout this chapter, we will refer to ourselves interchangeably as "teachers-in-training" and "teacher-learners."

Product outcomes of the autobiography assignment

Before embarking upon this assignment, most of us had not given a great deal of thought to the particular characteristics and behaviors of our past teachers. However, as a result of the autobiography task, we realized that our learning experiences had influenced our criteria for judging our language learning as successful or unsuccessful. In our discussions, we found several similarities in the themes running through the autobiographies. Our analysis of these themes revealed factors that influenced whether we perceived a language learning experience as successful. The main factors we identified were related to our teachers' beliefs and behaviors – specifically, expectations, reciprocal respect, maintaining motivation, and affect and atmosphere. The following list summarizes the contrasting themes which emerged as product outcomes of our analysis:

1. Teacher personality and style versus methods and/or materials
2. Our concepts about "good" and "bad" teaching
3. Teachers' high expectations for students' success, and/or teachers' friendly, supportive attitude
4. Teachers' respect for learners and learners' respect for teachers
5. Students' responsibilities for maintaining their motivation and/or their teachers' responsibilities for supporting the students' motivation
6. Comparison of the learning atmosphere in formal instructional settings versus naturalistic acquisition

What is noteworthy here is not just these themes themselves, but the fact that they were revealed as we wrote our autobiographies. Of course, we were aware of the importance of these issues in an academic sense, because we had discussed them in our graduate classes; however, they became much more real – more tangible – for us when we discovered that they had played a role in our own past learning experiences. It was particularly useful for us as teachers-in-training to realize that we already had our own (in some cases inexplicit) teaching philosophies, which had been molded by our language learning histories, and that what we had been learning in our M.A. program did, to a large extent, relate to our past learning experiences. However, there were also instances where our experiences ran counter to what we had come to view as successful teaching, based on our teacher education program. (We will return to this point later.)

Teaching behaviors and beliefs

One important part of the autobiography was recognizing that both "good" and "bad" teaching models were evident in our histories. Writing our autobiographies and then using them as data brought the "beliefs, based on previous teaching and classroom experience, about what is 'good' and 'bad' teaching" (Good et al. 1975: 32) into our conscious awareness. For example, it became clear through the autobiography assignment that the teacher factor in general was more important to us as learners than were materials or methodology per se. It was surprising to note how frequently this distinction was made in our retrospective accounts, usually discounting the importance of the method and/or materials used in favor of the person behind the method. For instance, in our group, one teacher-in-training wrote:

> I think that the "teacher factor" is perhaps even more important than methodology or materials because I know that I learned a great deal in an educational situation that did not conform to many of the principles we have learned in the TESOL Program as constituting a successful language learning environment.

We find this contrast intriguing, given that methodology courses are emphasized in language teacher education, and that the issue of teacher personality, or style, is so little understood.

The value of both positive and negative learning experiences became evident through reading our autobiographies. We benefited from examining the positive characteristics of our past teachers because their behavior could be emulated. As a result, our own teaching styles could evolve, influenced by a purposeful selection of the best traits of the teachers we most admired. However, we realized that we had also been witness to numerous poor teaching models. In this way, perhaps, we began to be able to learn how we should not teach, and this knowledge, too, contributed to our beliefs about the kinds of teachers we want to be. It became clear that we had internalized specific behaviors as "good" or "bad" and that this internalization of values might affect us as future teachers.

An analogy to the concept of "parenting" will illustrate our point. It is a truism that people often raise their children in the same way they were raised. This is how many patterns in dysfunctional families have been explained: When parents are tired or under pressure, they revert to the parenting styles they experienced as children. We believe that a similar pattern could emerge when we become teachers. When we are faced with difficult situations, we may revert to teaching in the way we were taught, and this could cause us to use behaviors that are not conducive to the learning environment we hope to foster. We will have chosen them by default (Freeman 1992; Kennedy 1990). Such behaviors arise naturally, since they were ingrained during our "apprenticeship of observation." During stressful times, especially through the "induction years" (Kubat 1990), the approaches that we have learned in our pro-

15

fessional preparation as teachers will not necessarily be immediately accessible to us during the difficult moments. As Kennedy (1991: 16) states:

Often, despite their intentions to do otherwise, new teachers teach as they were taught. The power of their "apprenticeship of observation," and of the conventional images of teaching that derive from childhood experiences, makes it very difficult to alter teaching practices and explains in part why teaching has remained so constant over so many decades of reform efforts.

Although it may seem that history is destined to repeat itself and that we do, in fact, teach as we have been taught, we believe that conscious knowledge of our histories may help us to overcome the tendency to imitate, unwittingly, the behavior of others.

Through the autobiography assignment, we were able to examine the "good" and "bad" teaching in our learning histories and to predict how those models might affect us in the future. By becoming aware of our beliefs with regard to those teachers we have witnessed, we can begin to develop teaching philosophies based on choice: We realize that we do have control over our own actions and beliefs. We may model our behavior after that of others, but it will be because we have made conscious, informed decisions to do so. Our "apprenticeship of observation," like our childhood, will affect us to the degree and in the manner that we allow.

Emphasizing expectations

One thing that our "good" teachers seemed to have in common is that we felt that they cared about us, that they were genuinely committed to us as students and to their profession. These impressions were conveyed to us by way of clear expectations that we would work hard and learn a great deal.

We were surprised to find in our data that the teachers we valued were not always humanistic, warm, and friendly – qualities that many have claimed improve language learning opportunities by reducing anxiety and stress in the classroom (Curran 1976; Dulay et al. 1982; Krashen and Terrell 1983). Some of the teachers that we considered the best were perceived as successful because they were demanding and strict, rather than displaying supportive behavior. These strict teachers were sometimes remembered as inspiring their students to work harder and achieve more than did the more pleasant teachers, as illustrated by the following remarks about a teacher that appeared in one autobiography:

She does not tolerate mistakes or those who do not work to the level she sets. She is strict, she is terrifying, she is unyielding and she is the best thing that ever happened to me in a language class. She pushed me to work to my full potential.

In our autobiographies, the perceptions of "good" teaching vary somewhat: A teacher that one student finds strict and overbearing, another may see as challenging, or even inspiring. Despite trends in teacher education that may discourage a demanding teaching style, our data suggest that students can still have positive learning experiences with strict teachers.

Furthermore, in our retrospective accounts, some very pleasant teachers were seen as less than successful. Depending on the class, it is possible for the teacher to fail by being too nice:

Needless to say, as typical high school students, we took full advantage of his good qualities. If we didn't want to study, we convinced him to plan a party or found a good cultural question to spend an hour discussing. After three years of Russian, I knew almost as much as most first year students at other high schools.

This sort of example made us reconsider our assumptions about "good" teachers. Apparently, for teachers to be sympathetic, friendly, and supportive was not enough for us. Our autobiographies documented several cases of "nice" teachers who did not seem to promote learning. In contrast, we recall learning languages in classes where high expectations were communicated to the learners, regardless of the teachers' affective characteristics. As one teacher-learner wrote: "I have found that I work much better in an atmosphere where expectation is a major motivator."

Richards (1987: 217) has identified "high expectations for student learning" as a consistent finding in the research on teacher effectiveness. Crookes and Schmidt (1991) also discuss the importance of expectations with regard to motivation. The notion of teachers' expectations, which arose repeatedly in our autobiographies, was capsulized in the following comment: "I felt that she was giving me her best, so I could not possibly give her less than my best." Thus we discovered that our own experiences meshed with the research finding that teachers' expectations play an integral role in influencing students' expectations for themselves and their subsequent achievement. As Rose has stated: "Students will float to the mark you set" (1989: 26).

Reciprocal respect

Respect is a related issue that appeared repeatedly in these autobiographies. Our data suggest that teachers' respect for students cultivates a positive learning environment in the classroom. For example, the following comment from one autobiography connects the teacher's accessibility and listening skills to the language learners' affective state: "She was often available and actually LISTENED to what we had to say. . . . I wasn't worried about making mistakes or being embarrassed." This attitude on the teachers' part apparently results in students, in turn, respecting their instructors. The following illustrates the motivational importance of teachers' respect for students:

What impressed me as the greatest difference between C. and most other teachers was the respect with which she treated her students. . . . I told myself at that time that if I ever wanted to be a teacher (heaven forbid!), I would want to teach like C.

Such reciprocal respect was mentioned regularly, as in the following summary statement: "The teachers I respected the most were those who also respected me as a language learner, with my own opinions and needs."

Maintaining motivation

Although we perceived our teachers as very influential, our own goals and motivation when we were language learners were as important as (and sometimes more important than) our teachers' personalities and behaviors. This idea is illustrated by the following comment: "I was internally motivated despite my teacher's style. The teaching method used was less than memorable."

The fact that, as students, we were motivated to learn languages despite limitations in teacher behavior, methods, or materials attests to the importance of intrinsic motivation. As one teacher-learner wrote: "What became evident from this experience is how my motivation could fill in any teaching gaps." This point also made us realize that the responsibility for creating a successful learning experience does not reside solely with the teacher. Students who are faced with what they perceive to be less than ideal teachers, materials, methods, etc., can still learn if their own motivation to do so is strong enough.

In these autobiographical accounts, we reported maintaining our interest and motivation when we were able to find practical, social, intellectual, or emotional uses for our learning:

My motivation and interest levels had now been through many combinations of intensity and it started to become clear that I worked better when I was not only involved in class, but was also learning "useful" skills.

When teachers focus on language skills perceived as useful and relevant by students, they support students' intrinsic motivation. In our data, materials and assignments that required creativity and emphasized multiple skills were often recalled as having perpetuated the students' desire to learn the language:

[The presentation assignment] required a variety of different skills from the students, much more than grammar drills had. Students researched the topic, chose relevant information to share with classmates, translated unknown vocabulary, designed visual and linguistic materials, and presented new information to the class. I was inspired by this challenge. I enjoyed working independently and studying real people and places.

Curiosity emerged as an important motivating factor in our learning. Crookes and Schmidt (1991: 26) suggest that "interest is closely related to curiosity." The puzzlelike nature of languages appealed to many of us. For example, one teacher-learner wrote: "Learning a language at that time (and even today) was for me like solving a cryptogram or similar puzzle – rewarding in the activity itself, not just for the sake of communication." The metaphors of solving a puzzle or breaking a code were often used to describe the language learning process: "What was still a code of gibberish to me was somebody else's language. It was fascinating. . . . I ate up the language like a hungry child."

In fact, continued motivation to learn emerged as a criterion for defining a successful language learning experience, even in cases where the learner did not actually retain the target language, as in this comment about a high school teacher: "Although [the teacher] did not make us linguistic geniuses, I must give him credit for fueling my interest in Russian." In some cases it was not until much later that learners resumed their study of the language: "I consider my third grade Japanese class to have been a success, for although I lost the language for several years, the experience left me with a yearning to relearn it."

Affect and atmosphere

The importance of atmosphere is that it defines the context in which students can (or cannot) concentrate on learning and feel safe taking risks, as depicted in the following comment: "The strength of this teacher was providing an enjoyable class atmosphere where her students learned German in a fun atmosphere." In the autobiographies, some of

19

us commented on the role of our classmates as well as our teachers in setting a positive tone:

I learned at a great rate because I learned useful, practical things, developed
a personal relationship with my instructors and classmates, and learned a
lot of what I wanted (at the same time that I learned what they wanted).
Everyone was supportive and encouraging, and I was motivated.

Several of the teacher-learners had also had experience learning languages naturalistically outside of formal instructional settings. In our autobiographies, there were several explicit comparisons between these settings and classroom language learning, such as the following: "I feel I learned more Spanish informally from interactions with my host family than from language class." For some the excitement of learning a language outside of school and having positive experiences living in another culture led to language teaching as a possible career choice:

It was too good to write off as another personal enlightenment travelling
story. I knew I would want more of it. And the only way to get more was
to share it. Written in my journal are the words: "I had . . . no idea that
learning a language could be this much fun. Can I take this into a classroom?
I think I've found my calling."

We realize that we may not be "typical" language learners, and therefore what we have discovered in our autobiographies may not pertain to others. However, we assume that we are representative of the learners who choose to become language teachers. We have not been consistently good language learners, nor have we succeeded in mastering all the languages we have attempted. What we do have in common is that somewhere in our histories we each became excited about careers in language teaching – sometimes because of and sometimes in spite of our "apprenticeship of observation."

As we have discussed, in our perceptions of what makes a learning experience successful, there seems to be an interplay between the various aspects of teacher beliefs and behavior, and motivation, respect, and expectations. This suggests that the two parties in the teacher-student relationship have their own responsibilities, their own contributions to make to the learning process. Teachers contribute their knowledge, pedagogical skills, and dedication to the students and to their profession. Students contribute by being motivated to learn and by being curious and interested in seeking knowledge. Both the teacher and the students contribute to a positive learning environment by respecting each other and by being committed to doing their best. (See Allwright and Bailey 1991: 23–28, for a discussion of how learners and teachers "co-produce" language lessons.) As a result of writing and collaboratively analyzing our autobiographies, we feel we will be more aware of our students' needs, wants, and expectations and that we will respect and respond to them, thereby creating a positive atmosphere for language learning.

The apprenticeship examined

By reading the autobiographies of our peers, we have been alerted to the importance of respecting our students as individuals as a central issue in creating a positive learning environment. We also saw that in our data the "teacher factor" was considered to be more important than methodology. We noted that the teachers we valued may have exhibited different characteristics, some apparently inconsistent with a humanistic teaching model, but that when teachers cared about their students and communicated high expectations, the language learning experience was judged to be successful.

As teacher-learners we felt sure that we could benefit from examining our "apprenticeship of observation." One teacher-in-training recast Lortie's apprenticeship metaphor:

I have seen brilliant teachers and others I would never wish to resemble in any way. As a teacher, I hope to be able to sort the wheat from the chaff and to become a better teacher for having witnessed the successes and failures of others. If I have completed this apprenticeship successfully, I will use this knowledge to better instruct my students in the future and to help other teachers avoid the same mistakes.

As a result of such reflections, we felt as a group that this assignment had helped us and that we could help others when, in the future, we become teachers and teacher trainers.

Process outcomes of the autobiography assignment

While we clearly benefited from discovering the product outcomes of our autobiographies, we were more intrigued by the process outcomes. In writing these autobiographies, we documented our experiences in order to help clarify our current beliefs, and the process was both thought provoking and affirming. The following comment exemplifies this point: "Until I began writing this paper, I did not realize to what extent my concept of a good language teacher has been molded by my experiences as a language learner."

When writing our autobiographies, we rediscovered memories that we had almost forgotten, and developed from them a new perspective on teaching. That is, the process of reexamining our past helped many

21

to discover the "why" behind our beliefs, while others articulated their beliefs for the first time:

> While writing this learner's autobiography, many of my accepted realities have been disturbed from their pleasantly anonymous resting places. I find that the more I sort through the neatly boxed memories, the more I discover that I am a summative product of these important denials.

Moreover, reexamining our histories gave us a chance to bring our own identities to the theoretical material we had been studying, and to interpret that material in light of our own experiences. From this foundation, we could begin to build the bridge to our future as language teachers.

The process of writing this autobiography assignment gave us insight into the beliefs and perceptions formed during our "apprenticeship of observation." It helped us to clarify our values and to begin thinking about their implications in the choices we will make in teaching. The additional processes of discussion and analysis allowed the eight co-authors collaborating on this chapter to benefit from shared insights and our emerging awareness of common concerns. As one teacher-learner noted:

> Introspection is very important. If not for this class on teacher ed., if not for this assignment requiring me to state my own theory of effective teaching, I might never have thought about this sort of thing and sorted it out in my mind. Often it's only when we're forced to do such activities that we do them and then (possibly) reach new levels of professionalism through self-awareness.

This process also represents a first step in becoming "reflective" teachers. In discussing teacher development, Bartlett (1990: 212) states: "Becoming reflective forces us to adopt a critical attitude to ourselves as individual second language teachers – to challenge our espoused personal views about teaching." The assignment, then, served as a springboard: We must now move from thinking critically about the behaviors of others to thinking critically about our own beliefs and behaviors.

During the past three decades, our field has seen tremendous development in theories of language and of learning (Richards and Rodgers 1986), but we seldom speak about a theory of teaching (Larsen-Freeman 1990). By thinking carefully about our own experiences, we began to articulate our own theories of teaching. This is indeed a personal as well as professional responsibility, because it is this theory that guides each of us in the classroom. It is what guided our teachers, whether they were aware of it or not. It is only when we are aware of our theories of teaching that we can examine them and alter them as needed.

Teachers as learners: The dialogue

This assignment proved to be important for the professor as well. Discussing the learners' autobiographies with the class members gave her a fresh outlook on her own career as a teacher, as well as her role as a teacher educator. It prompted her to examine her own behavior and reflect on her own theory of teaching. The following comments are taken from a journal entry that she wrote after we discussed what we had discovered in our autobiographies:

Reading the students' autobiography assignments is a profound (and humbling) experience. I find myself wanting to ignore the correspondence that must go out tomorrow, forget the Faculty Assembly, stay home Friday morning and read these fabulous stories, these self-accounts of evolving educators. . . . I think – no – I *feel* that I have chosen (or been chosen by) the right profession. Teaching works for me, because every day I learn something and almost every day I have fun learning.

The importance of the professor's journal response to us as teacher-learners was that it triggered a dialogue. While the autobiography assignment was not intended to provoke an ongoing journal exchange between the teachers-in-training and the professor, the process did result in such a dialogue (continued in written journal entries, ongoing seminar discussions, and – for some seminar participants – the writing of this chapter). One benefit of such a dialogue is that "the traditional relationship between teacher as all-powerful knower and student as apprentice learner move[s] toward a relationship of greater equality, of colleagues in a profession where each has something of value to contribute" (Porter et al. 1990: 234). This exchange also created "interaction beyond the classroom, both between teacher and student, and among students" (1990: 236). In fact, several students set up an unscheduled class meeting to discuss the professor's journal entry. Thereafter two teachers-in-training wrote these reactions:

We discussed today in our chat how sharing the journal about [Bailey's] thoughts on the lesson discussing our autobiographies brought us into the position of colleague or peer, with whom our professor confided her professional self-criticism and doubts. Neat. Thanks.

I've just remembered how I felt when I first read your journal entry. Oh, I was moved. I knew with the first line that I would have to suggest to the class that we do something about it although I didn't know what. Actually, I had been really struck by wanting us to do something ever since that day in class when you had an idea going, some kind of research stuff. . . . WOW!! I thought – what can we do?! How can we help? . . . In your letting us into your teaching/research world, the channel is open two ways – Mutual Discovery. Teacher/learner roles become blurred: With teacher as learner, the

23

student feels s/he has something substantial to contribute. It's incredibly exciting to see *you* so interested in *us*.

It was exciting for us as teacher-learners to feel that we were part of our instructor's learning experience and were welcome to participate in her professional research agenda. Because the professor suggested that we collaborate on a research project, we realized that we had something valuable to offer. The most positive learning experiences seem to take place when there is a reciprocal recognition of worth (Curran 1976) on the part of both the teacher and the students. By sharing the journal entry quoted above, the professor validated us as emerging professionals. One teacher-learner reacted to the combination of the autobiography assignment and the professor's journal entry as follows:

I think that what was meaningful about the autobiography assignment is that it made clear how much of a resource students can be. I know that I will want to have students do some variation of this assignment in every class I teach not only because I think I can learn a lot about how my students have learned in the past . . . but also because it would remind me that students are a resource for my own growing, learning and development. . . . I think that it is essential that teachers, that people, in order to grow and change, continue to learn. And one way that I think, hope, all teachers develop is by continuing to learn. This is obvious in your journal to us because you mention your own learning many times. . . . I think maybe teachers forget that students can be so beneficial to their own growing process and should be respected and valued.

The dialogue between us and the professor, which started in the autobiographies and continued in the journal entries, gave us an opportunity to clarify our thoughts and informally take the assignment a step further. One of the teacher-learners wrote:

I want to thank you for sharing your journal with us. Its spark set off a whole wave of thought and ideas for me. . . . I finally had the ideas I needed to finish the autobiography in a way that satisfied me.

Thus the "instructional conversation" (Tharp and Gallimore 1988: 111) led to unexpected, autonomous learning. In a similar vein, Porter et al. discuss the benefits of journal writing in that it provides an opportunity for reflection and may "promote autonomous learning, encouraging students to take responsibility for their own learning and to develop their own ideas" (1990: 233).

The autobiography was powerful for both the professor and the teacher-learners because the assignment (and the subsequent collaborative research project) allowed for the development of mutual respect, which we have discussed above as promoting successful learning. In fact, many of us felt that we benefited as much from the follow-up dialogue (in the journals and seminar meetings) as we did from the original assignment:

It was really helpful to have a forum to discuss these issues and to see that others (even Bailey!) have the same concerns and are going through the same process of self-analysis, criticism, and doubt.

This dialogue, beyond the original autobiography assignment, encouraged us as teacher-learners to reflect on our "apprenticeship of observation" and helped us draw additional conclusions and further implications for our own careers as teachers.

Principles of language teacher development

One such continuation was in articulating two principles of language teacher development. These ideas may be found in the professional literature we read for our seminar, but in our ongoing course discussions they dovetailed very neatly with, and were often illustrated by, the experiences we had documented in our autobiographies. Through critically analyzing our own language learning, and discovering the value of these experiences, we learned first-hand, in retrospect, about two key principles of language teacher development.

First in our data, we noted what we began to call the "ownership principle," meaning that by giving students a voice in the classroom decision-making process, the teacher fosters a feeling of joint control and personal involvement. For example, one teacher-learner wrote, "I want to give my students a say in what they learn, as C. did, to make them feel they have something invested in the class." Another wrote, "I think that the most exciting teachers and the most inspiring classes are those where the students are treated as a part of a learning, growing process."

The importance of ownership is discussed by teacher educators and supervisors (see, for example, Kierstead 1985; Priller 1992; Reznich 1985). Kierstead (1985: 36) notes the value of ownership in problem solving: "On the personal side, engaging in a high level of interaction . . . immediately heightens the teachers' interest in and ownership of a joint problem solving process." In our case, the autobiography assignment engaged us as teacher-learners at the start of the course and set the tone for the entire semester.

We also articulated a principle that we call "modeling" (Macdonald 1993; Priller 1992). This is the idea that one effective way to teach is through consistently and repeatedly demonstrating the behavior (and attitudes) a teacher educator wishes to impart. Here the idea of modeling does not refer to an individual demonstration of a technique. In-

25

stead, by adopting modeling as a principle, we refer to the consistent enactment of a teaching philosophy over time, in essence to "practicing what we preach." The product outcomes of our study illustrate the importance of previous models to the formation of teaching behavior and styles. The process outcomes have made us very aware of how our behaviors and beliefs (above and beyond our subject- matter knowledge) will influence our students.

We do not know to what extent the principles of ownership and modeling are valid in other cultures. Our cultural and educational predispositions support these concepts as fundamental principles, which should be important in teacher education worldwide. However, much additional research by teachers educated in other traditions and working in other contexts would be needed before such broad claims could be made with confidence.

Conclusions

There are many implications of the autobiography assignment, in particular, and collaborative research, in general, for teaching and teacher education. First, we realized that the "apprenticeship of observation" has had an influence on the ways we will teach. We felt, on the basis of our data, that factors such as maintaining motivation, emphasizing expectations, and creating reciprocal respect will be important in working with our own students. We learned the importance of modeling the behavior we would like to encourage and of creating a positive environment in which our students can develop a sense of ownership.

By analyzing our autobiographies and journal entries, we experienced the value of maintaining a dialogue with an instructor as a means of motivating students and making them feel they are part of a larger community. We discovered, first-hand, that reflection and introspection are valuable tools for values clarification and for encouraging critical thinking. We learned from our professor's journal how students can play a role in a teacher's learning experience.

We have argued that the autobiography is a useful device for promoting professional growth. It has given us a foundation from which to articulate our own teaching philosophies and a way of connecting the theoretical literature to our experiences. As Larsen-Freeman has noted (1983), the first step toward changing our teaching practice is awareness. Such awareness may encompass what we currently do, the factors that have shaped us, and our options for change. [See Bailey (1992) and Freeman (1992) for discussions of teachers' efforts to change.]

Because each person is different, with his or her own unique history, writing the language learning autobiography gives the teacher-learner a great sense of individuality. Being the sole "owner" of these memories, the author is the only person who can analyze these past learning experiences and turn them into a resource for his or her own professional development. Through this process each person was able to identify what was most important to his or her emerging philosophy. The power behind the autobiography assignments is the individual's investment in it.

However, as collaborative researchers, we also were encouraged by the many commonalities we found in examining the repeated salient features in our data. We found similarities across these individual realizations which not only validated what each person thought as an individual, but also located us as emerging professionals in a worldwide community. After exposure to numerous theories about language and learning in our graduate program, the autobiography assignment prompted us as teachers-in-training to evaluate how we relate to these theories. Our collective reaction to both the product and process outcomes of our work is summarized in the following comment from one autobiography: "I often surprised myself by how insightful I could be if I only applied my own history. This is empowering."

A primary goal of a teacher education course should be to give teacher-learners tools for continuing professional development (Lange 1990; Pennington 1990). As Smith (1971: 100) points out: "Somehow the teacher education program is expected to lead the teacher to a better understanding of her own assets, beliefs, and values, and to help the teacher steadily improve her competencies." The autobiography assignment was a powerful tool for reflection, because it allowed us to do just that: It provided the framework for us to examine systematically our emerging teaching philosophies and goals, as well as to examine the "evolution of [our] professional identity" (Schechter and Ramirez 1992: 193). The further step – that of jointly analyzing our autobiographies as data in a collaborative research project – led us to broaden our concepts of that identity: to include (at least) an image of ourselves as teacher-researchers, working within a broad professional community.

References

Allright, D., and K. M. Bailey. 1991. *Focus on the Language Classroom: An Introduction to Classroom Research for Language Teachers.* Cambridge: Cambridge University Press.

Bailey, K. 1992. The process of innovation in language teacher development:

What, why, and how teachers change. In J. Flowerdew, M. Brock, and S. Hsia (eds.), *Perspectives on Language Teacher Education.* Hong Kong: City Polytechnic of Hong Kong, pp. 253–282.

Bartlett, L. 1990. Teacher development through reflective teaching. In J. C. Richards and D. Nunan (eds.), *Second Language Teacher Education.* Cambridge: Cambridge University Press, pp. 202–214.

Crookes, G., and R. Schmidt. 1991. Motivation: Reopening the research agenda. *Language Learning* 41(4): 469–512.

Curran, C. 1976. *Counseling-Learning in Second Languages.* Apple River, Ill.: Apple River Press.

Dulay, H., M. Burt, and S. Krashen. 1982. *Language Two.* Oxford: Oxford University Press.

Ellis, R. 1986. Activities and procedures for teacher preparation. *ELT Journal* 40(2): 91–99.

Freeman, D. 1989. Teacher training, development and decision making: A model of teaching and related strategies for language teacher education. *TESOL Quarterly* 23(1): 27–45.

   1992. Language teacher education, emerging discourse, and change in classroom practice. In J. Flowerdew, M. Brock, and S. Hsia (eds.), *Perspectives on Language Teacher Education,* Hong Kong: City Polytechnic of Hong Kong, pp. 1–21.

Good, T. L., B. Biddle, and J. Brophy. 1975. *Teachers Make a Difference.* Washington, D.C.: University Press of America.

Kennedy, M. 1990. *Policy Issues in Teacher Education.* East Lansing, Mich.: National Center for Research on Teacher Learning.

   1991. Some surprising findings on how teachers learn to teach. *Educational Leadership* 49(3): 14–17.

Kierstead, J. 1985. Supporting the evolution of effective teachers. *Teacher Education Quarterly* 12(2): 31–41.

Krashen, S., and T. Terrell. 1983. *The Natural Approach: Language Acquisition in the Classroom.* Oxford: Pergamon Press.

Kubat, G. A. 1990. Surviving your first year: Some things to think about. In *ASCUS Annual: A Job Search Handbook for Educators.* Evanston, Ill.: Association for School, College and University Staffing, pp. 26–28.

Lange, D. E. 1990. A blueprint for teacher development. In J. C. Richards and D. Nunan (eds.), *Second Language Teacher Education.* Cambridge: Cambridge University Press, pp. 245–265.

Larsen-Freeman, D. 1983. Training teachers or educating a teacher. In J. E. Alatis, H. H. Stern, and P. Strevens (eds.), *Georgetown University Round Table on Languages and Linguistics.* Washington, D.C.: Georgetown University Press, pp. 264–274.

   1990. On the need for a theory of language teaching. In J. E. Alatis (ed.), *Georgetown University Round Table on Languages and Linguistics, Linguistics, Language Teaching and Language Acquisition: The Interdependence of Theory, Practice and Research.* Washington, D.C.: Georgetown University Press, pp. 261–270.

Lortie, D. 1975. *Schoolteacher: A Sociological Study.* Chicago: University of Chicago Press.

Macdonald, E. 1993. Principle-based teacher education. Paper presented at the CATESOL State Conference, Monterey, Calif.

Murray, D. 1992. Collaborative writing as a literary event: Implications for ESL instruction. In D. Nunan (ed.), *Collaborative Language Learning and Teaching*. Cambridge University Press, pp. 100–117.

Pennington, M. C. 1990. A professional development focus for the language teaching practicum. In J. C. Richards and D. Nunan (eds.), *Second Language Teacher Education*. Cambridge: Cambridge University Press, pp. 132–151.

Porter, P. A., L. M. Goldstein, J. Leatherman, and S. Conrad. 1990. An ongoing dialog: Learning logs for teacher preparation. In J. C. Richards and D. Nunan (eds.), *Second Language Teacher Education*. Cambridge: Cambridge University Press, pp. 227–244.

Priller, M. 1992. Final report, Peace Corps, Pst Poland V. Unpublished manuscript. Washington, D.C.: Peace Corps.

Reznich, C. 1985. *Teaching Teachers: An Introduction to Supervision and Teacher Training*. Brattleboro, Vt.: The Experiment in International Living.

Richards, J. C. 1987. The dilemma of teacher education in second language teaching. *TESOL Quarterly* 21(2): 209–226.

Richards, J. C., and T. Rodgers. 1986. *Approaches and Methods in Language Teaching*. Cambridge: Cambridge University Press.

Rose, M. 1989. *Lives on the Boundary*. New York: Penguin Books.

Schechter, S. R., and R. Ramirez. 1992. A teacher-research group in action. In D. Nunan (ed.), *Collaborative Language Learning and Teaching*. Cambridge: Cambridge University Press, pp. 192–207.

Smith, P. (ed.). 1971. *Research in Teacher Education: A Symposium*. Englewood Cliffs, N.J.: Prentice-Hall.

Tharp, R., and Gallimore, R. 1988. *Rousing Minds to Life: Teaching, Learning and Schooling in Social Context*. New York: Cambridge University Press.

2 The vision versus the reality: The tensions of the TESOL practicum

Karen E. Johnson

When Maja entered her practicum placement that morning, she was greeted with a shout of, "Hey! You teacher today!" Trying to conceal her sense of panic, she walked to her desk in the back corner of the room, laid down her things, and smiled at the group of ESL students standing excitedly around her. Reality began to sink in. Joan, her co-operating teacher, had called in sick that morning and left her in charge of the entire teaching load. The high school vice-principal would eventually find a substitute teacher, or ask a study hall monitor to cover the ESL classes that day, but Maja knew what this meant. She would have to teach all day, and she wasn't ready. She walked to the front of the room and began searching among the papers on Joan's desk. She found a single sheet of paper, torn from a notebook, with a list of the periods for the day and a few scribbled notes. Some of the notes were crossed out and other directions were scribbled on top of them. When Maja spotted me entering the room for my weekly observation, she said, "You won't believe this, but Joan isn't here; her son is sick." Maja stared at the sheet of paper she was holding in her hand and said, "I can't believe I'm gonna have to teach all day and wing it."

Understanding the TESOL practicum

For most pre-service teachers, the TESOL practicum is considered to be one of the most important experiences in learning to teach; however, little is known about what actually occurs during the TESOL practicum (Freeman 1989; Richards 1987; Richards and Crookes 1988). In fact, most second language teacher preparation programs simply assume that once pre-service teachers have completed their required course work, they will be able to transfer their knowledge into effective classroom practices. Without a better understanding of how pre-service teachers conceptualize their initial teaching experiences, and what impact these experiences have on their professional development as teachers, the field of second language teacher education will continue to operate without a grounded theoretical framework of how to teach second language teachers to teach (Freeman 1989; Johnson 1992). The purpose of this study is to provide descriptive evidence of the initial teaching experiences of one pre-service teacher, Maja, during the TESOL practicum. Specifically, this study examines Maja's perceptions of her initial teaching experience, and how this experience shapes her understanding of herself as a teacher, of second language teaching, and of the TESOL practicum.

The practicum setting

Maja was placed in an urban secondary-level (9–12) ESL program for a fifteen-week practicum. Her cooperating teacher, Joan, was responsible for two different groups of ESL students. The first group were refugees, mostly Vietnamese and Amer-Asians, who lacked literacy skills and formal schooling in their native language. These students were placed in ESL literacy classes for much of the school day, where they received basic reading and writing instruction in English. For the remainder of the day, they were mainstreamed in elective courses such as home economics, industrial arts, or vocational-technical education. The second group were first-generation immigrants, mostly from countries in the former Eastern Bloc, China, Korea, and Puerto Rico, who arrived in the United States after having attended school in their own countries, and who were literate in their native languages. These students were enrolled in ESL content-based science and social studies classes which were team taught by an ESL teacher and a content-area teacher using a sheltered English approach. These students also took more advanced-level ESL composition and literature classes, designed to upgrade their academic reading and writing skills in English before they were fully integrated into the mainstream secondary school curriculum.

The ESL program was housed in the only racially mixed secondary school in the district, and most of the students came from the poorer neighborhoods on the south side of the city. Maja remembered seeing the school "bouncer," stationed just outside the main entrance to watch students as they came and went throughout the school day. She recalled walking down the hall on her first day amid groups of students lounging on the floor around their lockers. When she finally located the ESL classroom, she could see Joan through the window, but the door was locked. Later, she learned that classroom doors are always locked; if students are late, they have to get a pass from the main office. She described the deafening noise in the hallway when classes changed and how she learned to head for the teacher's lounge only after the bell had run and the halls had emptied. Despite her initial intimidation, Maja was excited about her practicum placement. These were the type of students with whom she wanted to work. This was the type of school where she wanted to teach.

After spending her senior year abroad as a German major in Austria, Maja decided she wanted to teach ESL. She enrolled in the M.A. TESOL program because she loved languages and she wanted to teach them. Learning languages had always come naturally to her. Her own experiences learning German, both in school and in Austria, were extremely positive. She felt that knowing another language opened up the world for her, and as an ESL teacher, she could do the same for others. After completing three semesters of course work in the M.A. TESOL program, she was ready for her first teaching experience.

Data collection

The methodology used to collect data in this study followed the participant-observation procedures outlined by McCall and Simmons (1969) and Wilson (1977). I arranged weekly observations of Maja's practicum placement in which I took descriptive field notes about what I saw happening during each class. I also arranged to interview Maja before and after each observation. In addition, I arranged to videotape three of Maja's lessons, and she agreed to participate in a series of stimulus recall exercises (Shavelson and Stern 1981). These exercises involved asking Maja to watch her videotaped lessons and stop the tape and comment at points where she recollected her thoughts and decisions while teaching. These stimulus recall reports provided a running commentary of her perceptions of her own teaching. Finally, Maja kept a written journal, which consisted of open-ended entries that represented her day-to-day reflections on her experiences during the practicum.

These descriptive data (field notes, interview data, videotaped lessons, stimulus recall reports, and journal entries) were then analyzed using inductive analysis procedures (Bogdan and Biklen 1992). These procedures involved identifying emerging themes and patterns from the data that represented Maja's emerging conception of herself as a second language teacher, the tensions she experienced between her own conception of second language teaching and the realities she faced during her initial teaching experience, and the strategies she developed to cope with the tensions of the TESOL practicum.

Results

Since the purpose of this study is to provide descriptive evidence of Maja's initial teaching experiences, the themes that emerged from the data analyses are presented using descriptive narration. We begin with

Maja's description of what she perceived as a gap between her "vision" of second language teaching and the "realities" of the TESOL practicum. Next, we experience those realities through descriptive accounts taken from field notes and transcripts of two of Maja's initial teaching experiences. Each account is followed by Maja's description of the tensions she experienced as a result of these initial teaching experiences. We also sense Maja's frustrations as she places blame for these tensions on the realities of teaching, her cooperating teacher, and the practicum experience itself. Finally, through a descriptive account of how she planned for and carried out an instructional unit for an advanced-level ESL literature class, we see Maja begin to develop strategies that enable her to cope with the tensions of the TESOL practicum. These results are followed by a more general discussion of how Maja's initial teaching experiences shaped her understanding of herself as a teacher, of second language teaching, and of the TESOL practicum.

The vision versus the reality

During our initial interview, Maja repeated that she had never taught before, but she knew in her own mind what good teaching was, and she had lots of ideas about what she would do as a teacher. She described this as her "vision" of teaching. This meant "knowing why you are teaching something, what the learning outcome is, and how it fits into the overall goals for the students. I have to know where I am going, and why I am going there . . . and I feel it is my responsibility as a teacher to let the students know where they are going too."

She described the importance of starting with what her students already know and building from there. Her vision of teaching also seemed to include careful planning – planning which is predictable, organized, and structured. Maja claimed that "Prediction is very important for learning and behavior management. . . . the students need to be able to predict what is coming next, know what is expected of them every day, and be ready for it."

Maja's vision of herself as a teacher is to organize an environment in which her students are "learning more than just the English language, but learning all sorts of new things through the English language. It's not that these kids can't learn, it's that they can't express what they learn, they can't raise their hands in class and answer the teacher's questions, they can't write up the lab reports . . . but they can learn . . . they really can learn."

In Maja's vision of herself as a teacher, she is a model, one who sets up the environment for learning to occur. Maja said: "It is important to show them what I expect of them by modeling it first, and then letting them experience it on their own. I want my instruction to make them feel prepared to be able to learn the things I am asking them to learn." Maja also defined her vision of herself as a teacher by what she calls her "limits." These limits seem to be certain boundaries which define what she believes is appropriate behavior, not only for herself as the teacher, but for the students. She admitted that she was not yet sure what these limits were, but she was going to find out.

The reality, as Maja described it, "is what life is really like in an ESL classroom." There is a constant flow of interruptions, such as "knocks at the door, announcements over the loud speaker, the attendance sheet, students flying in, students flying out. This bothers me! There is so much crap going on that has nothing to do with education, the bell rings and I don't even realize it, and that bugs me. That drives me crazy!" Time is also a major factor in what Maja called the reality. Frustrated by short, 38–minute class periods, Maja said, "there is a real tension between do I cover all the things I had planned and I know are really important, or do I say a quality discussion is more important."

Maja described the reality of teaching ESL to be a process of "dummying down" the instructional material. Appalled at the "intellectually dead" nature of the content taught in the ESL literacy class, Maja said, "I had to act out, I'm brushing my teeth with toothpaste, as part of a grammar lesson! I felt like a fool, standing there saying this sentence and expecting the students to take me seriously." Maja described what she called "a school-wide perception that ESL students are dumb, that they can't learn, and that they have to learn English before they can learn anything else." In the ESL science class, Maja said, "the regular science teacher thinks these kids can't learn so she gives them these silly experiments."

Maja characterized the ESL students as "unfairly segregated and taught as if they are incompetent." In fact, the entire ESL program seemed to have a low status in the school. Three ESL teachers share two classrooms and are forced to move with their students throughout the building to hold class. After arriving at one of the shared classrooms and finding the door locked, Maja complained, "This happens at least three times a week. They won't give me a key to the room and the guy who teaches here before me always locks the room and leaves. ESL classes are the lowest priority here, almost as if the programs we run don't really exist."

While Maja seemed to possess a strong image of the kind of teacher she wanted to be, as well as what she expected second language teaching to be like, her initial teaching experiences during the TESOL practicum did not match those images. In fact, Maja described this mismatch as "the gap between her vision and the reality of teaching."

The realities: The ESL literacy class

On the morning Joan called in sick, Maja had not yet assumed direct teaching responsibilities, but had mostly observed or worked with small groups of students on tasks assigned by Joan. As the students filed into the room that morning, Maja grabbed some papers from her bag, left the room, and returned a few minutes later. The students had begun to settle into their desks in anticipation of the first-period bell. Maja walked back to where I was sitting and handed me a copy of a hand-drawn map. She explained that she had drawn it last night and planned to use it with the low-level students with whom she usually worked during small group activities. Since the previous lesson had been on neighborhoods, Maja had planned to use a map of her own neighbor-hood as a way to get the students to talk about their neighborhoods. Maja said she was not sure whether this was going to work with the whole class, but she didn't have anything else planned, and Joan's note had said to review what they had done yesterday.

By the time Maja had passed out all the papers, the students were seated and had grown relatively quiet. She began.

Did everyone get a blank piece of paper with nothing on it, and a piece of paper with a picture on it? A map? . . . OK. Now I'm gonna tell you about this map. . . . This is a picture of my neighborhood. Remember yesterday we talked about neighborhoods?

At that moment, the substitute teacher entered the room. A student yelled out, "Excuse me, teacher. . . ." Maja turned, greeted the substi-tute, and they spoke quietly for a moment. As he walked toward the back of the room, Maja returned to the class. "Bin, what's a neighbor-hood? Do you remember? Can anyone tell me what a neighborhood is?" Bin replied, "Like friends." Maja smiled, "Friends? OK, yes, neigh-bors are your friends."

Suddenly there was a loud knock at the door. Maja opened the door, greeted the student sarcastically, "I'm so happy you are here," and held out her hand for a late pass. The student handed her a pass and shuffled to his seat, mumbling something about Joan not being there today. Maja turned back to the class and resumed. "All right, a neighbor, a neighbor is a friend. OK, Wang, can you tell me what a neighborhood is?

For the next ten minutes, Maja walked around the room leading the students through the map of her neighborhood. They identified a movie theater, a restaurant, a drugstore, a church, a park, and, of course, Maja's apartment building. As each location was named, Maja would ask, for example, "What do you buy in a drug store?" or "Do you have a drugstore in your neighborhood?" During this exchange, students called out without waiting for a bid. Seemingly unfazed by this, Maja responded to what they said, asked another question, or returned to the map. About midway through the lesson, Maja returned to the front of the room and explained:

OK, now what I want you to do, I also gave you a blank piece of paper. OK. You see the blank piece of paper? And, what I'd like you to do is draw your neighborhood, draw where you live, and then label it. Just like I did, but now this is going to be where you live."

To this, the students moaned, "Oh, no . . ." and "Oh, God. . . ." Maja responded cheerfully, "It's really not going to be that awful and I will come around and help you." She calmly went through the directions again as she strolled between the rows of desks.

Maja spent the remainder of the period helping individual students complete their maps. She stooped next to a Polish student and asked him some questions about his neighborhood. He mumbled quietly that he lived on Eastern Avenue and that he had a car. He said something about six cylinders, blue, and PRL 238. Maja repeated 238 and asked whether it was the number of his house. He shook his head, flipped over the map, and made a quick sketch of the back of a car. Maja gave him a puzzled look, but said nothing. He pointed to the license plate and spoke as he wrote PRL 238. Maja realized that he was telling her this was his license plate and these letters stood for Poland. He beamed at her with pride as she asked him about his car and where he lived in Poland.

Later, she moved to the back of the room and joined a group of students who had finished their maps and were talking quietly in Vietnamese. Maja began asking questions about their maps. One student described a church in his neighborhood that had a school, and all the students wore black pants, white shirts, and ties. He said he was glad that he didn't attend that school; he liked it at this school better.

By this time most of the students were finished and several were walking around the room. Maja made no effort to get the class to quiet down or to try to get the wandering students to return to their seats. Instead, she went from student to student, checking that they had finished their maps and asking a few questions. Without warning, the pledge of allegiance began to blare over the loudspeaker. Several students stood up, Maja put her hand on her heart, and they began mumbling the pledge. The bell rang and the students began to scatter around the room to collect their things before moving on to their next class.

THE TENSIONS

Reflecting on this lesson, Maja began to describe some of the tensions she was experiencing as a result of the TESOL practicum. She began with her concern over the lack of meaningful instructional activities in the ESL literacy class. She said, "We are supposed to be teaching them English but unless the stuff they talk about is meaningful, the kids don't care about it, and it becomes a silly exercise to fill up time." She complained, "One week we talk about neighborhoods and the next week it's going to the movies, but none of this seems very meaningful to the students. . . . Some of them really get into it, but others just don't seem to care. They are like that with Joan too. They just don't care."

Maja also described the tension she experienced over her lack of knowledge about the students. She described not knowing how to gear her instruction to the individual needs and/or interests of her students. This was particularly evident when I asked her about the Polish boy in the ESL literacy class. She recalled, "Yeah, his car! Did you catch that? He was telling me about his car! He wanted to talk about his car and his neighborhood in Poland, not here. He probably doesn't feel like he has a neighborhood here. I didn't even think of that." Maja went on to say that if she was going to have any impact on these students during the practicum, she would have to get to know them individually.

The time factor, as Maja called it, also seemed to cause her a great deal of tension. She described how "they are all coming in, I know it's getting late and I got their journals to deal with, and I got the attendance to deal with, and I got these pictures I want to show, and I got this other stuff I gotta do, and I'm not going to get to it in 38 minutes." She described the tension she felt between getting through all the material and spending time on individual student's questions. She said, "I don't like it when I see myself teaching this way. I want it to be more student-centered not teacher-centered, but sometimes it's just easier to stand up there and tell them what they need to know. This is not my vision of good teaching but sometimes I find myself doing it anyway."

The realities: The ESL science class

Maja described the ESL science class as a sheltered English class designed to support the mainstream science curriculum. ESL students who passed this class received equivalent mainstream science credits. Maja indicated that the class was team taught, although not well, since Joan knew little about science and the regular science teacher taught the class only grudgingly.

After the bell rang, the science teacher shouted, "Get in your seats and get ready for the test!" One student, arriving late, danced into the room and sang, "Hello my beautiful teacher." This sparked a stiff reprimand: "Get in your seat!" The science teacher then turned to the class and shouted, "While I'm talking no one else should be talking." Although the students were in their seats, you could still hear other languages being spoken and students shuffling papers and books. The science teacher waited for what seemed like an eternity and then shouted, "You're wasting time, you should know that by now, you can take as long as you want, I don't care. I don't care if you waste all period, then there will be no time for the test and you will all fail!"

The science teacher explained, "Correct test decorum is to work in silence. If you have a question, you should raise your hand and we will acknowledge it." A student raised his hand and asked, "Is this a real test?" The science teacher smiled and said "Yes, this is a real one, and you should do well." Another student called out, "Can I pass it?" To this the science teacher shouted, "Scientists are not fools, and you are acting like fools. I will not have fools in my classroom so stop acting like fools, act like scientists!" At this point, Joan moved over to quiet a group of students and whispered to others to pay attention. Once the test began, Joan and Maja roamed the room assisting students who seemed confused or asked for help. The science teacher busied herself at her desk. As Maja moved from student to student, she used objects or actions to explain the meanings of unfamiliar words. She explained "squeeze" by squeezing a student's arm. She illustrated "movable" by sliding a desk next to her. She acted out "attached" by removing and refastening a pen cap.

About halfway through the test, the science teacher stopped the class and explained that the answer sheet did not correspond correctly to the test booklet. She said quickly, "Cross out number 40 on your answer sheet and put number 1, 2, 3,. . . . Does everyone understand?" For the next few minutes, Joan and Maja helped students modify their answer sheets. This seems to cause a lot of confusion. A quiet Chinese student in the front row indicated to Maja that she was confused. As Maja scanned the test to find the confusing question, the science teacher walked by and said, "She should know this, it was in their books, and we talked about it in class. She should know it!" Maja shrugged and walked to the back of the room, where Joan was helping a group of students. Suddenly the science teacher shouted, "Seven more minutes!," at which the students stiffened and shuffled their test booklets. One student called out, "Can we finish tomorrow?" Maja followed Joan's lead in nodding quietly to the students that they could finish during the next ESL support class. Joan and Maja circulated around the room collecting the tests. The bell rang and the students grabbed their things and scattered from the room.

THE TENSIONS

In Maja's mind, the ESL science class epitomized the "realities" of teaching. She found herself faced with a situation in which she had no

academic preparation in the content area, no power to alter these realities is any substantive way, and no support from the science teacher.
She seemed to be aligning herself with the students against these realities
– almost as if, by enabling her students to cope, she would be able to
cope as well. Despite all this, Maja seemed challenged. She was determined to help the students to succeed in the ESL science class.

She explained that the science teacher's lessons were so far over the
heads of the ESL students that Joan ended up reteaching the entire
lesson in the support class. She thought she might get a copy of the
science textbook and teach the lesson before the students went to the
science class. That way, she hoped, they would already know the answers before they got to the science class. Her plan was to stay a step
ahead of the regular science teacher, instead of "playing catchup" as
she felt Joan did. She also admitted that to do this would take a lot of
extra work on her part. She would not be able to wait until the science
teacher taught a particular lesson; she would have to anticipate what
needed to be taught, and then make sure she covered it during the
support class.

Referring to some of the more disruptive students in the ESL science
class, Maja also described the tension she felt when these students tested
her limits. She admitted, "Since at the beginning they don't know what
my limits are, they unknowingly crossed over the boundaries of what I
think is acceptable. Maybe I should lower my limits. But I'm not comfortable with this sort of behavior and I don't think it creates a good
learning environment for the other students." Maja felt that the only
way she would be able to maintain the limits she had set for herself as
a teacher was to establish a relationship with the students. She felt that
this relationship had to be built on mutual respect and understanding
and it would occur when the students and Maja came to understand
each other. However, Maja felt that this sort of relationship takes time,
time that the practicum experience does not allow her. Thus more tension . . .

The blame

At times, Maja seemed to resolve the tension she was experiencing by
placing the blame elsewhere. Mostly she blamed the practicum itself.
Maja described her presence there as being "a moment in time for me
and these students and no matter what I do ' feel I will not have an
effect on them." Maja talked about having "no control over what I
teach, they aren't my students, they don't really know me, and I have
no time to change things." Maja stated, "This whole practicum thing
is such a joke. It's not real teaching and there isn't anything I can do
about it, so I'll just do my time and hope I survive." These concerns

were also evident in Maja's journal entries. For example, about midway through the practicum she wrote:

I don't feel like I'm really "teaching" this semester. Part of the problem is simply that she [Joan] decides what needs to be done, and so there doesn't seem to be much room for changes. This sort of upsets me because it seems that I have to fit into what she wants me to do, even though I don't really feel comfortable with it. I'm not really uncomfortable, but I know if I had my own class, I'd do it my way. I guess it's just part of this practicum thing. It's not *real* teaching!

Maja also blamed Joan, her cooperating teacher. She described Joan's teaching and planning as "winging it" and "picking and choosing." She explained, "All they do is dittos, there are mountains of dittos. She just picks out activities for the day and there is no well thought-out plan for why these activities are done." She said, "all of the assignments are disconnected and unrelated to each other. The stuff they do in class has no purpose, is never corrected, and the students know this, so they really don't care about any of their assignments." Maja explained, "It is not that Joan is a bad teacher, but that she has a different vision of what she believes is good teaching."

Halfway through the TESOL practicum, Maja's initial enthusiasm had dissolved into complaints about "realities" that seemed beyond her control. The realities of teaching had begun to overwhelm her to the point that she appeared to be separating herself from the practicum experience. Her sense of having no control over what happened during the practicum seemed to trouble her the most. She seemed ready to give up, and might have done so if Joan had not suggested that she take over the advanced-level ESL literature class for the remainder of the practicum.

Coping with the realities: The advanced-level ESL literature class

Joan told Maja that she could teach whatever she wanted in the advanced-level ESL literature class as long as the students read some literature and wrote about it. This opportunity seemed to excite as well as frighten Maja. During our next interview, Maja pulled out a unit plan she had been working on in her university methods course. She said, "This is 17 pages, and I keep coming up with other instructional support ideas which could make it even better. It is supposed to take between 3 to 4 weeks, but as I look it over I think it might take all 6 weeks." Maja began by describing what she called the "conceptual framework" within which she had designed the unit. She described the importance of prediction: that the students needed to be able to predict what was expected of them so that they could participate to the best of their abilities. She talked about how prediction was also important for her as well. She explained, "I told my supervisor that I wanted my lessons to be organized, that I couldn't stand up in front of them without things all laid out. So she helped me plan out each week, all organized, all related to each other, all leading up to a final project." She also described wanting the students "to learn English as they are learning something else . . . something meaningful, that they care about, that's relevant to their own lives." This meant, as Maja described, selecting a piece of literature and creating activities that would help the students relate it to their own lives. In coming up with the activities for the unit, Maja said it was essential to find out what the students already knew and plan her lessons accordingly.

MEANING-BASED INSTRUCTION

Maja characterized her unit as a combination of literature and social studies that centered around the play *The Diary of Anne Frank*, set within the historical time period of World War II. Maja said she did not want the students just to read the play but to experience it from the point of view of the characters. She wanted them to understand the first impressions the characters give, how they develop during the play, and eventually, how the layers within characters, their roles and personalities, evolve throughout the play. Maja planned to accomplish this in several ways. To start, the class would focus on how the play was put together: the format of the script, the set designs, the costumes, and the character descriptions. Most of the actual reading would be done at home, but the students would have questions to answer about what they read. These questions, Maja explained, were not to test the students to see if they had read the material, but to help them relate the characters to themselves, to help them predict what might come next, and to question what they understood about what was going on in the play.

PLANNING AND PREDICTABILITY

Maja then went through each day of her unit and described what the students would do and what was expected of them. The unit included a weekly schedule of class activities with daily homework assignments. The students would read a short segment of the play, answer a series of questions, discuss different aspects of the characters, write a series of journal entries through the eyes of their assigned characters, and design a collage depicting their characters. Some sections of the play would be read and discussed in class. She hoped the students would be able to share in the experience of what it must have been like to live in hiding during World War II. She felt that many of the students could

41

Karen E. Johnson

relate to this sort of experience, since many had come to the United States under harrowing political and social conditions.

During the second half of the unit, Maja planned to assign groups of student to gather biographical information about a national leader during this historic time period. The groups were to investigate the personal and professional backgrounds of leaders such as Churchill, de Gaulle, Hitler, Mussolini, Stalin, and Roosevelt, and to characterize their political perspectives. Maja had collected biographical information on each leader and prepared reading guides and organizing questions to help the students understand the information. She also created a class vocabulary list that students would expand as they moved through the unit. The groups would eventually write character sketches on their leader, illustrate three key political decisions their leader had made, and present what they had learned about each leader to the class in a formal in-class presentation. Maja hoped that the activities they were doing for the first half of the unit would carry over to the second half. She wanted the unit to fit together, not only in terms of the content covered, but also in terms of the skills the students would need to complete the unit.

A SENSE OF CONTROL

Having been granted some control over this class, Maja quickly seized the opportunity to shape the curriculum, the instructional activities, and the classroom environment to be more consistent with her vision of second language teaching. Her unit plan reflected her earlier comments that she needed to know why she was "teaching something, what the learning outcome is, and how it fits into the overall goals for the students." The structure of the unit plan reflected her need to build predictability into her lessons. This would, in her words, enable "the student to be able to predict what is coming next, know what is expected of them everyday, and be ready for it." This was her chance to arrange the classroom environment in such a way that it would be, in her mind, conducive for "not just learning the language, but learning *through* the language."

Reaching her vision: The formal presentations

On the morning of the formal in-class presentations, Maja explained that the students had been working on the Anne Frank unit for almost five weeks and today was what she described as the culminating event. Two groups of students would be giving their formal presentations today. One group of students entered the room carrying a stack of books and two large posters. They were talking excitedly and, without direction from Maja, began setting up their things at the front of the room. One student placed the posters on the chalkrail, while another started writing some information on the blackboard.

Maja had arranged the desks in a semicircle and placed two sheets of paper, face down, on each desk. She explained that after each group presentation the class would fill out these evaluation forms. The form had three sections; the first asked the students to describe three new things they had learned about this leader from the presentation, the second asked them to describe two things they liked best about the presentation, and the third asked them to rate the presentation and describe why they gave it this rating. Later, Maja explained that she hoped this would help the other students play a more active role in the presentations, and she felt that it was important for the groups to receive feedback from their classmates as well as from her.

As the rest of the students filed into the room, Maja greeted each by name and asked some sort of question or made a comment. Later, in our interview, she told me that her university supervisor had suggested this strategy as a way to get the class started on time. She described it as "connecting up" with each student, and it was intended to give them the impression that class started as soon as they entered the room, not after the bell rang. This in turn, meant that she could take care of checking journals and homework assignments, fill in attendance forms, and make any informal announcements before the bell rang. She also mentioned that this strategy took a while to "work," since the students had to get a sense of "what she expected of them."

Maja made a few opening comments, explained how to fill out the evaluation forms, and quickly turned the class over to the first group of presenters. A Puerto Rican student began by describing the biographical information written on the board. Glancing at note cards, she described three interesting facts about Roosevelt's life:

. . . and Roosevelt was the thirty-second president. He was elected four terms, that's sixteen years, but he had a disease and he died. He was president when he died.

As she spoke, a Chinese student walked around the semicircle holding a large picture book open to a photograph of Roosevelt. The Puerto Rican student went on:

He had polio, that's a disease and your muscles can't move, so you can't walk, so he had a wheelchair . . . he had to sit in a wheelchair.

At this point, a student seated in the semicircle asked, "He was president? He couldn't walk?"

The Chinese student holding the picture book responded:

43

Many peoples think he's OK, because he was a good president, so it doesn't matter.

Maja interjected into the discussion:

That's right, a lot of people thought he could walk because they used to prop him up when he gave speeches. . . . They would stand him up on crutches so people didn't realize he couldn't walk. That probably wouldn't happen today, with TV and everything, but back then most people only heard him on the radio. They didn't seem him on TV like we do now.

The discussion went on for a few more minutes. The students seemed genuinely amazed that a president could be confined to a wheelchair. Then the other members of the group began to describe the posters on the chalkrail. The first poster depicted three major decisions that Roosevelt had made during World War II and a blow-up of a political cartoon of Roosevelt, Churchill, and Stalin. The Chinese student described it:

Yeah, this picture, yeah, Roosevelt smoking a cigar, and here, Churchill smoking a cigarette, one of those long things . . . a holder, you know, and Stalin, he not have anything. . . . They're smiling, like friends, and it say "Just Perfect Harmony" here.

The second poster depicted the bombing of Pearl Harbor and a timeline showing when the Americans entered the war. The Korean student explained:

. . . America say, their problem not us, so they want people mind their own business, but then Japanese bomb Pearl Harbor and America say OK. . . .

Both the political cartoon and the photos of Pearl Harbor generated a lively discussion which continue until Maja called time and asked the class to fill out their evaluation forms while the second group set up for their presentation.

MAJA'S REACTION

After class, Maja exclaimed, "Wow! They really know this stuff! These kids give me chills!" She seemed pleased that the students had learned so much about each leader and had clearly understood what she had expected them to do. Maja qualified this by saying, "These kids are great, they really take off on something. They know more about these leaders than I ever thought they would. It's them, not me." She went on to say that she felt she had provided just enough instructional support for them to be able to do what she was asking, and this was why they had done so well on their projects.

Later, as she watched the videotape of the presentations, she recalled,

"If you think about it, in the short time that I've been teaching them, this whole packet, and my whole system has really fallen into place. The difference between today and a few weeks ago is amazing. Considering all this stuff is new to them, it's really amazing. It's a credit to them that they can pick this up so fast." At the end of the videotape Maja recalled proudly:

My first impression is that I'm very confident and on top of things, but you know, I'm not overbearing either. I encourage them to talk and I really am interested in knowing what they have to say. I see myself wanting to connect with them, and I guess I do. I sound like I really know what I'm talking about. The lesson was so organized, and this is nice, this is my vision of good teaching and I think that's pretty good!

For Maja, her long-range planning and the strategies she had developed to cope with the realities of the classroom seemed to enable her teaching and her image of herself as a teacher to move a bit closer to her vision and lessened some of the tensions she had experienced earlier in the practicum.

Discussion

Maja's perceptions of the TESOL practicum seemed to be shrouded in tensions – tensions that seemed not only to affect what she said and did, but also her understanding of what teaching is and what it means to be a teacher. For Maja, the most overwhelming tension rested in the gap between her vision of teaching and the realities she faced in the classroom. To a large extent, she perceived these realities as being due to the nature of the TESOL practicum itself. Maja complained that these were not her classes, the students were not her students, nor was there enough time to establish a relationship with them. She complained of constantly having her limits tested, of spending more time and energy dealing with behavior management than actual teaching, and of feeling that these realities were beyond her control. Unfortunately, Maja's experiences are not unique. In mainstream educational research, a large body of recent research suggests that the realities of the classroom rarely conform to pre-service teachers' expectations or images (Kagan 1992). Moreover, since pre-service teachers generally lack the practical knowledge they need to deal with these realities, they tend to teach in ways that fail to promote learning, but instead simply maintain the flow of instruction and classroom order.

Throughout the TESOL practicum, Maja's conception of herself as a teacher, her conception of second language teaching, her knowledge of the students, and her ability to cope with the realities of the classroom

45

did not evolve separately, but seemed intertwined. As Maja discovered what her students were capable of doing, she was better able to tailor her instructional activities to match their abilities. As she began to establish a relationship with her students, she was better able to anticipate where they might have difficulties and how she could best help them. One of her later journal entries focused on her growing understanding of her students:

In class [the university methods course] we talk about "the students" as these generic things, like faceless blobs, that are always out there waiting for us to teach them. But now when I think of students I see faces and names, and personalities, and real people who have real experiences, and I know these people. I know what they like and don't like. I know how they will act and what they will say if I call on them. Now that I know them, I can teach them. Before, it was just a shot in the dark, but now I know what I'm aiming at.

Maja's initial tensions may have been due, in part, to the fact that most pre-service teachers enter the practicum with a critical lack of knowledge about the students (Book et al, 1983; Brousseau and Freeman 1984; Kagan 1992; Weinstein 1989). This lack of knowledge makes it difficult for pre-service teachers to see what their students are learning from their instructional activities, and thus, they tend to focus more on themselves than on their students. Pre-service teachers, like Maja, may first need to come to terms with their own images of teachers and teaching, and gradually begin to use what they are learning about their students and the classroom to modify, adapt, and reconstruct those images. However, for this sort of change to occur, it may be necessary for pre-service teachers to experience some sort of dissonance during the practicum experience (Kagan 1992). Such dissonance may force pre-service teachers to resolve these conflicting images, and in turn, begin to focus less on themselves and more on what their students are doing and learning.

Maja's conception of herself as a teacher and the limits she had set for herself and for her students also began to evolve during the TESOL practicum. As Maja began to recognize the limits of what she believed to be acceptable classroom behavior, she was better able either to adjust those limits or at least make them explicit for her students so that they knew what was expected of them. In her journal she wrote:

Joan and I have different limits. She is much more tolerant of things. This was hard for me to deal with at first because I'd observe her and say, "I wouldn't do it like that" or "That won't happen when I teach." But now that I've been teaching for a while I see why Joan lets the student do certain things and I'm OK with that. There are certain things I won't tolerate, but if students know what these are, they don't seem to cross them. Deep down, I think they want to fit in, they just have to know what fitting in means.

As Maja came to terms with the realities of teaching, she began to develop strategies to cope with them. This meant anticipating the ways in which these realities would affect what went on in her classroom, and then arranging her classroom instruction in such a way as to deal with the realities up front; in doing so, her lessons would have the best possible chance of proceeding in the way she envisioned them. While Maja's vision of teaching did not change drastically over the course of the TESOL practicum, her understanding of how to create a classroom environment in which that vision could become realized did. And in the process, she began to develop instructional strategies that enabled her to cope with the social and pedagogical realities she faced in the classroom. In our final interview Maja explained:

I've learned a lot through all of this. Mostly what it's really like out there. I guess nothing prepares you for what it's really like, but I got through it, and so did the students. I think I learned more from them than they did from me.

Conclusion

While the TESOL practicum is only one experience in the long-term development of an effective second language teacher, a better understanding of pre-service teachers' perceptions of the practicum may enable the field of second language teacher education to better understand how second language teachers learn to teach and how teacher preparation programs can effectively enhance this development process. Maja's perceptions of the TESOL practicum suggest some rarely cited implications for second language teacher preparation programs. First and foremost is the need for teacher preparation programs to put forth a realistic view of teaching that recognizes the realities of classroom life and adequately prepares pre-service teachers to cope with those realities. This means providing pre-service teachers with knowledge about how classrooms work, or procedural knowledge about the day-to-day operations of managing and teaching in real classrooms. It also means providing pre-service teachers with knowledge about what students are like, to see students, not as "faceless blobs" but as individuals with unique needs, interests, aptitudes, and personalities. In addition, it means providing opportunities for pre-service teachers to come to understand who they are – their conceptions of themselves as teachers, of their "limits," and of their "visions" of teaching. It also means granting them a reasonable amount of control over what and how they will teach during the practicum, so that they can test their emerging conceptions of teaching. Finally, putting forth a realistic view of teaching means providing pre-service teachers with realistic expectations about what the practicum teaching experience will be like and what they can expect to gain from it.

I would argue that the view of teaching described above is virtually ignored in most second-language teacher preparation programs. On the contrary, it is assumed to be "on-the-job" knowledge that can be learned only through experience. Maja's perceptions of her experiences during the TESOL practicum attest to the trial-and-error nature of how she acquired this knowledge, and point to the importance of making such knowledge an integral part of any teacher preparation program. Teacher preparation programs that continue to present a theoretical view of teaching, without recognizing a more realistic one, are in essence sending pre-service teachers into the practicum ill-prepared to learn to teach. Those pre-service teachers, like Maja, who have strong images of themselves as teachers and of teaching may be able to overcome the realities of teaching without succumbing to them. But what about the pre-service teachers who do not? More important, will Maja be able to sustain her vision of teaching throughout her professional career, or will that vision be slowly eroded by the realities of teaching that appear to be inherent in most educational institutions? How much tension, or dissonance (Kagan 1992), is helpful (or harmful) to pre-service teachers as they learn to teach? How much control should pre-service teachers be given over what and how they teach during the practicum? How might a teacher preparation program have made Maja's practicum experience less like "hazing" and more like professional development? These are questions that must be answered by further explorations into pre-service teachers' perceptions of what actually occurs during the TESOL practicum and beyond.

References

Bogdan, R., and S. K. Biklen. 1992. *Qualitative Research for Education: An Introduction to Theory and Methods*, 2nd ed. Boston: Allyn & Bacon.

Book, C., J. Byers, and D. Freeman. 1983. Student expectations and teacher education traditions with which we can and cannot live. *Journal of Teacher Education* 34 (1): 9–13.

Brousseau, B., and D. Freeman. 1984. Entering teacher candidate interviews – fall 1982. Research and evaluation in teacher education. OPE Technical Report No. 5. East Lansing: Michigan State University (ERIC Document Reproduction Service ED 257 800).

Freeman, D. 1989. Teacher training, development and decision making model: A model of teaching and related strategies for language teacher education. *TESOL Quarterly* 23: 27–45.

Johnson, K. E. 1992. Learning to teach: Instructional actions and decisions of preservice ESL teachers. *TESOL Quarterly 26*(3): 507–535.

Kagan, D. M. 1992. Professional growth among preservice and beginning teachers. *Review of Educational Research 62*(2): 129–169.

McCall, G. J., and J. L. Simmons. 1969. *Issues in Participant Observation.* Reading, Mass.: Addison-Wesley.

Richards, J. C. 1987. The dilemma of teacher preparation in TESOL. *TESOL Quarterly 21*: 209–226.

Richards, J. C., and G. Crookes. 1988. The practicum in TESOL. *TESOL Quarterly 22*: 9–27.

Shavelson, R. J., and P. Stern. 1981. Research on teachers' pedagogical thoughts, judgments, decisions, and behavior. *Review of Educational Research 51*: 455–498.

Weinstein, C. S. 1989. Teacher education students' preconceptions of teaching. *Journal of Teacher Education 40*(2): 53–60.

Wilson, S. 1977. The use of ethnographic techniques in educational research. *Review of Educational Research 47*: 245–265.

3 Student foreign language teacher's knowledge growth

Gloria Gutiérrez Almarza

> We play school. Grace has a couple of
> chairs and a wooden table in her cellar,
> and a small blackboard and chalk. . . .
> Grace is the teacher, Carol and I the
> students. We have to do spelling tests
> and sums in arithmetic; it is like real
> school, but worse, because we never get
> to draw pictures. We cannot pretend to
> be bad, because Grace doesn't like
> disorder.
>
> (Atwood 1990: 53)

This chapter describes part of a ten-month longitudinal study of the process of learning to teach foreign languages, which I carried out at the University of London during the academic year 1990–1991. The study was not about the content or structure of a particular teacher education programme, nor was it about what student teachers should know or how they should perform while teaching. It was not meant to evaluate student teachers' practice according to a set of predefined criteria, nor was it meant to be an assessment of the knowledge they had about teaching and learning a foreign language. Rather, it grew out of a concern to uncover some of the issues that characterize the process of learning to teach a foreign language from the student teachers' perspective, and more specifically to analyze the origin and content of student teachers' knowledge, the changes it undergoes during an initial teacher education course and how it relates to the way they teach during teaching practice. The study also aimed to explore to what degree qualitative research techniques can be used as teacher education techniques.

The study focused on how four foreign language student teachers (Beth, Melani, Rachel and Ronan) developed their professional knowledge about foreign language teaching, namely, student teachers' pretraining knowledge, the interaction between pretraining knowledge and

I would like to thank Fernando Beltrán and Martin O'Shaughnessy for their suggestions on the manuscript and the Spanish Ministry of Education for their financial support to carry out this study.

50

teacher education knowledge and how this knowledge related to practice while participating in a pre-service teacher education programme (Post-Graduate Certificate in Education).[1] In contrast to studies which have tried to establish some sort of relationship between teachers' pedagogical knowledge and actual classroom performance by assessing their performance against prespecified sets of criteria (see Kagan 1990), this study aimed to address one of the areas which has not received attention in pre-service foreign language teacher education research: what kinds of relationships exist between knowledge and action with reference to the student teachers' thinking, rather than to an external framework. So the research objectives were embedded within the general theoretical frameworks of teachers' thinking and teacher socialization.[2] Studies like this one tend to emphasize what teachers are, rather than what they do. There is a vast corpus of data which has provided evidence to support the idea that student teachers tend to recall and build upon their own experiences in classrooms. Teachers have internalized models of teaching by "apprenticeship of observation," which they activate once they are in a classroom. These early school experiences seem to constitute a more powerful influence than teacher education programmes on the process of learning to teach, both in the way student teachers interpret their training and teaching and in the way they teach (Lortie 1975). However, it is not only the time spent "watching teachers" on which student teachers base their knowledge; they have also had informal language learning experiences to which they attach different meanings (Freeman 1991; Horwitz 1985). If this is so, it is rather surprising that teacher training courses do little to make this experiential perspective explicit. There are two points worth mentioning here. First, this knowledge, which is based on different personal learning experiences, is rich, diverse and complex, and probably different from the prescriptive mode of knowledge with which they are presented during teacher education. Second, teachers' professional courses do not seem to make much difference, due to the well-rooted nature of the assumptions and experience that student teachers bring with them.

Drawing on the assumption of research on teacher thinking that teaching situations are singular and on qualitative research which focuses on studying concrete, singular situations without aiming at generalizations, no previous hypothesis or prespecified categories guided the data collection. This made it easier to understand the process from

---

1 These were a priori categories of analysis, which were understood in their full meaning after the data analysis. Pretraining knowledge was understood, from the beginning, as the ideas student teachers had about language, language learning and language teaching before they began the teacher education programme.
2 See, for example, Calderhead 1981, 1988; Clark 1986, 1988; Clark and Peterson 1986; Freeman 1989; Lortie 1975; Mitchell and Marland 1989.

the participants' points of view. Nevertheless, this approach should not imply that the findings are anecdotal and that they do not make sense in other situations.

The chapter also discusses the qualitative techniques used to collect the data, how they proved very helpful in examining student teachers' knowledge and suggests ways to describe and analyse the process of learning how to teach and thus design teacher education courses more in line with this process. Finally, it discusses the analysis of the data by describing the origin and content of student teachers' pretraining knowledge, documenting the changes in pretraining knowledge during the teacher education course and drawing the relationship between student teachers' knowledge and their practice.

Research methodology

The full period of data collection covered nine months – the length of the Post-Graduate Certificate in Education (PGCE) course – during the 1990–1991 academic year. The methods of data collection included a blend of qualitative techniques: semistructured interviews,[3] journals,[4] classroom observations[5] and stimulated recall procedures.[6] The qualitative data gathered by these different complementary methods were designed to capture student teachers' knowledge about foreign language teaching and to understand its influence on teaching. In a similar fashion to Woods's study (1990), these methods were designed to gain access to aspects of student teachers' knowledge at two levels, theoretical and classroom activity. At a theoretical level, they aimed to elicit student teachers' ideas about language and about teaching and learning languages. At a classroom level they focused on the activities and learning experiences selected by the student teacher and how these were used within the teaching-learning process (Richards 1990), together with the "definitions and process by which they are manufactured" (Bogdan and Biklen 1982: 33). Using Butt and Raymond's (1987: 71) words:

[The] interest [was] in teacher thinking and its interrelationships with action. It is logical, then, that we focus directly on the qualitative nature of teacher's

3 See Bogdan and Taylor 1984; Brenner et al. 1985; Burgess 1988; Butt and Raymond 1989; see also Gutiérrez Almarza 1992 for a detailed description of the way the interviews were conducted in this study.
4 See Bailey 1990; Goetz and LeCompte 1984; Porter et al. 1990. See also Gutiérrez Almarza 1992 for a detailed description of the way the diaries were conducted in this study.
5 See Black and Champion 1976; H. Burgess 1985. See also Gutiérrez Almarza 1992 for a detailed description of the way the observation was done in this study.
6 See Calderhead 1981; Clark and Peterson 1986.

thoughts and actions. . . . What teachers do and think within their professional lives depends . . . upon the meanings those individuals hold and interpret within their personal, social, and professional realities and everyday-life situations. Just observing an event or a phenomenon, even through the eyes of a participant is not sufficient. One needs to go further to understand the relationship among antecedent, subsequent, and consequent events through engaging in dialogue with the teacher.

The data gathered consisted of transcribed interviews, journals, transcribed classroom recordings and documents (e.g., planning protocols, photocopies of classroom materials used during the lessons).

Data analysis consisted of, first, coding one of the student teacher's data both deductively by using the general categories derived from the literature and the research questions, and inductively by identifying the concepts which formed these categories as they emerged from the data, as Figure 1 shows. The data do not fit categories neatly because human consciousness is far from neat and has many implicit and ill-defined connections. Modifications and expansions of categories took place throughout the analytical process until the material was finally arranged in a meaningful way.

A second analytical stage was an inductive process of defining and redefining the initial broad categories, after new readings of the data. As I was reading, I was jotting down the ideas and concepts which seemed to be embedded in the data. These made up the content of each of the categories, for example, 'language functions', 'two different language learning processes', 'means of expression'.

Third, I revised and modified the a priori coding themes. Following the traditional 'cut-and-paste' technique, I gathered all the chunks of data belonging to the same category together. This was completed by written summaries of each different category (Hewson and Hewson 1989). The same process was followed with all of the student teachers. This served as a way to validate the categories and themes which emerged from the data.

Four main themes were finally clearly identified (pretraining knowledge, teacher education or transfer to the concept of teaching method, relationships between students' knowledge and teaching practice and relationships between pretraining knowledge and posttraining knowledge), by means of which I described student teachers' knowledge, how it developed, and the relationships between knowledge and teaching. These became the organizing themes of the case studies. The analysis was completed by writing up the individual profiles in a case study format which described the most salient features of each student teacher's knowledge and in a cross-case study format which brought together common trends within the group. The complete research process is summarised in Figure 2.

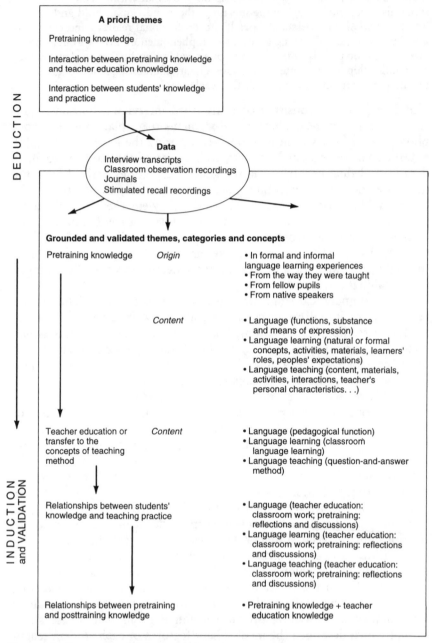

Figure 1. Summary of data analysis.

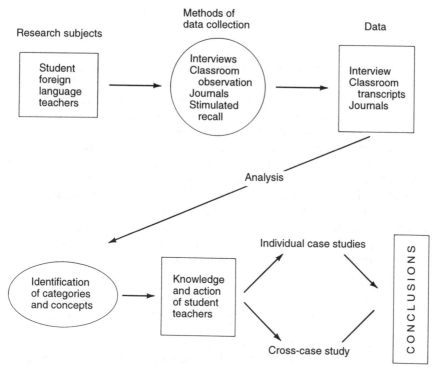

Figure 2. Research process.

Discussion of results

Drawing on the analysis of the data and the theoretical framework, I will now discuss the process of student teachers' knowledge growth, which encompassed the following themes: student teachers' pretraining knowledge: origins and content; teacher education: the transfer to the concepts of teaching method; teaching practice: the relationship between knowledge and practice; and the relationships between pretraining knowledge and posttraining knowledge. It is impossible in the space of this chapter to show the richness of the data or the complexity of the analysis. The only thing I can do is provide a few examples in the form of quotations from interviews and classroom observations to illustrate the most relevant issues found at the different stages in the process of learning to be a foreign language teacher, as summarised in Figure 1.

Gloria Gutiérrez Almarza

Student teachers' pretraining knowledge

All four student teachers had memories of their language learning experiences on which they built an initial conceptualisation of their profession. These recollections were based on their own learning experiences (formal and informal) as well as on the way they were taught: their "apprenticeship of observation" during their schooling years. They learned not only from their teachers but also from fellow pupils and other people with whom they interacted, and they assigned different meanings to their individual learning experiences. This is particularly relevant to foreign language students, who, apart from learning foreign languages in formal contexts (school grammar-based language teaching and college literature-based work), spend a considerable amount of time interacting with native speakers in informal and naturalistic situations in the countries where their foreign languages are spoken. Melani saw these two experiences in the following terms:

In and out of the classroom context, it was a complete involvement. I had to function in the language as a complete human being in all different ways, so it is the whole personality that is involved. In the classroom you are given tasks to do. It is an intellectual exercise, and you are meant to express your thoughts, opinions or whatever in the language, but you thought 'What's the point? My language isn't French. If I really wanted to say it, I'd say it in English', but when you are in the country and you want to say how you feel about something you have to use the language [It is] the whole person as opposed to just the pupil.

Ball and McDiarmid also argue that 'understandings of subject matter are acquired in significant ways outside of schools; to assume that teachers' subject matter preparation is confined to experiences of formal schooling would be to ignore a major source of teachers' learning and ideas' (1990: 446). Regardless of the specific origins of student teachers' knowledge, what is relevant is the description of the content of this existing pretraining knowledge, which I will describe next.

CONTENT

The four student teachers began their education courses not only with general ideas about the dynamics of teaching and learning and about the general and interactional aspects of teaching and teachers' roles, but also with subject-specific knowledge and knowledge about learning and teaching particular subjects. Thus student teachers' pretraining knowledge was subject specific about the subject matter – language – and also about ways of learning and teaching it. All four had a rich understanding of language, language learning and teaching.[7] The two different contexts in which they learned language meant that they defined language and language learning according to these contexts. They all had at this stage, though to different degrees, a functional view of language. They generally saw language as having different functions, substance and means of expression (oral or written) in the two contexts (classroom and natural). Language as a subject in the school curriculum was seen as a formal system and as mainly written language. Ronan remembered the language he had learned at school:

There was not much oral expression, there was basically sitting down in front of your exercise book and writing out little sentences, and getting your very basic, very rigid grammatical background, which does have its advantages, I mean, you need to know that stuff but perhaps. . . .

In a natural context, the four understood language in a much wider sense, mainly as a way of exploring personal experience and as interpersonal communication involving meaning, paralinguistic features and spoken language. While the system of the language was the focus when they talked about language in the classroom, meaning, fluency and a cultural component formed the substance of the language outside the classroom. Rachel remembered the contrast between the language she had learned at school and the language she needed in a natural interactive situation:

I stayed with a French family for a week and we were at the table and I wanted to ask for some butter and I came up with something very formal, very polite, and they all laughed and, you know, that's how we were taught at school . . . I think language provides a framework for your personality and thoughts, the way you see things, I don't know, I don't know exactly what it is, a different language can make you see things differently.

They all understood language learning in relation to natural or classroom contexts, as they involve learners in different kinds of activities, in using different kinds of materials and language, playing different roles and achieving different learning outcomes. They all included learner-related factors in their discussion of language learning. Rachel made a clear distinction between these two ways of learning French,

---

7 Most studies on teachers' thinking and some studies on teachers' knowledge assume that teachers bring with them general concepts about teaching. For example, Zeichner et al.'s (1987) belief inventory includes the following categories to describe teachers' perspectives: teacher's role, teacher-pupil relationship, knowledge and curriculum, student diversity, role of the community in school affairs and role of school in society. Richards (1990) summarises the categories which have been used to describe effective language teaching as classroom management, structuring tasks, student groupings, time on task and feedback.

emphasizing the contradictory things people expected of her in the class-room and in a natural situation:

I found I wasn't really expected to produce perfect sentences [in France], in fact people were surprised I spoke as much and as well as I did . . . So I think I did start to relax about absolute perfection and at the same time I began to feel more and more confident about doing things in the language. . . . It was completely different to go from learning verbs to actually having to talk to people. We hadn't done much work in listening. . . . I don't think we ever learned at school . . . how to do useful things with the language, we never learned how to get a train ticket . . . so that was something you had to learn from scratch. . . . During my first week, when I spent time with a family, I took it as a personal challenge to get every single word I uttered right, but when I went to Paris with the daughter of the family I found I wasn't really expected to produce perfect sentences.

The same contrast is highlighted by Beth:

It is very different because probably, people who were my teachers might say something like: 'Come on, you have to get your French a bit better, it is not that good, this is wrong, this is wrong'. When you go to the country . . . they would say 'Your French is good, you sound like you're French' and all this . . . People are much more enthusiastic . . . and you know it is not true, but it does encourage you, whereas some of the teachers some time ago were saying 'That's dreadful . . . you are not using the subjunctive or something'.

Regarding teaching, they not only mentioned general concepts about or attitudes towards teaching but instructional subject-specific aspects (teaching content, materials, activities), interactional aspects and teach-ers' personal characteristics. They conceptualised language teaching mainly as establishing successful relationships with the students, organ-izing activities (learning and managerial) and selecting materials and content. Melani said that 'you have to be very much in control and confident. So not only do you know what you are doing and you want to do it, but you know how to do it because that can be felt instantly'. Rachel's main concern was how to re-create a natural process of lan-guage learning within the constraints of a classroom:

As a teacher now it worries me that even the most realistic, meaningful type of classroom activities that I can possible imagine, will never manage to recreate the incredible experience and excitement of learning a language abroad. I do realize that the two learning processes are completely different in terms of time, input, practice, etc. But it worries me that I lack the power to, albeit artificially, reproduce only the excitement of the experience . . . It should be, but I just don't know how to do that, but it would be brilliant to make the classroom what, say, Wales, was for me when I started learning English; it just happened. I mean if you can make the classroom as close as possible . . . to what happens outside, the pupil might have a better chance of learning a language.

Beth and Ronan do not share the same view about whether a language teacher should or should not be a native speaker:

In a way I think it is nonsense to teach a language which is not your own. . . . I can talk, my English is a million times better than my French, so really I should teach English . . . unless you can say that you've seen the problems of the learner because you've learned it. . . . I don't know.

When I did my year teaching in Mexico I got quite frustrated as an English teacher and when someone put a very specific grammar question to me I found inevitably 9 occasions out of 10 I couldn't answer it, I could put things into context, but the times I was asked a purely grammatical question I used to say 'well, I can't give you a rule, but I can tell you that this is right and this is wrong' but when I was in Mexico I also taught French at L'Alliance Francaise to a little beginner group and as I had learned French from scratch myself I knew the grammatical background, I enjoyed that more and the questions that were put to me I could answer.

These were the major themes of the four student teachers' conceptions of language, teaching and learning language as they entered the pre-service programme. The concepts (language functions, different language learning processes, etc.) which formed the content of the student teachers' pretraining knowledge are extremely valuable because they are the 'cogs' we can use to link *their* knowledge with *our* theory during teacher education. Although their ideas might not have been put forward in an academic discourse, they may serve as a basis on which to make the connections between theory and practice which are crucial in their professional development. Yet we won't be able to establish what kind of contribution teacher education courses make to student teachers' development and how they contribute to student teachers' education if we do not know what was already there and how this old knowledge relates to practice.

Teacher education or transfer to the concept of teaching method

Five weeks into the programme, student teachers' pretraining knowledge became a compound body of knowledge encapsulated in the method student teachers were trained to use during teaching practice.[8]

---

8 This is the way Ronan described the method they learned during teacher education:
COANT, a visual input for vocabulary you build gradually in the oral process, after which you can consolidate the language by writing:
C = c'est . . . (e.g., vocab input, e.g., hay una cerveza)
O = oui/non (e.g., ¿hay una cerveza? si/no)
A = alternatives (e.g., ¿hay una cereza o hay un café? – hay un café?)
N = negatives (e.g., ¿hay un café? – no, hay una cerveza)
T = target (e.g., ¿qué hay? hay una cerveza)

This method amalgamated a view of language, a view of how people learn a language and a particular series of learning activities, mainly a sequence of teachers' graded questions and pupils' answers.

From now on, having a definite, clear method became the most important aspect of Melani's knowledge about teaching. In different entries to her journal she wrote that having a method meant having clear and unambiguous materials, well-defined lesson plans and being able to handle equipment successfully. By carrying out the sequence of activities dictated by the method, learned during teacher education, she measured both her pupils' progress and her own success as a student teacher:

Now having applied it [the method] with . . . both classes and private students, I can see why it's been called the 'miracle' method! Even my least confident students have been speaking the language with good pronunciation and without making mistakes and I know they'll never forget what they've learned. . . . With this method they never hear an incorrect version – so, of course, they don't make mistakes. . . .

The method was without question the decisive factor in my carrying out teaching practice successfully. It gave me absolute confidence and it had a positive effect on the pupils towards French or Spanish and towards me, as it allowed me, for the first time, to really achieve something in the language and feel that they had achieved something.

The confidence she experienced from having this method also affected the relationships she maintained with the rest of the teachers in the school department and her attitude towards coursebooks:

They [the teachers] didn't try to interfere in what I did – partly because they simply didn't realize that different methods of language teaching existed! Recent developments in modern language teaching have simply not reached them and their lessons are clear examples of language teaching without method. . . .

Having had the experience of looking critically at coursebooks I can just see how defective all the coursebooks currently available are, the methodology enabled me to do this for myself. . . . Now I feel confident that I won't need a coursebook to give me the progression of structures to follow but will be able to build up a course myself, selecting the structures to be taught and deciding in which order to present them.

By contrast, Ronan thought:

[I]t's going to be a lot of trial and error over the next six weeks . . . because I suppose every teacher is unique. There is no model because you cannot apply the model, a model can't be applied to a particular personality, that's not going to work for every one. So it is a matter of me testing the models and finding my own . . . own sort of niche and then realizing it with the pupils.

The main theme which ran through the way Rachel understood foreign language teaching was the resistance she offered to the new method she was trained to implement during teaching practice. In contrast to Melani, who adhered to the new knowledge, or in contrast to Beth, who rejected it and adhered to the way she had been taught at school, Rachel found herself uncomfortable with the new knowledge because it conflicted with previous teacher training and teaching experiences. And, like Beth, she felt guilty:

I hope I am not going to be too critical about this, and not just, I suppose I shouldn't really say this, but I feel tempted to experiment when there isn't going to be an observer, whereas when I am going to be observed I'll do things that he [tutor] is expecting me to do and, I don't know, I may be a bit selfish, in a sense, that, you know, I am asking for time to experiment but there are children there that have to learn, and using those children for guinea pigs which isn't perhaps a good idea. But I don't know . . . but I just feel that there are ways that children or students can learn, can enjoy lessons more even if it has to take a longer route.

She did not believe in a methodology which did not consider the learner as the center of the learning process. Her main consideration was to motivate the students: 'It seems to me that it [Q/A – question and answer] is a shortcut, but in which you are going to get people stuck. Pupils are going to lose motivation or not see language as something that can help them do things, other than getting the question right'.

More specifically, the range of language functions which appeared in their pretraining knowledge was reduced to that of language performing a pedagogical function, with an emphasis on structures and forms and no real difference between the written and the spoken means of expression. For example, Melani wrote in her diary, 'after having [taught] for a year or so, I would get to know in what order to present grammatical structures'.

Two of the student teachers did not accept this new view of language that was different from their own. In response to a phrase-based view of language, Beth rehabilitated an academic view of language with an emphasis on language competence and knowledge of the underlying grammatical system, which would allow learners to generate language in different contexts in contrast with the limited generating capacity of narrowly contextualised phrases:

Whereas I can generally accept that oral work, conversation, etc., is a more realistic presentation of language, language within a realistic context, I can't quite invalidate some of the ways I learned, e.g., memorizing lists of vocabu-

61

lary for weekly tests. I understand the rationale that is discussed here but it is tempting to think – what's wrong with the way I was taught?

Rachel reacted against this view of language she found in the course on the basis that language was devoid of meaning and relevance for the learners:

I am reacting quite strongly against the methodology that is being advised here. . . . For example, encouraging us to begin presentation with what they call 'C'est un livre' 'This is a book', 'This is a chair', 'What is this?' 'Is this a book?' . . . I just feel I don't like to say: 'Right this is an orange, you have to learn this' . . . They've sort of advised us to use a warm-up. But the reasons for using that warm-up seem to be to get the students to revise language which is going to be met later in the class . . . but there are no implications about whether that warm-up is also there to interest the students in the language they are about to learn.

In all four student teachers, the conceptualization of language learning now focused on classroom language learning, based on the teacher's mediation in the learning process by implementing a method which prevented pupils from making errors. Most of them found it difficult to relate their own learning processes as successful learners to the learning processes of the secondary pupils they encountered during teaching practice. For example, Melani saw the process as an interplay between the teacher's intervention (presenting a good language model which prevents learners from making mistakes) and pupils' attitudes. These ideas bear a close resemblance to behaviourist language theories, in contrast with her pretraining knowledge which included what seemed to be more learner-related factors contributing to language learning. She emphasized the idea that learning could be manipulated from the outside, namely, by using a method, at the expense of the learners' contribution to their learning process. While Melani understood language learning as a question of creating the necessary external conditions for learning the language, Rachel insisted on a more cognitive view of language with an emphasis on the learners' interests and motivations:

I feel first that it is not respecting the students' intelligence, in a way. Students may not have the word in the foreign language for a book or a chair, but they know very well that it is a book and a chair and to have to spend ten minutes arguing or not arguing, but deciding that this is a book and this is a chair, seems is to insult the students. . . . The students may not be very motivated by that kind of presentation. Why should the student want to learn, I mean, to learn those items in the first place? . . . I am just wondering to what extent, where is the balance on that scale, where can you sort of exert your knowledge as a teacher in order to choose the right kind of input, to guide the students to look into, let's say, certain texts, or certain whatever, but at the same time keeping up motivation in the student.

During teacher education, student teachers acquired some pedagogical knowledge (a method) which they lacked and some ideas about language learning processes, while their subject matter knowledge remained largely the same and was, in some cases, a source of friction with the new teacher education knowledge. The four student teachers seemed to modify their pretraining knowledge in response to pressures which came from the university rather than from the classroom, and so they performed their task during teaching practice in a similar way – although they voiced reservations about the way they taught in their discussions about their teaching, as we will see below. Whereas the teachers studied by Wilson et al. (1987) developed their pedagogical content knowledge during practice in different ways to respond to different sets of students, different schools, time or content, all four student teachers implemented the same method regardless of any of these elements.

Relationship between knowledge and teaching

Documenting the complex relationship between knowledge and action was at the heart of this study. Although at times it was not easy or clear, I will try to discuss how the student teachers' practice was rooted in different knowledge sources. Student teachers used pretraining knowledge and the new teacher education knowledge in a variety of ways during teaching practice. Although an analysis of their behaviour showed a homogeneous way of dealing with subject matter, in that they followed the same method, the interviews I conducted on the way student teachers were teaching showed that student teachers' knowledge had not been made homogeneous, and during teaching practice and at the end of the year they maintained different views about language, teaching and learning languages. Melani's view of language, a rehearsal stage for the real experience, drew on her pretraining knowledge (developing language competence), and teacher education knowledge (focus on accuracy by practicing surface structures and a progression from oral to written skills). The substance of the language she selected and taught was basically structural, as the following quotation shows:

It's simply an exercise but it'll still be interesting and fun for them to do and although they aren't actually communicating in the language, they are speaking the language and pronouncing it correctly and getting the feel of speaking it which will be of value to them when they communicate and also I think it can be an enjoyable way of using the language because they don't have to think about what meaning they want to communicate, that's all done for them, all they have to do is speak the language and understand it. It's much easier for them to do so, once they are freed of all concern about content, message, they seem to enjoy the Q/A, because, I think, it gives them a sense of achievement. They are actually being given the chance to speak the language without having to think of what to say.

She also conceived of language as underlying rules or patterns, because that way students 'take the whole thing as a whole' and ' . . . after the presentation [I was] asking them about the pattern, it's a way of focusing attention on the form: getting them to put circles around them makes it even clearer'. During teaching practice she appreciated that her multifunctional and meaning-based approach to language was only possible outside the classroom, so she followed a structural approximation to language with some systemic knowledge and a limited level of communication:

There isn't yet anything that they want to find out about through the language or communicate to other people through the language. What all this is is a preparation for sometime in the future when they may well want to find out about something through the medium of Spanish and communicate it through Spanish. So it's like a role-play or rehearsal for the actual event, but just like in the theatre there has to be a certain suspension of disbelief, they have to imagine that this is something they actually want to find out about, so that they'll be able to do it when the time comes.

She realised that she had to keep the real world and the classroom separate. For example, when she saw language as communication and as a means of expression, she thought it could be achieved only outside the classroom context.

Rachel, similarly, drew on the knowledge she acquired during teacher education when she presented language as structures and phrases and progressed from oral to written skills. She incorporated part of her pre-training knowledge when she directed pupils' attention to grammar rules. The next quotation shows her dissatisfaction with the kind of language she was expected to teach:

But it still worries me, do they know that, why are they using the plural there? Do they know why they are using the singular in 100 gramos de merluza, for example? I tried to ask at the end of the presentation of food why we'd say, try to elicit, but there wasn't time, I am not sure that things are so clear. . . . I don't know whether they would be able to take those items and use them in a different context when they need to use the article. . . . If I had had the class from the start, I would have made sure that they had some kind of awareness of gender from the very start and they would be able to make links with the articles, with different kinds of articles, so that it didn't have to be taught every single time when the word came out.

Although she felt guilty about favouring language as a rule-governed activity over contextualized phrases, Beth dismissed the learning of contextualized phrases on the grounds of their limited generative potential in new situations and the fact that the ability to speak may not lead to knowledge of the system:

It's so strongly inbred into you, as a result of being here and because of the school I was in, that you don't overdo the grammatical side of things. Personally I'd rather have a rule which tells you that there is more than one thing you put the *s* on the end of the adjective, personally that's what I like. . . . Sometimes I think it is easier to see it as a sort of . . . as rules really, I mean, I think that can sometimes make learning a lot easier because you can apply the rules to a lot of different circumstances whereas in a communicative approach I think you can get stuck just at what you've been taught. Purely communicative means you can't move on to things you haven't met before, I think. I am saying this and I am thinking, 'Oh my God, am I the only person who has thoughts like these', you know, it seems like really appalling.

In Rachel's view, classroom language learning was a question of learning the code, of acquiring language competence by mastering the underlying rules of the language. During teaching practice, Rachel focused on performance by practicing correct language structures in a process of pupil recognition and production of language carefully selected and graded by the teacher. Underlying Rachel's practice there was a gradual process of recognition, production, consolidation and reinforcement:

Well, basically, the oral question and answer just takes them very gradually . . . from the mere recognition of the language to the full production orally. And then the worksheet, in a way, reflects that as well; it takes them from merely having to recognise the new language, by ticking or crossing where they are not expected to produce anything yet [and then] they produce the language by copying and then the next activity they have to, not to exactly copy, but they'd be able to use a model and change it and then the very last activity that they are expected to produce it on their own. So the idea is that everybody can start, and everybody will be able to recognise when they are copying, and most people would be able to gradually use the language on their own, just very gently.

At the same time, drawing on her pretraining knowledge, she expressed doubts about this and saw a need for an understanding of the underlying grammar rules. She expressed doubts about whether by focusing on and practicing only the explicit forms of the language, pupils would also acquire the underlying rules and would be able to use the language in different contexts. She commented, for example, that 'they did very well and . . . they know how to use all this language, but I don't know if they know anything about it when you teach it in another context' or 'how to handle the language if they are left on their own with those phrases. Will they know how to put the bits together?'

65

Melani, by contrast, thought that by using the method she could compensate for the inadequacies of the classroom to learn a language and that a teacher-led Q/A activity would reproduce the immersion process which characterizes natural learning in the classroom:

Q/A activity does the same thing [as when you are in the foreign country] but because you haven't got a year or a long time it's doing it in a short length of time by selecting the language and so on. It's like a very intensive immersion session in the sense that the pupils are doing what I did when I was learning, which is to proceed by trial and error, but they haven't got the [time] that I had, so it doesn't take the same length of time. They are supported in the way that I wasn't and at the same time it's immersion in Spanish, the whole thing is in Spanish.

Melani's ideas about language learning seemed to be based on her teacher education knowledge: an inductive way of acquiring linguistic competence by focusing on performance. This was complemented by her pretraining knowledge, which made her see the need to focus on the underlying grammar rules. Her pretraining ideas about achieving communication were postponed for a future when pupils were free from classroom constraints.

Similarly, Ronan first introduced the language, made pupils repeat after his model and involved them in choral and individual repetition exercises, followed by positive reinforcement, as learned during teacher education:

The exercises are always the same, usually listening, speaking, a bit of writing and a bit of reading and have it progress from the simplest to the difficult. To start off with the simplest you can get: 'yes/no answers' you can have 'either/or' and they say it is one or the other, then go onto the negative versions when they say, you say: 'is it such and such thing?' and they say 'no, it's such and such a thing' and you move on to the target question where there is no indication as to what they are required to answer. So at the start all pupils can get an answer and you go up, you're gradually testing, building up their confidence, testing them more and more, as it goes on you try to keep that kind of format with everything progressing from simple to difficult.

Regarding teaching, Rachel and Beth, although they implemented the method very efficiently, showed a greater degree of resistance towards the modifications not only in their pretraining subject-matter knowledge but also in the knowledge about language learning imposed by the new methodology. Beth's lessons followed what she called the 'institution' methodology. This embodies the underlying learning principles of teacher's correct modelling, pupils' repetition and teacher's reinforcement by a sequence of questions and answers. The role of the teacher is to model correct language and provide feedback, whether in the form of reinforcing the language and praise or correcting mistakes. She was rather torn between the ideas underlying what she did and what she really believed in. At the same time as she disagreed with the underlying assumptions of what she was taught during teacher education, she came to value the way she had learned when she was at school:

I think the fact is, you know, that I learned French in a very traditional way and so it's very difficult to distance yourself from that kind of learning and my sort of learning was very much learning lists of vocabulary with English down one side and French down the other. Now personally I find that a much easier way of learning something than the way they are doing it here.

Beth understood foreign language teaching as something more than the controlled practice of phrases in the Q/A sequence on four grounds. First, it limited pupils' independence:

The other thing I feel is that we're halfway through the lesson now and it's still very teacher-dominated work and they put up with it and they reacted very well. But because of the length of time spent on the presentation right at the beginning it means that you are just continually dominating, you have to get through a certain amount before you can let go and do things and that's why I think there might be a quicker way to introduce the information at the beginning to allow them to go off and do things.

Second, it took too long:

Part of me would think that it might be easier just to give them a list of vocabulary. . . . It'd save a lot of time . . . just to tell them this means such and such and swap them round to get different meanings. . . . It just takes a hell of a long time to get them to learn a few very simple phrases and I just don't know if that's the most efficient way . . . of teaching something.

Third, she did not seem to be very convinced of the way Q/A practice produced learning. She thought it might be rather superficial and routine, and would not help learners to internalize the language system. She was not convinced by the absence of explicit grammatical rules:

Personally, I'd rather have a rule which tells you that there is more than one thing you put the *s* on the end of the adjective. But there is very much, particularly at this school, the softly-softly approach to it and it is let the pupils infer it rather than you tell them. . . . It's learning by your own discovery rather than having the teacher telling you, which just takes a lot longer. I am just so reactionary.

Fourth, she didn't agree with a rigid progression from oral to written work on the grounds that different pupils have different learning styles, as she saw in her classes:

There is very much this sort of you must do, listening, speaking, reading, writing. I am someone who likes seeing things written down and, I don't know, I thought that was quite interesting when I saw that. . . . I am so sort of programmed into that I almost said 'Oh no don't write it down yet, . . . we are still at the oral stage,' which is like ludicrous, but I mean that's how strong the feeling is, you shouldn't be seeing it written down, if we haven't said it enough times.

From her own experience she commented: 'I'd rather link a word with something right from the beginning, so I can start linking how something might sound like something that it's written down like that'. She argued that although she had been taught to delay letting students see the written forms, 'by keeping things orally you keep things a bit untenable, you can't really get hold of them'. To solve this conflict between her experience and teacher education, she learned to feel guilty about her real thoughts: 'It sounds really traditional, doesn't it, I am ashamed of myself'. In contrast, the following quotation illustrates the way Melani reflected on the teaching method:

This next activity is . . . still part of the preparation, but it's further work on the language in the text. We are still not using the verbs in the future but they are using the verbs and they are using all the other words in the text and in the Q/A sequence you're taking them step by step as it were, first of all they just recognize the language, then they start using it with less and less support, and finally you ask them a question and they answer using language from the text. . . . It really is the essence of the method, this Q/A sequence, because it's the activity that links the language to their thought processes. That's why it's the most important part of the lesson.

Her choice of learning activities was based on this method she had acquired during teacher education. The next quotation shows some of her postteaching reflections on it:

[The lesson] simply went very smoothly, according to plan. I mean that's the beauty of having a method, that whatever you have to do, whatever you have to teach you know how to do it. It's just a question of finding materials and finding exactly what way to do it.

This method dictated most of the activities she implemented. The scope of maneuver she had within this method was in the sequencing of the activities. She discussed teaching in terms of the implementation of this specific method which governed teaching materials, activities, order of skills, progression of activities, selection and grading of language. Her understanding of language learning underlying her practice emphasized the external intervention of the teacher (providing activities which focus on explicit linguistic behaviour and grammar rules) rather than the contribution of the learners' personal background. This shift from what seemed a cognitive view of learning in her pretraining knowledge to a more behaviourist-oriented position can be traced to teacher education.

The above quotations show clearly that pretraining knowledge was apparent not so much when the student teachers taught, as when they discussed their teaching. In most cases teacher education did not alter significantly the knowledge the student teachers brought to the course, regardless of the similarity with which they carried out their instruction during teaching practice.

Pretraining and postteaching knowledge

Despite the homogenizing effect of the teaching method on student teachers' performance during teaching practice, the fact was that at the end of the course, they left with different kinds of knowledge about the dynamics of teaching and learning languages. To a considerable extent these variations were rooted in their pretraining knowledge. For example, once Melani finished teaching practice and saw herself free from the constraints imposed by the context of the classroom, she was back in a position in which she could continue to explore the ideas she had about language prior to the beginning of the course. More than ever, she then saw how difficult it would be to reconcile her ideas about language and the limited possibilities that a secondary class can offer. For example, at the same time as she emphasized the poetic function of language, she underlined the limited possibilities that secondary classrooms allow for the teaching of languages:

Really, foreign language learning in this country is a desperate battle for
the impossible. First of all, especially in the state schools, that everything,
literally everything is against you, including the National Curriculum. . . .
Yes, foreign language learning in this country is a hopeless task.

As a way of bridging the differences between the classroom and natural settings, and successfully reproducing a natural learning process in the classroom, Melani understood language teaching as following a specific teaching method. Beth, on the contrary, left the course with reinforced ideas based on her own learning experiences, particularly that more emphasis should be put on developing language competence – understanding grammar rules – rather than on the practice of samples of performance which might impair future possibilities of using language in different contexts. What concerned Beth was not so much the limiting possibilities of the method over her professional development, but the limiting possibilities it had over the pupils' learning, as the following quotation illustrates very vividly:

I have just seen situations when you get to the stage of just having phrasal learning without the pupils actually understanding individual words within the phrase. I just don't know whether by avoiding too much emphasis on rules and fitting words into patterns, and things like that and just relying on talking to them in the target language, I just wonder if that makes it more difficult. . . . I saw a lot of kids who . . . were bright enough [and] didn't have the ability to, they couldn't understand that certain things were transferable and that they could adapt things and switch them into different sentences. . . . Watching my videos I was so bored because, . . . half an hour would be doing activities with the colour of somebody's hair and . . . I really can't believe that . . . when I was teaching, that the kids seemed fairly interested, like it was all new stuff and that is definitely something that you don't realize. . . . I just think, 'Oh God!, it's so boring', but they actually seem to still find it interesting.

To have a method gave Rachel a vital sense of professional security, 'that method has sort of defined a way of carrying out a lesson with confidence', but she was worried that it might also turn into a straight-jacket:

I felt that my lessons were becoming very mechanical because I seemed to have found a way. . . . We were shown a way here of going through a lesson of presenting and practicing language which I found was quite successful and it was very easy to stick to that method, but I did feel that it was a bit mechanical in the end. . . . I don't know whether it'd stop me from looking at other things and from, I don't know, developing other ideas, examining other ideas, I mean I am frightened of the sheer bulk of the timetables and, you know the exhaustion that it would drain me and I wouldn't have time or energy to consider other possibilities. I'd like to, but I don't know.

Rachel, although unable to go beyond the method, could not deny its efficiency:

I don't actually like the Q/A, but I like the way it guides students through different processes and I like the way it guides students from just being able to recognize a pattern to being able to play with it and actually produce it.

Thus during teacher education, student teachers progressed differently despite their similar behaviour during teaching practice.

Summary and conclusions

The student teachers' contributions have become central to understanding the process of learning to teach. If given the chance, they reflect not only on their activity during teaching practice but also on their own language learning experiences. These reflections provide them with a springboard to explore the theoretical aspects of the profession in initial teacher education, without necessarily having to postpone it until they are full-fledged classroom teachers. This is contrary to suggestions that only experienced teachers have the faculty to reflect.

These four student teachers efficiently implemented during teaching practice the method learned during teacher education, yet the degree of acceptance was subject to a great deal of variation. There is much evidence that the methods and content knowledge introduced to students in campus courses have little influence on the subsequent actions of students even during initial training (Zeichner et al. 1987). Researchers have found different explanations for the fact that student teachers find teacher education knowledge either irrelevant or difficult to grapple with. For example, beginning teachers may base their teaching goals and the way they teach on their undergraduate disciplinary backgrounds (Wilson and Wineburg 1988). Socialization studies view formal teacher education as largely failing to alter the effects of the socialization of students by observation of their own teachers. The little impact that teacher education courses have on how teachers think about their work is related to the influences that teachers bring with them, shaped by years as 'teacher watchers' (Barnes 1989; Feiman-Nemser and Buchmann 1986a; Pennington 1990). On the contrary, others argue that practical experience in the classroom is the source of student teachers' knowledge (Calderhead and Miller 1985; Shulman 1986, 1987).

The picture which emerged in this study is more complex, since during teaching practice student teachers drew on different sources of knowledge. My data suggested, first, that a large proportion of the transformations in pretraining knowledge had its origin on campus during the teacher education programme and before student teachers took up their school placements. These changes were related to the way they selected content, provided explanations and organized activities during teaching practice. Supporting evidence that it was the teacher education programmes which induced this particular behavioural transformation could be found in the fact that the four student teachers presented the subject matter to their pupils in the same way, regardless of different contexts, content or learners. While experienced teachers[9] have been found to develop their pedagogical content knowledge from practice, student teachers in this study were taught during teacher education courses a particular way of organizing the subject matter to make it

---

9 Gudmundsdottir and Shulman (1987) suggest that there is no indication that teachers are taught to organise their content knowledge the way they do. Instead, teachers invented the teaching models themselves during years of practice. Freeman, in line with the findings of studies on the socialisation of teachers, found that teachers' 'norms of experience and those embedded in the norms of the school environment converge to provide them with a highly traditional teacher-centred concept of classroom practice' (1991: 444).

accessible to pupils, which student teachers implemented during teaching practice. Thus, teacher education played a very influential role in shaping student teachers' performance during teaching practice. It was the knowledge learned during teacher education which became apparent during teaching practice. Second, although the method newly acquired during teacher education contributed to the learning activities and the selection of content, pretraining knowledge formed the basis for the discussions of the way they taught. More specifically:

1. All student teachers implemented a view of the subject matter which was different from their pretraining conceptualization. Basically, they shifted from a combination of what we could loosely call a functional approach to language and a concern for grammar rules to a more structural or phrasal approach to language.
2. There seemed to be a common shift from an intuitively based cognitive approach to language learning, which emphasised the active role of the learner, to a more behaviourist-oriented position, with an emphasis on external action.
3. Although all student teachers implemented a specific learned behaviour during teaching practice ('the method'), this may be only superficial behaviour, which teachers may shed once they do not feel they have to conform to certain standards. Some of the ideas they expressed in the interview conducted at the end of the year offered initial support of this idea.
4. Student teachers internalized the teaching method learned during the teacher education course and reacted to it in different ways. While there were some who found the method to be their main way to approach teaching but still included some ideas from their pretraining knowledge (Melani, Ronan), others followed the method with little modification on their part, despite misgivings about it (Rachel, Beth).
5. Despite the homogenising effect of the teaching method on student teachers' performance during teaching practice, the fact was that, at the end of the course, they left with different kinds of knowledge about the dynamics of teaching and learning languages. To a considerable extent these variations were rooted in their pretraining knowledge.

In summary, student teachers' development during pre-service programmes cannot be attributed to one single influence. It is important to find out what particular experiences contribute, so that the learning process can be enhanced rather than hampered. More research is needed to explore these different, at times conflicting, influences in student teachers' practice.

Implications for teacher education

Content of teacher education

This analysis has shown the presence of a number of recurrent themes in student teachers' knowledge before they enrolled on a PGCE course. These have a number of implications relevant to the content of foreign language teacher education. First, rather than present student teachers with a given curriculum, based on a transmission model, starting with and building on these themes would contribute to more active participation of student teachers in a shared curriculum and lead to more effective learning. It would also alleviate the endemic problem of lack of time in pre-service teacher education courses, continuously voiced by teacher educators, by which we tend to justify transmission models. The themes which were of general concern to the four student teachers were a discussion about language, which includes its functions, substance and means of expression; a discussion about language learning, which involves a concept or theory of language learning, individual learners' factors, and L1 – L2 learning; and a discussion about language teaching, which incorporates the role of the teacher and a concept of teaching. These categories cover a lot of what happens in the classroom and are the focus of current research. Second, if teacher educators have an understanding of student teachers' knowledge, it may help them to design teacher education strategies and to specify the content of teacher education in ways which can develop that existing knowledge more effectively. So it can be argued that pre-service education is not just what happens after students enter training institutions but also previous learning experiences. Helping students to be aware of the understandings they bring to formal education is only the first step in the transition to professional thinking, in which students learn to look beyond the familiar worlds of teaching and learning (Feiman-Nemser and Buchmann 1986b: 225).

Process of teacher education

First, it seems that, regardless of whether teacher training institutions are progressive in the content they convey, teacher education should not be a question of imposing traditional or progressive teaching models on student teachers. It should be about establishing connections with the student teachers' personal understandings and building on their knowledge. If we accept that the learner's personal contribution has an influential role in learning new material, teacher education courses should aim to provide space and means by which student teachers can bring up and examine their pretraining knowledge in order to see how it relates to teacher education knowledge, so that learning is more meaningful. Hewson and Hewson (1989: 195) argue that in the same way that teachers need to know what their students' conceptions are and why they hold them, teacher educators need to know their student teachers' conceptions of teaching to make new conceptions of teaching intelligible or create, if necessary, dissatisfaction with existing conceptions which may conflict with those taught. In the same way that teachers are concerned about pupils' knowledge and the role it plays in the school curriculum, teacher educators concerned about the way student teachers learn should make sure that student teachers' previous knowledge has a legitimate status in the college curriculum. If we consider this knowledge as meaningful for prospective teachers' development, we will be bridging the gap between student knowledge and college knowledge. It is clear that the growth of student teachers' knowledge depends on the opportunities students are provided to make their preexisting knowledge explicit, to examine and challenge it (Calderhead and Robson 1988). Helping students reveal, think about and check their perspectives about teaching and learning is essential to educating them in the process of reflection (Clandinin 1986). Only when we, teacher educators, understand student teachers' perceptions of teaching when they enter teacher preparation programmes, can we adjust appropriately the course content to overcome any misconceptions that might be getting in the way of pre-service teachers' learning (Book et al. 1983). While some foreign language teacher education models contemplate only a two-phase teacher education model (pre-service and in-service), these data add more weight to including pretraining experiences and the meanings student teachers attach to them as an integral and legitimate part of any initial teacher education. We will not be able to establish the kind of contribution teacher education courses make to student teachers' development and how they contribute to student teachers' education if we do not know what was already there and how the old and the new knowledge relates to practice. In other words, these results, I think, provide enough empirical evidence to advocate teacher education rather than training, not only during in-service teacher education but also during pre-service courses.

Second, we have seen that student teachers modify their pretraining knowledge during teacher education, not only their knowledge about the discipline they are going to teach, but also about the way it is learned or taught. They teach in a way which does not bear much resemblance to their pretraining knowledge, although this does not mean that this knowledge does not influence the way they think about their activity. What remains an open question is whether this particular transformation is the only one possible, or whether different transformations should be made available to the students; and whether this particular pedagogical content knowledge is the only one desirable or whether this induced change into a teaching method is the best way to promote teachers' ongoing development in the very varied and rich contexts in which they will have to work. Research on teachers' thinking points out how unrealistic it is to conceive of teacher education as imparting a set of preformulated ideas or principles to be implemented by teachers (Calderhead 1987). These ideas are necessarily filtered and adapted by previous knowledge. Pre-service teacher education courses should help student teachers to be in more control of their professional development and provide them with the opportunity to approach the profession from a much broader perspective than as merely a method. Student teachers should be taught the skills and confidence to analyse and articulate their thinking.

Third, since it is clear that teaching performance and competence are not the same, evaluating student teachers' observable behavior may not provide enough information about the way they have or have not internalized the new knowledge presented to them during teacher education courses.

Fourth, the use of interviews, together with observational records, has proven to be invaluable in exploring student teachers' knowledge, particularly by providing evidence that teaching is more than observable behaviour. Consequently, teacher educators, should include techniques to evaluate teaching practice which can reveal the assumptions and beliefs which lie behind student teachers' actions. Strategies that get student teachers to talk about their work in different kinds of recorded interviews and recorded observations of their work can provide materials so that teaching can be individually and collectively analysed. Moreover, the use of transcripts can provide a fruitful stimulus for discussion, in that 'examples of teaching by students may be at least as valuable as those showing experienced teachers because of the turn which events can take under less experienced guidance' (Westgate 1988: 149). As Ramani (1987: 3) argues:

The responses of student teachers to classroom data can be used to raise theoretical questions which can then be linked to current conceptual issues. These questions will suggest the areas which need to be read up on or investigated for clarity and deeper understanding. Such an approach to theory, which is rooted in teachers' own intuitions and which encourages them to move from the specific to the general, is seen as being more meaningful than one which is based on theoretical inputs from trainers.

The videotaping technique can be a valuable means of allowing student teachers to develop an understanding of their thinking and the ability to verbalize and think through what they are doing (Woods

1990), thus enhancing their responsibility for and understanding of their classroom decision making. Recordings offer the possibility of making explicit the possible divergent assumptions about procedures and processes held by teacher, tutor and student teachers.

Finally, if we design teacher education programmes without an understanding of what student teachers' conceptions are and the role they play in their education, we are implicitly assuming that our conceptions and theirs are the same (Cooney 1984; Weinstein 1989). Most teachers would agree that pupils' learning rarely matches curricular aims. Similarly, most teacher educators should accept that student teachers' learning is unlikely to be synonymous with curriculum aims. It seems necessary that student teachers' conceptions and understandings of their subject matter, teaching and learning should provide a foundation for teacher education. Serious consideration of student teachers' pretraining knowledge will also encourage us – teacher educators – to examine our implicit theories. This will lead us to explore whether our programmes are consistent with our underlying assumptions (Weinstein 1989).

Finally, understandings such as these 'can enable us to examine critically our current teacher education practices and to build teacher education courses which equip teachers not only with basic common competence but with the knowledge, skills and confidence to continue learning' (Calderhead 1988: 63). I want to point out that four case studies can only provide more questions about teacher education which need to be addressed in further in-depth studies about the process of learning to teach. How is student teachers' existing knowledge taken account of? Is student teachers' knowledge challenged and furthered during teacher education? What kinds of interactions are allowed between students' knowledge and teacher education knowledge?

References

Atwood, M. 1990. *Cat's Eye*. London: Virago Press.

Bailey, K. M. 1990. The use of diaries in teacher education programs. In J. C. Richards and D. Nunan (eds.), *Second Language Teacher Education*. Cambridge: Cambridge University Press, pp. 215–226.

Barnes, H. 1989. Structuring knowledge for beginning teaching. In M. C. Reynolds (ed.), *Knowledge Base for the Beginning Teacher*. Oxford: Pergamon.

Bogdan, R. C., and S. K. Biklen. 1982. *Qualitative Research for Education: An Introduction to Theory and Methods*. Boston: Allyn & Bacon.

Bogdan, R. C., and S. J. Taylor. 1984. *Introduction to Qualitative Research Methods: The Search for Meanings*, London: Wiley.

Book, C., J. Byers, and D. Freeman. 1983. Students' expectations and teacher education traditions with which we can and cannot live. *Journal of Teacher Education* 34(1): 9–13.

Brenner, M., J. Brown, and D. Canter (eds.). 1985. *The Research Interview: Uses and Approaches.* New York: Academic Press.

Burgess, H. 1985. Case study and curriculum research: Some issues for teacher researchers. In R. Burgess (ed.), *Issues in Educational Research: Qualitative Methods.* Lewes: Falmer, pp. 177–196.

Burgess, R. 1988. Conversations with a purpose: The ethnographic interview in educational research. *Studies in Qualitative Methodology* 1: 137–155.

Butt, R., and D. Raymond. 1989. Studying the nature and development of teachers' knowledge using collaborative autobiography. *International Journal of Educational Research* 13(4): 403.

Calderhead, J. 1981. Stimulated recall: A method for research on teaching. *British Journal of Educational Psychology* 51: 211–217.

Calderhead, J. 1987. Teaching as a professional activity. In J. Calderhead (ed.), *Exploring Teachers' Thinking.* London: Cassell, pp. 1–19.

Calderhead, J. 1988. The development of knowledge structures in learning to teach. In J. Calderhead (ed.), *Teachers' Professional Learning.* Lewes: Falmer, pp. 51–64.

Calderhead, J., and E. Miller. 1985. *The Integration of Subject Matter Knowledge in Students Teachers' Classroom Practice.* University of Lancaster School of Education.

Calderhead, J., and M. Robson. 1988. Images of teaching: Student teachers' early conceptions of classroom practice. Paper presented at the Annual Conference of the British Educational Research Association, Norwich.

Clandinin, D. J. 1986. *Classroom Practice: Teacher Images in Action.* Lewes: Falmer.

Clark, M. C. 1986. Ten years of conceptual development in research on teacher thinking. In M. Ben-Peretz, R. Bromme, and R. Halkes, (eds.), *Advances of Research on Teacher Thinking.* Lisse, Netherlands: Swets and Zeitlinger, pp. 7–20.

Clark, M. C. 1988. Asking the right questions about teacher preparation: Contributions of research on teacher thinking. *Educational Researcher* 17(2): 5–12.

Clark, M. C., and P. Peterson. 1986. Teachers' thought processes. In M. C. Wittrock (ed.), *Handbook of Research on Teaching,* 3rd ed. New York: Macmillan, pp. 255–298.

Feiman-Nemser, S., and M. Buchmann. 1986a. Pitfalls of experience in teacher preparation. In L. Katz and J. Raths. (eds.), *Advances in Teacher Education.* Norwood, N.J.: Ablex, pp. 61–73.

Feiman-Nemser, S., and M. Buchmann, 1986b. First year of teacher preparation; transition to pedagogical thinking? *Journal of Curriculum Studies* 18: 239–256.

Freeman, D. 1989. Teacher training, development, and decision making: A model of teaching and related strategies for language teacher education. *TESOL Quarterly* 23(1): 27–45.

Freeman, D. 1991. 'To make the tacit explicit': Teacher education, emerging discourse, and conceptions of teaching. *Teaching and Teacher Education* 7(5/6): 439–454.

Goetz, J., and M. LeCompte. 1984. *Ethnographic and Qualitative Design in Educational Research.* New York: Academic Press.

Gudmundsdottir, S., and L. S. Shulman. 1987. Pedagogical content knowledge:

Teachers' ways of knowing. In A. L. Stromnes and N. Sovik, (eds.), *Teachers' Thinking: Perspectives and Research*. Trondhiem, Norway: Tapir, pp. 51–83.

Gutiérrez Almarza, G. 1992. Towards developing a qualitative perspective of student foreign language teachers' knowledge, its origins, development and relationship to practice. Ph.D. thesis, University of London.

Hewson, P., and M. Hewson. 1989. Analysis and use of a task for identifying conceptions of teaching science. *Journal of Education for Teaching 15*(3): 191–209.

Horwitz, E. K. 1985. Using student beliefs about language learning and teaching in the foreign language methods course, *Foreign Language Annals 18*(4): 333–340.

Kagan, D. M. 1990. Ways of evaluating teacher cognition: Inferences concerning the Goldilocks principle. *Review of Educational Research 60*(3): 419–469.

Lortie, D. C. 1975. *The Schoolteacher: A Sociological Study*, Chicago: University of Chicago Press.

Mitchell, J., and P. Marland. 1989. Research on teacher thinking: The next phase. *Teaching and Teacher Education 5*(2): 115–128.

Pennington, M. C. 1990. A professional development focus for the language teaching profession. In J. Richards and D. Nunan (eds.), *Second Language Teacher Education*. Cambridge: Cambridge University Press, pp. 32–151.

Porter, P. et al. 1990. An ongoing dialogue: Learning logs for teacher preparation. In J. Richards and D. Nunan (eds.), *Second Language Teacher Education*. Cambridge: Cambridge University Press, pp. 227–241.

Ramani, E. 1987. Theorizing from the classroom. *ELT Journal 41*(1): 3–11.

Richards, J. C. 1990. The dilemma of teacher education in second language teaching. In J. Richards and D. Nunan (eds.) *Second Language Teacher Education*. Cambridge: Cambridge University Press, pp. 3–15.

Shulman, L. 1986. Those who understand: Knowledge growth in teaching. *Educational Researcher 15*(5): 4–14.

Shulman, L. 1987. Knowledge-base and teaching: Foundations of the new reform. *Harvard Educational Review 57*(1): 1–22.

Weinstein, C. 1989. Teacher education students' preconceptions of teaching. *Journal of Teacher Education 40*(2): 53–60.

Westgate, D. 1988. Initial training of foreign language teachers. *British Journal of Language Teaching 26*(3): 147–152.

Wilson, S. M., L. S. Shulman, and A. E. Richert. 1987. "150 different ways" of knowing: Representations of knowledge in teaching. In J. Calderhead (ed.), *Exploring Teachers' Thinking*. London: Cassell, pp. 104–124.

Wilson, S., and S. Wineburg. 1988. Peering at history through different lenses: The role of disciplinary perspectives in teaching history. *Teachers College Record 89*(4): 525–539.

Woods, D. 1990. Studying ESL teachers' decision-making: Rationale, methodological issues and initial results. Carleton University.

Zeichner, K., B. R. Tabachnick, and K. Densmore. 1987. Individual, institutional, and cultural influences on the development of teachers' craft knowledge. In J. Calderhead (ed.), *Exploring Teachers' Thinking*. London: Cassell, pp. 21–60.

4 Learning to teach together: Teaching to learn together

Anné Knezevic and Mary Scholl

The growing recognition that the knowledge base of effective language teachers includes not only linguistic and pedagogical theory, but also the wealth of their individual experience, has led to reconsideration of the role of reflection in teaching and teacher education. Reflection has the power to help the teacher connect experience and theoretical knowledge in order to use each area of expertise more effectively. Teaching is complicated, large-scale, hard to define, and close to the soul (Duckworth 1987). Though the reasons for our decisions and actions as teachers are within us, it is often difficult to articulate how we know what we do when we teach. Without reflection, teaching is guided by impulse, intuition, or routine (Richards 1990), and subsequently kept within the realm of tacit knowledge. Shulman (1988) called for teacher educators to help learners make this tacit knowledge explicit through reflection upon practical experience and theoretical understanding. Collaboration is a powerful vehicle for exposing and developing knowledge of teaching.

Collaboration – shared responsibility inside and outside the classroom – gives teachers an opportunity for heightened reflection. The need to synchronize teaching acts requires team teachers to negotiate and discuss their thoughts, values, and actions in ways that solo teachers do not encounter. The process of having to explain oneself and one's ideas, so that another teacher can understand them and interact with them, forces team teachers to find words for thoughts which, had one been teaching alone, might have been realized solely through action. For these reasons, collaboration provides teachers with rich opportunities to recognize and understand their tacit knowledge (Polanyi 1966). We believe that collaborative teaching merits further exploration as a means of learning about teaching.

We are students of the teaching of languages. Both of us came to language teaching from similar preteaching interests: politics and social change. We were both interested in public service but were frustrated with our jobs at the time. For us, teaching was a marketable career choice that also fulfilled a need to be a part of a multicultural, inter-

We would like to express our gratitude to Steve Cornwell and Miki Knezevic for their thoughtful assistance in editing this article. We would also like to extend our thanks to many others for their valuable contributions to our work.

national community. In May 1992, we completed coursework for a Master of Arts in Teaching (MAT) degree in English and Spanish at the School for International Training (SIT) in Brattleboro, Vermont. There, the faculty challenged us to explore and reflect upon our knowledge and beliefs about teaching and learning. They led us to work out our own thoughts about teaching and learning. Throughout the year, we began to develop an awareness of the processes through which we learn and teach. In turn, this knowledge has helped us to make more critical, rational teaching decisions.

During the second semester of our coursework, we were hired to team-teach an undergraduate-level Spanish class. The joint responsibility and experience of teaching our own class gave us many shared experiences which became stories. We told these stories to each other, to our colleagues, and to our students. We told them for comic relief, we told them to share our joy and pain, and quite often, we told them because we wanted to make sense of something that had happened. Each "telling" of a story gave us an opportunity to reconsider events and interactions that had happened both inside and outside the class-room. We reconsidered our thoughts and actions. We questioned what we might change in ourselves in the future. Telling our stories to our colleagues often resulted in dialogues about teaching issues which we were all working to understand. We became aware of how the telling of the stories helped us to think and talk about teaching.

In this chapter, we relate two stories from our team teaching experience that led us to new understandings of teaching and learning. As background for the stories, we first introduce our teaching context: our class and the graduate program which influenced our thoughts about teaching. The first story illustrates our planning process. Through a story about the development of lesson plans around a Mexican poster, we came to recognize the benefits and patterns of our collaborative planning. In the second story, we replay events that occurred within a brief time frame in order to examine a series of spontaneous decisions that guided our classroom behavior. As we analyze the steps in our responses to this situation, we show how working with a teaching partner can help make more critical, rational decisions in the pressures of the moment. In conclusion, we assess the effects and benefits of collaboration in the development of our overall understanding of teaching and learning.

The MAT program and the class we taught together

In many ways, our class provided an ideal teaching situation. It consisted of nine students from all programs at SIT and one professor from the MAT program. All learners were highly motivated; they were studying Spanish out of a personal interest, and most had traveled to Spanish-speaking countries. The diversity of proficiency levels in the group, from advanced beginner to high intermediate, presented us with the challenge of creating multilevel lessons in which all students would be learning.

On a deeper level, the students contributed some interesting dynamics not usually found within a language classroom; six students were our classmates from the MAT program. As classmates and colleagues, we were all wrestling with new ideas and our evolving understanding of teaching, and they were as eager to look at their learning and our teaching as we were. Spanish class gave us a common experience which supplied a background of mutual understanding on which we could "project" our remarks (Dewey 1933). MAT coursework gave us a shared professional discourse to use in understanding the class (Freeman 1991a).

The presence of a faculty member in our class created another unique teacher-student dynamic. At first, the prospect of teaching a faculty member seemed daunting; however, we quickly realized the benefits. He played an important role in coaching (Schön 1987) our teaching by helping us think through our plans, by giving us useful feedback about our teaching, and by talking with us about how he was learning. He spoke using the terms, language, and ideas that the MAT program had been teaching us, and this helped us relate our experiences to the pedagogical theories we had been studying.

Logic dictates, and research substantiates, that we are in many ways products of our education. It follows, then, that we teach as we were taught (Goodlad 1983). Each student beginning a teacher preparation program brings a legacy of experience of schools and schooling with him or her. Memories of foreign language study in school, as well as experiences in living abroad, in our case, served as our "apprenticeship of observation" (Lortie 1975). A concern of many graduate teaching programs, including our own, is to work with this diverse experience base that students bring to their studies. The MAT program stressed the value of critical thinking and reflection; it encouraged us to become "reflective practitioners" (Schön 1987). It helped us expand our knowledge by giving us not only a new language to use but also a framework with which to reflect on teaching. It has been argued that, when teachers are encouraged to reflect critically on their teaching, the quality of their work experience is improved dramatically (Gomez and Tabachnick 1992). By learning to reflect, we were able to begin to transcend the paradigms we had developed during our years of language learning.

Being in the MAT program enabled us to reflect upon our teaching. It gave us language with which to describe the interactions and experiences we were having as teachers. We used these new tools in examining our mutual experience of teaching together. We found storytelling to be a powerful method of reflection because it was a natural way of bringing forth and exploring tacit knowledge. Through telling our stories together, we came to know about our experiences in new ways. Consequently, we developed new insights into teaching. The following stories focus on two aspects of teaching: planning and decision making.

Collaboration in planning

Planning is a critical part of teaching, and teachers plan for several reasons. Planning can help to reduce uncertainty and to create a sense of direction; further, it can promote confidence and security. Planning can be a means to the end of instruction, serving to direct what happens. It is a time to establish both long- and short-term instructional objectives and to evaluate progress toward those goals (Clark and Peterson 1986). As team teachers, we found four additional reasons for planning together:

– To coordinate our actions and build a team identity
– To think through techniques for organizing the events of a class period
– To practice reflective dialogue
– To think creatively

In this way, planning, for us, was the time to shape a vision of our class.

The potential for creative thinking in collaborative planning was exciting because the joint product was greater than what we might have created individually. We each grew to appreciate the imaginative capabilities of the other as we bounced ideas back and forth. There was an element of adventure in exposing an idea to our co-teacher; we never knew where and how it would end up. There was room in our process for off-beat suggestions, as well as for elaboration of more rational possibilities. In order for one partner to work with the other, each of us had to clarify our statements and our reasoning more than we might have if we had been teaching alone. In this way, collaborative planning gave each of us a venue for a more thorough expression of our own ideas as well as the opportunity to work with our partner's contributions. Within this process, our evolving understanding of teaching emerged. The following story illustrates our planning process and highlights the creative thinking techniques and modes of communication that facilitated our work together. The discipline of forming this and the next story helped us bring our tacit understanding of teaching to light because it forced us to reach for insight into why events, ideas, and processes unfolded as they did.

Teaching teams often divide planning responsibilities among members, with each person being responsible for planning a section of the class period. However, we decided to plan the entire class period together throughout the semester. On average, we spent four hours per week together preparing for four hours of class. We had to be, and become, comfortable with our surroundings and with one another. We varied the routine by working at one of our homes, a local café, or a favorite restaurant. While enjoying a snack and the atmosphere, we chatted about the trials and tribulations of the week. Discussing these issues allowed us to get to know each other and gave value to our lives outside our work. We began to understand the feelings, thoughts, and ideas that each partner brought to the planning session. Talking about "life issues" also helped each of us to prepare ourselves for work by freeing our heads from these thoughts. Consequently, we were better able to focus on lesson planning. Being in a comfortable environment and taking the time for some personal discussion was a ritual that created a secure atmosphere in which to work. We acknowledge, however, given the busy schedule of today's teacher, that this luxury is not always possible.

Finding a focus

One spring afternoon, one of our students showed us a Mexican social science poster from the early 1950s. The poster was designed to warn readers of potential accidents that could occur in the workplace. It had thirteen vivid and somewhat gruesome drawings of accidents including an explosion in a dynamite factory, a butcher with his hand caught in a meat grinder, a train derailment, and a cowboy being thrown by a bull. As serious as the accidents were, we were amused by the carefully constructed details of each drawing and by the humorous titles beneath each one. For example, the explosion in the dynamite factory was entitled "Infrequent accidents," and beneath a picture of cargo falling on dock workers the caption read "Rare accidents." The artist cleverly contrasted "Accidents *in* the countryside" (falling into a well or getting stuck in barbed wire) with "Accidents *of* the countryside" (being thrown by a bull or being kicked while milking a cow). As we were chuckling, we realized that we both wanted a copy of the poster. We asked to borrow it, and our student agreed. As we were leaving, Mary said, "Wouldn't it be great to use this in our class?" Anné agreed. "How" was the question we began to answer in our next planning session.

Brainstorming

The first step in our lesson-planning process was brainstorming. Based on deferred judgment, brainstorming produces a creative atmosphere, encourages fanciful thinking, teaches receptive attitudes, and asks participants to consider many alternatives (Davis 1987: 57). We worked to consciously create just such a cushion for each other's ideas. We began bouncing ideas back and forth in an attempt to put as many suggestions as possible on the table. We tried to include ideas that addressed different skill areas and kept within the broad parameters of the presentation-practice-use model for setting instructional goals that we had learned in the MAT program.

With the Mexican poster, we thought of using vocabulary exercises, matching games, and descriptive writing. We refrained from judging the ideas. Instead, we helped each other express them more fully by asking questions to clarify and expand statements made. "What do you mean by a guessing game? How do you see us introducing the activity? Where do you see the activity leading?" were typical guiding questions. They helped to open communication between us, expand our thoughts, and bring us to a similar vision. Learning to express our ideas to one another and to ask nonjudgmental questions gave us a broad base from which to begin our teaching. Attitudes of open mindedness and flexibility toward the other and her ideas were essential at this point. As Bateson points out, "For complementarity to be truly creative, it is not sufficient for need to run in both directions; it is necessary to acknowledge that both contributions are of equal value and that both are freely given" (1990: 100). In order for our planning sessions to be successful, we both needed the opportunity to develop our ideas and make meaningful, creative decisions.

Narrowing the options

As we found ideas that we liked, we began to negotiate the choice of a theme. Critical-thinking and decision-making skills came into play in this phase. We tried to make decisions by consensus; layer upon layer of possibilities would be added and removed as we refined our ideas in order to arrive at a shared vision. For this lesson, we both agreed that descriptive writing about the accident or victim was a good direction to take. But this seemed limited. Next, we focused on the idea of a character study; but what, then, would tie the characters together? What would be the purpose of writing such a description? At this point, problem-solving skills helped us find and test alternatives.

Mary remembered an exercise she had done in another context. During college, she had participated in an activity in which each person was asked to create a character sketch of his or her ideal leader. Then, students came together in small groups to present their "leaders" and to decide which leader would be most appropriate for developing a community on another planet. It seemed as though the exercise might fit with the ideas we had been discussing. Suddenly, Anné had a golden idea.

Mary's story reminded Anné of an award given annually by a senator from Wisconsin for the most wasteful use of taxpayers' money. This memory prompted a thought: An award! An award for the "stupidest" accident! The finalists for the award could be the people in the poster! The students in our class could create character sketches in order to compete for the stupidest accident award. We thus had a concrete theme that enabled us to refine the idea into a lesson plan.

We would ask students to describe the person in their picture and the events that had led up to the work accident. Then we would ask them to form a committee to decide on the winning story. We realized that the committee would need a name and so "The Royal Academy for the Appreciation of Klutzy Moves" was born. The students would become members of this "Academy," and their responsibility would be to select and honor the winner. Toward the end of this flow of ideas, Anné recalled a term in Spanish used to describe a person who does silly things: pineapple head (*cabeza de piña*). This became the title of the award that was to be given by the Academy: the "Pineapple Head Award." While the resulting task seemed off-beat, we believed that it would give the students a relaxed opportunity to learn and use Spanish in the classroom.

Developing and refining selected options

Once we had figured out the general flow of our lesson, we were able to focus on how the activities would develop. The idea turned into a two-day lesson plan. Day 1 focused on writing and reading: First, we let each student chose a picture to work with. The students then wrote about the character of the person in the picture and the chain of events which had led up to the accident. At this point, our role was to answer questions and help them in their work. After they had composed a story, we began a peer editing session in which they helped each other with the writing. At the end of the hour, we asked the students to bring their character sketches back to the next class, to present to the group.

On day 2, the focus shifted to speaking and listening. The students became the members of the Academy for the Appreciation of Klutzy Moves. Their task was to present the Pineapple Head Award to one of the characters. First, we split the class in half and had each student present his or her story to their "Academy." Then, each group listened to the presentations, asked questions to learn more about each character and incident, and selected two semifinalists. Finally, the two groups came together, presented the semifinalists, answered questions, and selected a winner.

The culminating activity for the class was a regal ceremony in which the Pineapple Head Award was presented. The ceremony involved an opening statement by the head of the Academy of Klutziness (Mary) and a guest appearance by last year's recipient (Anné). After a brief introduction, the guest speaker, dressed in bandages and walking on crutches, told her wretched story and explained the picture of her accident. This model listening exercise gave the students an opportunity to hear the new vocabulary they had been learning. Next, the students presented their candidates for the award. After a period of questions and answers, we tallied the final vote. The celebration that followed included the presentation of the award and a snack of fresh pineapple.

We were interested to see how the lesson plan would be received by the students. We were pleased to find that we were able to follow our plan closely on both days. The activities seemed to provide the students with appropriate tasks and challenges. In this way, the students remained engaged and focused throughout both class periods. The students' creativity and abilities were extraordinary; the stories they wrote were impressive. The winning story was about an ESL teacher who taught workplace ESL in a dynamite factory. While this teacher was using sticks of dynamite to diagram sentence structures, his former wife entered the room with a lit cigar, dropped hot ashes on the dynamite, and caused the terrible explosion seen in the poster.

When teachers-in-training are taught about lesson planning, they are usually introduced to the notions of objectives, of specifying content or what they are teaching, and of blending that content into appropriate activities (Freeman 1991b). The MAT program presented these ideas to us, but we were also asked to develop a meta-awareness of what we thought about when we planned. This broad approach to lesson planning assured a balance between trying out established planning formats and developing planning strategies to suit our individual needs and teaching styles. Our version of collaborative planning was representative of this approach. Elements of structure that we learned formally and then adapted for our personal use made the process our own. The development of the Mexican poster lessons showed how our unwieldy ideas became manageable as we shepherded them through a collaborative planning process. The steps included:

- Finding a base to work from (e.g., the poster)
- Brainstorming ideas
- Narrowing options
- Clarifying selected options
- Brainstorming around these options
- Deciding on a theme to link the ideas within the option
- Developing a sequence to order the ideas
- Fleshing out specific activities
- Verifying logistical details of the lesson

Collaborative planning helped us both cognitively and interpersonally. Throughout the process there was a balance between "free-for-all" brainstorming and "give-and-take" negotiation of ideas between us. We worked to create a common understanding of ideas by asking questions and clarifying thoughts. Planning with a partner resulted in a more complete development of our ideas, and this led to more coherent lesson plans. We enjoyed planning together and often laughed at the thoughts that emerged. This laughter helped us explore and expand the limits of possibility in creating the lesson. Teaching seemed to be a perfect outlet for our creative thinking.

Perhaps the most important factor in the planning process was the respect and trust that we developed for each other. During the three months that we worked together, we came to genuinely appreciate the contributions the other made to our collective work. Because we had to develop clarity and precision of expression, our communication patterns improved and deepened. As a result, making the tacit explicit became easier. These dynamics enabled us to create our plan cooperatively and to enjoy the steps that led us to this goal. In a sense, we were building a team identity, and this image was crucial inside the classroom. The following tells a story of a series of interactions and decisions that occurred just minutes after we entered the classroom. In this situation, we faced every teacher's nightmare: We arrived for class without the materials for the two-hour activity we had planned.

Collaboration in the classroom

The joys of planning together come to fruition inside the classroom, as the lesson unfolds. Despite careful orchestration, though, Murphy's law dictates that nothing in life happens quite as planned. This truism applies to the classroom. Planning reduces, but does not eliminate, uncertainty about teacher-student interaction because classroom teaching is a complex social process that regularly includes interruptions, surprises, and digressions (Clark and Peterson 1986). Decision making is at the heart of the interactive stage of teaching. Often, these choices

must be quick and spontaneous. It follows, then, that if we can understand the processes and motivations behind intuitive, instinctive decision making, we can gain greater control over our interactions in the
classroom. Critical, rational decisions come from the teacher's awareness of his or her decision-making process and its results (Orlich et al.
1990).

Collaborative teaching provided us with an ideal opportunity to develop our critical, rational decision-making skills. By teaching with another teacher, we had a model to observe in the classroom. We watched
each other's actions closely, and this focus was critical to our synchro-
nization in the class. We considered one another's classroom behavior
both consciously and subconsciously. Often in reflection after the class,
one of us would ask, "Why did you do X?" Through modeling, dialogue, and discussion, we worked to understand each other's reasoning
and motivation.

Within the classroom, team teachers are an invaluable resource for
one another. There is a colleague within reach who can answer a question, confirm a hunch, suggest a new approach, and step in if needed.
Collaborative teachers give one another reinforcement and feedback. In
this way, a team is built. Our students commented that our teamwork
was smooth. For them, it often seemed as if a single teacher was teaching the class.

Examining our reactions, thoughts, and feelings when faced with unexpected situations in the classroom provided us with a window into
our collaborative teaching relationship. In the following story, we analyze a situation which occurred because we had to improvise the day's
lesson plan. There were split-second decisions that were made in order
to teach the class and then our reactions after reflecting upon the afternoon. While we learned from this predicament, we probably would not
have experienced the moments of tension had we been teaching on our
own. Because, in the words of James Joyce, "man's errors are his portals
of discovery," the value of this experience became clear to us only in
retrospect.

What led up to the problem

To truly plan for the reality of teaching, we must learn to expect the
unexpected. We usually did all that we felt was necessary to prepare
ourselves in every way for each lesson. Sharing responsibilities pushed
us to ask more questions and discuss details more thoroughly than we
would have done as solo teachers. In our planning sessions, we talked
until we both felt that we had a similar understanding of how the class
would progress. Normally, at the end of our planning sessions, we

would take a few minutes to summarize the decisions we had made regarding activities, materials, and details.

By this point in our team teaching experience, we had become quite comfortable with each other. We had established patterns in our interactions. Perhaps this ease allowed us to overlook the final planning step during the session prior to this particular class. We did not double-check the details of who would bring the student papers to class. The following shows our reactions to this crisis and our response to this unexpected lapse.

When the story began, we were entering the second half of a two-day project using a children's picture book, *Tuesday*, by David Wiesner. In this book, frogs have a magical ability to fly at night. The tale chronicles their adventures as they fly through town, dropping into homes, getting caught in sheets hanging on clotheslines, and commandeering TV remote controls. The book ends with a play on an idiom: The following Tuesday, pigs fly. We liked the book's beautiful illustrations, off-beat humor, and its lack of written text. We thought that *Tuesday*, in its light-hearted style, would stimulate the students to use Spanish.

During the previous class period, we had laid the groundwork for *Tuesday*, presenting vocabulary for writing the story and outlining our schedule for the two-day project. Then we divided the class into three groups and gave each group the task of writing a text for one third of the story. To keep an element of surprise in the exercise, we asked the students not to look beyond their part of the story. Each group spent the rest of the period creating text for their portion of the tale. Their work was to be used during the next class so we collected the writing at the end of the hour.

On the second day, we wanted the students to refine the texts they had created. They were to write their text on large paper and then go through a series of activities to correct and strengthen their work. Eventually we would have a final product created by the entire class. We planned to invite them to sit in front of the fireplace in the classroom, serve them cookies and milk, and have them read their parts of the story aloud. We thought that the humor of the situation would help them feel more comfortable as they shared their work by reading it aloud. It was a great plan, whose destiny, unfortunately, was not to be fulfilled that day.

The problem exposed

We were enthusiastic about the lesson to come as we entered the classroom and began setting up as usual. As Anné erased the blackboard, Mary put the chairs in a semicircle. Anné turned on some background music and Mary brought out sheets of newsprint to be used in rewriting the texts the students had composed. The students began arriving, and we greeted them enthusiastically, hoping that they would find the class as exciting and fun as we thought it would be.

Suddenly, we realized that neither of us had the student papers. Mary thought that Anné had them; Anné thought that Mary had them. Without the student papers, the class could not proceed as we had planned.

Responding to the problem: Improvisation

Given the dilemma, we began a mad scramble to come up with an alternative plan. If we wanted to work with the *Tuesday* book, we could ask the students to rewrite their texts. However, making the students redo their work because of our mistake seemed like a punishment. The fact that we did not have the students' work also seemed disrespectful on our part. So we decided, almost tacitly, to find something new. At this point, our individuality and our unique approaches to the crisis began to surface. We had a quick huddle in the corner of the classroom. The students were still arriving and greeting us as if it were a normal day. Mary felt pressure and panic. She did not want to let her classmates and professor down. She wanted the class to run smoothly, and she disliked public blunders. This, combined with trepidation about the immediate future, caused her stress. Anné approached the situation with a different mind-set. She was calm and intrigued by the potential for improvisation. She had confidence in Mary and faith that the class period was salvageable. To her, the situation was an adventure: It was a chance to try something spontaneous. At that moment, though, we had neither the time nor the inclination to discuss our attitudes.

Team improvisation, being together "on stage" in front of the class, can be difficult. Given our different feelings and mind-sets, we had a lot to balance in the few minutes we used to regroup and "plan" class. We had to consider alternative activities, our partner's state of mind, and the students' needs. We had to listen to each other while simultaneously thinking on our own. Most important, we had to come up with answers quickly. Words failed us more quickly because we did not have time to use them properly. We barely had time to explain an idea, much less include each other in its development. Something had to give way in the balancing act. In order to focus more on thinking about a solution, Mary limited her listening to Anné to the point that she did not hear her suggestions, nor did she explore Anné's ideas with her. This happened so quickly that words were a burden. Creating a similar vision of the class in both our minds seemed futile and impossible in this brief time.

Out of the depths of Mary's panicked thoughts and Anné's calm suggestions, an idea came. The plan needed little explanation because it was an activity that Mary had learned in a class at her university and had demonstrated in the advanced Spanish class they had both taken in the fall. Anné had been in that class and had participated in the activity, so she too had an image of how the exercise would proceed. Anné, noting Mary's rising blood pressure, readily approved the idea. Thus Mary took the lead with this exercise in the demands of the moment and few words were needed. We had developed our own style of communicating, even within the classroom.

We began the activity by dividing the students into pairs. Each pair was given a slip of paper with the names of two related inanimate objects on it, for example, "spaghetti" and "a fork" and "a car" and "a highway." We asked each pair to keep their objects secret. Their task was to personify these objects by developing and presenting a dialogue between them. They could not refer to either object by name, for it was the class's task to guess the objects from clues in the conversation. In a sense, it was like spoken charades. The absurd element of personifying an object and naming it gave the students an entertaining communicative activity. With Mary's discovery and Anné's acceptance of this activity, the major problem of what to do had been overcome.

Mary's panic started to subside as she passed out the slips of paper. We had overcome the significant challenge of finding an activity within minutes, but there were more obstacles ahead. As mentioned earlier, the class was filled with fellow MAT students. Many of our peers looked at the class as an opportunity to analyze learning and teaching. We wanted to provide the students with learning opportunities, and they, in turn, taught us a great deal in their reactions to these learning experiences. At times this meant that we addressed pedagogical issues together. At other times, however, we felt pushed into pedagogy and away from Spanish, and needed to take more control over the direction of class. After spending our off-campus teaching practicums working with children in elementary and middle schools, we discovered that coming to terms with our roles as teachers of adults was challenging. We were excited to be working with such capable and motivated students, yet occasionally we were unable to channel their energies as we would have wished. Now we would have to show some authority, a delicate undertaking in a group of peers.

One student in particular was an enthusiastic learner of both Spanish and teaching. She had been very attentive to the details of our teaching and her learning. This student contributed materials, ideas, and insight to the class, and we generally appreciated and benefited from her input.

On occasion, however, we felt pressured by her inquisitiveness. On the one hand, we wanted to provide a receptive environment in which the students felt comfortable expressing their needs. On the other hand, we felt an obligation to exert control in order to keep the focus of the class on learning Spanish. In the past, this student had challenged our understanding of this balance. On this occasion, she asked Mary a question which referred to an important pedagogical issue we had been examining in our MAT classes. Mary's response was a product of past interactions filtered through the present situation.

As Mary finished distributing the charade tasks, the student asked her how we planned to correct student errors in the exercise. The question itself was innocuous, yet the combination of the student's history in the class and the tensions of the moment made it seem overwhelming. Mary stopped in her tracks, knowing that she was not ready to respond as she would have liked. After a deep breath, she asked the student to wait a moment and turned to Anné for help. It took honesty for Mary to recognize and admit her limitations. While she wanted to give the student a respectful answer, she was angry and was not thinking clearly. The tension of the moment had blocked her ability to act. Looking to Anné for help gave her time to gather her thoughts and feelings, and it also gave Anné a chance to step in.

Anné had witnessed the interaction between Mary and the student, and she, too, knew the student's history and the stress Mary was feeling. When Mary turned to her, Anné saw that she was stunned, and Anné knew what had to be done. Anné also realized the value in the student's question, and diplomatically asked for the student to suggest an error correction strategy. With that comment, she diffused the volatile situation, and a thoughtful pedagogical discussion began. Later, Mary expressed relief at Anné's response because it both reflected their shared teaching values and gave her a chance to regain her composure before returning to the group. By asking the student to help answer the question, we gave her greater input into her own learning. Anné's question also opened up a discussion about what sort of correction would be useful in these circumstances, and we decided that both students and teachers would take responsibility in correcting errors. In the end, this exchange broadened the range of options and sharpened our response to the students' needs.

The lesson worked out well. The students enjoyed their roles as creators and actors. They took responsibility for helping each other examine errors seriously, and many interesting explanations arose from the questions they raised. We both felt a sense of relief as the class ended; our panic had turned into productivity. Now we could look at what we had learned from these interactions.

Lessons learned

The first lesson we learned was to plan details carefully and consistently. We could have avoided the whole situation by writing a checklist prior to class that day. Then, we would have discovered the confusion with the papers before class. We also realized how useful it is to have contingency plans. Had we taken some time earlier in our team teaching to discuss a potential "plan B" for unexpected situations, we could have avoided some of the tensions that arose in deciding what to do. But practicing improvisation allowed each of us to tap unexplored resources.

We saw that management in an adult classroom rests on striking a balance between care and control. Despite the pressure surrounding the student's question, the activity was enhanced a thousandfold by the issue she raised. This reinforced our belief in the importance of giving students input into their own learning process. Moreover, we learned the value of being attuned to signals in the class so that we could provide support for one another. We saw that one way of showing care was to share control of the direction of the class. Furthermore, this story demonstrates how our complex thinking skills and our tacit knowledge of teaching were operating quickly and in an integrated fashion in order to make necessary decisions. Through collaborative teaching, we started thinking on our feet in the classroom; we were "reflecting-in-action" (Schön 1987).

A musical metaphor helps define this process because at times our work that day resembled jazz improvisation: action smoothly integrated into ongoing performance. Schön (1987) writes:

Improvisation consists in varying, combining and recombining figures within a schema that gives coherence to the whole piece. As the musicians feel the directions in which the music is developing, they make new sense of it. . . . They reflect in action on the music they are making.

In this story, we could "improvise" together because our "feelings" and decisions about the direction of the class were rooted in the underlying structure of our shared vision of the class. This, in turn, was shaped by our evolving knowledge of teaching and our shared values. Thus we were able to test new ideas and adjust our incipient knowledge base. At the same time, we learned to be aware of the whole of the classroom situation while still experimenting with the specifics. We understand this integrated decision making as "reflection-in-action."

Our story shows commonality of purpose and an understanding of how to complement one another's efforts as our teamwork became more aligned (Senge 1990). Because we worked together, we each had a chance to solo while accompanying the other. Through teaching collaboratively, we pushed each other deeper in our understanding and provided one another with alternative suggestions that removed obstacles from our path. In this way, we balanced one another and delved further into the intricacies of teaching.

Collaboration leads to learning

> We shall not cease from exploration
> and the end of all our exploring
> shall be to arrive where we started
> and know the place for the first time
> T.S. Eliot

These stories are explorations into ourselves, our teaching, and our learning. Through the collaborative process of experience, and telling and writing these stories, we have gained a new understanding of our identities as teachers, friends, and colleagues; we have come to know parts of ourselves for the first time. Because we have reflected on common experiences using our shared professional discourse (Freeman 1991a), teaching concepts that began as words – and as symbolic representations of ideas – have become anchored in personal experience. In this approach to learning, moments or stories from practice have been attached to issues and concepts. With these vivid examples in place, we grasped their meanings and constructed our own interpretations of these teaching ideas. Consequently, this knowledge has become available to us as a resource for use in the future. In this way, our philosophies of teaching and learning have deepened as we have come to know "where we started . . . for the first time."

For us, *collaboration* meant consistently working together to accomplish a task; it was a series of actions that complemented those of our partner. In a deeper sense, it became a conscious way of approaching teaching, based on respect for and appreciation of the other's presence. We both left the experience open to the importance and potential of collaborative planning because we realized that plans we created together were greater than those we might have developed individually. Contributions from both of us led to more creative and complete lesson plans. In the future, we will look for opportunities to discuss plans with other teachers as a way of recapturing this benefit.

The story of collaboration in the classroom showed us how control in the classroom is subtly bound to the concept of care. Looking at our reactions to and reflections on the incident gave us insight into how our teaching processes are composed of a unique mix of tacit knowledge and pedagogical theory. Because these elements, both "hard to define and close to the soul" (Duckworth 1987) were challenged and examined through collaboration, we built a broader base from which to make intuitive decisions. This, in turn, shaped our understanding of teaching.

Collaboration can serve as a catalyst and a mirror for exposing, expressing, and examining ideas. It can lead to enriched learning and improved instruction. Teaching knowledge, after all, is developmental (Freeman 1991b). We recognize that our situation is not often available to most teachers or students of teaching. The question of how to create such opportunities for teachers to collaborate and learn from each other remains relevant and pertinent. How can we build bridges to connect teachers in meaningful experiences that provoke thought, dialogue, reflection, and learning? We believe that the prospects for improving teaching lie in the answers to this question.

References

Bateson, M. C. 1990. *Composing a Life*. New York: Penguin.

Clark, C., and P. Peterson. 1986. Teachers' thought processes. In M. C. Wittrock (ed.), *Handbook of Research on Teaching*, 3rd ed. New York: Macmillan, pp. 255–297.

Davis, G. 1987. How to get a hippo out of a bathtub or what to teach when you teach creativity. In R. Clasen (ed.), *Educating Able Learners: Book of Readings*, 2nd ed. Madison, Wisc.: University of Wisconsin, pp. 53–60.

Dewey, J. 1933. *How We Think*. Chicago: Heath.

Duckworth, E. 1987. *The Having of Wonderful Ideas and Other Essays on Teaching and Learning*. New York: Teachers College Press.

Freeman, D. 1991a. 'To make the tacit explicit': Teacher education, emerging discourse, and conceptions of teaching. *Teaching and Teacher Education* 7(5/6): 439–454.

Freeman, D. 1991b. Learning teaching: "Interteaching" and other views of the development of teachers' knowledge. Plenary given at the Washington area TESOL conference.

Gomez, M. L., and R. Tabachnick. 1992. Telling teaching stories. *Teaching Education* 4: 129–138.

Goodlad, J. 1983. A study of schooling: Some findings and hypotheses. *Phi Delta Kappan* 64: 465–470.

Lortie, D. 1975. *Schoolteacher: A Sociological Study*. Chicago: University of Chicago Press.

Orlich, K., et al. 1990. *Teaching Strategies: A Guide to Better Instruction*, 3rd ed. Lexington/Toronto: Heath.

Polanyi, M. 1966. *The Tacit Dimension*. Garden City, N.Y.: Doubleday.

Presseisen, B. Z. 1984. *Thinking Skills: Meaning, Models and Materials*. Philadelphia: Research for Better Schools.

Richards, J. C. 1990. *The Language Teaching Matrix*. Cambridge: Cambridge University Press.

Schön, D. 1987. *Educating the Reflective Practitioner: Toward a New Design for Teaching and Learning in the Professions.* San Francisco: Jossey-Bass.

Senge, P. 1990. *The Fifth Discipline: The Art and Practice of the Learning Organization.* New York: Doubleday/Currency.

Shulman, L. 1988. The dangers of dichotomous thinking in education. In P. Grimmet and G. Erickson (eds.), *Reflection in Teacher Education.* New York: Teacher's College Press, pp. 31–39.

5 Learning how to teach ESL writing

Amy B. M. Tsui

> Our students are all too often deprived of
> the joy of watching how their thinking
> goes onto the paper, how their ideas get
> shaped into words and expressions, and
> above all, to see how their buildings and
> castles could have always been rebuilt
> with blocks combined in new and
> different arrangements.
>
> Julie Li, a writing teacher—
> (Li 1991: 1)

This chapter describes how an ESL teacher, being dissatisfied with the way she had been teaching writing since she became a teacher, tried to introduce process writing to her students. It describes how she, after being introduced to the concept of process writing in an in-service initial teacher education programme, tried to implement it in her classroom, the dilemmas she faced, the decisions she made in resolving the dilemma, and her reflections on what she learned as a writing teacher over a period of nearly two and a half years.

Process writing

Recent studies in writing have shifted the focus from the artefact produced by a writer to the process in which the writer is involved when writing (Applebee 1984). This shift in focus has enabled us to perceive writing as a process of creating, discovering and extending meaning rather than a process of putting down preconceived and well-formed meaning (see Raimes 1985; Shaughnessy 1977; Silva 1990; Zamel 1983, 1987). This understanding of writing has important implications for the teaching of writing. Zamel (1983) points out that the writing teacher should provide students with the opportunity to actually experience the process of writing and to understand that writing is 'the mak-

I would like to thank Julie Li and her students for sharing their thoughts, experiences and feelings with me.

ing of meaning out of chaos' (1983: 199). They should provide a supportive environment in the classroom, in which students are encouraged to work through their composing processes collaboratively. They should act, not as assessors, but as facilitators who help students to develop strategies for generating ideas, revising and editing (see Silva 1990). How the writing teacher implements all of this in the classroom is still an empirical question, however, for there are a number of factors at work, such as the teacher's as well as the students' understanding of what writing is all about, institutional constraints, and so on. This chapter describes how a writing teacher in Hong Kong learned to implement process writing in her classroom, the constraints she had to work under, and how she dealt with those constraints.

Teaching writing in Hong Kong classrooms

In Hong Kong schools, the teaching of writing is predominantly product oriented (Pennington and Cheung 1993; Stewart and Cheung 1989). (For a review of approaches to L1 and L2 writing in the past thirty years, see Raimes 1991: 409–410.) A typical writing lesson in Hong Kong schools consists of two or three lessons of thirty-five or forty minutes each. The teacher gives students a composition title. Some teachers might spend the first fifteen to twenty minutes discussing with the whole class the points that could be included, and providing some vocabulary. Some teachers might require their students to write an outline before they start writing. Then students are given the rest of the double or triple period to write, at the end of which their compositions are collected, marked and graded. They are required to correct grammatical errors and resubmit their work.

In an ongoing study of the teaching of writing in Hong Kong secondary schools, Sengupta conducted a survey of 230 secondary school teachers and found that they assigned an average of twelve compositions a year to students. More than 90 per cent think that it is important for students to write the number of compositions specified by the school. More than 70 per cent think that it is important for students to produce the minimum number of words required. Although 90 per cent of the teachers give a mark for accuracy and content and more than 60 per cent give a mark for organization, fewer than 50 per cent actually write comments on students' compositions. Although about 60 per cent of the teachers say that students need to revise their work, nearly 90 per cent do not give students extra time for revision, which is understood largely as error correction. Sixty-five per cent believe that all errors should be corrected.

Data sources

The data used in this chapter consist of the teacher's report on her process writing project,[1] student writings, classroom observations, the writers' conferences with the teacher and interviews with the students, and the students' evaluation of the writing tasks and activities.

Anxiety in teaching writing

Julie is a young Chinese ESL teacher who has had nearly four years of teaching experience since she graduated from university. In her second year of teaching, she enrolled in a two-year part-time in-service initial teacher education programme at the University of Hong Kong, in which the author was her ELT methodologies tutor and practicum supervisor. Before she was introduced to process writing in the programme, she followed what other ESL teachers did in her school and how she was taught as a student. This was largely a product-oriented approach in which the emphasis was on grammatical accuracy and rhetorical organization.

Julie expressed unhappiness with the way she had been teaching writing. She knew that writing was a problem for her students because it had been a problem for her when she was young. She remembered that she used to associate writing with the words *stressful, lonely* and *nightmarish*. However, she did not know how to help her students, and sometimes she was frustrated because, even with thorough preparation, the activities or tasks that she tried to build into the writing lesson did not always work. In one of the conferences, she reflected:

I feel sometimes frustrated, um, even after I have been well prepared for a certain writing class, and I feel that some of the activities that, or some of the tasks that I tried to build in, into the whole writing class itself don't seem to work as I expected them to.

Her frustrations were shared by her colleagues, who found it difficult to help their students even when they knew that the latter had problems writing. They associated writing with the word *exhaustion*. Julie reported in one of the conferences:

Some teachers, when we share rather casually about what we do during writing classes, they think that it might be exhaustion for both the students and the teachers when the word *writing* comes to mind. I think this [what they mean] is probably due to the fact that students don't enjoy the activity. It's natural that when you enjoy something you never feel tired. So

1 This report was published in a departmental journal (see Li 1991).

they simply don't enjoy the activity and teachers don't enjoy teaching the students how to write.

Her colleagues felt that the writing lesson had become a free lesson for them, a lesson in which to catch up on their marking or to prepare for other lessons. They were unhappy with this practice. Julie further reported,

... despite the fact that they do it for most of the [writing] classes, they also feel that it is not the right thing to do.

Teaching writing as problem solving

To Julie, teaching is problem solving, and she has always seen her role as helping her students to solve problems. The problem she had to solve, as far as the teaching of writing was concerned, was how to turn writing into an activity that her students could enjoy. In order to do that, she felt that it was necessary first to understand the problem from the students' point of view. In reporting how she conducted a writing project with her students, she wrote:

I have got a student, Anna, who has so much to say: chatting with her neighbours, contributing in discussions. But when it comes to composition, she has amazingly little to write about. She says she hates it and that she feels bored. We sit and play with our babies. We give them toys, blocks and sand for building, modelling and construction. We praise them if they manage somehow to put the blocks together, we laugh with them when their castles collapse. And we encourage them to try out blocks of different colours, shapes and sizes in their various combinations to produce more buildings and more castles of different styles. But Anna (and most of our students, too) is usually given nothing more than a title and 60 minutes, and she has to sit still, to work quietly, to produce something all alone by her self in a composition. (Li 1991:1)

Not only are students deprived of help, support and encouragement that they need very badly, the demand that is made of them in a writing task is enormous. As Julie wrote, 'Teachers expect it to be a composition of a train of thoughts which must centre round a title or topic they choose for them, which is then to be carefully translated into written symbols, preferably to be organized into a framework with good opening, some sensible developing paragraphs and a sound ending. Better still, to be neat and tidy' (ibid.). All of this is to be done within an hour or so. And the product that they sweat over to produce is, as Julie points out, often read by the teacher with a frown. It is not surprising, therefore, that writing is an anxiety-generating activity for students and that they do not enjoy it.

The anxiety in writing that Julie's students experienced is commonly shared among L2 writers (see Blanton 1987; Bloom 1985; Daly 1985; Raimes 1985; Selfe 1985; Winer 1992).[2] In Winer's (1992) study of the attitude change of student teachers towards writing, dread of writing, particularly writing which is to be graded, was repeatedly identified as one of the problems. The student teachers reported that 'producing a piece of writing has always come after a period of suffering' and that they were '. . . experiencing complete and total anxiety over writing' (Winer 1992: 60; see also Daly 1985: 63). Writing was viewed by these student teachers as belonging to the same category as 'spinach' (Winer 1992).

In other words, writing is a high-risk, low-gain activity in which students are putting themselves at great risk of getting negative feedback from the teacher. Daly (1985: 43) describes it as 'unrewarding and even punishing for some students' (see also Selfe 1985: 85). The problem that Julie had at hand was how to change it to a 'low-risk, high-gain' activity. In order to achieve this, she had to identify and address the causes of anxiety in writing.

Identifying causes of writing anxiety

Grammatical accuracy

One of the major causes of anxiety identified by Julie was concern for grammatical accuracy. She reported that she used to understand writing as a mastery of technical skills which included such aspects as sentence connections, grammar and vocabulary. Because of the emphasis on accuracy, the students perceived the production of grammatically correct writing as of paramount importance (see also Hildenbrand 1985, cited in Zamel 1987: 705–706).[3] This could be seen from the comments that her secondary 3 (grade 9) students wrote in their evaluations of their writing lessons:

I think we should do more exercises on things like prepositions to help us improve and to get better marks on it in an exam.

I hope we have more grammar exercises to do because I think I am weak at grammar.

2 Shaughnessy (1977: 235) first talked of the 'written anguish' of L1 writers. Raimes (1984) points out that the anguish in L2 writers is even greater than that in L1 writers because, in addition to all the worries that L1 writers have in writing, L2 writers have to master grammar, syntax and mechanics.
3 Hildenbrand's 1985 ethnographic study of an ESL community college student's attitude towards writing found that if the classroom work was focused on accuracy of form, the student would see that as the main objective of teacher-assigned tasks.

I want the teacher gives us . . . more grammar exercises. I wish I can improve my English.

I hope I can use more new vocabulary that I learn in my writing and make less grammar mistakes.

In an interview that I conducted with Julie's secondary 5 (grade 11) students, the words *afraid* and *worry* were frequently used when they talked about their experiences [see also Selfe (1985: 85), in which a university freshman, Bev, used *hate* and *fear* in connection with her writing]. They reported that they were afraid of making grammatical errors and getting low grades as a result. Because of such worries, they found it very difficult to get beyond the first sentence, and when they eventually did, they found it very difficult to get beyond the first paragraph (see also Jones 1985: 97).

This undue emphasis on grammatical accuracy traps students within the sentence. As Raimes (1984: 83) points out:

They worry about accuracy; they stop after each sentence and go back and check it for inflections, word order, spelling and punctuation, breathe a sigh of relief and go on to attack the looming giant of the next sentence.

In addition to grammatical accuracy at the sentence level, Julie, like most writing teachers, tried to get students to organize their writing in large structural units such as the introduction, the body and the conclusion. She required them to practise writing in different organizational patterns such as narrative, description, exposition, argumentation, and so on. She asked her students to write an outline before they started to write. Consequently, as Silva (1990: 14) points out, 'writing is basically a matter of arrangement, of fitting sentences and paragraphs into prescribed patterns. Learning to write, then, involves becoming skilled in identifying, internalizing, and executing these patterns'.

The restrictive nature of imposing rules and patterns is well reflected in a commentary by an ESL student reported by Zamel (1987: 699):

My teacher emphasizes on the rules and limitations how to write a research paper, for example, avoiding a topic too broad, too subjective, too controversial, too familiar, too technical. . . . I feel I did not dare to strike even a step; all around me were abysses – each step was full of danger. I felt I was restricted and I could not write any more. I felt upset and frustrated. I lost my desireness and confidence to write.

This feeling is echoed by one of Julie's secondary 3 (grade 9) students, who wrote in her evaluation of the writing lesson:

It would be best if there is less boundary [restriction] in compositions in the future, like using some appointed phrases, words, because they would limit the creativity of us, and the earnest in writing.

And among the eight pieces of writing that the secondary 3 (grade 9) students did in this school year (1992–1993), 'The Shark Attack', which was a highly controlled composition in which students were asked to fill in blanks according to some pictures, was rated the lowest. The students, in these commentaries, pleaded that the teacher not give them similar exercises again.

Writing topics

Another cause of anxiety in writing, as related by both Julie and her students, is that students are often asked to write about something which is irrelevant or of no interest to them. Julie recalled that in her experience as an ESL learner, her anxiety over writing came partly from the fact that she was often required to write on topics about which she had very little to write or about which she did not particularly want to write. In my interview with Julie's secondary 5 (grade 11) students, they gave the following titles which they had been asked to write about but which they disliked intensely: 'The First Day of School', 'School Picnic', 'Sports Day', 'Parents' Day', 'Speech Day', 'Swimming Gala'. These topics are very common writing topics in Hong Kong schools. They explained that they had to write on these topics year after year and in both their English and Chinese compositions. These schools events, according to them, were typically uneventful. Consequently, they found it very difficult to produce the minimum number of required words. Hence they were preoccupied with filling up the page rather than with communicating their ideas and feelings. When I asked what they would like to write about, they said that they would prefer to write about the picnics they had with their friends than about the school picnic, because the former were usually more fun. They also preferred topics such as 'A Wonderful Day', about which they could write anything, or writing letters to friends because it would make the writing task more real.

The views of these students were echoed by Julie's secondary 3 (grade 9) students, who, in their reflections on their writing lessons, wrote:

I like to write about free association of ideas. It's much more interesting. And things like 'The Shark Attack' is very boring. So please try to avoid similar exercises.

I like to write composition freely. Although I've got some problems when I started writing, I found that it is interesting when writing a composition by my own ideas.

If all the writing exercises can give us more opportunities to imagine more and think more, I think the compo[sition] will be better. I don't like the teacher to fix the writing topic for us.

103

I like writing letters, postcards or some short paragraphs which I can express my feelings more freely.

I want to write more about ghost stories or children stories during the writing lessons, or write something freely.

Writing environment

A third cause of anxiety that Julie identified is the fact that there is a lack of a 'safe' environment for writing. As writing is taught in schools, it is a lonely activity which has to be completed within a very short period of time. Teachers are often very critical and unsympathetic. This, Julie pointed out, is another major cause of anxiety.

They [students] fear compositions because they are always supposed to generate ideas, elaborate on them, write them out, synthesize them, then organize them, revise them and edit them all at the same time. Worse still, they are expected to do these all by themselves. They fear compositions because they know the audience is going to be the teacher who will read it with a red pen and, more often than not, with a frown. They simply don't feel free to use language naturally. (Li 1991: 1)

As many writing researchers have pointed out, a supportive and friendly environment, in which students feel free to take risks, is essential. Students need the support of their peers as well as their teachers (see Dunn et al. 1985; Hildenbrand 1985, cited in Zamel 1987; Jones 1985; Kantor 1984; Selfe 1985). The following commentaries from Julie's secondary 3 (grade 9) students illustrate the point.

We have many discussion in the class. It is very interesting. I can ask help from my classmates. If I should write the composition all by my ownself, I feel quite difficult and bored.

I like writing the dialogue very much because I can work in groups and discuss with my friends. It is much interesting than writing a piece of composition on my own. I hope the teacher will give us more dialogues than composition to write.

In the future, I think the teacher may give us more interesting exercises, exercises that require group discussion.

I think that some discussion before writing can make us feel safe to write.

In the preceding discussion, we have seen the three main causes of anxiety Julie identified: undue concern for production of accurate form rather than content, uninteresting writing topics on which students were required to write a specified number of words and an unfriendly and unsupportive environment in which students had to work under the pressure of time.

Addressing writing anxiety

Julie was first introduced to process writing in the in-service teacher education programme in which she enrolled during her second year of teaching. According to Julie, the concept of process writing changed her perception of what writing was all about. She began to wonder whether the students' as well as teachers' anxiety about teaching writing had to do with the approach to writing. In a conference with me, she described how she usually taught writing:

I followed what the panel suggested. . . . I used every single double period to do it. I did writing in alternate weeks. . . . I would start off with some preparation work, sometimes in the form of free discussion, sometimes in the form of reading materials that were related to what they were going to write about, sometimes in the form of listening. That usually took fifteen to twenty minutes. Then the topic was given. And in the last ten minutes or so in the first period, they wrote an outline and I would usually go around checking their outline and they wrote for thirty-five minutes and handed it in. Comments and feedback were given to students but they were not supposed to get another draft done. That's the end product. They get a mark.

According to Julie, neither the students nor the teachers enjoyed it. 'So they simply don't enjoy the activity and teachers don't enjoy teaching the students how to write. And I think that has a lot to do with the approach'. She felt that she needed to reflect upon familiar teaching routines and try to see teaching and learning differently (see Li 1991: 11). She was attracted by the idea of allowing students to experience the process a writer actually goes through in writing, by asking them to go through several drafts on the basis of comments given by the teacher. She recalled her experience of establishing a dialogue with her students through the comments she made on their writing and their responses to her comments.

One of the girls, when she was introducing herself to me in one of the compositions at the beginning of the year, she said that she likes collecting stamps and she likes collecting stickers and then I said I like collecting stickers too. I said I like little twin stars most and then she said she likes Hello Kitty most. After a few weeks which I have already forgotten that I have written that on her paper, she met me in the corridor and she said 'I've got a little twin star in my album'. It was just a casual thought together with other comments and I know from that that they take comments from the teacher very seriously.

She was also attracted by the idea of allowing students to share ideas and to get comments from their peers when they were going through the drafts because, from her own experience, she knew that students loved sharing ideas. She reported, ' . . . not every comment is really that

105

useful. But they enjoy doing it like that. Actually they like sharing ideas with their peers very much. That's the impression that I get'.

Julie decided to try and address the anxieties that students have about writing with her secondary 3 (grade 9) class. She felt that secondary 3 was a more suitable level for experimentation than secondary 4 or 5 (Grade 10 or 11), because the former were not under the pressure of public examination. There were two more years before they had to sit for the Hong Kong Certificate of Education Examination, which is a public examination for all secondary 5 school leavers.

Providing a creative topic

To make writing enjoyable, Julie said that to inculcate a favourable attitude towards writing was very important. She reported:

While writing is both an intellectual process as well as a technical skill to be acquired, it is also a creative activity, an art to be enjoyed. I attempted, therefore, to inculcate favourable attitudes to writing and I chose to do this by teaching students to write stories for children. (Li 1991: 2)

In one of her conferences with me, she pointed out that 'students like stories and they like to talk about things which may not seem to be allowed in the classroom, things which allow imagination and freedom to write what they have in mind'. Moreover, she knew that her students were all familiar with the elements of a story, and that they all liked films and juicy stories. She felt that the latter are sources from which they could get ideas of a framework which would hold together characters, time and place, plot, development and outcome.

Providing a safe environment

Apart from starting with a familiar topic which gives plenty of room for creativity and imagination, she also tried to create a 'safe' and supportive environment. She organized students into groups of five and six so that they did not have to struggle on their own. They stayed with the same group throughout the whole writing process: from writing, to revising, to the actual production of a story book. To enhance support and solidarity within the group, she asked them to give their groups a name. The students came up with names such as 'Perfection', 'Cats' and 'The Lovely Ones'.

However, when group discussion first started, the students were inhibited and their pace was very slow. The students politely took turns speaking, and one member kept a record of the points made. In my post-observation conferencing with Julie, I drew her attention to the role of the teacher when students are conducting group discussions. I suggested that, instead of withdrawing entirely, she could act as a facilitator to help groups which appeared to need some support. So Julie encouraged them to think critically and, instead of agreeing or disagreeing with the students, she suggested alternatives. Her encouragement gave them more confidence, and the discussions became more reactive and evaluative. In other words, simply putting students in groups did not necessarily provide a safe environment, especially when they were not used to group work. The teacher had an important role to play in helping students ease into group interaction.

In an interview with Julie's secondary 5 (grade 11) students who had done story writing when they were in secondary 3 (grade 9), the students unanimously voiced the feeling that group discussion was something they enjoyed very much because it helped them to get over the anxiety of not having enough ideas to write about, of having their ideas rejected by the teacher and of having to produce the required number of words. As a result of sharing ideas, they had so much to write that the required number of words was no longer a concern. They felt safe in a group, and they were more willing to take risks. [See Sweigart (1991: 484), which shows that students wrote better after group discussions than after class discussions.] One student, who had had her ideas rejected by the teacher as crazy, said that when working in a group, she no longer feared that her ideas would be rejected by the teacher, because if her ideas were accepted by the group, then she would have the whole group to back her up if the teacher rejected the ideas. Another student said that she never thought that she was imaginative and had good ideas because she had received many negative comments from the teacher. But when she worked in a group to write stories, she found that her ideas were always accepted by her peers and were considered good. She was now much more confident and felt that she was an imaginative person (see also Hildenbrand 1985, cited in Zamel 1987).

Generating ideas, organizing and revising

To prepare students to write stories, Julie read extracts of stories from children's literature such as 'Cinderella' and 'The Hare and the Tortoise' to refresh their memory of how children's stories are constructed. The students also drew on their own knowledge of television series, films and stories, and together with the teacher, they identified the basic elements of a story, such as the plot, the leading and supporting characters, the setting, the scene and the title. For the plot of the story, they identified the components of situation, problem, events, climax, resolution, and evaluation.

Instead of putting a straitjacket on her students by asking them to start with a story outline and work from the beginning, Julie encouraged her students to start working on any of the elements of the story with which they felt most comfortable. In her lesson plan, she put down the following as the objective:

To introduce students to the idea of constructing a sequence of ideas in the framework of a story, alerting them to the fact that there are many ways to 'get things started' while organizing and selecting at a later stage should help to 'get things done'.

She selected one element and demonstrated to her students how they could start with that element and develop the story. The students then jotted down any words or phrases that they could think of in association with the elements. 'Thus their fear of putting down the first sentence was dispelled', Julie reported. They discussed how one element was related to another and how one shaped the other. Ideas and thoughts associated with the elements were jotted down on worksheets and kept in their folders for later use. By doing this, students were encouraged to generate and share as many ideas as they could without worrying about putting them in a logical sequence or in a particular structural pattern. Julie reported:

They are no longer restricted by the idea of having a good outline first before they start to write. They know they are allowed to add or to drop ideas, to shift the order of different chunks of details. (Li 1991: 3)

Zamel (1983: 165) points out that the process of writing is a 'a non-linear, exploratory, and generative process whereby writers discover and reformulate their ideas as they attempt to approximate meaning'. To help students understand such a process, Julie asked her students to revise their drafts on the basis of her comments as well as their peers' comments. She tried to make it clear to her students that revision is not the same as editing errors. It is a process in which new ideas may be generated and old ideas dropped. It is also a process in which ideas get re-organized and re-formulated. In my post-observation conferencing with Julie, as well as on the supervision feedback sheet, I asked Julie to pay special attention to the way students revised their stories. The students' stories went through four drafts before the story book was produced, and Julie kept all the drafts. This proved to be very useful when Julie tried to analyse and understand the thinking that her students had gone through.

To prevent students from being inhibited by concern for grammatical accuracy, Julie did not do anything about grammatical errors when she went through the drafts. She tried to 'reply' rather than 'assess' (Barnes 1976: 111), by responding to the plots and ideas and by telling them that she would be interested to know the details of their descriptions.

In other words, instead of being an examiner holding a red pen with a frown, Julie assumed the role of the reader for whom the story was written.

In recalling their story-writing experience, the students told me that they found it very enjoyable. They liked the idea of being given the opportunity to revise what they wrote before their writings were finally assessed by the teacher. Julie, in one of the conferences with me, reflected:

It is the process itself that enjoyment comes from, and when we do the process approach, students can actually see how they improve from one draft to another, and they enjoy actually making changes in their own work rather than seeing how their work has been marked. This is what they enjoy most. . . . I mean their confidence is built up when they receive the third or fourth draft. I think they like, they welcome getting back the papers from the teacher, much more than they did before. I feel that they like to see what is happening this time. . . . I feel this is what makes it enjoyable for students.

According to Julie, this part is also what Julie enjoyed most as a teacher. She used to think that the teaching of writing was the assessment of student writings by the teacher. However, as she went from group to group, helping students when they had questions, her perception changed. She felt that her role is not that of an assessor (see Applebee 1984), but that of a coach, a facilitator and a supporter (see Applebee 1984; Dunn et al. 1985; Hartwell 1985; Kantor 1984; Newkirk 1984; Zamel 1987).

Creating a genuine writing environment

The importance of creating a genuine environment for writing is well documented in the literature. For example, in Arnt's study (1990: 58) of six ESL writers in the People's Republic of China, the writers unanimously expressed hostility towards 'school-set writing assignments', but expressed the feeling that they would find writing less burdensome and even enjoyable if they had a genuine message to communicate (see also Applebee 1984; Blanton 1987; Raimes 1984, 1985; Zamel 1985).

In getting students to write stories for children, Julie said that her students would have a more real sense of writing in a genuine environment if she asked them to actually produce a story book with cartoons or pictures together with an accompanying tape, so that they could show the book and play the tape to their younger siblings or relatives. Most of her students did in fact read the drafts of the story to their younger siblings or relatives.

With their child audience in mind, the students were better able to make revisions when going through their drafts. The following is an example of how, under Julie's guidance, one group revised their drafts with their child audience in mind. This was a group called 'Perfection', which wrote a story called 'Lego Wonder', about twin sisters, Apple and Pie, whose animosity, generated by vying for love from their parents, changed to love after Apple was rescued by Pie during their dangerous journey to the Lego Empire. The following is an excerpt from the second draft of their story.

Suddenly, I was caught by a soldier. He took me to a dark room where there were a lot of children. I learnt from the children there that I had to answer three questions if I wanted to leave this place. After a while, a group of soldiers came and asked me three questions. I couldn't answer them, so . . . I was regretful that I didn't study hard!

Julie wrote in the margin, 'your child audience would love to see the place and try their wit, too!', and in the final draft, the excerpt was revised to read as follows.

Suddenly, I heard a voice behind me. 'Don't you like our Lego Empire? I'll take you to the Palace to visit our King'. I found myself sitting on a soft lump. It was a piece of cloud! I was floating in the sky. I looked down and saw a lot of Lego houses, Lego men. Then I couldn't steer the cloud and I fell down into one of the chimneys. I fell down, down, down. After a while, I heard a boy scream painfully. Then there was a sudden silence. 'The little boy had been transformed into a Lego soldier! If you can't answer the questions, you will become one of us', the guard told me.
    I saw him smile as cunningly as a fox. And I shivered. 'What are the questions?'
    'The first question is three plus four times six divide by nine. Second one, until now how many world wars were there in your world? Third one, what were the causes for the world war?' Oh, oh, how difficult. . . . Oh, if I study hard, I should have answered them all! How wonderful it would be if Pie were here! What should I do? Could you please help me? (Li 1991: 5–6)

As we can see from the revision with the child audience in mind, this group gave a much more detailed description of the Lego Empire and actually spelt out the three questions. The revision made the story not only more vivid but also more appealing to children (for more examples, see Li 1991; see also Urzua 1987: 291).
    The story-writing task took two months to complete. The project was evaluated highly by the students. In my interview with them, they described the experience as 'unforgettable', as having changed their perception of what writing was all about.

Reverting to product writing

According to Julie, although both she and her students enjoyed the process very much, she was faced with two problems: First, it took much longer to complete a writing task using the process approach than it did with the product approach. As a result, her students were writing far fewer compositions than other classes. Second, her students were making far more grammatical mistakes than before. She became worried when even her top students began to slip in terms of grammatical accuracy. Julie's dilemma was whether to carry on or go back to the product approach. She was afraid that carrying on would disadvantage her students in public examinations, given the importance attached to grammatical accuracy. In addition, although the English panel chair, who led the ESL teachers in the school, very much appreciated her effort and the work produced by the students, she was not ready to encourage more of this kind of writing or to encourage more teachers to adopt this approach. Julie reverted to the product approach during the following school year. Julie's decision reflected the typical curricular constraints that override teachers' attempts to introduce innovation in teaching (see Pennington and Cheung 1993; Stewart and Cheung 1989; see also Sola and Bennett 1985, cited in Zamel 1987: 704).

However, after going back to the product approach for more than a year, Julie found that her students no longer enjoyed the writing lessons. This was confirmed by an interview I had with the students who had written stories for children. In comparing what they were presently doing with what they had been doing in writing stories, they felt that they had enjoyed writing much more then. They said that their anxiety about writing had come back when the teacher went back to the product approach.

Julie also found herself not enjoying teaching writing any more. In one of our conferences, she said:

I didn't enjoy it either when I went back to the old approach. I have too little to contribute. I have too little to do. What I did was starting them off with the discussion, marking the exercise, writing a comment or two and then I have to think of the next topic or the next kind of writing to expose them to. But when I did the process approach, I think I have so much to bring in to the classroom. The relationship between myself and my students seems to be so much closer.

According to her, this was due largely to the fact that the product approach no longer allowed her to establish a dialogue with her students. When her students were going through drafts in writing, she felt that she got to know them much better, that she was getting into their worlds, sharing her thoughts with them and providing them with support. Each time she gave them back the drafts, she felt that her students were eager to read the comments. But since she had gone back to the product approach, the comments were no longer received with such eagerness. She realized that she was sacrificing enjoyment for quantity,

111

which she believed was positively correlated with grammatical accuracy. To resolve the dilemma, she decided to modify the process approach.

A modified version

When I asked Julie what decisions she had made when she modified her classroom practice, she reported that the guiding principle was to retain the essential elements of process writing but to reduce the amount of time needed to complete one writing task. She felt that providing a genuine writing environment was one of the essential elements. In one of the writing tasks she gave to her students this year, she asked them to write a postcard message to a tourist, introducing places of interest in Hong Kong. She actually sent these messages on postcards to the Tourist Association in Hong Kong, which replied to the students. She also felt that providing a topic which gave students plenty of room for imagination and creativity was another essential element. In one of her writing tasks, she gave the titles 'Friends', 'Romance', 'Rainy Days' and 'Examinations', as it was near examination time, and students were asked to freely associate ideas and write whatever came to mind.

These two tasks were highly rated by her students. The following are some excerpts from their evaluations.

I like to write about something like 'Friends', 'Romance', 'Rainy Days' 'Examination' which can let me write freely.

I like the postcard writing and the four passages (free association of ideas). They are interesting and special.

I like writing postcards because I was writing to somebody.

Do more interesting pieces, like the postcard message. The idea of free association is good, I can write it freely and I like it.

I would love to have more writing exercises on free association of ideas. The postcard message to a tourist is interesting as well. . . . I would like to have more funny [interesting] writing exercises in order to make us feel that writing is funny [interesting], not frightening.

We can do something more on e.g. the postcard message, something like that. I also like free association of ideas. We can write whatever we like and don't have to limit to one topic, e.g. 'Friends'. we can write anything about friends, and I think that's very good.

A third essential element, according to Julie, was providing a safe and supportive environment in which students were willing to take risks. Therefore, she decided to retain the brainstorming stage, in which students are allowed to freely associate ideas with their peers in groups and in which they are not required to write in complete sentences or in readable, acceptable paragraphs. She also felt that although group discussions might be more time consuming than teacher-fronted discussions with the whole class, the former could not be replaced by the latter. In one of the conferences I had with her, she reflected:

In student–student interaction, besides feeling more confident because they've got more ideas to write, they also feel much more safe because they know that even if they're wrong, it's not going to do them harm. . . . If it's sharing within a group, there isn't an authority. . . . In teacher-fronted discussion, even if the atmosphere has been very friendly and pleasant, they feel sort of inhibited because they know that you are the authority; although you are kind and friendly and you want to hear what WE think, they also feel that – 'Let me think about it very carefully before I start talking about it'. But in student–student sharing within the group, they can talk very freely.

Another stage she kept was asking students to read each others' work, in pairs or in groups, and give comments to each other for revision before the final draft is handed in and assessed by the teacher. Given that students have developed mutual trust, peer feedback contributes very much to providing a safe and supportive environment in which to develop thinking and writing (see Hedgcock and Lefkowitz 1992: 257; Mangelsdorf and Schlumberger 1992: 235). According to Julie, her students enjoyed getting peer feedback on their drafts:

. . . they enjoy doing it. They like sharing ideas with their peers very much. . . . The only thing that makes them fear doing it is that others will know how much they get for the paper or the grade they get for the paper. So if they are still in the process instead of the real product itself, then they have nothing to fear. They think that it is still a rough piece of work yet to be refined and so if you give me an extra idea, I welcome it. If you hate my idea, then I'll explain to you why [I have such an idea]. But then if I ask them to exchange it after a test, after I have already given them marks and I ask them to exchange test papers, then they wouldn't do it because it has already been given a mark. They would fear how people would look at them.

She also kept the stage in which teachers provide comments and suggestions for revision. She felt that this is a stage which is very helpful in improving content. It is a stage in which the teacher can abandon his or her role as a knower or a figure of authority and assume the role of a supporter and facilitator or, in Zamel's words, 'a co-inquirer in an intellectual enterprise' (1987: 710). It is also a stage in which the teacher develops a close relationship with the students. In one of the conferences, Julie reflected:

The more you write the comments in a personal way, the more they feel that they are writing something for you to read rather than for you to assess. . . . They told me that when they write, they will say to themselves this is something that Miss Li will enjoy reading.

She felt that developing a dialogue with the students in this manner could help to improve her relationship with the students, especially in her school, where students are not allowed to go into the staff room and therefore communication with them is very limited. Hence, the modified version required students to produce a draft, revise it after getting feedback from peers as well as the teacher, and produce a final draft for the teacher's assessment.

When I asked Julie what was her basis for reducing the number of revisions, she said:

From what I read from the exercises [writings], I see that they have already shown very evident improvement in all the three aspects [language, content and style] after one draft and then I feel that they also feel very confident to finalise whatever they have got and hand it in as a product.

However, she also pointed out that the number of drafts that students needed to go through actually depends on the topic. For some topics, such as writing a letter to a tourist introducing Hong Kong, one revision before the final draft was sufficient. For other topics, however, such as story writing, students did need to go through several drafts for the story to take shape.

Student performance in the process and product approaches

Even though Julie came up with this modified version, she did not use it for all writing tasks. Of a total of eight writing tasks that she gave to her secondary 3 (grade 9) students in the 1992–1993 school year, only three were done through the modified process approach. In exploring the reasons behind this decision, Julie admitted that she was not convinced that the approach was good for her top students, despite all the positive feedback from students and the enjoyment that she shared with her students. She said:

The top students sacrifice accuracy for ideas. I mean they used to be very fluent and accurate when I tried to give them one hour and they hand in the product in the old way. But when I asked them to do it in the modified process approach, then they sacrifice accuracy. I don't know if it has something to do with their eagerness to include a lot and they tend to forget about organization, they tend to forget about tenses and all that. . . . But in terms of the content, it's very interesting. Much more has been included and I think they enjoy it much more than they do for the one hour thing.

The weak and average students, however, benefited from the process approach. She said, 'I think the [process] approach is definitely worthwhile for the weaker students, judging from what they did'. She compared their performance in the two different approaches and found that they scored higher in both content and language when they were doing process writing. In one of the conferences, she said:

> For the weaker ones, the problem is actually twofold. One is language and the other is pressure of time. So for the process approach, I think they benefit from the approach because both problems are solved. I mean with more time given to them and without the stress, they would tend to write more comfortably and then comes accuracy. I mean they lack the confidence that the top students have.

The performance of the average students was similar to that of the weaker ones: They improved in terms of content and accuracy (cf. Carroll 1984).[4]

For the class that went back entirely to the product approach, which is now in secondary 5 (grade 11), Julie found that the top students improved steadily in accuracy but not in content, whereas the average and weak students did not improve in either accuracy or content. All three groups of students found writing less enjoyable than before, as mentioned above.

Integrating the process and product approaches

On the basis of her analysis of the performance of her students in process writing and product writing, Julie raised the following questions: Is it true that the process approach is suitable only for average and weak students, and not for good students? Must accuracy be achieved at the expense of content, or vice versa? Could students not achieve both at the same time? How can one resolve the conflict between a process approach in the teaching of writing and a product approach in the assessment of writing in public examinations?

Once again, she reviewed what she had done with her students in process writing. She found that in all the stages of process writing, that is, generating ideas, drafting, revising and editing, her emphasis had been on content and not form, even in the editing stage. In product writing, by contrast, her emphasis had been more on form than on content. However, both content and form are important. As Raimes (1985: 247–248) points out, writing teachers should

> . . . consider the need to attend to product as well as process. Our students should be taught not only heuristic devices to focus on meaning, but also heuristic devices to focus on rhetorical and linguistic features after the ideas have found some form.

---

4 Carroll (1984) points out that the process approach is believed by many teachers to be inappropriate for students whose English is limited.

In other words, it is not a matter of adopting one approach for certain students, but rather a matter of marrying the two (see also Conner 1987; Raimes 1986, 1991). This is something that Julie would explore with her students in the following school year.

Learning about writing and the teaching of ESL writing

In this discussion, we have seen how an ESL writing teacher took the teaching of writing as a problem-solving activity and tried to come up with solutions as she encountered them. Julie, in reflecting upon what she had learnt in the past two years or so as a writing teacher, felt that her perception of writing and the teaching of it definitely changed as she took her students through process writing. She used to think that writing was mastering of technical skills. Now, however, she feels very strongly that writing is a creative activity and that it is inextricably linked with thinking. In one of the conferences, she said:

It [writing] involves a lot of thinking. I think if a student can think in a logical way, she is able to develop ideas, she is very likely to be a good writer. It has got a very direct relationship with fluency. . . . Thinking affects writing and thinking determines writing, what the written product is going to be like. . . . And on the other hand, writing also develops thinking.

In terms of the teaching of writing, she used to think that so long as she is well prepared, she would be able to teach successfully. She also thought that whether students were able to produce good writing depended on how much effort they made. However, in the course of teaching writing, she became more and more aware of the fact that success depended on efforts on both parts.

I always feel that if something is successfully done, it must have both the students' effort plus the teacher's. And with the process approach, both can be assessed . . . because much of the success of the approach depends on how much the teacher has prepared herself, how much the teacher has been sensitive . . . to the needs of the students at different stages. . . . I found myself in situations which I had to abandon what I planned and react to the the needs of students. I need to be not only more sensitive to needs but also more flexible.

She felt that, in the course of exploring how to teach writing, she has become more confident. She is no longer anxious about what is going to happen next, whether her plans will work or not, whether she will be able to keep to the schedule, because she knows that being flexible and being able to respond to the needs of her students on the spot are the keys to success. Her flexibility and sensitivity to student needs are fully demonstrated in her going from a product approach to a process approach, from a process approach back to a product approach, and from the latter to a modified version of the process approach.

What Julie has done with her students, the decisions that she has made in responding to needs and her commitment to making writing enjoyable are nicely summed up in Bartholomae's (1986: 5) description of writing teachers:

> What characterizes writing teachers . . . is not that they have a set of 'methods' for the teaching of writing, but they have a commitment to writing as an intellectual activity and to what that activity can produce in the classroom.

References

Applebee, A. N. 1984. *Contexts for Learning to Write*. Norwood, N.J.: Ablex.

Arnt, V. 1990. *Writing in First and Second Languages: Contrasts and Comparisons*. Research Report No. 1, Department of English, City Polytechnic of Hong Kong.

Barnes, D. 1976. *From Communication to Curriculum*. London: Penguin.

Bartholomae, D. 1986. Words from afar. In A. R. Petrosky and D. Bartholomae (eds.), *The Teaching of Writing*. Eighty-Fifth Yearbook of the National Society for the Study of Education, Part II. Chicago: National Society for the Study of Education, pp. 1–7.

Blanton, L. 1987. Reshaping ESL students' perceptions of writing. *ELT Journal* 41(2): 112–118.

Bloom, L. Z. 1985. Anxious writers in context: Graduate school and beyond. In M. Rose (ed.), *When a Writer Can't Write*. New York: Guilford, pp. 119–133.

Carroll, J. A. 1984. Process into product: Teacher awareness of the writing process affects students' written products. In R. Beach and L. S. Bridwell (eds.), *New Directions in Composition Research*. New York: Guilford, pp. 315–333.

Connor, U. 1987. Research frontiers in writing analysis. *TESOL Quarterly 21* (4): 677–696.

Daly, J. 1985. Writing apprehension. In M. Rose (ed.), *When a Writer Can't Write*. New York: Guilford, pp. 43–82.

Dunn, S., S. Florio-Ruane, and M. C. Clarke. 1985. The teacher as respondent to the high school writer. In S. W. Freedman (ed.), *The Acquisition of Written Language*. Norwood, N.J.: Ablex, pp. 33–50.

Hartwell, P. 1984. Grammar, grammars, and the teaching of grammar. *College English* 47: 105–127.

Hedgcock, J., and N. Lefkowitz. 1992. Collaborative oral/aural revision in foreign language writing instruction. *Journal of Second Language Writing 1* (3): 225–276.

Hildenbrand, J. 1985. Carmen: A case study of an ESL writer. Doctoral dissertation, Teachers College, Columbia University, New York.

Jones, S. 1985. Problems with monitor use in second language composition. In M. Rose (ed.), *When a Writer Can't Write*. New York: Guilford, pp. 96–118.

Kantor, K. J. 1984. Classroom contexts and the development of writing intuitions: An ethnographic case study. In R. Beach and L. S. Bridwell (eds.), *New Directions in Composition Research*, New York: Guilford, pp. 72–94.

Li, J. 1991. Getting students to write stories for children – A project in process writing. *Curriculum Forum 1*(3): 1–17.

Mangelsdorf, K., and A. Schlumberger. 1992. ESL student response stances in a peer-review task. *Journal of Second Language Writing 1*(3): 235–254.

Newkirk, T. 1984. Anatomy of a breakthrough: Case study of a college freshman writer. In R. Beach and L. S. Bridwell (eds.), *New Directions in Composition Research*. New York: Guilford, pp. 131–148.

Pennington, M., and M. Cheung. 1993. Factors shaping the introduction of process writing in Hong Kong secondary schools. Unpublished manuscript, City University of Hong Kong.

Raimes, A. 1984. Anguish as a second language? Remedies for composition teachers. In S. Mackay (ed.), *Composing in a Second Language*. Rowley, Mass.: Newbury House, pp. 81–97.

Raimes, A. 1985. What unskilled ESL students do as they write: A classroom study of composing. *TESOL Quarterly 19*(2): 229–358.

Raimes, A. 1986. Teaching writing: What we know and what we do. Paper presented at the Annual Meeting of TESOL, March 3–8, 1986, Anaheim, Calif.

Raimes, A. 1991. Out of the woods. *TESOL Quarterly 25*(3): 407–430.

Selfe, C. 1985. An apprehensive writer composes. In M. Rose (ed.), *When a Writer Can't Write*. New York: Guilford, pp. 83–95.

Sengupta, S. Ongoing research. The teaching of writing in Hong Kong secondary schools. Department of Curriculum Studies, University of Hong Kong.

Shaughnessy, M. 1977. *Errors and Expectations*. New York: Oxford University Press.

Silva, T. 1990. Second language composition instruction: Developments, issues, and directions in ESL. In B. Kroll (ed.), *Second Language Writing*. Cambridge: Cambridge University Press, pp. 11–23.

Sola, M., and A. T. Bennett. 1985. The struggle for voice: Narrative, literacy and consciousness in an East Harlem school. *Boston University Journal of Education 167*: 88–110.

Stewart, M., and M. Cheung. 1989. Introducing a process approach in the teaching of writing in Hong Kong. *ILE Journal 6*: 41–48.

Sweigart, W. 1991. Classroom talk, development and writing. *Research in the Teaching of English 25*(4): 469–496.

Urzua, C. 1987. 'You stopped too soon': Second language children composing and revising. *TESOL Quarterly 21*(2): 279–303.

Winer, L. 1992. 'Spinach to chocolate': Changing awareness and attitudes in ESL writing teachers. *TESOL Quarterly* 26(1): 57–79.

Zamel, V. 1983. The composing processes of advanced ESL students: Six case studies. *TESOL Quarterly* 17(2): 165–187.

Zamel, V. 1985. Responding to student writing. *TESOL Quarterly* 19(1): 79–101.

Zamel, V. 1987. Recent research on writing pedagogy. *TESOL Quarterly* 21(1): 697–715.

Section II Transitions: Learning in the practice of teaching

Section II consists of four chapters that focus on the practice of teaching. The issue here is not entry into the profession or starting out in the classroom, as in Section I, but various examinations of the teacher's work in action. These studies look at teaching from various research perspectives, through narrative and life history, teacher decision making, and classroom discourse combined with the teacher's stimulated recall. The studies have in common a concern with transitions in classroom practice: an experienced teacher moving from teaching one subject matter to teaching another, a study of a teacher who is teaching her first beginning-level class, a teacher working with college-bound immigrant students as they move into the demands of university classrooms, and an examination of teachers in the practice of teaching adult learners.

The first chapter in the section, by Patrick Moran, is a unique examination of a high school English teacher who teaches herself to be a Spanish teacher. While there is a good deal of research on teachers' acquisition of subject-matter knowledge, there is nothing in the literature on teacher learning that examines such learning as a self-directed process outside the structure of formal teacher education. Moran's study chronicles how a skilled, experienced teacher builds her own competence and understanding of a new subject matter. Using the tools of a narrative research, Moran and the teacher co-construct an account of the experiences and factors that contribute to her learning to be a teacher of Spanish. This chapter picks up, in an interesting way, where the chapter by Kathleen Bailey and colleagues in Section I leaves off, by taking the "apprenticeship of observation" another step to an "apprenticeship in subject matter."

Anne Burns's chapter tells of one teacher, Sarah, who participated in a larger study of experienced teachers' pedagogical beliefs. Faced with a very beginning-level ESOL class of adult immigrants, Sarah talks of "starting all over again." Through this commonplace, naturally occurring transition in teaching situation in which a teacher faces students at a new level, Burns is able to bring to the surface the complex interaction of context, learners, and curriculum within which Sarah must revise her view of teaching. This study of the cognitive context of teaching offers intriguing parallels to the chapters by Johnson and by Gutiérrez Almarza in Section I. Together these three studies confirm the interpretative nature of what teachers know and provide insights into teachers' thought processes as they encounter and work with the fabric of the language classroom.

The chapter by Polly Ulichny presents a detailed study on one experienced teacher's classroom practice. Working closely with the teacher, Wendy Schoener, Ulichny analyzes audiotapes of an advanced reading class that prepares students for university-level course work. The study provides a grounded account of Schoener's teaching in action, giving a view of teaching methodology from the inside out. Ulichny's work is in many ways pioneering because it reveals how the external prescriptive views of method that generally prevail in the field of language teaching bear little resemblance to teachers' and students' lived experience of methods in the classroom. In focusing on a teaching method in practice, this chapter offers an interesting parallel to Tsui's study in Section I. While the two studies differ in the classroom contexts, skills being taught, and cultural backgrounds of students and teacher, they demonstrate how the concept of teaching method needs to be researched and critically reexamined from the teacher's perspective.

The last chapter in this section, by Deborah Binnie Smith, presents findings from a larger study she did on teachers' beliefs and their classroom practices. Smith's chapter offers a broad comparative look at teachers in the practice of teaching, through the research construct of instructional decision making. Her study shows the benefits that such exploratory research can bring a fuller and more textured understanding of how language teachers work and what their teaching entails in practice.

The four chapters in this section show language teaching in practice. They suggest the complexity of subject matter (Chapter 6), of working with a variety of students (Chapter 7), of teaching method (Chapter 8), all against the backdrop of instructional practice (Chapter 9). Together this type of research demonstrates what can be gained from critical, inquiry-based perspectives and understandings of the commonplace elements of language teaching – what is taught, to whom, and how it is taught.

Suggestions for further reading

The following books and articles are suggested as further reading on the key topics in this section.

On teachers' acquisition of subject-matter knowledge
Shulman, L. S. 1987. Knowledge-base and teaching: Foundations of the new reform. *Harvard Educational Review* 57(1):1–22.

Wilson, S., L. Shulman, and A. Richert. 1987. "150 different ways" of knowing: Representations of knowledge in teaching. In J. Calderhead (ed)., *Exploring Teachers' Thinking*. London: Cassell, pp. 104–124.

On learning to represent subject matter to learners
Grossman, P. 1990. *The Making of a Teacher: Teacher Knowledge and Teacher Education*. New York: Teachers College Press.
Grossman, P., S. Wilson, and L. Shulman. 1989. Teachers of substance: Subject-matter knowledge in teaching. In M. Reynolds (ed.), *Knowledge-Base for the Beginning Teacher*. New York: Pergamon Press and the American Association of Colleges of Teacher Education, pp. 23–36.
McDiarmid, G. W., D. Ball, and C. W. Anderson. 1989. Why staying one chapter ahead doesn't really work: Subject specific pedagogy. In M. Reynolds (ed.), *The Knowledge-Base for Beginning Teachers*. Elmsford, N.Y.: Pergamon, pp. 193–206.

On narrative research
Connelly, M., and D. J. Clandinin. 1990. Stories of experience and narrative inquiry. *Educational Researcher 19* (5): 2–14.
Cortazzi, M. 1993. *Narrative Analysis*. London: Falmer Press.
Kelchtermans, G. 1993. Getting the story, understanding the lives: From career stories to teachers' professional development. *Teaching and Teacher Education 9*(5/6): 443–456.

On teaching method
Clarke, M. 1994. The dysfunctions of the theory/practice discourse. *TESOL Quarterly 28*(1): 9–26.
Pennycook, A. 1989. The concept of method, interested knowledge, and the politics of language teaching. *TESOL Quarterly 23*(4): 589–618.
Prabhu, N. S. 1990. There is no best method – Why? *TESOL Quarterly 24* (2): 161–176.

On studies of teachers' decision making
Kagan, D. 1988. Teaching as clinical problem-solving: A critical examination of the analogy and its implications. *Review of Educational Research 58* (4): 482–505.
Shulman, L., and A. Elstein. 1975. Studies in problem-solving, judgment, and decision-making: Implications for educational research. *Review of Educational Research 3*: 3–42.

6 "I'm not typical": Stories of becoming a Spanish teacher

Patrick R. Moran

> "I'm not typical," Katherine said as she erased the blackboard, part of her clean-up ritual at the end of the teaching day. "I didn't go through what typical high school Spanish teachers do, I'm afraid. So I'm not sure how helpful I can be to your study."

This chapter relates a series of stories about what "Katherine Russell" (a pseudonym) "went through" in becoming a Spanish teacher, and also about what may or may not be "typical" in that process. Some of the stories take place in the midst of her year-long internship as a Spanish teacher in a small, public high school in rural New Hampshire. Others are situated in her experiences prior to this time period. When Katherine Russell decided to add Spanish teaching to her responsibilities as an English teacher six years ago, she set out on a journey both to teach herself Spanish and to teach herself how to teach Spanish. In her mind, her experiences were unlike "typical" Spanish teachers in the United States, who major in Spanish at the undergraduate level, study abroad in a Spanish-speaking country, do a teaching practicum, graduate, and land a job in a high school. Perhaps she is right. Perhaps her journey to becoming a Spanish teacher is "not typical." On the other hand, her experiences may be more typical than she realizes. After all, what is "typical" in becoming a foreign language teacher?

In the following pages, I recount Katherine Russell's stories of becoming a Spanish teacher. I use the word "stories" because I found that her journey was not a linear series of events that flowed smoothly in a logical sequence, like a carefully arranged line of falling dominoes, from past to present. Rather, it unfolded like criss-crossing ripples from many intersecting key events, with few (if any) straight lines of cause and effect. Structuring her experiences as stories seemed an apt means of expressing this complexity.

The chapter, as a result, is set within an emergent concept in research on teacher knowledge: "story" (Carter 1993; Clandinin and Connelly 1991). Consistent with similar concepts, such as "narrative" (Clandinin

125

1992; Clandinin and Connelly 1988; Connelly and Clandinin 1990),
"biography" (Butt and Raymond 1987; Goodson and Walker 1990),
"life history" (Knowles 1991; Woods 1987), these approaches to research focus on the individual teacher and his or her experience, and
on the critical importance of portraying this experience from the teacher's point of view. In a review of the literature, Carter (1993) describes
how story is used to address three aspects of research in teacher knowledge: (1) as "a way . . . of capturing the complexity, specificity, and
interconnectedness of the phenomenon" (p. 6) – as an effective means
of reporting research; (2) as "a way of knowing and thinking that is
particularly suited to the explicating the issues" (ibid.) – in effect, the
means by which teachers perceive and express what they know; (3) as
a "product of a fundamentally interpretive process that is shaped by
the moralistic impulses of the author and by narrative forces or requirements" (p. 9) – in other words, a description of the narrator's views
and intentions. While I cannot claim that Katherine perceived her experience as stories, I do recognize that these stories of Katherine's experiences are as much my construction as they are hers. Even though
she read and commented on them, it is I who structured the inquiry,
framed the analysis, and tell the stories.

I gathered data from five papers that Katherine wrote as part of her
student experiences for her internship year, from three classroom observations, and through six hour-long interviews with Katherine over a
three-month period. (The source of the data is indicated in parentheses.)
My research methodology is based on the "grounded theory" approach
(Glaser and Strauss 1967), where theory is generated and modified
through the process of data gathering and analysis. I shared my analyses
with Katherine, and modified hypotheses based on her commentary.

In keeping with the image of multiple stories, this account is organized as a series of stories, all treating a different dimension of Katherine's experiences. It begins with a chronological snapshot of Katherine's
seven-year journey, "Settings for Stories," a sort of aerial map of her
experience, including this inquiry. Katherine's particular efforts in learning the subject matter are described next, in "Learning Spanish." From
there, the account shifts to Katherine's autodidactic pedagogical journey, "Teaching Spanish." Then, with her entry into a graduate program
in teaching second languages and direct teacher education interventions,
the account switches to "Learning to Teach Spanish." In "Other Stories," the account then delves more deeply into specific themes that have
surfaced in previous sections, and attempts to posit a relationship
among them. In the final section, "Questions," I ask the reader to consider to what extent Katherine's becoming a Spanish teacher may be
"typical."

Before beginning these stories, it may help the reader to be aware of dominant themes in Katherine's stories, themes that I identified from analyzing our interview transcripts. I will sketch these here, and refer the reader to "Other Stories" for a fuller discussion. Briefly, then, in Katherine's quest to become a Spanish teacher:

- She drew upon a nexus of *core values* that she used to guide her teaching. Prominent among these was *legitimacy* – a fusion of feelings, values, and practices to define what it means to be (or become) a Spanish teacher.
- She relied on her views of *students and learning*, to the extent that their reactions to her teaching practices provoked her to reflect upon and to make changes in her practice, as did her own learning experiences as a graduate student in the teacher education program.
- She developed *a feeling for subject matter*, Spanish language, and Hispanic culture, specifically of its importance to her mission as an educator, which also motivated her efforts to change her teaching.
- She consciously employed *models of teaching*, Spanish teachers who had taught her, fashioning to varying degrees her own teaching practices after these teachers.

My hope is that, through the telling of these successive stories, the reader will perceive not only the emergence and importance of these themes, but also the relationships among them. Because I conducted and completed this research project during Katherine's internship experience in the teacher education program, all these stories are recounted within the time frame of one school year.

Settings for stories

Katherine Russell, a lively white-haired woman in her mid-fifties, has been teaching English in this small New Hampshire high school for about thirteen years. The high school building is a relic from an earlier era, built in the late nineteenth century, four stories of red brick with an empty wooden belfry on the roof. A small wooden addition stands alongside, housing the library and a reading room. The maple floorboards have been varnished many times over, and they snap and groan under even the lightest footstep. There are fewer than a hundred students in the high school; more than once, the school district has threatened to shut the high school down and move the students to a nearby regional high school, but the community resists, successfully so far.

At the time of the study, enrollment in Katherine's Spanish classes was small. The largest of her classes had twelve students, the smallest six. She was teaching three levels of Spanish, primarily to students interested in going on to college. Since she also taught English, her classroom was decorated with posters and paraphernalia for both languages, including bullfight posters, impressionist painting reproductions, even a model of Shakespeare's Globe theater. There were labels written in Spanish taped under, alongside, or on many objects all around the room.

Students were either from homes in the surrounding countryside or from the village, so small that there are just a few places of business and a post office. The nearest larger town lies across the river in Vermont, and even that is not much bigger. Dartmouth College and the cosmopolitan community of Hanover are about a half-hour's drive away, but Katherine reported that "the kids never go there." Katherine herself lives outside the community and drives about thirty minutes to get to school.

Katherine's teaching was highly participatory, with the students rarely in their desks for the whole period. They moved their chairs about into work groups, or they left them to carry out various tasks around the room. More often than not, these involved manipulating a wealth of objects stored in a large cardboard box behind Katherine's desk. Students used the objects and the clothing to act out skits in Spanish. Katherine spoke to them almost all the time in Spanish. During my first visit in November, the bustle of activity in Spanish and the interest of the students seemed such an accepted set of activities that I was surprised when Katherine later told me that her classes the year before had been quite different.

Katherine was originally an English major in college, and had taught high school English for five years in New York before she moved north to this area with her family. Six years ago, she began teaching Spanish in this high school. At the time, Katherine was convinced that Spanish could not possibly be that difficult, since in her own high school experience, the teacher had not demanded much from students. Also, she was interested in finding more committed students, since some of those in her English classes were not motivated and caused problems. This decision to become a Spanish teacher sparked a significant effort on Katherine's part to gain knowledge of the subject matter, Spanish.

For the previous six years, she had sought to improve her own understanding of Spanish and her ability to teach it, since she had not been trained as a Spanish teacher. Every summer, she attended a Spanish language program of some sort, ranging from college summer programs in Vermont and New Hampshire to programs in Spain and Central America.

In her Spanish classes, she began by applying models of teaching Spanish that she had experienced as a student in the programs and courses she had taken. These models of teaching were based on grammatical views of language, not a communicative view. Even though she herself enjoyed learning the structure of Spanish, she eventually discovered that her students did not. They preferred more immediate, communicative uses of language, "everyday things." Largely because of their reactions, Katherine saw that she, too, needed more of this kind of language in her own repertoire.

However, she did not know how to teach this kind of communicative language in her classes. She had no relevant teaching models to draw upon; none of the Spanish teachers who had taught her had used a communicative approach to teaching language. At this point, even though she felt "competent" as a Spanish teacher, she admitted to herself that her teaching was "mechanical" and "boring." In fact, she had reached a point of "stagnation," not knowing what to do, but sensing that there were surely techniques and methodologies for teaching communicative language. Her drive for "legitimacy" – a sense of conscience about striving to be a "good teacher" – pushed her to take action.

At this juncture, after five years of teaching and learning Spanish, Katherine entered graduate school, a Master of Arts in teaching (MAT) program in foreign languages conducted over two consecutive summers with an interim-year practicum. This structured experience of teacher education set in motion a catalytic constellation of events that precipitated change in Katherine's teaching.

In Katherine's remaking of her teaching, her summer course work in the MAT program appears to have been one major catalyst in stimulating change. This summer experience consisted of many other events, some of which Katherine described as especially important: "Angela's Spanish class" (in which Katherine was a student), and "the demonstrations of [teaching] methods." In addition, her experiences as a student during the summer triggered her own "awareness of what it was like to feel exposed, to feel dumb, to feel the pressure to do things quickly," which had the effect of "sensitizing [her] to students' fears and anxieties."

A second key event was the "reflection" period that occurred from the end of summer course work to the beginning of the school year, when Katherine took up her Spanish classes again. As she put it, "I needed time away to internalize things, because at the time, I couldn't see how they applied to my situation." In the several days before the beginning of the school year, Katherine gathered her thoughts and set down on paper the changes she wanted to make in her teaching.

The third key event, then in progress, was her teaching itself, infused with the added dimension and responsibility of an "internship" or "interim-year practicum." During this time, Katherine was expected to implement changes in her teaching, which she did. She had to write four progress reports on her teaching, and a teaching supervisor from the graduate program made three visits to observe and discuss her teaching.

129

More significantly, however, Katherine was able to see changes in her students' responses to her teaching and to Spanish. This change that Katherine fashioned in her teaching was at the heart of the story of her development as a Spanish teacher.

Another part of the settings for these stories was the intervention of this research project in this chronological snapshot. I was the supervisor of Katherine's internship for the graduate program, and I visited Katherine's classes, discussed them with her, read her written reports, and jointly set and evaluated teaching goals with her throughout the year. In February 1992, I proposed a research project to her, an inquiry into her acquisition of Spanish and Hispanic culture and its influence on her language teaching. She agreed, and alongside our supervisory relationship, I carried out the research into her personal history as a language and culture learner, mainly through a series of six hour-long interviews over a three-month period, but also drawing upon my classroom observations and her written reports. As it turned out, not until the third interview did I stumble upon the significance of the change she had undertaken in her language teaching. With this discovery, I shifted the focus of my inquiry to exploring this change. Not until the penultimate interview did the concept of "legitimacy" emerge, an element that seemed to weave through all aspects of Katherine's stories. In any case, my dual role as internship supervisor and as researcher undoubtedly affected the inquiry, though I did not explore this as part of my study. Even though the above summary account is presented as a chronology, this is not the way it surfaced from the interviews. Rather, this is how I eventually pieced together information from the interviews.

Thus, Katherine's development as a Spanish teacher seemed to consist of three ongoing stories: her own study of Spanish, her evolving teaching practice, and her return to graduate school – respectively entitled "Learning Spanish," "Teaching Spanish," and "Learning to Teach Spanish." Even though these stories interweave and influence one another, I will tell each of them separately. This interweaving is then explored in "Other Stories," followed by "Questions," a series of speculations on the relevance of Katherine's stories to other language teachers.

First, though, Katherine's experiences with Spanish.

Learning Spanish

Let us begin with the story of Katherine's self-directed learning of Spanish. As mentioned, Katherine began this journey with "high school Spanish." From this foundation, she structured her own learning of Spanish, mainly through summer programs in the United States and

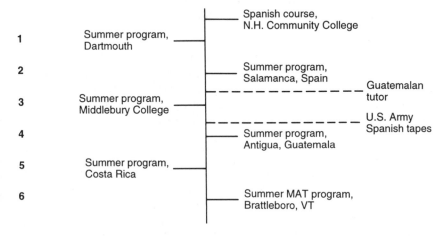

Figure 1

abroad, gradually building fluency and accuracy to the point where she is now at ease in the language.

Six years previously, when Katherine had proposed the addition of Spanish to the curriculum of the high school, she had a "naive" conception of what it would take to be Spanish teacher.

I had no idea what was involved in getting fluent in a language. I guess I was a bit arrogant in that I even thought it was a possibility. . . . All I had was essentially high school Spanish, but I thought it was possible given the way I was taught Spanish. I mean, all I did was listen. I don't think I even said a word the whole time. I thought that obviously I could do that. But I didn't have any idea about fluency – what it took to learn Spanish. But I began looking around for a program. (Interview)

Figure 1 shows the initiatives that Katherine undertook to learn Spanish and to develop her teaching practice. This time line illustrates the organized programs and other initiatives that Katherine undertook for six years, as part of her self-designed program of preparation to "get myself qualified," as she put it. She took courses, studied abroad during summers, worked with a tutor, and studied Spanish on her own using U.S. Army audiotapes, along with books and materials for learning Spanish on her own, what she referred to as her "regimen."

As she progressed through these programs, her own understanding of the subject matter, Spanish, evolved. As she said,

I think that my ideas about what I was trying to learn changed . . . because I don't think I understood what was really involved in learning a language when I began. I somehow looked upon it much more as an academic exer-

131

cise, that I was basically learning different kinds of formulas that I could pass on to somebody else, and help them learn to do the formulas. (Interview)

By "formulas," she is referring to grammatical patterns or structures, and vocabulary – an emphasis on the forms of language rather than its uses in specific cultural contexts. As a matter of fact, her experience in Salamanca did bring her into contact with the demands of developing "fluency" and communicative ability in Spanish.

Well, when I originally, when I went to Salamanca, I remember my Spanish teacher – who was actually a Latin American woman – telling me, "Oh, when you come back, you're going to be fluent. Isn't that wonderful!" And I really believed her. I thought, "Well, she wasn't lying." I just believed that that was probably what was going to happen. And of course, it didn't. So, I was very discouraged, because then suddenly I realized how hard it was, and how much was involved in really learning a language. (Interview)

From that point on, she redoubled her efforts to master Spanish, and began working regularly with a tutor, a Guatemalan student at Dartmouth College. The following summer, she attended the Spanish immersion program at Middlebury College, where she was expected to speak Spanish all the time, not only in class but outside class as well, with other students of Spanish at all levels of proficiency. This forced immersion had an important impact on her:

Even though I didn't think about it at the time, but it's something I'm using now, I think, that it wasn't "good" Spanish really, but it was making an effort to use the language to say things all the time to people. And to say things that were sophisticated, really, because you didn't know these people, and you wanted to let them know who you are, and you wanted to find out who they were, and that sort of thing. So it was more than just "How much does this cost?" and "I like that," or something like that. And so that was, I guess, very important. (Interview)

This sort of learning experience, however, was not what she was getting in the formal classes she was taking. Her Spanish teachers at Middlebury (and in the other programs) used teaching approaches that were "structural"; that is, they did not feature communicative use of the language. As she progressed from one summer program to another, she began to realize what her Spanish classes were missing.

None of the programs I've ever been involved in have used situational-type things. Here you are in a store; here you are here; here you are there. What are the kind of . . . conventional sorts of things people say to one another in those sorts of circumstances? You know, what are the sorts of formulaic things that people say with the language, because everybody has them. And so I would know all sorts of fancy words – and I do, I have a rather extraordinary vocabulary – but I wouldn't know the ordinary things. But how would you say "this," which everybody says every day, all the time? I wouldn't know. (Interview)

The "situational-type things" and the "ordinary things" that "everybody says every day" became more of a priority for Katherine. Since she was not able to get them in her formal classes, even in Spanish-speaking countries, she made a decision about two years ago to do it on her own.

That's what I've been trying recently – I mean, recently, within the past two years or so – to try to accumulate. For myself. . . . I think it was just an awareness that all this effort I was putting into structures was important, but that I would ultimately, I mean, have all these structures and endlessly be able to transform this and that – and nevertheless, there are idioms that I just didn't know! Like how do you say, "How about this?" or "How about that?" You know, something silly like that. (Interview)

Katherine then transformed her conception of what she needed in order to attain more of this "everyday" language. Interestingly, she thought of it as acquiring another set of "formulas."

. . . because language for the most part, when people speak to one other, is made up of a lot of formulas. And I never learned those formulas, because that wasn't the way that any of the classes I ever had dealt with things. (Interview)

She identified these "formulas" as "idioms," and as part of her "regimen" of self-study, she undertook to learn these on her own, primarily from books. It appeared to be a process of building more vocabulary, albeit specific to "situations" one could find in the culture. She gave an example of the kind of idioms she was working on:

Well, OK, like this one here that's . . . it doesn't seem to be able to stay in my brain, like "I dislike to/I hate to." And it's basically, it's *se me hace cuesta arriba*, which means "it makes a lot of costs above." I mean, it doesn't make any sense, if you try to translate it. But this book is just very . . . it's an old, old book . . . that was published maybe, oh I don't know, I don't know if it's even 1940, that early . . . well, 1920. It has little situations, and lots of idioms. (Interview)

This sort of study, however, was very painstaking, and Katherine felt frustrated in working alone with her books and tapes.

Well, I've been trying to work on it. It is frustrating, because it's not the way to go about it – the way I go about it. I mean, that's not the most efficient way, which is basically all by yourself in your own head . . . at least not for me. Maybe somebody else could do it this way and be effective, but it's just . . . it's a difficult thing, because I don't hear the language. (Interview)

Learning these "formulas" in isolation, without being able to "hear the language," has been an uphill struggle for Katherine. When she dreams of what would help her get the "everyday language" she needs, she envisions an extended stay in a Spanish-speaking country, where she would have an immersion experience, not unlike that of the Middlebury program.

So, maybe something like that in which one goes somewhere where there are maybe not very many English-speaking people, and there's some situation in which you have to be with people and talk to them, and listen to them, and listen to their family life, or something, you know, if you live with a family. Somehow or another, what would really be ideal would be truly to have something, some plan of study in which I'm just stuck for six months, let's say, in a place. . . . (Interview)

Katherine knows that this kind of situation would allow her both the time and the opportunities to learn the sorts of things that she cannot seem to do on her own.

It would just be the time. It would give me the time to absorb an awful lot. Because I'm really at a fairly advanced level, and I think that if I just had the time, to just hear and hear and hear, and listen and listen and listen, and have to push to say and say and say, that I would be where I would like to be. . . . Just having to be . . . having to use language. And to just listen to it and respond, and think. . . . (Interview)

Her extended stays in Salamanca, Guatemala, and Costa Rica have given her opportunities to learn about Hispanic culture, which she seems to see as a sort of informational overlay which she can use in her classes as an interesting and realistic backdrop for the language. Interestingly, these opportunities apparently did not provide her with the sort of interactions with native Spanish speakers of which she dreamed.

The story of her acquisition of Spanish and Hispanic culture, then, is one of her own making. She chose her programs and courses of study with an eye to improving her knowledge of the language and the culture. Her journey as a learner is one of climbing a series of hills, each one illuminating a wider and more profound perspective on the language and culture. She traveled from the simple formulas of high school, to the grammar and vocabulary patterns of Dartmouth, to the challenge of the fluency and culture in Salamanca, upward to the thrill and excitement of speaking in the Middlebury immersion experience, on to the awareness of "everyday" and "situational-type" language, and eventually to the desire for an in-depth immersion experience in a Spanish-speaking culture with much interaction with the people there.

Along the way, Katherine has developed a high level of linguistic competence in Spanish; she has an extensive vocabulary and a wide range of grammar structures at her command. She speaks accurately, without hesitation, in a natural manner, with many expressions and interjections that native speakers would use. She has worked hard and diligently to reach this level.

This story may sound separate, but in fact, it was intimately linked with her experiences with the students in her Spanish classes at the high school, as we shall see in the next of her stories.

Teaching Spanish

The essence of this story is Katherine's efforts over five years to forge an effective practice as a Spanish teacher. This consisted of conscious attempts to model other teachers, to respond to her students' requests and interests, to meet her own standards of acceptable teaching. Eventually, she reached the limits of her ability to cope on her own. She was thus left with a feeling of "stagnancy" and a desire to attain "legitimacy" as a Spanish teacher.

Katherine's Spanish teaching practices followed models of Spanish teaching that she had experienced as a student. In effect, she seemed to piece together her methodology from teachers and from the textbook she used. She did this until her models failed to elicit students' interest or overcome their resistance, as we shall see shortly.

Remember that Katherine's original motivation to teach Spanish was derived directly from her own high school Spanish experience. In essence, she assumed that there was not much to teaching Spanish.

Anyway, all I had was essentially high school Spanish, but I thought it was possible, given the way I was taught Spanish. I mean all I did was listen. I don't think I even said a word the whole time. I thought that obviously I could do that. (Interview)

However, as she realized the challenge of becoming "fluent," she became more concerned about reaching an adequate level of proficiency. During her summer program at Dartmouth College, she consciously compared herself with other participants in the Rassias[1] program, searching for some reassurance that she was capable of teaching Spanish.

Then I went to Rassias's program one summer. There were other teachers in the course learning Spanish. Some of them were French teachers who were

1 John Rassias, a well-known foreign language educator, advocates breaking down students' inhibitions through teachers' use of drama and theatrics. His approach has a strong emphasis on grammatical patterns and learning through habit formation – accuracy through drill and repetition.

going to have to teach Spanish in their schools. And I saw that my Spanish was as good as theirs. So that made me feel that I could do it. (Interview)

At this stage of her development, Katherine appeared most concerned about her mastery of subject matter, as opposed to a mastery of language teaching methodology. After her summer at Dartmouth, she began her career as a Spanish teacher. She employed the methodology that she had experienced there, an emphasis on grammar and vocabulary ("formulas"), on pattern practice, repetition, drill, and on accuracy and avoiding errors.

Well, I suppose I really didn't know what to do when I first started out, but I had been through that Rassias course, and I guess that was the model for me, the approach. (Interview)

One important reason that she used this approach as a model was that it had worked for her: She had learned Spanish. In turn, she assumed that it would work for her students.

And so I used various things that – I guess exercises, one would call them – that had been used with me when I was in that Rassias program for the summer, and that had to do with drills with verbs – I found that very helpful. I mean, I did myself. It just really did sink in. To try to bring some humor into repetition, and uh . . . I did not use the dialogs. (Interview)

I tried to bring in lots of different real objects, things from . . . that would be pertaining to the things we were doing. And, anyway, then I thought that I was doing really well, and the students were doing OK. I mean, as far as what my goals were, the students were doing OK. (Interview)

However, her students reacted to these teaching practices in a way that she hadn't expected.

One of my brighter students told me, "You know, we can do all these things, but we don't know what they mean." That's when I got the idea that meaning was important. (Interview)

Students were able to go through the drills and practice exercises, but they did not know what they were saying. This seed of student resistance and discontent took root and grew in importance over the next four years, eventually culminating in a teaching impasse, as we shall see later. For the time being, however, Katherine continued her efforts at learning Spanish and broadened her exposure to other models of Spanish teaching. The next summer, she went to Middlebury and had her immersion experience. There the teaching was different, since she was now at the "intermediate level" and was placed in a higher class.

When I went to Middlebury – the same. I mean, it was essentially that. It's very conventional, very orthodox. Very dull. In Middlebury, they didn't use pattern drills at all. . . . I think they do it in the very elementary stages, but . . . it was more . . . the study of literature. And the teacher lectures in Spanish. Conversation, in which we all sort of hem and haw, and try our best, and we have a topic, and then we talk about it. (Interview)

The following summer, Katherine went to Salamanca and found the program there to be similar: traditional.

The approach to teaching there in the program was very academic. . . . Well, it was through the University of Salamanca. My teacher was just very, very traditional. (Interview)

Following this, her third summer program, Katherine did not have any further student experiences in a classroom with other Spanish students until she entered the MAT program three years later. Instead, in subsequent summers in Guatemala and in Costa Rica, she was assigned a tutor and worked in a one-on-one situation. In Guatemala she learned a lot of Spanish, but not much about teaching.

The language program there was staffed by amateurs, not trained teachers. It's based on one-on-one instruction. They liked me. I worked with adults. They were intelligent, professionals. I learned many things. (Interview)

In Costa Rica it was slightly different, but in terms of developing her teaching of Spanish, the result was the same.

Because I was on such a *lofty* level [said in a slightly self-mocking manner], they put me into a one-on-one program. They put me with someone who didn't know much about teaching language. We would talk, but after a while you get lazy. This person would never prepare anything. As a teacher, I have an eye for a person who has prepared or not. Still, he was personable and bright. (Interview)

Meanwhile, as a teacher in her own Spanish classes, Katherine was doggedly implementing the teaching practices that she had adopted from her student experiences in the Rassias program at Dartmouth College the summer before her first year of teaching. She had not experienced any classroom teaching since then that seemed worth emulating. At the same time, the students' reactions had not changed. They "resisted" the emphasis on learning patterns, and the lack of attention to "meaning." Katherine was sensitive to these reactions to students, and she made attempts to modify her teaching.

And so, that . . . they were obviously missing a certain . . . the concept that the verb changes, and what happens when the verb changes, and so forth, because I was approaching it, really, just completely mechanically. So then, I had to . . . I decided, "Well, I'd better explain." And I explained endlessly. And that was kind of boring. (Interview)

137

These attempts were fruitless, and Katherine summed up her feelings about her teaching this way:

I think I was pretty stagnant, as a matter of fact. (Interview)

At this point, Katherine had reached an impasse. She had recognized students' resistance and their desires, and she had also set about learning more "everyday" language in her own study of Spanish. However, she did not feel able to teach this kind of language with any success. Her development as a teacher up until this point was stymied, in a way, which led her to describe her situation then as "stagnant." She described what this meant:

With English, I can always see all kinds of possibilities, somehow. With Spanish, it was basically . . . I didn't. Different ways of going about things. Different ways of relating teacher to student, student to student, and that sort of thing. And so, I had evolved basically a rather mechanical approach, I think, to organizing class periods. I just didn't really see a way out of it. I understood that there had to be some techniques for bringing in speaking, and that sort of thing, but I really didn't know how to do it. And when I tried doing things, I just felt they weren't very successful. Whatever it was didn't work out, and I didn't know how to go about making it work out. (Interview)

She decided to enter graduate school, motivated by more than just a desire to find "techniques for bringing in speaking." There was also a strong feeling about herself and her work:

I really felt that if I'm going to continue, I have to have, in my own mind, more legitimacy. (Interview)

This sense of "legitimacy" mirrors fundamental values that Katherine holds dear, about being a "good teacher" in her "own mind," in her own estimation.

It's like saying that I'm a good teacher, that I'm an effective teacher. And if I'm not one, in my own mind, then I don't have legitimacy. (Interview)

In the high school where she taught, Katherine, felt no pressure to excel in teaching, not from the school administration, nor from her colleagues. For her, holding to this value of good teaching, the "flame," as she called it, was a matter of personal "conscience."

You have to keep the flame alive. There's no one [in the school] who holds you accountable for being a good teacher, except yourself. It's your own conscience. You have to have a very strong conscience. (Interview)

Katherine was now approaching her sixth summer of work on her teaching, about to enter the MAT program, motivated by a strong desire to attain "legitimacy" as a Spanish teacher. She knew that she needed to bring more "everyday language" into her classes so as to overcome students' resistance and her "mechanical" teaching.

Her experience in the language teacher education program is the next of her stories.

Learning to teach Spanish

Until this point in her development as a Spanish teacher, Katherine had been teaching herself to teach, in a manner of speaking. She had drawn upon her own experiences as a classroom learner of Spanish, upon Spanish teachers she had observed (primarily in the Rassias program at Dartmouth College), and on her own resources. However, she had reached her limits of self-resourcefulness. She was stymied and feeling "stagnant." By entering the MAT program in teaching foreign languages, Katherine triggered a series of catalytic experiences that resulted in a transformation of her teaching. The first was the summer program, followed by a period of reflection, and culminating in her return to the classroom and the changes she made.

The MAT program consists of two consecutive summers, separated by an interim-year practicum, an internship. The first summer session is eight weeks long, and comprises an intense schedule of coursework, interaction and collaboration with peers, and structured reflection on one's learning and teaching. For Katherine, three dimensions of this summer experience stood out as particularly pivotal: her experience as a student of Spanish in Angela's Spanish class, her overall experience of being a student, and demonstrations and discussions of language teaching methodologies.

The intensity of the summer program was followed by a period of reflection, in which Katherine "internalized" through reflection what she had learned, and articulated learning goals for herself and her students. Then, returning to her Spanish classes, she implemented changes in her teaching. She tried out techniques, materials, and ways of interacting with students that she had seen during the summer. She saw positive results. Students responded differently than they had before. Her efforts had paid off.

The summer coursework and Katherine's learning experiences presented her with insights into the dilemma she had been facing in her Spanish classes. One very powerful source of insights – and teaching strategies – was her Spanish teacher, Angela.

But also, really, to have a really extraordinary model in my own Spanish teacher, who used so many things, and she saw that as a mission on her part, to bring to us different ways to go about doing things. (Interview)

139

Not only did Angela show Katherine different ways to teach Spanish, her manner and attitude affected Katherine as well.

She kept saying, "Oh, don't think I'm so wonderful. You know, I've just read about these things." She didn't want us to think that she was the originator. And then she told me about different books, with activities, which I bought at the end of the summer. (Interview)

Remember that Katherine had an "eye" for effective teachers, whether they were "prepared or not" or knew what they were doing. Angela fit the bill, showing Katherine techniques and giving her resources. In addition, Katherine was looking for a teacher who could give her ideas about how to "get students to use Spanish in class." She got all sorts of teaching ideas from Angela, as well as from the methodology course. These techniques involved using commands to get students up and about and manipulating objects, tapping into students' imaginations to get them to create stories and characters, adopting a playful manner in class, giving students opportunities to induce grammar rules, and to identify things they wanted to say in Spanish. However, Katherine came to understand that teaching techniques were not all that she needed to get her students to speak Spanish.

Angela, through her strategies of error correction and her attitudes toward errors, showed Katherine how students' attitudes and feelings – in this case, Katherine's feelings – could affect students' speaking Spanish. Angela, in effect, modeled a teacher attitude and error-correction strategies that had a significant impact on Katherine.

And I would say [Angela was a model] then, just for basic enthusiasm, I mean, and also how very kindly she corrected people. . . . I think it was very important, because, after all, we were all adults. And adults are much more sensitive to being corrected than children are, for one thing. And then, she was very, very tactful with us. (Interview)

In addition to showing Katherine a viable model of Spanish teaching, this experience of correction seemed to unlock in her an experiential awareness of the role of students' feelings in learning. This awareness was corroborated in other courses, particularly in the language teaching methodology course. Katherine drew connections from the more "student-centered" approaches and from thinkers and researchers in the foreign language teaching field, and she linked this to the anxiety and trepidation she felt in speaking Spanish. At the end of the summer, in her final paper for this course, she presented a coherent and in-depth discussion of her philosophy of teaching, devoted almost exclusively to setting the proper environment for learning.

The learner's basic need . . . is security. The teacher is central in reducing the learner's struggle with the loneliness and threats to self-esteem that are so often a part of the classroom environment. In addition, learning in itself may be perceived as potentially dangerous. The self, secure in what it is, may be suspicious and resistant to that from outside that involves change. The teacher's responsibility is first to address the issue of security and to create an environment that is safe. (Final paper)

By this time, at the end of the summer, Katherine had consolidated her views on the role of affect in learning languages, and she had already seen her high school students bathed in an affective light, as learners with feelings. Her experiences as a student in the various courses of the summer allowed her to empathize anew with her students.

The other thing – and this [the summer MAT program] – is my own awareness of how hard it is for me to feel exposed, and to feel dumb, or unable to do things very quickly, and somehow I think that was very important – in terms of sensitizing me to the importance of students' fears and anxieties. (Interview)

This new awareness of students' experiences was not limited just to emotions, however. Katherine also became conscious of what it was like simply to be in one place all the time during class. She transferred this awareness to her students, too.

And so, I think part of that realization was this summer, how I hated sitting all day long. I hated it. I still hate . . . I hate sitting. And I thought, just the physical . . . this physical problem that I'm having, and just think of someone who's fourteen! (Interview)

Her summer experiences accumulated, but it was not until courses ended and she had time to think things over that she began to put them together.

I just needed time away from the school to really internalize a lot of it, because at the time, I didn't really see how I was going to use anything . . . much. (Interview)

During this time of reflection, she drafted her statement of learning goals for the interim-year practicum, the upcoming school year. Not surprisingly, most of her goals dealt with promoting a positive learning experience for her students.

I began the semester with both eagerness and a degree of trepidation, determined to put to use what I believed I had gained from my summer experiences. . . . I hoped to shape classroom experiences in such a way that would break down the resistance I had encountered in the past from students in regard to learning another language and that would also encourage and sustain enthusiasm for learning Spanish. I also felt that a learning environment that seriously took into account the issue of security would, in addition, address itself to the goal of student retention of material, freeing the intelligence to open itself to new material and to receive this material and willingly incorporate it. (Report)

Once she got under way in her Spanish classes, she implemented the changes she had envisioned. Student "security" was high on the list, and she went about creating a safe learning environment for her students and putting into practice teaching ideas she had seen and experienced in her summer classes. By December, halfway through the school year, she had made great strides toward her goals.

I believe that I have been successful in addressing the issue of student security. The level of enthusiasm in all three classes is high. Students have told other teachers and their parents how much they like learning Spanish. (Report)

She saw results, which was of critical importance. Now, students were positive, taking initiative, relaxed, and more communicative with the language. Katherine was well on her way toward continued transformation of her teaching. Whereas prior to her summer experience she would have referred to herself as an English teacher but not as a Spanish teacher, now she is able to call herself both an English and a Spanish teacher.

I've always been very proud of what I've done in English, but in Spanish, I always felt as though I was getting by. . . . I was trying. In my own mind, I was "competent" and "all right," but I didn't see that I was doing anything that good. I guess that's the difference. Not that I'm saying that I'm doing anything that's extraordinary now, but in my own mind, I'm doing something that is special, and so I see it as having validity – my own work as having the same validity. (Interview)

Katherine has achieved "legitimacy" as a Spanish teacher, as she says – "in my own mind." She feels that she has achieved a measure of self-respect as a Spanish teacher that she did not previously have.

Other stories

In this section, I recount other stories that derive from the previous ones. In the first instance, I combine them into a single story of Katherine's change. In the second, I look beneath the surface of this transformation for stories that may explain it.

First, then, Katherine's story of transformation appears quite straightforward. She sought legitimacy in her teaching. Fueled by a feeling of stagnation and inability to cope, she entered graduate school. There she found in Angela a new model of Spanish teaching, new ideas about teaching foreign languages, and she discovered the importance of feelings in learning languages. She reflected on what she had learned during the summer, set goals for her teaching, and when she returned to her classroom in the fall, she made changes. The students responded positively. Katherine felt good about the changes, and that she could now call herself a Spanish teacher. A simple story.

Figure 2 portrays these elements and events of transformation in Katherine's teaching. Viewed in a chronological fashion, Katherine passed from a feeling of not being a legitimate teacher of Spanish to being a more legitimate one. As Figure 2 indicates, the dominant elements in Katherine's changes dealt with teaching practices, models of teaching, and sensitivity to students' learning experiences and environment. These, in any event, were the primary areas in which Katherine effected changes. Her primary interest was in "getting her students to speak Spanish" and "to break down resistance." This amounted to changing her teaching practices through emulation of the model teacher (Angela), increased sensitivity to her own affective language learning experiences, and exposure to teaching approaches, philosophies, and techniques that reinforced these aims.

In contrast, her view of the subject matter – the Spanish language and Hispanic culture – did not alter significantly as a result of her summer experience. However, as explained in the next story, it played a powerful, "subliminal" role in her teaching. The influence of her teaching context was also negligible. Long ago, it seems, Katherine had resigned herself to the solitary venture of maintaining her good teaching at this high school.

This said, however, there is a second, deeper story. This deeper story of Katherine's changes in her teaching revolves around the dynamic relationship of four elements: core values, students and learning, a feeling for subject matter, and a quest for models of teaching. As we shall see, these four elements are in flux and evolving. They are not static, but dynamic.

Core values

Katherine possesses a strong set of values about education and about herself as an educator. She has stood by these values in the face of an indifferent school administration for the past thirteen years.

Her standards of "legitimacy" as a Spanish teacher derive from her sense of self-respect and standards of excellence that she has set for herself. In her words, to be "all right" as a Spanish teacher did not sit well with her, especially when she juxtaposed this against her English teaching, where she is "proud" of what she has done, where she is able to "see the possibilities." Her "conscience" drove her to "keep the flame alive."

143

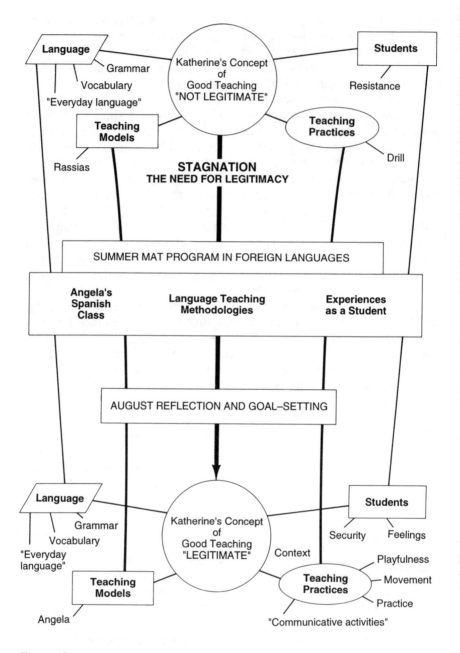

Figure 2

These "possibilities" are linked to her educational "mission," as she describes it. Katherine has an overriding purpose as an educator. Her interest in "legitimacy" goes beyond developing expertise in teaching techniques.

Because I think that everything is ultimately moral. And all teaching is ultimately moral. So, however it is, that's the basis of things. That permeates everything. It's just not manipulating techniques, whatever the techniques happen to be. (Interview)

Her "stagnation" was, then, more than a simple feeling of inability to "get her students to speak Spanish" and to overcome their "resistance" to Spanish and her teaching. More likely it constituted a profound inner dissonance between her core educational values and what was happening in her classes. She was not able to achieve her mission in her Spanish classes.

I just had a feeling without having any ways of doing something with the feeling. And feeling frustrated because I didn't. And what I was doing was that I wasn't accomplishing anything much along the lines of what I deeply wanted to do. (Interview)

Students and learning

What Katherine "deeply wanted to do" was to help students "make connections" with other people in the world: peaceful, empathetic, and tolerant connections. This lies close to the heart of her educational mission, what she wants to help students achieve.

I somehow see being a language teacher the same way I see being an English teacher. And I feel that what's central – one of the central things about teaching, about being a teacher – is to help people make connections. To feel connected and rooted. And in this sense, it's a different material from English, but in this sense, the language is not simply a set of techniques to use, to say this and that. But it's really a way of people having a sense of the humanity of other people who use that language. And when you have a sense of the humanity of other people, it's very hard to hurt them. You're less likely to, even if you're angry with them. (Interview)

This desire for evoking a "connected and rooted . . . sense of the humanity of other people" is indeed an educational mission that goes beyond the subject matter, whether it be English or Spanish. It goes beyond simply saying things in another language or manipulating techniques. It touches the core of Katherine's vision of herself as a teacher. As she says, "all teaching is ultimately moral." Her morals here relate to shared humanity, tolerance, and peace.

At the same time, Katherine must grapple with the reality of the stu-

145

dents in her teaching situation. She has other "moral" standards of behavior and attitudes, such as "taking responsibility," "being accountable," and "keeping your word." Yet she has realized that she must accept students as they are, and she has "bent" toward acceptance of behavior that she does not support or tolerate in herself.

Through her awareness of the role of students' feelings in their learning, and through her successful attempts at breaking down their resistance by emphasizing student security and initiative, Katherine has seen new behaviors and attitudes in these students. "Resistance" has given way to "enthusiasm." "Endlessly explaining" has yielded to inductive learning, sparking students' interest and involvement. "It's better than being told," they say. Being "professorlike" has been overshadowed with eliciting "feedback" from students, which has contributed to "a sense that the students and I are mutually engaged in a challenging adventure."

In short, Katherine appears to have tapped into a primal force, the power of learning, and this is affecting her educational mission as well. It seems more related to the process rather than the outcomes of her mission. In order to make the "connections to a sense of humanity," it makes a difference how students are invited to do so.

A feeling for subject matter

Katherine believes that the subject matter, Spanish and Hispanic culture, is a strong motivating force in her change as a teacher. In fact, culture is a key to her mission to "help students make connections." Her own experiences with the language and the culture seem to have given her an experience in this sort of connection with other Spanish-speaking people.

In some ways, it is centrally motivating, but on a more subliminal level. In the sense that because I have been a person that's been to some other countries, I have developed a feeling for friendship for certain people in other countries, and also anger toward people in other countries, as well. I have liked things in other cultures, and not liked things, too. (Interview)

The force of culture in her teaching, however, is "subliminal" and "implicit." It seems to be a "feeling" or a sense that she has about speaking Spanish and learning Hispanic culture. She talks about her desire to get her students to take on a new, Spanish-speaking "identity" as a means to a shared sense of humanity.

If I do feel that way [about the language and culture], that somehow I have to get people – I mean it sounds so God-like, and I don't mean it to sound this way, but it's hard for me to put this into words – but to get people to use the language in a real way for them, in a sense of taking on another personality. They're becoming a Spanish-speaking person, in a way. And as a Spanish-speaking person, this identity of a Spanish-speaking person is a possibility for themselves, so therefore there's a kind of identity that's established with people who really are Spanish-speaking people. Because they're not "those" people any more. In a sense, it's me. Or it's . . . we are these people. (Interview)

Katherine has a desire for students to develop a "we" feeling instead of a "those people" feeling. She appears to have equated this transformation in students with their using "the language in a real way for them." Or with speaking Spanish. It appears that her intention to "get students to speak Spanish" also carries the hope that students will make an identity shift. She realizes that this is "subtle" and that it is a "feeling," yet it is very important.

By the same token, Katherine's own development of a "Spanish-speaking identity" is another factor in her perception of this feeling. When asked if she feels different speaking Spanish, she speaks of "coloration of personality." Nonetheless, she is not "a different person."

It's like another color of a personality. And it's fun. Well, it's not that I'm a different person. I'm not. But it's as though I have another coloration, or . . . like wearing, not like really "clothes" but something that's . . . trying on something different. And also, there are ways of . . . I mean a language is a whole point of view, so there are different expressive possibilities in Spanish that even me, with my limitations, that . . . for me with my limitations, that don't exist in English. (Interview)

Although her own summer sojourns in Spanish-speaking countries allowed her the opportunity to learn a lot about the people, their customs, and their history, they also affected her concept of "identity."

Well . . . the sense of common humanity is one that I think anybody who goes anywhere . . . if you're basically open, that's one thing that you do see. And then the differences, which can be very hard to take. Some, which you say, "Gee, I wish my culture were more like that." And then . . . an awful lot which are hard to take. And . . . just, I don't know, one really learns to accept them. I guess you have to if you're going to be there long enough. I never was long enough that I really had to do that. So things like different attitudes towards time . . . I never was there long enough that I had to really adjust, in the way you do if you live someplace for a long time. I could say, "Well, I'm here for just a little while," and be an observer, you see, so I really didn't have to really come to terms with the differences. (Interview)

The distance of the "observer" role, and not having to "really come to terms with the differences" suggests that adopting a Spanish-speaking identity is perhaps more of an intellectual undertaking in Katherine's mind. One can achieve "tolerance" and acceptance of others, but the fact that Katherine was not really staying there allowed her a different kind of adjustment, so that she "didn't have to really come to terms with the differences." Again, this suggests a kind of dissonance, in this instance between Katherine's value of "identity" and the reality of her own experience in learning Spanish.

Katherine also seems divided on this matter in terms of her teaching. In describing how she goes about teaching culture, the following exchange with me brought out another view. Katherine gave an example of how she deals with cultural issues in her Spanish classes:

And then, I remember one time, one girl said, "Well, that's the way they do it, and we do things differently. That's all." And that's basically the way things are.
Is that basically where you want people to be?
I think that's the only way you can. I mean, you can't change yourself. I mean, you might want to, but most likely you're not going to. But it's a kind of . . . I think a certain kind of tolerance, and understanding, and lack of feeling self-righteous and superior.
Sort of a "live and let live"?
That sort of thing. You know, "That's sort of interesting. Well, how do they do that?"
You said you don't think they can change themselves. What did you mean by that?
Well, it's not . . . I mean, you'd have to be part of a culture, and really become . . . you know, be married to somebody, or live in some place, and make these little modifications in their personalities. But they're in a language class . . . as ours is, you know. . . .

This seems to be in opposition to Katherine's view that students need to change identities. Here, she says point blank: "You can't change yourself. You might want to, but you're certainly not going to." This suggests another sort of dissonance simmering within Katherine. On the one hand, she has a "deep feeling" about the importance of taking on a Spanish-speaking "identity," yet on the other hand, she believes that "you can't change yourself" in this way. This element, a feeling for the subject matter, also seems to be in flux, unresolved.

Models of teaching

As we have seen, Katherine actively seeks out models of teaching as a means of changing her own teaching. She relies on seeing or experiencing teaching in action, whether this is done consciously or otherwise.

The things that I do well – in any of the things in my teaching – are mainly because I've seen them done. And I say, "Oh yeah. Let me try that." Whether I said it consciously or not. (Interview)

Her quest for models of teaching has led her from Rassias to Angela. From each of her models, she has emulated or incorporated aspects of their manner or their methodology to fit her core values, her students, and her sense of the subject matter. Model making is a primary means that Katherine employs to reach her own teaching goals.

At this point in her development, however, Katherine has not yet discovered a model of teaching that will show her how to help students adopt Spanish-speaking identities. She is left with this "deep feeling" but not any "ways of doing something with the feeling."

I think in a somehow very subtle way, that this feeling I have, I think it's always been there. It probably became more blossomed perhaps because of the summer experience, and also seeing that there were possibilities for doing things to help people to get a feeling for being Spanish-speaking people. I didn't really have a kind of a means, or techniques, or approaches, let's say. I just had a feeling without having any ways of doing something with the feeling. (Interview)

Of the teaching models who were non-native speakers of Spanish, like herself, none has apparently provided her with the model of how to help her students achieve the kind of "identity" that she feels is so important.

Let us turn now to a story of Katherine's tacit orchestration of these diverse and dynamic elements in her teaching. Figures 3 and 4 illustrate their interplay in Katherine's movement toward change.

Figure 3 portrays my explanation of the dynamic interaction of elements that Katherine Russell (KR) uses in furthering her teaching practice, namely, her *mission*, her *context*, and her *teaching practice*. Katherine experienced a tension or dissonance between her mission and the context of her teaching situation: school, students, colleagues, and community. To resolve this tension, Katherine made use of models of teaching that she had observed or experienced.

When she adapted these models to her teaching practice, Katherine seemed to evaluate them in terms of how they reflected her educational mission, as well as how they applied to her perception of her teaching situation. In other words, she looked for compatability with her educational mission and values, and she also looked for signs of validity in her teaching situation. For example, when her students resisted the drills in her teaching practice and lost interest in Spanish, this created tension with both her educational mission and her teaching practices. She sought a model to accommodate this tension. Not finding one on her own, she eventually resolved this through her work in graduate school.

Figure 4 represents another story of the dynamic relationship among another three key elements that Katherine uses to guide her change: her

Patrick R. Moran

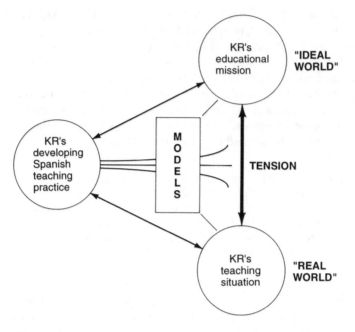

Figure 3

conception of and relationship to Spanish; her fundamental values and outlook on life; and her views of students and learning. The relationship among these elements is dynamic because each affects the other and depends on the others in some way. For instance, Katherine's value of "legitimacy" as a Spanish teacher pushed her to develop mastery in the subject matter, Spanish. In turn, this led to a deepening awareness of the "human connections" that are possible in learning another language and to communicate with Spanish speakers. This led to attempts to encourage this awareness in her students. Another instance involved her increased understanding of the affective dimension of learning, which has led her to greater acceptance and tolerance of differing learning styles – a fundamental value – and, in turn, to shifting her views of Spanish by accepting students' communicative interests in the language and in the culture.

In these "deeper" stories, I have suggested explanations of how Katherine has changed her teaching through her tacit orchestration of these four elements. I have also suggested that Katherine has experienced, or possibly employed, dissonance within and among these elements as an integral part of the process of change in her Spanish teaching.

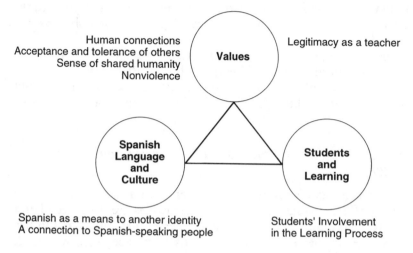

Figure 4

Questions

At the beginning of this study, Katherine made a point of saying that she considered her own development as a Spanish teacher to be out of the ordinary, not following the traditional path that foreign language teachers take. For her, this traditional path meant an undergraduate major in the foreign language, an experience abroad, teacher preparation in the foreign language, followed by entry into a school as a young teacher. As she put it succinctly, "I'm not typical."

Perhaps Katherine is right. Her entry into foreign language teaching may well be out of the ordinary, atypical. On the other hand, Katherine's process of developing a Spanish teaching practice may not be that different from that of other foreign language teachers. At the very least, her experience of change and growth may resonate with or replicate other teachers' experiences.

In this section, I will indulge in some speculation about those aspects of Katherine's stories that may be true for other non-native foreign language teachers like her. I will pose these speculations as questions.

What role do models of teaching play in teachers' development of teaching practice?

Certainly, Katherine made use of models of teaching in her own development as a teacher. Yet models do not necessarily meet all a teacher's needs and desires, as Katherine certainly seems to have glimpsed. Katherine has a desire, a mission in her teaching, for which she has not discovered a model.

Are models temporary learning strategies for teachers? To create the new, a teacher needs to recombine the old in a different way. Is Katherine on the threshold of casting aside a dependence on models and creating her own teaching paradigm for her mission, values, and students?

What role do values and morals play in teacher development and change?

This study suggests that Katherine's values were a predominant force behind her efforts to change and grow. Her values are deep-seated and "permeate everything." Yet, as Katherine herself has discovered in her attempts to enact her own values (responsibility, keeping your word, striving for achievement), this is not an easy undertaking. Are there certain kinds of core values that are necessary for growth and development as a language teacher?

Does dissonance between what a language teacher wishes and what she or he sees provoke growth and change?

In Katherine's story, the tension that existed between "legitimacy" in her own mind and the lack of legitimacy in her Spanish teaching appeared to be a clear line of development. For example, she wanted to "get her students to speak Spanish" and set out to achieve this, with success. Now, she wants to get her students to adopt a Spanish-speaking identity but does not know how to go about it. This dissonance seems to lie at the nexus of change.

What role does a non-native foreign language teacher's "identity" in that language play in the development of his or her teaching?

Katherine seems caught between a desire to achieve this "identity" in her students and the limits of her own experience with it in her own learning of Spanish and Hispanic culture. Can one teach what one has not experienced?

What influence does the expectation of change and one's accountability for it have in a teacher's development?

Katherine initiated these seemingly sweeping changes in her teaching during a supervised teaching internship, where it was expected that she would identify areas to change in her teaching. The teacher education coursework clearly had an impact, and the supervision served to reinforce the importance of change and that Katherine account for it. How important is this sort of expectation and accountability to teacher change? Also, along the same lines, what effect does telling one's story of development as a teacher, as a public accounting of oneself, have on one's development as a teacher?

These questions have emerged from Katherine's stories, and there are certainly others that I have not posed. These are questions, I believe, that can be asked of the development of any teacher. Therefore, although the circumstances of Katherine's becoming a Spanish teacher may be unusual, they may be much more "typical" than she realizes.

In closing, I am tempted to write a final word about Katherine Russell and her process of changing her teaching. However, if there is one thing that I have learned by getting to know Katherine through her stories it is that change defies finality. Although we may describe stories with beginnings and ends, I am not sure that it is useful to describe teachers in the same way.

References

Butt, R. L., and D. Raymond. 1987. Arguments for using qualitative approaches in understanding teacher thinking: The case for biography. *Journal of Curriculum Theorizing* 7(1): 62–93.

Carter, K. 1993. The place of story in the study of teaching and teacher education. *Educational Researcher* (Jan.–Feb.): 5–12.

Clandinin, D. J, 1992. Narrative and story in teacher education. In T. Russell and H. Munby (eds.), *Teachers and Teaching: From Classroom to Reflection*. Philadelphia: Falmer.

Clandinin, D. J., and F. M. Connelly. 1988. *Teachers as Curriculum Planners*. New York: Teachers College Press.

Clandinin, D. J., and F. M. Connelly. 1991. Narrative and story in practice and research. In D. A. Schön (ed.), *The Reflective Turn: Case Studies in Educational Practice*. New York: Teachers College Press, pp. 258–281.

Connelly, F. M., and D. J. Clandinin. 1990. Stories of experience and narrative inquiry. *Educational Researcher* 19(5): 2–14.

Glaser, E. M., and A. L. Strauss. 1967. *Discovery of Grounded Theory: Strategies for Qualitative Research*. Chicago: Aldine.

Goodson, I. F., and R. Walker (eds.). 1990. *Biography, Identity, and Schooling: Episodes in Educational Research*. Philadelphia: Falmer.

Knowles, J. G. 1991. Life history accounts as mirrors: A practical avenue for the conceptualization of reflection in teacher education. University of Bath, U.K., Conference on Conceptualizing Reflection in Teacher Development, March.

Woods, P. 1987. Life histories and teacher knowledge. In J. Smyth (ed.), *Educating Teachers: Changing the Nature of Pedagogical Knowledge*. New York: Falmer.

7 Starting all over again: From teaching adults to teaching beginners

Anne Burns

This chapter examines the nature and processes of language teaching as they are viewed by a teacher. A key question is how the underlying thinking and beliefs the teacher brings to the classroom shape the processes and interactions that occur. My aim is to explore the notion that what teachers do is affected by what they think (Clark and Yinger 1979) and the kinds of pedagogical beliefs that they hold. In doing so I draw on research conducted in six beginner learner classrooms in the Australian Adult Migrant English Program (AMEP). An underlying assumption in this chapter is that experimental and descriptive accounts of the language classroom are necessary but insufficient, and that they need to be complemented by the perspectives and perceptions of classroom teachers themselves. As Breen (1991: 213) suggests, 'the mere description of effective teaching is partial. We need to explain good teaching – to uncover the reasons that motivate and sustain it.'

Through the illustration of a collaborative case study, I attempt to draw out two propositions. The first is that the thinking and beliefs teachers hold are fundamental in motivating classroom interactions. They determine what is represented for learning and how the representation of content takes place. The second is that the critical, and therefore the most meaningful, changes and advances in professional growth involve close and deep engagement with the actual processes of the teacher's own classroom. The focus on the teacher is not intended to imply that the perspectives of learners are not also important (see, e.g., Allwright 1990; Slimani 1992), but rather that the teacher is a crucial and important starting point for considering alternative routes and pedagogical insights for teacher education.

The study

Six experienced teachers, working with beginning adult language learners who were newly-arrived immigrants to Australia, agreed to being contacted by the researcher to participate in the study. They were all recognised by the program administrators within their teaching centres as skilled, experienced and committed language teachers. The duration of their individual experience within the AMEP varied from three

154

months to eighteen years. At various stages during their teaching careers, most of them had undertaken specialist TESOL training, and they had all participated in in-service courses offered through their teaching centres and the centralised curriculum support unit of the organisation in which they worked.

The research focus

A particular area of interest in this study lay in attempting to identify the extent to which internalised understandings and beliefs created and explained the approaches teachers took to instruction with beginning second language learners. As the teachers were already experienced and informed members of the profession, a further area of interest concerned the nature of their reflection on practice and whether and how forms of practice could change through close reflection. Two main questions motivated the investigation which was carried out.

1. What was the nature of the thinking and beliefs that these experienced teachers brought to classroom processes, and what impact did these beliefs have on classroom practice?
2. How might changes and developments occur in teachers' beliefs?

It was anticipated that gaining insights into these questions would contribute to understanding the nature of the thinking and beliefs which informed the teachers' planning, decision making and curriculum enactment.

The teachers and their classes

The six classes comprised a broad range of learners, assessed on a seven-point oral-proficiency speaking scale (see Brindley 1979, 1989) as beginner speakers of English, during their pre-course interview. As they were all permanent residents, within one year of their arrival in Australia the learners were enrolled in courses intended to provide initial general instruction in English, as well as information required for successful settlement in the country. Across the six classes, the students could be said to be representative of learners typically enrolled in initial AMEP classes. They were from diverse first language and ethnic backgrounds, including Vietnamese, Turkish, Lebanese, Korean, Chinese and Spanish. Mixed nationality groups existed in each class, in addition to mixed ages, educational backgrounds and gender.

The teachers followed the decentralised, needs-based and learner-centred approach to curriculum development adopted by the organisation in which they worked [for an extensive description of this curriculum approach within the AMEP, see Nunan (1988)]. The teachers received support in the processes of developing their individual courses and teaching programs through National Curriculum Frameworks (Nunan and Burton 1988–1991), in-service sessions and curriculum support teachers in their teaching centres. However, decisions relating to the identification of their learners' needs, the planning and sequencing of course content and materials, and assessment tools, tasks and procedures within the classroom rested with the teachers themselves.

Procedures

The procedures adopted for the study were collaborative, the researcher aiming to explore with each teacher not only what was occurring in his or her classroom, but why it was occurring. An ethnographic and interpretive approach was employed, consistent with 'hermeneutic' investigation (Oschner 1979). In other words, the emphasis in the collection and evaluation of the data was on understanding, interpretation and explanation. The events observed were viewed as 'intended, motivated actions on the part of reasoning actors' (Reynolds 1982: 44). A major consideration was that the research should attempt to investigate a multiplicity of features which would reflect the particular classroom contexts in which the teachers worked. These features included the organisational settings, the content, interactions, participants and methods observed in the classrooms as well as the interpretations of the teachers themselves.

Qualitative research procedures (Bogdan and Biklen 1982; van Lier 1988), were used in both the collection and analysis of the data. Two major complementary sources of data collection were used: (1) classroom observation and (2) ethnographic interviews. The procedures adopted in collecting the data were as follows:

1. A series of audio-recorded classroom observations of lessons conducted by the six teachers was carried out. The observations occurred midway through the learners' ten-week courses, which varied in intensity from twelve hours to twenty hours a week. The duration of each lesson was approximately one and a half to two hours, and the observations encompassed complete lesson units which were part of regularly scheduled classes, as recommended by van Lier (1988).
2. Each lesson was transcribed by the researcher for use during subsequent discussions with the teachers.
3. A preliminary analysis of the lesson structure was carried out to identify emerging patterns of interaction and the sequences of tasks and activities presented.
4. Ethnographic interviews using a semistructured approach and stim-

ulus recall procedures were then conducted. They were designed to elicit reflections and descriptions of the thinking informing classroom instruction and interactions. Before the interviews, the researcher and teacher reviewed the preliminary analyses of the lesson structure and the materials used in order to gain agreement on the analyses. The purpose of the interview and the stimulus recall procedure were also discussed, and any areas for clarification in relation to these procedures were reviewed.

5. The teachers were then asked to review the transcriptions, to listen to the recordings and to verbalise their reflections on what was occurring in their classrooms. Each interview was recorded with the teacher's permission, and the verbal protocols were matched against the portions of transcribed classroom interaction to which they related.

Data analysis

The methodologies selected for data analysis placed emphasis on indepth description, analysis and interpretation. As well as analysing particular aspects and features of classroom instruction, they sought to take into account a 'macro' view of the classroom as a social context. This was an important consideration in identifying what influence the settings for the interaction had on the relationships between thinking and action (van Lier 1988). Through a content analysis procedure (Bogdan and Biklen 1982), which identified emerging patterns and themes, the interview data were coded and sorted into descriptive categories. The data from two of the teacher-stimulated recall interviews were analysed by a rater trained in the use of ethnographic data analysis, and an interrater reliablity of 87 per cent was obtained. All other data were coded by the researcher.

The research yielded a substantial amount of information on the nature of classroom interaction and the intricacies of its relationship to teachers' beliefs. Something that was immediately obvious was that the scope and nature of the beliefs expressed by the teacher were immensely complex and emerged from interrelated contexts, networks and levels of thinking. These complex cognitive interrelationships were reflected in and influenced instructional practice in a number of interconnected ways.

Different contextual levels of thinking about the classroom

As the data were analysed, it emerged that the teachers' thinking cohered around interconnecting and interacting 'contextual' levels, as il-

157

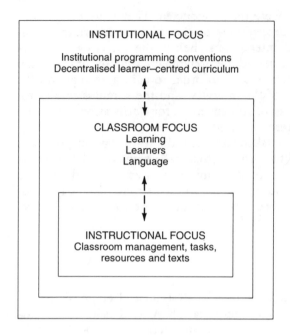

Figure 1.   The intercontextuality of teacher thinking and beliefs.

lustrated in Figure 1. At the broadest level was an institutional focus, which involved the 'normalised' or conventionalised ways in which particular organisational ideologies or philosophies were interpreted by the teachers. This contextual level formed the 'institutional culture' which created the cognitive frameworks for thinking about their specific teaching programs and classes.

The second contextual level involved the personal philosophies, thinking, attitudes, beliefs and expectations that the teacher had developed about language, learning and learners. These beliefs, which the teacher brought to the individual classroom situation, shaped overall planning approaches, the selection of content and the forms of interaction which the teachers believed should characterise their classrooms. At the third and most specific level were the thinking and reflections which went on about specific forms of instruction that occurred, the tasks to be undertaken during the lesson, the decisions made in preparing for and carrying out these tasks, the resources and materials used and the teacher's own role in managing various forms of classroom interaction. Thus there appeared to be networks of 'intercontextuality' in operation. Thinking at one level interacted, became interdependent with and was influenced by beliefs operating at another level. The framework as shown in Figure 1 and discussed below attempts to capture the embeddedness of these different contextual levels.

'Theories for practice': A case study

I will focus on one teacher, Sarah, to illustrate how these interconnecting contextual areas operated in her classroom and at the same time to explore further the two major propositions put forward earlier. Sarah's learners were a small group of mixed-nationality learners who were attending their first English course in Australia, for sixteen hours a week. Because of the learners' fairly limited levels of formal learning in their first language and their lack of experience of previous language learning, six of those hours were spent with Sarah so that they could receive more individual attention than in the larger general class. Sarah briefly described her learners and the timetabling arrangements for the class as follows:

Hung and Tan are Vietnamese. Lian is from mainland China . . . Chinese, yeah. Ding is Vietnamese too and Susanna is from Sao Tome. There are a couple of South American women in the group as well. This is two hours everyday . . . no, not every day. Two hours Tuesday, Wednesday and Thursday from one o'clock till three.

Sarah felt that to a certain extent she was 'starting all over again', as she was much more familiar and experienced with groups of more advanced learners and had not taught 'slower-paced' beginners before. Although she was a highly experienced teacher, she admitted to feelings of uncertainty about the best way to proceed. The model proposed here suggests that there are different contextual factors motivating the cognitive processes which intersect with classroom instruction. It provides a framework for discussing the impact of Sarah's thinking and the nature of her explicit and implicit beliefs on her classroom interactions and activities, and the changes which emerged as she reflected critically on particular dimensions of these interactions.

The institutional context

Institutional beliefs and philosophies were expressed in terms of issues such as the widely-accepted approaches towards curriculum development, the commonly adopted programming conventions or the thinking behind class composition within the particular teaching centre where Sarah worked. She described, for example, how the placement of the learners in this particular class had happened in accordance with the

159

broad procedures and approaches to learner placements, programming and timetabling in the teaching centre:

I suppose the first thing I should say is that this is a withdrawal group from a larger core class. After the first week we sat down and talked about those people. What we do when we go through the interviewing process, we interview all the students . . . and we actually had discussed all of these students . . . and had decided on having a module for those types of students on the interview day. And then the first week of class, we withdrew that group.

The organisational orientation towards decentralised and needs-based curriculum development also framed the broad perceptions which underlay Sarah's individual thinking about her own classroom:

We just had a general idea of what we think is the best way of using the teaching staff to cater for learners' needs.

The withdrawal was . . . I think it was basically just the people we thought were . . . um, going to be the slow learners.

Perceptions of the institutional considerations and norms surrounding the specific classroom situations with which they were associated were evident in one way or another for all the teachers in the study. They framed the subsequent levels and networks of thinking and beliefs which converged at and so mediated the more individualised classroom situation.

THE INFLUENCE OF THE INSTITUTIONAL CONTEXT ON
CLASSROOM PRACTICE

Sarah's awareness of the organisationally-contextualised nature of her class as a 'withdrawal group from a larger core class' had an impact on her thinking about lesson planning and therefore on the nature of decisions she made about lesson content:

Within the larger core class they're getting a lot more, um, what do you say . . . more traditional, structural models and written practice. And they're getting, they were watching audiovisual [material]. So I felt that this was an opportunity, because . . . what often happens in those larger classes is that the low levels tend to become rather passive and quiet . . . that I'd use this to try and draw them out and get them talking.

I wanted as much as possible to use what they were bringing to class from their everyday lives, so that's why I don't often prepare very much . . . in terms of materials.

Classroom interaction in Sarah's class also reflects its genesis in her thinking and beliefs about the institutional arrangements and procedures established for her learners. She is aware of their exposure to other teaching methodologies and so her own classroom processes reveal her desire to offer alternative forms of content which are relevant to her learners' needs and 'everyday lives'. These awarenesses are found in the rather loosely-structured lesson planning, in the content of the classroom tasks and in the nature of classroom discussion. A lesson extract illustrates how her teaching approach is contextualised within her overall awareness of the institutional programming arrangements.[1]

Transcript 1: How was your weekend?

Li: I . . . went to Chinatown.
T: So how was your weekend? Lian? What did you do at the weekend?
Li: I . . . went to Chinatown.
T: Oh, great! What day . . . what day, Lian?
Li: Uh . . .
T: On Saturday or Sunday?
Li: Er . . . Saturday.
T: Ah, fantastic. And who did you go with?
Li: Er . . . husband.
T: With your husband.
Li: Yes.
T: Ah, right . . . right. Any friends?
Li: No . . . er . . . husband . . . go.
T: Just the two of you . . .
Li: Yes
T: Right. Was it good?
   (Lian laughs and nods)

The interaction in Transcript 1 reveals Sarah's consciousness of the broader organisational setting of the learners' experiences. It suggests the contrast she wishes to present with the 'more traditional, structured models and written practice' of their core class. In the smaller group, she seeks opportunities to make her learners less 'passive and quiet' and attempts 'to cater for learners' needs' by aiming 'to use what they were bringing to class from their everyday lives' and 'to draw them out and get them talking'.

The broader social and institutional contexts in which classrooms are located are frequently overlooked in research involving the analysis of classroom data. For Sarah, however, as for the other teachers in this

---

1 In the transcript examples, T represents turns taken by the teacher, while the learners are identified by the first two letters of their names. One-second pauses are represented by '.'; eg., '. . . .' equals four seconds, and overlapping speech is indented. Nonverbal information is provided by parentheses. Single unidentified students are designated S.

study, these were clearly contextual and conceptual starting points that operated interactively with the specifics of their classroom situations. Van Lier (1988: 47) points out that:

[Classroom] interaction consists of actions – verbal and otherwise – which are interdependent, i.e. they influence and are influenced by other actions. Pulling any one action, or a selection of them, out of this interdependence for the purpose of studying them, complicates, rather than facilitates their description, just as a handshake cannot be adequately described, let alone understood, by considering the actions of the two persons separately involved.

The notion of the interdependence of actions may be a profitable one to extend to a parallel notion of the interdependence and interrelatedness of the contexts of teachers' thinking. It may be relevant in enhancing our understandings of the relationships between what teachers think and what teachers do when they teach, in terms of what is 'thinkable' and 'do-able' within institutional constraints.

The classroom context

Sarah's thinking, belief and, as a result, decision making at the classroom level were framed as already suggested by organisational exigencies. Thinking about the specifics of the classroom was in turn influenced by further concepts or concerns, which focused on (1) the nature and characteristics of the learners; (2) beliefs about learning and appropriate learning strategies for beginners; and (3) views on language itself. These three major focus areas appeared to construct the 'conceptual guidelines' which overlay more specific areas of decision making, such as the tasks to be undertaken, the materials to be used and the various forms of interaction planned, which were determined either before the lesson commenced or interactively, as it proceeded.

THE NATURE AND CHARACTERISTICS OF THE LEARNERS

In shaping her understandings of what should be planned and attempted in her classroom, Sarah alluded frequently to the attributes of the learners making up her class. Descriptions of the learners and their characteristics, their existing abilities and skills and their likely progress were important conceptual schema which interacted with more specific decisions about classroom content and the roles which could be taken by teacher and learners. Sarah's thinking about her learners interacted with notions of their capacity to learn and what learning entailed. It was also located within the organisational parameters which had already determined the nature of the learners' profiles and characteristics, before their placement into Sarah's class:

I think it was basically just the people who we thought were going to be the slow learners. It wasn't based on age or nationality at all. It was just within a group, you can usually see who are the people who are going to be, sort of taking off and the others are going to be [struggling].

Other dimensions of her thinking and beliefs about the learners emerged in connection with her own distinctive and individual experiences of working with and planning for this particular group of learners:

Well, in the past there've been problems with literacy, but I'm lucky in this case because all of them can read and write.

Well, yes there are problems with mother-tongue interference and readings and unfamiliarity with words, so that they will try and pronounce something phonetically and they wouldn't understand.

Um, so yes I think if it was a class with literacy problems as well, I wouldn't do these things like, write the sentence on the board.

THE NATURE OF LEARNING IN THE CLASSROOM

Related to her thinking about learner characteristics were beliefs about the nature of learning and about the learning roles and responsibilities learners should adopt. For Sarah, a major principle guiding her desired approach was that the learners should be self-directed and encouraged to interact with each other in the classroom:

I think basically it's the confidence building and communication that's the rationale behind it and I want it to be as student-directed as possible. And hopefully, er . . . to start getting them talking to each other as a sort of ultimate aim of the class.

She referred also to the desirability of the learners' continuing to be self-directed in their learning beyond the classroom, giving examples of how individual learners carried out extra tasks:

Lian often goes home and does an hour each evening and goes through all of the sheets she gets in the general class. And then, you know, read and . . . sometimes write something for me. And Susanna too, she . . . just looks at . . . looks at the words and I'll say, 'Did you remember that word?' But the others, not so. . . .

The particular distinctions and concepts which shaped Sarah's notions of the learners' characteristics, abilities and learning roles appeared also to set up expectations about classroom content and the particular forms of interaction which could be assumed to enhance learning. Closely aligned to her concepts of the roles and responsibilities of the learner were interpretations and perceptions of the nature of language learning and what forms it would or should take, given her

163

understandings of the particular characteristics of the learners in the group. A central philosophy was Sarah's view that learners should be self-directed. In her thinking about her class, this re-emerged as a desire for learner-centred interaction and teaching content:

Because I come immediately out of a class that I teach till one [o'clock], I'm often a bit late into the class. But I find that this is a really good thing. I was worried about it and apologising profusely to them as I race in with my cup of coffee, but I find it's really useful, because they automatically start talking to one another in a small group.

She touches on this theme again when explaining her purposes in the 'What did you do at the weekend?' discussion task:

I think I want . . . I want to teach them something that's directly relevant to their lives. And I didn't want to just kind of pull vocabulary or exercises out of a text that would kind of impose that. So I was trying to increase their vocabulary and their ability to talk about things that they did every day . . . er, just trying to elicit from them things that they did.

I think that's really important . . . just, you have to . . . in order to foster communication, it's got to be relevant to them.

Learner-centred learning is believed to be further enhanced by positive classroom relationships and by ensuring that the learners' affective needs are considered. Her conceptualisations of the nature of beginning learner characteristics and abilities frame her convictions of the importance of increasing their confidence and establishing a positive and nonthreatening classroom environment. For example, continuing her comment on her lateness in class and the interaction among the learners which it produced, she states:

And that did really great things for the group dynamic, right from the beginning and I think they feel quite confident. Because it started off in L1 with the Vietnamese people chatting and then as Susanna came in and Lian didn't understand [and] they had to start using English.

A further comment arises from discussion of one of her classroom tasks, when she extrapolates on the general principles informing her planning for these learners:

In general I want them to come away feeling that they've communicated something in English, that's something they'd wanted to say about themselves and that, er it was something that, er . . . gave them confidence. And to think that they weren't, you know . . . they weren't completely isolated. I think it . . . I think the confidence building thing was the most important aim.

The conceptual orientation to learners and learning that emerges from Sarah's comments is reflected in her instructional approach. Transcript

2 reveals how her evaluations of the learners' learning level, skills and abilities combine with her philosophy of self-directed, relevant and empathetic forms of interaction.

Transcript 2: I did some ironing.

T: Susanna, what about you?
Su: Uh?
T: What did you do at the weekend?
Su: Weekend. . . . . . . stay oos.
T: Sorry, I don't understand. (laughs) Say that again please.
Su: Oos . . . I can't say. Oos.
T: At home. At home, yeah, stayed at home.
Su: Yeah.   Yeah, cook.
T: Really? What?
Su: Biscuit . . .
T: Biscuit. Everybody understand? Biscuit. Biscuit (writes 'biscuit' on board.)
S: Biscuit. Yeah.
T: Cook. Cook biscuits.
S: Ah, yeah. Cook.
T: You like biscuits . . . Tan?
Su: Ah, food . . . food.
T: Food . . . yes. Lunch, dinner, yes. (Susanna makes ironing motion and giggles) What's that? What's this? (T also motions ironing. Some learners discuss in first language. Lian looks up her dictionary.) In English? (Lian laughs and so does T.)
Li: Oh. . . .
T: What is it?
Li: Ironing.
T: Ironing. Right . . . do the ironing. Yeah. (T writes 'iron' on board and draws a picture of an iron. Beneath iron she writes 'ironing' and beneath this 'I did some ironing'.) Yeah. OK. Iron (Learners speak in first language and copy words as teacher writes.)
S: Ironing.
T: Ironing. So you can say, 'On the weekend, I did some ironing. I did some ironing.'

Sarah's underlying concern to enhance her learners' ability to communicate with others on personal and relevant topics is revealed in Transcript 2. She has selected a lesson topic, 'talking about weekend activities', which she believes is appropriate for beginning learners and allows them to speak about themselves, in order to extend their potential to communicate with native speakers. It is a topic highly prevalent in casual social exchanges in Australian culture, which links with Sarah's wish to 'increase their vocabulary and their ability to talk about things that they did every day'. It suggests again her goal of making her learners more confident and self-directed.

THE NATURE OF LANGUAGE IN THE CLASSROOM

Also reflected in the classroom interaction above is Sarah's implicit assessment of her learners' existing language skills and abilities. Her awareness of the learners' relatively limited speaking level, but also of the fact that she was 'lucky in this case because all of them can read and write', emerges in the particular forms of classroom interaction and instructional practice we see in the extract. Although she constantly expresses her aim of encouraging self-direction in her learners, in actual fact, the teacher takes most control of the interaction. She also makes the assumption that she can transcribe the learners' contributions on to the whiteboard and that this will facilitate general comprehension and vocabulary development.

The classroom language produced by both Sarah and her learners is suggestive of the 'intercontextuality' between and within the various levels of belief alluded to earlier. Throughout the discussion, Sarah makes frequent assertions that language use in the classroom should be 'communicative', as the following comment illustrates:

In this class I want it to try and be, as much as possible, fairly natural kinds of conversations. And I often find that with those more structured surveys or questionnaires that students tend to stick methodically to the questions and it doesn't kind of take off into their sort of everyday lives at all. So that . . . I think that was one of the reasons I was trying to stick as much as possible to continuing a flow of conversation.

At the same time, however, she is clearly alert to the limited language proficiency of her beginning learners, to the less well developed learning strategies which had placed them in this class, as well as to the slower pace of learning which seemed to be assumed. Therefore, accommodations began to appear in her thinking about language. They reflected something of the implicit tension she felt, between language 'use' or 'words and sentences as manifestations of the language system' and language 'usage' or 'the way the system is realised for normal communicative purposes' (Widdowson 1979). These tensions emerged in comments such as:

If they're unable to explain, I'd try to give them the language in simple units, but as naturally as possible. I'd try to give them a little chunk that would make sense if they were having a conversation with a native speaker.

It's a kind of gradual process of building up from simple units . . . yeah, isolated units . . . into something a bit more . . . what's the word? Co . . . more in a context.

Transcript 2 suggests the nature of the accommodations 'in action' which were made by Sarah. Despite her expressed desire to provide opportunities for 'natural conversation' and 'communication', the exchanges in this classroom excerpt are more suggestive of traditional patterns of initiation, evaluation and response (Sinclair and Coulthard 1975) than genuine, 'natural' conversation (see also Nunan 1987).

The instructional level

At the third most specific contextual level, the teacher reflected on distinctive areas of instructional planning: the various tasks, materials and forms of classroom management that she implemented. Shavelson and Stern (1981: 477) suggest that when teachers are engaged in making decisions about planning,

. . . they are faced first and foremost with deciding what activities will engage learners during the lesson or, put another way, the teacher must decide how to entertain his or her audience while attending to curriculum. Activities then and not the prescriptive model are the focus of teacher planning.

For all the teachers in the study, the lesson 'task', the setting up and managing of activities and the materials associated with the task, emerged as the major and focal unit of reference for classroom planning. Their thinking about lesson content and processes centred primarily on the tasks and activities considered appropriate, given their evaluations of the proficiency levels and learning strategies of the learners.

INSTRUCTIONAL TASKS, TEXTS AND RESOURCES

Sarah commented frequently on the kinds of activities she included in her lesson planning and how she organised those activities:

They write down their first sentence and try to add to that. So it's like a little diary or something that's like building up a little story each week.

It's often revising . . . um, the form-filling that would happen in the other class or, occasionally people from the other class bring in things like a social security letter. Sometimes there are surveys where they just have to write in, you know . . . one or two words.

Maybe a little cloze or something. I'd start off with all the sentences on the board and then start rubbing out words and asking them to come up to the board and write things in and then gradually you sort of basically got

167

nothing left on the board and you know they're coming up and they're writing out the whole story for you.

Interestingly, there were few or no explicit references to the specific purposes of the tasks or how these tasks articulated into sequences of planning related to broader course goals. Again, Shavelson and Stern (1981) suggest that while teacher training in curriculum planning emphasises models which commence with the specification of objectives, this model is not reflected in teachers' actual planning behaviour. This study and others (cf. Nunan 1990), suggest that their findings may also apply to language classrooms.

In Sarah's thinking, tasks were the major concepts informing the structuring of lesson planning, and not the course goals or objectives. Being asked to reflect on why certain tasks were chosen and the purposes of the tasks proved somewhat challenging, in fact, as the comments below reveal. Here, she is expanding on the 'diary activity', in which students wrote down personally-relevant sentences:

I know for some of the people in the class it was really useful. The South American woman found it very useful and Susanna and Lian and Tan the Vietnamese guy. Not Tan, hang on . . . there's another younger man and he's very conscientious, so yeah. . . . It doesn't sound great does it. It doesn't sound like I've really thought through this very much.

A further comment highlights the relative vagueness Sarah begins to perceive in her thinking about overall goals and purposes. It revisits the underlying orientations of her beliefs about learning and positive classroom relationships, which were suggested at the broader classroom level:

I think . . . the confidence building was the most important aim and um . . . that they also had something, you know to take away with them from the class that they could refer to. But more often, I think, you know, more often just the laughter and the general kind of camaraderie in the class was . . . um. I mean, it doesn't seem like a good educational goal, does it? I feel like it's all very . . . sort of very vague.

Yet another comment encapsulates her frustration in attempting to articulate more clearly her goals and purposes and points to the value she perceives in reflection which has challenged her assumptions about her classroom. She returns to listening to the classroom recordings with the comment:

Yeah . . . I guess, you know . . . now I come to think of it . . . I think, oh God, what was my rationale? I'm sure I had one. It's good for you.

Sarah's responses suggest a tentativeness in planning which is further increased by her feelings of unfamiliarity with beginner learner groups.

This tentativeness was equally in evidence for other teachers in the study. Despite the fact that they were experienced teachers, it was frequently the case that they suggested they were 'feeling their way' when planning for their learners. Sarah's comment suggests that, while she attempts to draw on her previous teaching experience to test out successful approaches to planning, at the same time she still feels unsure:

Well, you see, I've never really had . . . that is the first really low level class I've taught. So I'm kind of feeling my way and just doing I suppose what comes naturally. I don't feel confident about teaching low level reading and writ . . . you know, literacy at all. You know, I haven't worked on any materials and I'll probably go screaming around the place and saying who's done what . . . and give it to me.

While it may be premature, as Nunan (1990) suggests, to assume that planning, including the formulation of objectives, can be removed from the instructional equation, the reflections of this highly-experienced teacher seem to further highlight the mismatch which exists between conventional 'ends-means' models of curriculum planning and delivery traditionally taught in teacher pre-service and in-service programs and the realities of the intricate and multifaceted processes of the classroom (Cumming 1989). The complexity of the intercontextualities, the moment-by-moment classroom interactions, the accommodations and tensions which characterise the relationships between thinking, beliefs and behaviour and the need to shift and adjust previous expectations, experiences and conceptualisations to meet specific, and possibly new, classroom situations point to the need to rethink and reorient current modes of teacher education.

Prevailing models for language teacher education may, as Freeman (1989: 29) suggests, have proceeded in the wrong direction, assuming that research in second language acquisition and methodology are primary, rather than ancillary to language teaching itself. Critical insights into what constitutes language teaching need to give voice to the perspectives of teachers themselves. They need to identify and track the routes of professional growth through collaborative partnerships between teachers and researchers and to investigate the classroom-based questions generated by teachers. This may lead to more effective understandings of what is meant by learning how to teach.

Making the implicit explicit

A further examination of Sarah's classroom suggests that increased awareness through close and critical engagement with classroom data can be a catalyst for the re-evaluation of thinking and beliefs and for

169

the development of alternative modes of instruction. A notable insight in this study was that the conceptual frameworks motivating classroom action and the unconscious accommodations within those frameworks, such as those already suggested, were not necessarily salient to the teacher. Having an opportunity, however, to give close attention to classroom data was clearly a powerful motivational factor. For Sarah, it produced a reflective and critical re-evaluation of her classroom practice as well as heightened awareness. Listening to the audio recording and reading Transcripts 1 and 2 challenged her assumption that the interaction in her classroom was directed by her learners. Her reflective comment on this connected with her other beliefs about learner-centred learning and interaction:

I mean, just listening . . . it is very much teacher–student, teacher–student the whole time . . . and er, obviously it would have been good to try and get them to interact. Possibly this was the problem, I think with this class . . . was that it was very much, you know one-to-one, teacher–student. I mean it kind of glares at me at the moment . . . you know, when I'm looking at it now.

Discovering that she 'controlled' much of the classroom questioning and interaction, she began to contemplate ways to involve the learners more actively. She decided that one of her strategies might be to draw on and acknowledge the learners' own well-developed first language resources:

Well I think using L1 is probably one of the best ways to get people confident about talking to one another at the beginning.

Attempting to incorporate this teaching strategy at particular stages of lesson planning and classroom interaction, she reported later that she felt some success had been achieved. The result had been more opportunities for student-centred interaction, with the learners successfully assisting and supporting each other as they prepared to communicate personal information in English:

You leave them to it and then you say, 'Well all right, can you explain to me or to the other people in the group?' Um, somehow when they're . . . two minds are better . . . two heads are better than one, so that if someone is not confident to explain to the rest of the group what they did on the weekend and they're on their own . . . I found that the husband and wife might chat together or the two Vietnamese guys who sat next to them might chat together and the two of them kind of combined the fragments of language that they have in order to explain that to another person, . . . the South American lady sitting next to them or whatever.

170

Other insights which came from a close examination of classroom data challenged some of Sarah's beliefs about the communicative rationale she had assumed to characterise the oral activities and tasks:

Er, it's interesting. I didn't think I was working as much on pronunciation. It's a kind of pronunciation . . . um, fairly kind of primitive . . . that I was doing with them. I was trying to get people to be comprehensible, in the sort of short chunks of what they were saying. I did do a little bit on the question asking that we spent time on. But for most of these things it was just getting the sounds correct. Um . . . oooh, I feel stupid.

Despite her feelings of self-consciousness and of being 'stupid', Sarah displayed considerable open-mindedness, increasing reflection and heightened professional awareness through her willingness to deliberate closely and critically on the data. She also alluded to the positive value she saw in this kind of critical reflection, commenting, 'It's a very good learning experience'.

Close reading and discussion of the classroom transcript prompted particular insights and reflections. Transcript 3 continues the 'ironing' discussion from Transcript 2 and features one of the Vietnamese learners, Ding (Di), his wife, Tan (Ta), and Lian (Li).

Transcript 3: Did you do some ironing at the weekend?

T: Ding, do you iron?
Di: Yeah . . . yeah, yeah.
T: Yes? Sometimes?
Di: No.
T: No?
Di: I. . . . er, at home . . . times.
T: Yes, you?
Ta: Sometimes . . . yes. Sometimes . . . yeah. (breaks into Vietnamese)
T: Aha . . . and your wife?
Di: No.
T: Your wife . . . doesn't iron? (learners speak in L1)
Di: No.
T: OK. Did you do some ironing on the weekend? Did you do some ironing on the weekend? (exaggerating intonation)
Di: Yeah, yeah. Yeah. (speaks in L1)
Li: Saturday and Sunday.
Di: Saturday and Sunday.
T: Saturday and Sunday? That's a lot. (laughter) OK, what about Hung? Do you do ironing?

Listening to the recording and focusing on the interactional data in Transcript 3 prompted Sarah to challenge her assumptions that her classroom tasks provided opportunities for the learners to engage in communicative interaction. She began to critique various aspects of the interaction, which she had assumed she did not use and which she judged to be uncommunicative or 'not spontaneous', and to consider possible strategies for changing the patterns of classroom interaction:

That's something I would never do with a general class. This 'DID you DO some IRONING at the WEEKEND'. Um . . . on the whole I used to cringe when I'd hear, you know, myself or other teachers . . . um, making the normal speech so stilted and slowed down. Um, I think . . . I think, listening to that, I'd probably . . . yeah, I'd like to change that. I would.

Um, I'd probably like to think I could still put a stress on the most important word. 'Did you do some IRONING at the weekend'. But not break that down to those sort of . . . like it is there. Because it completely . . . it doesn't help them at all with their listening or when they come to do pronunciation work later on. But it's funny how you're not aware of things, you know that you . . . sort of, normally say that you don't do. It's very useful . . . very much.

She realised that the learners were experiencing oral interaction predominantly as rather individualised sentence level utterances in the 'weekend' lesson. As a result, she set about attempting to create opportunities for more prolonged and 'natural' communicative interaction.

Changing classroom practice

Sarah decided that she would try to focus on more extended personal accounts of the learners' activities outside the classroom. She decided to facilitate this process by giving them more time to combine their first language resources, in order to help each other construct accounts of recent events. This decision was consistent with her belief that lesson content should be relevant, drawing on the learners' daily lives and enabling them to participate in casual conversations.

Transcript 4 provides an example of the interaction occurring, with Tan as the main speaker, as a result of attempting these strategies.

Transcript 4: You caught ten kilos of fish?

Ta: Evening . . . husband go to the car Newcastle. Fishing. Ten kilo.
Li: Ten kilo.
T: What?
Ta: Yeah. Yeah.
T: You caught ten kilos of fish? (turns to Tan's husband, Hung)
Hu: Yeah.

T: Fantastic . . . but not in Cabramatta [shopping centre]? (laughter)

Ta: Cabramatta . . . vegetables, food. Er . . . er, evening . . . Sunday go to the car my friend husband. Ten kilo fish!

T: Fantastic . . . so. . . .

Ta: Yeah, er . . . evening eigh . . . eight o'clock. Three A.M. . . . five o'clock A.M.

T: From eight o'clock . . .

Ta: Yeah, P.M. Five o'clock A.M. (Ding and Tan speak in L1.)

T: OK, wait a minute. I don't understand. (Ding discusses in L1 with Tan.)

Di: Er, tomorrow, five o'clock.

Li: Tomorrow . . . five o'clock Sunday . . . Saturday.

T: Ah, so from the evening to the morning. All night? Fishing all night?

Ta: All night, yeah.

T: (laughs) And where did you go fishing? Was the fishing in a river or at the beach?

Ta: Er no beach . . . er . . .

T: Did you have boat? (draws picture of boat on the board.)

Ta: No . . . no.

Di: No boat, no boat (learners discuss in L1 as Ding goes up to the board and draws a picture of a man standing next to a river.)

T: River . . . mmm. OK, thank you, Ding (learners discuss in L1). River (she writes 'river' on board.)

SS: River . . . river.

What is immediately obvious in this transcript is the greater quantity of language produced by the learners, as well as the more equal roles taken by both the teacher and the learners in creating the discourse. The teacher is not in control as she was in the earlier interactions, and the typical classroom 'initiation – response – evaluation' pattern of the previous transcripts is much less in evidence. Interestingly also, the teacher no longer addresses and questions one individual learner at a time in the way that characterised her earlier tasks. In this interaction, several of the learners, Ding, Lian and Hung, enthusiastically combine both their first and second language resources to construct their account of the fishing expedition jointly. Sarah's reflections on the lesson suggest that she feels there is greater cohesion here with the beliefs that motivate her thinking about learning opportunities:

I think they were patient and willing to wait for . . . you know someone to look up a word in the dictionary or um, . . . have that little conversation before things came back into English. And I think they realised that it was, you know, really useful for them, because they could then be co-teachers.

They could be helping one another and it was a kind of cohesive thing, rather than something that split students apart. I mean I wanted everybody to be able to contribute.

For Sarah, close engagement with data from her own classroom was an enlightening process and a significant means of professional growth. It allowed her to reflect deeply and to articulate her thinking as she evolved greater awareness of the actual and complex interactions in her own classroom. At the same time, through this heightened awareness, she challenged and questioned what she saw as inconsistencies between classroom interactions and her own thinking and beliefs. Articulating these inconsistencies enabled her to develop learning strategies for her beginning learners which accorded more closely with what she believed met her learners' needs outside the classroom.

Briefly, the following processes were key factors in illuminating Sarah's experiences of teaching these beginning learners. Close engagement with data from her classroom and reflection on classroom processes resulted in:

1. Articulation of the nature of her own views and beliefs and to what extent they were reflected in classroom practice
2. Heightened awareness of her own style of teaching and the typical patterns of her classroom interaction
3. Greater understandings of the consequences, effects and outcomes of particular forms of interactional patterns
4. Planning, reflections and strategies for alternative courses of action based on informed understandings
5. Appreciation of the value of engagement with classroom data and the processes of thinking consciously about the classroom
6. Growing confidence in making decisions based on informed knowledge about own classroom

Discussion

The case study of Sarah's classroom suggests that interconnecting networks of belief appear to be foundational to classroom operations, constituting the theories, prior texts or schemata (Woods 1990) which are manifested in instructional practice. Theories *for* practice, as distinct from the theories *of* practice typically taught in teacher education programs, construct the cognitive structures for planning, decision making and teaching behaviour in the language classroom. The thinking and beliefs which are brought to bear on classroom processes appear to be highly significant but are frequently unconscious and implicit. Nevertheless, these implicit theories for practice, motivated by the multilevel contexts surrounding specific classroom activities, appear to activate and shape patterns of classroom interaction, roles and relationships and, therefore, to create for learners particular kinds of opportunities for learning. Personalised theories for practice, then, should be considered not as adjuncts or ancillaries to classroom behaviour but as the motivating conceptual frameworks shaping what teachers do when they teach.

If theories for practice are essential forces in determining behaviour in the classroom, implications are then raised for how teacher education conceives of and represents to classroom practitioners the concepts of *theory* and *practice*. Stern (1983: 23) has commented that:

Language teachers can be said to regard themselves as practical people and not as theorists. Some might even say they are opposed to 'theory', expressing their opposition in such remarks as 'It's all very well in theory, but it won't work in practice'.

However, as Stern further points out, and as Sarah's commentaries on her classroom reveal, 'theories' are nonetheless embedded in classroom practice. The distinction commonly made between theory as the province of researchers and academics and practice as the 'real stuff of the chalkface' may be essentially misleading, as it negatively reinforces the traditional dichotomies which still exist between theorist and teacher.

For teacher education, a much more useful concept, from the practical point of view of the classroom, would be the notion of *theories for practice*, together with investigation of the important influences they clearly have on classroom processes and interactions. Finding strategies and procedures for teachers and researchers jointly to investigate and reflect upon these processes and to articulate the implicit thinking which underlies them would contribute to and strengthen the conscious development of informed theories of practice. As Breen (1991: 232) comments:

By uncovering the kinds of knowledge and beliefs which teachers hold and how they express these through the meanings that they give to their work, we may come to know the most appropriate support we can provide in in-service development.

Such an approach implies the development of a different and more cooperative relationship between researcher and practitioner. What is required are not prescriptions for teaching, but exploratory and collaborative approaches to understanding how teachers learn their skills (Allwright and Bailey 1991). A collaborative relationship would greatly facilitate our knowledge of the reflexivity between theory and practice. It would enable researchers to test empirical theories against the actual processes of real classrooms and assist teachers to question assumed understandings and implicit theories for practice. Not only would it allow teachers to develop renewed vigour and enthusiasm for teaching, it would also create greater interest in theoretical knowledge, encouraging teachers to test prescriptions for teaching against their own experiences of being and thinking in the classroom (Gebhard 1989; Nunan 1991). By exploring and identifying how thinking and beliefs give meaning and shape to classroom work, we would also gain critical insights into the nature of professional growth and the forms of in-service and professional development support which would most appropriately enhance it.

References

Allwright, D. 1990. The characterizations of teaching and learning environments: Problems and perspectives. In K. de Bot, R. B. Ginsberg, and C. Kramsch (eds.), *Foreign Language Research in Cross-Cultural Perspective.* Amsterdam: John Benjamins.

Allwright, D., and K. Bailey. 1991. *Focus on the Language Classroom.* Cambridge: Cambridge University Press.

Bogdan, R., and S. K. Biklen. 1982. *Qualitative Research for Education: An Introduction to Theory and Methods.* Boston: Allyn & Bacon.

Breen, M. P. 1991. Understanding the language teacher. In R. Phillipson, E. Kellerman, J. L. Selinker, M. Sharwood Smith, and M. Swain (eds.), *Foreign/Second Language Pedagogy Research.* Clevedon: Multilingual Matters.

Brindley, G. 1979. *The Assessment of ESL Speaking Proficiency through the Oral Interview.* Sydney: Adult Migrant Education Service.

1989. *Assessing Achievement in the Learner-Centred Curriculum.* Sydney: National Centre for English Language Teaching and Research.

Clark, M. C., and R. J. Yinger. 1979. Teachers' thinking. In P. Peterson and H. J. Walberg (eds.), *Research on Teaching.* Berkeley, Calif.: McCutchen.

Cumming, A. 1989. Student teachers' conceptions of curriculum: Towards an understanding of language teacher development. *TESOL Canada Journal* 7(1): 33–51.

Freeman, D. 1989. Teacher training, development and decision making: A model of teaching and related strategies for language teacher education. *TESOL Quarterly* 23(1): 27–45.

Gebhard, J. G. 1989. The teacher as investigator of classroom processes: Procedures and benefits. Paper presented at the 23rd Annual TESOL Conference, San Antonio, Tex.

Nunan, D. 1987. Communicative language teaching: Making it work. *ELT Journal* 41(2): 136–144.

1988. *The Learner-Centred Curriculum.* Cambridge: Cambridge University Press.

1990. The language teacher as decision maker: A case study. In G. Brindley (ed.), *The Second Language Curriculum in Action*. Sydney: National Centre for English Language Teaching and Research.

1991. Methods in second language classroom-oriented research. *Studies in Second Language Acquisition* 13: 249–274.

Nunan, D., and J. Burton (eds.). 1988–1991. *National Curriculum Project Frameworks*. Sydney: National Centre for English Language Teaching and Research.

Oschner, R. 1979. A poetics of second language acquisition. *Language Learning* 29: 53–80.

Reynolds, M. J. 1982. The choice of frame and focus in a data-driven case study: A description of a research process. In S. Dingwall and S. Mann (eds.), *Methods and Problems in Doing Applied Linguistic Research*. University of Lancaster: Department of Linguistics and Modern English Language.

Shavelson, R. J., and P. Stern. 1981. Research on teachers' pedagogical thoughts, judgments and decisions and behavior. *Review of Educational Research* 51: 455–498.

Sinclair, J., and M. Coulthard. 1975. *Towards an Analysis of Discourse*. Oxford: Oxford University Press.

Slimani, A. 1992. Evaluation of classroom interaction. In J. C. Alderson and A. Beretta (eds.), *Evaluating Second Language Education*. Cambridge: Cambridge University Press.

Stern, H. H. 1983. Language teacher education. In J. Alatis, H. H. Stern, and P. Strevens (eds.), *Applied Linguistics and the Preparation of Second Language Teachers: Towards a Rationale*. Washington, D.C.: Georgetown University Press.

van Lier, L. 1988. *The Classroom and the Language Learner: Ethnography and Second-Language Classroom Research*. London: Longman.

Widdowson, H. G. 1979. *Teaching Language as Communication*. Oxford: Oxford University Press.

Woods, D. 1990. *Studying ESL Teachers' Decision-Making: Rationale, Methodological Issues and Initial Results*. Ottawa: Carleton University Papers.

8 What's in a methodology?

Polly Ulichny

Introduction

How does a teacher teach? To answer this question, researchers have studied teachers and their classrooms in numerous ways. Some, looking for effective teaching practices, have conducted empirical research that identifies isolated teaching behaviors and correlates them with student achievement measures. Brophy and Good (1986) and Rosenshine and Stevens (1986) summarize this research in a variety of elementary and secondary classrooms. Chaudron (1988) summarizes the second language classroom research in this tradition. A second strand of research on teaching investigates teacher thinking and decision making. Clark and Peterson (1986) describe the literature that investigates teacher theorizing, planning, and thinking outside the classroom. Both of these approaches propose a view of teaching that is rational and technical and that can be synthesized into a set of principles that define expert knowledge within the profession.

In contrast to this technical-rational definition of the knowledge base of teaching, an alternative view that presents teacher decision making as more complex, contextually determined, and personally constructed has emerged (Connelly and Clandinin 1988; Elbaz 1983; Louden 1991; McDonald 1992; Olson 1992). In this chapter I present a case study demonstrating this alternative view of the teaching moment. I maintain that a teaching event is a constant mediation between enacting planned activities and addressing students' understandings, abilities, and motivation to carry out the activity. How a teacher determines which activities to engage the class in, how she assesses the students' participation in the task, and what she determines are reasons and remedies for lack of adequate participation are the basic units of the teaching moment. The particular construction or "sense-making" of the moment is a product of an individual teacher's past learning and teaching experiences, beliefs about teaching and learning – from both professional training as well as folk wisdom gleaned from fellow teachers – and her particular personality.

This chapter will present a portion of a case study of an ESL teacher engaging her students in a classroom activity. In an effort to understand how one teacher teaches, I have examined how she plans her lesson, introduces it to the class, interprets student feedback as they engage in the task, and modifies her task and interaction with the class based on that assessment. The understanding of her personally constructed teaching method is based on a detailed microanalysis of the discourse of this event, coupled with the teacher's own reflections and interpretations of the classroom talk. This method embraces Breen's (1985: 140–141) suggestion that:

For us to begin to understand language learning experiences in the classroom, the researcher must discover what teacher and taught themselves perceive as inherent within the discourse of lessons. . . . The reconstructive cognition of learners and the social psychological forces which permeate the processes of teaching and learning must reside within any explanation concerning how and why people do what they do when they work together on a new language.

The analysis presented here reveals the moment-to-moment "in-flight" decisions (Jackson 1968) that a teacher makes to mediate between task and student performance. The interpretations she makes "on-line" are a product of her beliefs about her students and the learning task at hand. These, in turn, are formed by her past experiences as teacher and learner as well as her personality. Together they form her knowledge base for teaching and provide her with a *weltanschaung* of the teaching-learning moment from which her unconscious decisions to direct and redirect classroom interaction emanate.

I conclude the chapter with a brief discussion of the changes that occurred in the teacher's mediation of task and student performance during the course of the collaborative study in which we engage. Just as discovering a teacher's methodology of instruction requires investigating the belief system that lies beneath the surface of planning and executing classroom activities, change requires reflection on these underlying principles and conscious attention to modifying the roots as well as the consequences of these beliefs.

Background of the case study

The episode I present is part of a larger ethnographic investigation of a semester-long noncredit college ESL reading class (Ulichny 1989). In order to investigate what actually goes on in a given classroom, I carried out a detailed discourse analysis of multiple episodes of the class over time. The microanalyses of talk were embedded in a larger ethnographic investigation that explored the context of situation of the class (Malinowski 1961) as well as the teacher's interpretation of the interaction. In following Breen's recommendation, I looked at the larger context of the class in order to characterize the participants' own understandings of their behavior.

To carry out this investigation I attended and audiotaped twenty hours in this ESL classroom over the course of a semester. In addition, to get the insiders' perspectives, I interviewed each of the students once. Since I was concentrating on the teacher's method, I conducted fourteen hours of taped interviews with her about her classroom practice. The interviews followed a particular format. First, we listened to segments of the tape of classroom interaction based on what the teacher wanted to listen to and comment on. The teacher stopped the recorder any time she wanted to comment or felt that something noteworthy was happening. On the basis of these comments, I probed the teacher about her observations. This led her to further question and reflect on the conscious and unconscious choices in the ongoing classroom dynamics. These probing questions elicited aspects of her teaching philosophy, her personal history as a teacher, her assessments and impressions of students in her class in terms of their culture, personalities, strengths, weaknesses, styles of learning, and preferences in the classroom, her current dilemmas in her classroom and her career, and her description of the institution she worked in. In the process of carrying on this work, we also became close friends and confidantes. Many more conversations took place outside the official taped interview sessions, which also informed the microanalysis of the classroom.

While there are many aspects of this project, I describe what a teaching methodology looks like in action. I hope to show how utterly complex a moment of teaching is – how it is made of fits and starts, retrackings and unconscious decisions that happen moment by moment, and how it is not the result of a grand plan, as a methodology textbook would lead us to believe. Second, I hope to show what went into the method of discourse analysis, which allowed me to characterize the evolution of the teaching and learning (by all concerned) that took place during this ESL course. In other words, I will show the building blocks of the other aspects of this project. Third, I describe the changes over time in this teacher's approach to teaching this class based on the collaborative work we did in this study.

Building the context: The teacher

The teacher of this class, Wendy Schoener,[1] had been an ESL teacher for eight years at the time of the study. She was one of two full-time

---

1 I am using the real name of the teacher in this study. It is customary in academic research to ensure the anonymity of the subjects, thus protecting their privacy. With Wendy's permission, I use her full name. Since Wendy was such an instrumental person in the construction of this analysis, masking her true identity would be the

ESL teachers at the university in which the study took place, and was considered a very good teacher by colleagues and by former students. Wendy was not as convinced as they were, however, that she was as good a teacher as she could be. She took her career in ESL very seriously. She read professional literature and designed her own courses rather than relying on course books. Her philosophy of teaching included beliefs that:

- Students learn best by engaging in content-based instruction rather than focusing on isolated language exercises or even reading strategy exercises.
- Authentic readings (meaning those intended for native speakers) are better than simplified texts because they give students an experience of reading that is closer to real life.
- Students need encouragement, understanding, and nurturing in order to succeed in the mainstream. They do not need to be told what they are not doing, as much as what they are doing well.
- Attention must be paid to all learners in the class, not just the ones who understand and seem to follow the lesson. The lowest-level students serve as the barometer of where to engage the class. This may not, however, serve the needs of the more advanced students. Thus, more advanced students need adequate time to talk in order to stay interested in the class and to be patient with the weaker students' progress. This, Wendy recognized, created a constant tension in her assessment of how she judged her teaching effectiveness.

She also believed that the expectations for her course – to provide students of diverse backgrounds and abilities with the experience and tools necessary to negotiate mainstream college classes successfully – were impossible. Nevertheless, she took the task and the unrealistic goal extremely seriously.

Wendy's methodology was – in the grand sense – content-based and followed a communicative-competence approach to teaching. However, she was eclectic in her choice of tools to accomplish her goals. Her personality and what she had learned from her past experience as an ESL teacher were as important as her educational beliefs in determining what she did in the class.

Wendy was an extremely sensitive and nurturing person. When called upon (and also when she was not), she would go to great lengths to support her students. In addition to listening carefully to what each student had to say, she spent many hours carefully commenting on stu-

same as publishing this chapter under a pseudonym. Moreover, without Wendy's generous collaboration and openness, this work would never have been accomplished. Using her real name is a modest way of recognizing her valuable contribution.

dents' work – both in writing conferences and in written feedback on their work. Her care and support extended outside the classroom. She helped her students through a variety of life-related tasks – filling out registration forms and applications, finding jobs, even filling out their tax forms.

Wendy was mindful of the stress of encountering a new language and culture and was very reluctant to push anyone when he or she showed resistance. She would rather lower her expectations for individual performance than pitch a class above the heads of her students. This particular trait came from her own experience as a timid student from a working-class environment who felt totally unprepared for oral participation in college seminars. In addition, her early years of teaching, when she had occasionally prepared "fantastic" lessons which met with silence because the tasks were beyond the ability of her students, remained strongly and embarrassingly impressed on her memory.

Wendy viewed her students and her job through the lens of her personal history of being an outsider and, therefore, an unentitled participant in the world of academia. She saw her students as being marginalized immigrants and outsiders. Likewise, she saw her profession as being marginalized within the university system – she was not a "real" professor by university standards, although her work was certainly equivalent to that of a professor. Thus, Wendy stood with her students on the outside and tried to ease their way into the mainstream, rather than positioning herself in the mainstream and requiring students to meet her there. Her personality and desire to nurture her students to success made her more willing to take on the hard work herself than to demand uncomfortable work from others.

As a result of these connected experiences of nonentitlement, Wendy was very critical of her ability as an ESL teacher. While she knew that she dedicated her life to her students, she often wondered whether she was more of a mother than a teacher. She was concerned that she misrepresented the "system" to students by being so understanding. She was also concerned that she was not teaching them that to survive in the mainstream one has to work hard. This dilemma of who did the work was a critical motivator in Wendy's teaching style. When she encountered the conflict in her own moment-to-moment teaching, she thought that things were not going well and assumed that the fault was hers.

Building the context: The class

The class that we investigated was a noncredit, ESL reading class required of incoming university students whose English was judged too limited for them to manage a full-time regular student load successfully. Some of the students were taking only ESL classes in preparation for the next semester; others were taking one or two mainstream classes along with the ESL reading class.

There were eighteen students in the class, representing twelve countries and nine languages (Spanish, Chinese, Vietnamese, Cambodian, Arabic, Farsi, Haitian Creole, French, and Turkish). Their ages ranged from late teens to mid-thirties. Along with their extremely varied cultural and linguistic backgrounds, they brought with them a wide variety of schooling experiences and literacy backgrounds. Some of the students had had minimal schooling in their own countries (the Southeast Asians) and had received their formal schooling in bilingual programs in the United States. Others had completed secondary school in their own countries and were beginning university in the United States. Still others had had some university training in their own countries before beginning their U.S. university careers. The greatest extreme in preparation was between a student who had had a seven-year gap in her schooling in Cambodia, had completed a U.S. high school bilingual program, and was now entering the university at age eighteen, and a thirty-four-year-old Iranian professor of psychology who had completed a Ph.D. in Finland. The variation in English language ability among the students was not necessarily in keeping with the amount of schooling each student brought to the class. It ranged from rather fluent to minimal expressive ability. According to tests, however, their comprehension of written English and grammar was good enough to allow all of them to enroll in the university.

Wendy was free to design the reading course as she wished. Rather than following an ESL textbook for intermediate readers, she chose to design the course around chapters from the introductory textbooks that the students would encounter in their first courses in the university. The subject areas from which she chose materials were sociology, economics, psychology, and biology. In addition, the class read a novel and a play. The sources of the reading and the main focuses of the classroom discussions are listed here. Each subject area was discussed over approximately two weeks of class time.

Course sequence
1. Teaching the syllabus and reading strategies (understanding meaning from context)
2. Sociology textbook chapter: modes of family organization and competing sociological theories to explain them
3. Economics textbook chapter: the world economy and reasons for the differential distribution of wealth among the nations of the world

4. *Animal Farm*, a novel by George Orwell
5. Psychology textbook chapter: child language acquisition from first words to syntax
6. *A Raisin in the Sun*, a play by Lorraine Hansberry
7. Biology textbook chapter: Mendel's genetic experiments

The specific piece of teaching that this chapter examines comes from about two weeks into the semester. The class is reading the sociology chapter, which introduces students to functional and critical theories of family structure. In this section they are discussing why in industrialized nations, the nuclear family structure is more functional than extended families. Wendy has picked this chapter because she thinks that it will be particularly engaging and provocative for students who come from cultures with extended families.

Wendy's method of teaching is to go through the chapter section by section, breaking it down into comprehensible chunks. She does this through a variety of activities and techniques. In the passage that follows, she has assigned a section of the chapter as homework. She has also given the class a simplified lecture that restates the five reasons why, according to the book, nuclear families are more functional in industrialized societies, and she is planning to have the students locate the five points at which the reasons are given in the text. This is the planned activity she introduces to the class.

After her short lecture, which resembles a dictation more than a college lecture, as she responds to student pleas to slow her pace, she asks the students to rephrase the five main points from their notes. This is intended as a brief recap, but as we will see, it turns into a major portion of the lesson. She discovers that student comprehension of her lecture is unclear. Their oral reproduction of their notes comes in scattered words, without the logical relationships she has presented. Even after helping the class, she cannot elicit an orderly set of ideas – so she changes plans "in flight" and works on building their comprehension of the five points of her lecture. The aim of the lesson stays the same – facilitating their understanding of the text – but she finds herself working on creating comprehension where she did not expect she would have to. As we will see, she makes constant adjustments to meet their level of understanding. That, I will argue, is the real stuff of her teaching method: the constant adjustments to make the text and the classroom talk comprehensible to the students.

Discourse analysis

A detailed analysis of the elicitation from student notes of the first lecture point follows. The transcript of the discussion is divided into four segments, with the microanalysis of the discourse following each. The segments illustrate the progression of assessments and adjustments that Wendy makes in order to match student performance to the task.

Segment 1: Discovering a problem[2]

Wendy asks Khiet, a rather shy and soft-spoken Vietnamese student, to read back her notes.

```
 1  W:      Let me write down just a few main words from your notes.
            What did you say number one was, what kinds of notes
            did you have, uhm. Khiet..[ . . . ] uhm That's a hard one.
            What did you have (sounds very encouraging).
 5  Khiet:  Higher status?
    W:      Higher status? OK (writes it on board).
    Khiet:  Or monies. monies
    S:      Money
    W:      Uh huh. Ok or money (writes)..Want some help?=
10  Erol:   =Choice
    S:      Free choice
    W:      Something about being free to choose OK (writes) I did
            give you a lot of ideas
    Ss:     Yah (complaining intonation) [ . . . ?]
15  W:      OK. Unfortunately that's how some lectures are OK?
```

Wendy is expecting this exchange to be a straightforward report of what she has just said in her lecture, namely, that children in nuclear families have the possibility of assuming a social status different from that of their parents because they are free to choose jobs, spouses, and living quarters outside their family network. She remarks on this class segment in the interview as follows:

Those were hard ideas. I spent some time beforehand trying to distill it down into something that would then correspond to what they saw in the book. . . . I did this expressly because I think it's a little speedier. That might not be true if I see how much time [it took in class].

---

2 Transcription Key

.	one conversational beat pause
?	rising intonation
,	falling, clause-ending intonation
=	latched talk (no pause between speakers)
*	onset of overlapped speech
CAPS	slow delivery parallels writing on board
[..]	unclear talk, not transcribed
( )	transcriber comments

Instead, she discovers immediately that they have not understood her simplified version because they cannot reproduce it as a structured argument. Students seem to have a few of the key words she has mentioned, but they cannot connect the words in any sort of general statement or example.

This is clearly evident when Wendy asks Khiet to read back her notes. As a policy, Wendy does not call on students, much less the shy Asian women, unless she is sure that they are able to answer her. She does not want to put less able students on the spot or to embarrass them. Khiet answers very tentatively and quietly, with the help of other students. But her answer is not a sufficient restatement of the first lecture point. It is a series of unconnected words, "higher status," "money," and "free choice," that must be arranged into propositions in order for them to make sense. When Wendy sees this, she backs up and writes "free to choose" on the board, indicating that this is the central notion and that something more must be said about it.

In addition, Wendy means to encourage the students by telling them that she has given them "a lot of ideas" in her lecture, underscoring the fact that she sympathizes with the difficulty of the task. The students recognize this compassion and let her know that they agree. Wendy then tells them that "unfortunately" for them, "that's how a lot of lectures are," in order to justify the difficulty and indicate that she is not going to let them give up. This personal interjection into the content is indicative of the classroom ethos.

Segment 2: Fine-tuning the hints – Assessing the source of the problem

Cycle 1
1	W:	But. what did I say about higher status and money?.
	I:f	
	S1:.	If they are free to choose
	Erol:	If they accept
5	S3:	If they * try. If they want

Cycle 2
	W:	* uh hmm Can they have it?
	Ss:	No
	W:	Can people have higher status or money than their family more money?
10	Ss:	hmm hmm
	W:	Is it possible?
	Ss:	It is, Sure, uh hmm*

Erol: It is.

14 W: OK (writes on board). So it's possible to have higher
status and money

In Segment 2, Wendy begins cycles of fine-tuning to get the students
to produce correct answers. The first cycle provides the students with
the next part of the proposition, higher status and money, and provides
them with the logical relationship that binds the two element by starting
their sentence with "I:f" (line 2). She supplies the ingredients and suggests the conditional framework into which they fit. The students
sometimes need a little jog of memory to start them on the right answer,
and in this case Wendy gives all the hints she believes they need in order
to answer. She even starts them off by elongating the vowel in "if" and
pausing, which indicates that the sentence pattern is what she is asking
for. Several students respond in staggered overlap. S1 has the right beginning, "If they are free to choose" (line 3), but it gets lost in the other,
less felicitous answers: "If they accept . . ." (line 4) "If they try . . ."
(line 5) and "If they want . . ." (line 5). Perhaps Wendy does not hear
the "right," answer, or she is distracted from it by the louder answer,
Erol's "If they accept (line 4).[3]

In the hint to elicit the first lecture point, Wendy has structured the
surface level of the proposition for them. It seems as if she has decided
that the problem is basically one of language and they merely need a
scaffold to put the right words together. However, even with blatant
hints, they cannot link the two elements into the conditional proposition. None of the students seems able to get beyond the "if" clause.
When she sees that her strategy is not working, Wendy steps back and
tries again; however, this time she does not work at getting the right
sentence out of them. In the second cycle, she gets the students to display the meaning of the statement by constructing the background sup-
position it entails. She reasons that, if the language is not the problem,
a basic lack of comprehension must be the problem. She thus tries to
come closer to their level of ability by downshifting the difficulty of the
task to build a scaffold which demonstrates what the first point means.

The first part of the demonstration is problematic, which seems to
indicate that she is correct about what they had understood. When she
asks the students: "Can they have it" (line 6), with falling intonation,
she is trying to establish the point that children may obtain a higher
social status than their parents. The students respond rather confidently:
"No" (line 7), perhaps because in their experience this is not the case.
Having understood the question correctly, they are answering it from
their own knowledge base and not from her lecture. In any case, Wendy

3 When she listens to the tape later, she criticizes herself for not having picked up S1's
answer and for not giving the students enough time to develop their answers further.

seems to have located the source of the problem. Rather than assume that the students believe that children cannot attain a different social status from that of their parents, she treats her own question as an insufficient expression of what she is asking. In her next utterance she rephrases the question, filling in all the pronouns with their referents: "Can people have higher status or money than their family, more money?" (line 8) The students still respond negatively, although the answers are less confident.

I cannot verify my interpretation of what is happening here, because I have no direct supporting information from the students. However, I have many examples of similar exchanges which support the hypothesis that the students are reacting to the repetition of the question and are therefore more hesitant in the second response. If a teacher asks the same question a second time, students can be reasonably sure that their first answer was not evaluated as correct and that is the reason for the repetition. Because Wendy does not overtly evaluate responses, but almost uniformly waits or probes until she hears something she can work with, the students have most likely learned to adjust to her style. However, given that she repeats the question in a way that clarifies what she intends to ask, it is possible that the students understand something different in the case of the first question. At any rate, the third question, "Is it possible?" (line 11) again rephrases the original question by indirectly asking the students to reconsider their response. This time the students rally around an affirmative answer: "It is," "Sure," "uh hum" (lines 12, 13).

Wendy accepts this answer by repeating it as a conclusion: "So it's possible . . ." (line 14) and by writing it on the board. I cannot be certain from this interaction, however, whether the students understand what she is asking, whether they believe what they answered correctly, or whether they merely understand the kind of answer Wendy is looking for and supply it. A subsequent interaction, however, lends support to the interpretation that the students do not believe the answer they gave but have understood what Wendy was after in this exchange.

Segment 3: Doing the work for the students

1	W:	Where does the freedom to choose come in. * What about it?. . . .
	S1:	* School
	Erol:	Freedom
5	Norma:	She need uh to choose=
	Gilbert:	= To have a better education
	Norma:	her school

```
W:      OK. So if you want this?=
Erol:   =House
10  W:  You need this? Does that make sense to you?
    Ss: Yah
```

Up to this point in the dialogue, Wendy seems to have established the presupposition for the conditional statement she is trying to demonstrate, namely, that children can have more money and higher social status than their parents. With that agreed to, she moves on to a more open-ended question which again asks the students to link the two themes of the conditional: "Where does the freedom to choose come in . . . What about it?" (lines 1 and 2) The students answer with single words. "School" (line 3) needs to be expanded as an example of a choice that might make a difference in one's status to count as an answer to her question; likewise "Freedom" by itself is merely a repetition of what Wendy had said. The students, stuck at a one-word stage of retelling "text" concepts, do not present their answers in well-formed utterances. They throw out words that Wendy had provided in the lecture and this discussion and expect her to do something with the words to fashion answers.

Finally, Norma and Gilbert team up to provide the most connected answer so far: "She need to choose her school" [To have a better education]. Their words, incidentally, are taken directly from the lecture, even in the selection of "she," but they still do not link this idea in words to obtaining higher status. They provide a better response than the one-word answers, but they do not go beyond a single clause. Wendy no doubt recognizes that the production of the conditional statement linking the two ideas is beyond the students' ability at the moment, so she relents and demonstrates it. She calls attention to the phrases on the board, "higher status" and "money" on the one hand and "freedom to choose" on the other. Tapping on the board, she creates the relationship visually and verbally for them: "So if you want this . . . you need this."

However, her demonstration is interrupted by Erol's response, "house." He is still providing one-word examples of the kinds of things one must have the freedom to choose. Wendy's subsequent "Does this make sense to you?" (line 10) is a genuine appeal for feedback about their understanding of the basic concept. She says it slowly and with high-pitched, rising intonation, indicating that it is more than a routine comprehension check. She communicates that she is doubtful that they have understood. The students, however, respond "Yah" (line 11) with confidence.

In this exchange we see the distance between Wendy's ideal of what students should be doing – dealing with the concepts in the reading –

and their ability to comprehend and speak English. The students have not demonstrated that they can produce the first main point of the lecture, or that they understand it. Upon careful examination, it appears that they have simply demonstrated that they are attuned to the rules of the interaction: recycling of questions means that the first answer is wrong; questions tapping comprehension need a "yes" answer and if they give Wendy enough words to work with, she will create well-formed utterances. At this point, there is nothing Wendy can do to bridge the comprehension gap. She cannot be sure that they are being truthful or that they have understood. Their answer to her direct question about their understanding defies their demonstrated comprehension. This is her worst-case scenario. She has lost the students and cannot assess where they really are because what she has proposed is too difficult. If she cannot make the input comprehensible to them, she has not taught them.

As we see in Segment 4, her recourse is to return to language and to an activity that focuses on constructing a correct sentence. Sentence-level work is the lowest level of difficulty in her assumed hierarchy of tasks, and so she decides to write the sentence that they will produce on the board. Given the amount of trouble they have had so far, she takes on the responsibility of constructing a sentence and requires them only to ratify her solution.

Segment 4: Doing what they do well together

1	W:	OK. So. (writes on board) what could we say? BUT PEOPLE . NEED *I guess (spoken slowly as she writes on board) ooh woops
	Norma:	*Need
5	W:	(corrects spelling on board) FREEDOM TO CHOOSE. And what kinds of things do they have to- They have to cha:nge, be different from what their families were=
	Erol:	=Yes
	W:	sometimes. So what did they have to be free to choose?
10		Any examples?
	Norma:	*Eschool
	S2:	*Education
	W:	School or education? (writes on board)
	Ss:	House, spouse, job (These are overlapped and "house"
15		and "spouse" are both said more than once. Many students are answering here.)
	W:	House, job, spouse, OK, good (writes on board).. Good. You got it.

Not only has Wendy gone to the lowest level of task, but she has abandoned the idea of a conditional sentence which seems beyond their ability, and she has taken on the work herself. Rather than constructing a scaffold and guiding the class to the solution of the problem, she writes the sentence on the board. Although she does elicit nominal participation, it is totally gratuitous, as the transcript reveals. She asks: "what could we say?" (line 1) but without pausing for an answer, she begins to write. She also elongates the word "people" (lines 1 and 2) seeming to ask the students to supply the next word, but does not wait for their response. She decides on "need" (line 2), which Norma repeats as Wendy writes in a delayed response to the slot-filler elicitation. Wendy ignores Norma and goes on to complete the phrase. It appears that Wendy's tolerance for students' mistaken guesses has reached a limit. There seems to be no sense, in her mind, in requiring them to do things that are beyond them. Her first recourse in the face of difficulty is to simplify the level of the task and to provide the class with more guidance to complete it. But when these techniques fail, she pushes them forward onto the next question by completing the task herself.

Wendy's next step is to bolster their confidence again by asking them to do something she is sure they can manage, namely, to give examples of things they must be free to choose. She is confident that the students can do so because it requires only the type of one-word answers they are good at supplying. Further, they have already provided a number of examples that were not mentioned in the lecture itself. Thus the final fallback in the face of serious breakdowns in comprehension is to do things together that they all know they can do well [cf. Jordan and Fuller (1975) for discussion of this strategy in cases where speakers share minimal common language].

There is one wrinkle, however. When Erol answers "Yes" (line 8) to her open-ended request for examples, "What kinds of things do they have to- they have to change, be different from what their families were," perhaps he has understood the question as a repetition of the earlier exchange in which Wendy asked three times whether it was possible for children to be different from their parents. Here she interrupts the question to reestablish the presupposition that caused so much trouble earlier. She also hedges the statement with "sometimes" (line 9) in order to make it more acceptable to their knowledge of the world. Erol's inappropriate answer is treated as a comment of agreement, and Wendy rephrases the question: "So what did they have to be free to choose? Any examples?" (line 10) In this rephrasing she makes the question more explicit and identifies the type of answer it requires, thus meticulously guiding the students to the correct solution to the problem. The interaction ends with more and more students supplying correct one-word examples.

All the answers come from the previous discourse, either the lecture itself or from this reporting activity. In addition, they bear a phonetic resemblance which suggests that one word may serve as a clue leading to another. For example, Norma's Spanish pronunciation of "school" places an /e/ before the /s/ + consonant cluster, thus possibly triggering the similar initial-sounding "education" that overlaps with her response. "House" and "spouse," which are both said several times, quite possibly reinforce each other because they rhyme. Wendy ends this difficult interchange by repeating and writing their correct answers on the board and explicitly commending them on their success: "OK, good. . . . Good. You got it" (lines 17 and 18).

Summary

This picture of early classroom interaction illustrates the work that an experienced ESL teacher undertakes in bringing complex text information within the grasp of a diverse group of learners. Teacher modeling emerges as the basic form of instruction at this early stage of the course, although this is not a conversation class about texts. However, in this episode Wendy models the kind of talk she expects students to produce in U.S. university courses. Through sensitive, fine-tuned guidance, she assesses the students' comprehension and production, she models and scaffolds the content, and, more important, she packages the information from the text these students will need to acquire in order to succeed in college. This picture of classroom interaction further shows how complex and encompassing Wendy's thinking and actions are as she tries to coordinate the students' understanding of task and text simultaneously. It is important to note that Wendy's choices are not premeditated. In fact, they are not even talked about in this detail in our interviews. A complete picture of her "in-flight" decisions is available only upon reflection and careful scrutiny of the classroom discourse. The importance, however, of these unconscious decisions is obviously great.

These episodes show that to understand a teaching methodology, we need to examine much more than overt decisions like curriculum choices, tasks, or seating arrangements. We first need to establish what actually happens for students and teacher in particular exchanges in the class. A reflective examination by the teacher, based on actual data or discourse analysis as I have demonstrated here, is effective in revealing the fabric of learning. In my analysis, I have paid particular attention to the nature of the task required of the students, the students' responses to it, the teacher's assessment of these responses (deduced from what she does as well as what she says), how the interaction develops and is satisfactorily resolved, and what happened to make the exchange satisfactory.

Second, linking what actually happens to what motivates the teacher's choices is a crucial ingredient in discovering a teacher's method. It allows us to grasp, in Breen's terms, what working on a language means to teacher and students. In Wendy's case this analysis results from a combination of the following things: her goal for the class to discuss authentic readings, her philosophical commitment to concentrate on exchanging meaning and not on correcting student utterances as linguistic forms, and her personal commitment not to discourage students by pitching the lesson too high for them.

While the particular constellation of factors in Wendy's case is unique – her personality, professional choices, and institutional constraints – I believe that this episode represents a familiar moment in ESL teaching practice: trying to coordinate comprehension and task completion simultaneously. If we look closely at ESL teachers' practices, we will see, as we did here, that in the "black box" of teaching (Long 1980), the act of making the lesson comprehensible *is* the art and the method of ESL teaching. Particularly when the background knowledge of students and teacher differ and English as the language of instruction is not shared equally among participants, cues of student comprehension, or lack of it, guide the teacher in mediating the talk and the task to meet students' performance and abilities. When the language is both the substance and the medium for the instruction, the teaching methodology lies in how that particular teacher makes task and talk comprehensible.

Change over time

Wendy listened and reflected on this portion of the class during the course of the study, and she was disheartened by what she heard. Instead of encouraging rich discussion of the topics covered in the reading, she felt that she was asking students to participate in a quiz show of "fill in the teacher's slot." Our careful listening to and discussion of the classroom talk identified places to begin to modify aspects of her method of instruction. In her view, not only was the language of the text too difficult for the students, the notion of talking about an author's meaning was a new experience for most of her students. These factors were further complicated by the fact that the author's meaning ran counter to the students' experiences in the world.

When Wendy realized these contributing factors, she modified the structure of classroom talk. In subsequent lessons she introduced the students to the content of the textbook chapters by discussing what they knew about the subject. By raising their consciousness of their background knowledge and by exposing possible areas of conflicting beliefs, the students were able to engage in more complex discussions of the content. In addition, before she attempted to elicit specific text content from the whole class, Wendy had the students formulate their responses in small groups. These rehearsals encouraged careful listening to each other and helped them compose more linguistically complex contributions to the discussion. Both strategies helped to shift most of the comprehension work to the students. Wendy did, however, maintain a nurturing, accommodating style in her discussions with the whole class as she helped them construct and display meanings from the text. Microanalyses of subsequent segments of the class reveal that the students, in fact, learned to imitate her style of discussion. They learned to package their arguments and explanations in the same way Wendy had done in the early lessons.

As Wendy reflected on the class's progress and modified her strategies accordingly, she came to understand three levels of what Schön (1983) refers to as the "action-present" – the zone of time in which action can still make a difference to the situation. Her first level of reflective intervention was mechanical. It involved immediate changes in the way she structured discourse opportunities for the class as I described above. This was the simplest modification to undertake and yielded immediate, positive results. Her second level of intervention was structural. This included her choice of topics and readings for the class. Reflection on the discourse over time revealed that Wendy became better at fostering rich discussions among the class when both she and the students were familiar with the subject matter being discussed. She realized that her choice of separate chapters from a variety of subject areas put everyone in the position of novice. Further, she noticed that, when the topic was unfamiliar, she tended to monitor the form of the students' contributions rather than the content. In order to feel confident in her teaching, she needed to present the students with material she understood well. This enabled her to stand back during the discussions and to help them construct new meanings for themselves.

This structural modification, however, was not immediate. During the semester she was confined by the syllabus she had already created for them. In subsequent semesters, however, she modified her syllabus by planning thematic courses on such topics as immigration, growing up in different cultures, and the 1930s and 1940s in the United States. The readings for these courses included original documents, academic writings, and fiction. By spending an entire semester on one basic theme, students gained knowledge in the content area with which to begin to speak authoritatively about the texts.

Wendy's third area of the action-present was the most difficult to modify. She called it her "congenital problem area," a term that referred

194

to the personality traits which sometimes led her to do too much of the work for her students. Throughout the course of this study and in subsequent classes, Wendy struggled with her sense of when and how much to simplify the task for the students. She realized that some of this work was necessary and in fact made her an excellent teacher. But she was also convinced that she could do too much of this work, and that did not necessarily benefit the students.

This last area was the most difficult to change. Because there was no easy answer to the question of when and how much to intervene on students' behalves, making a conscious effort to modify this aspect of her practice involved constant judgments in individual instances. Changing behavior patterns in the class would also mean changing her assessment of teacher and student roles. In addition, because her judgment to nurture students was deeply connected to Wendy's worldview, it surfaced in her moment-to-moment decisions on how to direct and redirect the interaction of the class. As such, it was far less amenable to conscious scrutiny and purposeful change. Wendy understood this part of her teaching style to be a potential problem, something she needed to be mindful of in each class in order to incorporate the insights from her reflection into her practice. She hoped that this general attention would find its way into her ongoing decision making in her classes.

Conclusion

In this chapter I have argued that understanding a teacher's method of instruction is far more complex than either technical-rational models of expert knowledge or textbooks describing various curriculum approaches and teaching methods would have us believe. As the case I have presented demonstrates, after the initial syllabus or lesson planning, much of a teacher's methodology resides in the way she interprets and acts on information from the ongoing classroom interactions. The interpretive framework she brings to the class is based on her past experiences as a teacher and learner, her professional knowledge and folk wisdom about teaching, and aspects of her personality. These factors shape the quality and kind of information she receives from the class. The ongoing interpretation of how well the class is performing the task at hand influences immediate decisions on how to direct and redirect interaction as well as how to plan subsequent lessons and activities. Paying attention to the ongoing decisions and uncovering their sources can provide a tool for analyzing the work of teaching and the thinking that it embodies. More important, however, it provides us with a place to discover the action-present in which teachers can reflect and modify their practices.

References

Breen, M. P. 1985. The social context for language learning – A neglected situation? *Studies in Second Language Acquisition 7:* 135–158.

Brophy, J. J., and T. Good. 1986. Teacher behavior and student achievement. In M. C. Wittrock (ed.), *Handbook of Research on Teaching*, 3rd ed. New York: Macmillan, pp. 328–375.

Chaudron, C. 1988. *Second Language Classrooms: Research on Teaching and Learning.* Cambridge: Cambridge University Press.

Clark, W., and P. Peterson. 1986. Teachers' thought processes. In M. C. Wittrock (ed.), *Handbook of Research on Teaching*, 3rd ed. New York: Macmillan.

Connelly, F. M., and D. J. Clandinin. 1988. *Teachers as Curriculum Planners: Narratives of Experience.* Toronto: OISE Press; New York: Teachers College Press.

Elbaz, F. L. 1983. *Teacher Thinking: A Study of Practical Knowledge.* London: Croom Helm.

Jackson, P. W. 1968. *Life in Classrooms.* New York: Holt, Rinehart & Winston.

Jordan, B., and N. Fuller. 1975. On the non-fatal nature of trouble: Sense-making and trouble-managing in Lingua Franca talk. *Semiotica 13*(1): 11–31.

Long, M. 1980. Inside the "black box": Methodological issues in classroom research on language learning. *Language Learning 30*(1): 1–42.

Louden, W. 1991. *Understanding Teaching: Continuity and Change in Teacher's Knowledge.* New York: Teachers College Press.

Malinowski, B. 1961. *Argonauts of the Western Pacific.* New York: Dutton.

McDonald, J. P. 1992. *Teaching: Making Sense of an Uncertain Craft.* New York: Teachers College Press.

Olson, J. 1992. *Understanding Teaching.* Buckingham, U.K.: Open University Press.

Rosenshine, B., and R. S. Stevens. 1986. Teaching functions. In M. C. Wittrock (ed.), *Handbook of Research on Teaching*, 3rd ed. New York: Macmillan, pp. 376–391.

Schön, D. A. 1983. *The Reflective Practitioner: How Professionals Think in Action.* New York: Basic Books.

Ulichny, P. 1989. Exploring a teacher's practice: Collaborative research in an adult ESL reading class. Doctoral dissertation, Harvard University, Cambridge, Mass.

9 Teacher decision making in the adult ESL classroom

Deborah Binnie Smith

Background to the study

In the English as a second language (ESL) literature, theorists present a variety of approaches, strategies, and techniques for the ESL practitioner. Underlying these approaches are theoretical assumptions concerning the nature of language and perspectives on how second languages are most effectively taught and successfully learned. However, little research has been conducted concerning the assumptions and beliefs about language learning and instruction that ESL teachers hold and how these inform their decision making.

This chapter describes a study which explored the ESL instructional context from the teacher's perspective. More specifically, the study examined the pedagogical decisions made by experienced ESL teachers and the role that L2 theory, individual teacher beliefs, and contextual factors play in this decision making. The intention was not to test the effectiveness of a particular theory of instruction nor to evaluate the planning and implementation practices of the teachers involved. This was an exploratory study which focused on a relatively recent area of research interest in the adult ESL context – teacher decision making.

In the literature, two differing perspectives of language learning have dominated in ESL pedagogy: a product view and a process view.[1] In theoretical models reflecting a product-oriented or "formalist" (Rivers 1987) position, language is viewed primarily as an object to be mastered. Two mainstream approaches adopting this perspective, the audiolingual method and the cognitive code method, focus on learner mastery and accurate use of discrete language items through a transmission model of teaching. On the other hand, underlying the process-oriented models there is an assumption that language is an activity, not a product, and emphasis is placed on the use of language for communicative purposes. This perspective underlies both the communicative language

---

1 Although the terms *product* and *process* are usually associated with teaching writing, these terms are used here to differentiate between a view of language teaching which emphasizes mastery of discrete language items (a product approach) and a view of language teaching which emphasizes use of language for communication (a process approach). A similar distinction in teaching-learning approaches is made by Widdowson with the terms *use* and *usage*.

teaching approach (Littlewood 1981; Savignon 1983) and task-based teaching (Long 1985). These process-oriented teaching approaches emphasize student-centered classrooms in which teachers are facilitators rather than directors and activities which focus on communication of meaning rather than accuracy and form.

Eskey (1983) has suggested that the ESL field "has always suffered from a pendulum effect" in that there is a "melodramatic swinging back and forth between (these) two extreme positions" (p. 315). This characterization of the ESL field as one dominated by "extreme positions" is certainly evident when examining the literature. For example, classrooms are described as either student-centered or teacher-directed; teachers are facilitators or information givers; a teaching approach is transmission or interactive.

While it has been argued by practical knowledge researchers that teachers personalize theoretical ideas and make them practical for the classroom situation (Connelly and Clandinin 1986), the extent to which ESL practitioners' personal theories of instruction reflect these contrasting theoretical perspectives has not been a major focus in ESL research. The majority of ESL classroom-based studies have been concerned with the learner and the impact that particular classroom processes have on language learning outcomes.[2] While researchers have been investigating teacher decision making in the "regular" classroom context for the last decade,[3] only a few, relatively recent studies have examined the ESL context from the teachers' perspective.[4] This study sought to contribute further to our understanding of teacher decision making in the ESL classroom.

Design of the study

Since the study was concerned with the teacher's perspective on ESL instructional tasks and context, it was conducted from a qualitative methodological perspective. In this approach, detailed descriptions of people's perceptions are developed on the basis of many observations in the setting. From these descriptions, an understanding or theory is

2 See Allwright (1983), Chaudron (1988) and Long (1983) for extensive reviews of classroom-based research.
3 See Clark and Peterson (1986) for a review of research on pre-active (before teaching) decision making and interactive (while teaching) decision making. For research on the role of teachers' practical knowledge in decision making, see Clandinin (1986), Connelly and Clandinin (1986), and Elbaz (1983).
4 Cumming has investigated student teachers' conceptions of curriculum (1989) and how experienced teachers approach curriculum planning (1991). Woods (1989a) has investigated the types of curriculum and lesson decisions that experienced teachers make.

formulated (Bogdan and Bilken 1982). The following broad research questions provided a sensitizing focus for the collection and analysis of the data in the present study:

1. How do experienced ESL teachers approach instructional decision making?
2. Is teacher decision making influenced by individually held beliefs about L2 teaching-learning and perceptions of the instructional context and task?
3. How do context factors (institution, setting, students) affect ESL teachers' planning and implementation decisions?
4. Are teachers' instructional decisions consistent with theoretical ideas about planning and instruction?

In addition to the broad research questions, a framework of relationships was developed in order to guide the direction of the study. This framework, shown in Figure 1, emerged from the literature review of teacher decision-making research and regular and L2 classroom-based research. It provided initial direction for the emergent research design of this decision-making study of ESL teachers.

1. *Pre-active factors:* Pre-active factors (on the left-hand side of Figure 1) included teacher characteristics and context factors, since both have been shown in previous studies (e.g., Shavelson and Stern 1981) to affect teacher planning and implementation decisions. *Teacher characteristics* identified as particularly relevant to examine included individual beliefs about teaching and learning ESL, perceptions of the instructional task and context, and L2 theoretical knowledge. It is important to note here that this study was concerned with stated beliefs and evidence of beliefs provided by observed classroom practices. In the case of the latter, researcher hypotheses concerning teacher beliefs were validated with the teacher participant in the post-observation conferences and final interviews. *Context factors* selected as pertinent for this study related to the institution (e.g., administrative expectations), the setting (e.g., classrooms and audiovisual resources), and student characteristics. It should be noted that the examination of context factors included two different types of data. First, information was gathered from both institutional documents and the participating teachers about the program and students. Second, teacher statements provided data on individual teacher's perceptions of the context and the impact these had on decision making.
2. *Decision making:* Planning and implementation decisions are shown in the right-hand side of Figure 1. In order to analyze the classroom data, *lesson task structure* and *participation structures* were selected as the central units of analysis. The term *participation structures*

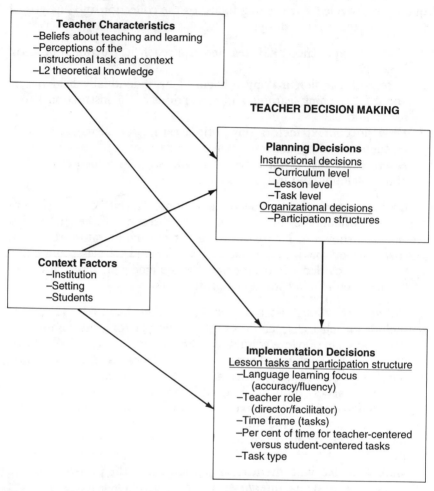

Figure 1. Framework of relationships.

refers to the way in which students are organized for particular tasks: as a whole class, in small groups, in pairs, or as individuals. These constructs have been used as units of analysis in both regular and L2 classroom-based research. In regular classroom studies, researchers have examined how task and participation structures serve to organize the academic and social structure of lessons (viz., Erickson 1986; Doyle 1983). Second, task and participation structures are not only key concepts in ESL instructional theory, that is, communicative language teaching and task-based language teaching, but also a focus of considerable research activity in ESL classroom research (see, e.g., Pica and Doughty 1985a, 1985b; Pica et al. 1990). Thus the conceptualization of the present research and the development of the framework of relationships guiding the study drew from several areas in the research and theoretical literature: findings from decision-making studies, both regular and ESL classroom-based research, and ESL instructional theory.

Data sample

Teachers

Nine ESL teachers in three adult education institutions participated in this study. Three teachers from each institution were selected so that individual perceptions of institutional features (e.g., type of students, administrative expectations) and how these affected planning and teaching decisions could be explored for differences among teachers working in the same setting. This provided a basis for comparison in terms of contextual variables within and across the three institutions. The nine teachers were selected by a process of judgment sampling. This involved selection "according to the number of criteria established by the researcher . . . that endows them with specialized knowledge" (Burgess 1984: 55). For this study, criteria included a minimum of three years' experience teaching adult learners, prior experience teaching in the present institution, and prior experience in teaching courses which focus on developing listening and speaking skills. There was no attempt to "screen" teachers according to methodological preference such as the communicative language teaching approach for teaching listening and speaking skills. Rather, a criterion for selection was that the course each was teaching was described by the institution as one which promoted speaking and listening skill development. The reason for this sampling focus was the researcher's interest in how individual teachers "operationalized" courses with similar skill objectives. This allowed for a comparative analysis of individual approaches to teaching, speaking, and listening across all nine teachers and the three institutions. Second, it was not the intention of the study to evaluate how strictly individual teachers adhered to practices identified with a specific approach such as the communicative approach. Rather, the aim of the study was to examine individual teacher decisions for classroom practices and the role that teacher characteristics and context factors played in their decision making.

The teachers participating in the study had all taken undergraduate teacher training courses in TESL; many had completed or were in the process of completing a master of education degree in TESL. In terms of teaching experience, they ranged from eight to thirteen years; in the current institution, experience varied between three years and eight years. In short, this was a group of ESL instructors who had not only extensive experience in the classroom but also a solid background in second language acquisition theory and pedagogy. In addition to their formal ESL training and teaching histories, most had a wide range of experiences working with second language speakers. Many had been volunteers in second language classrooms (including French and ESL) before beginning their teaching careers. Many had been involved with various local immigrant services societies helping refugees and new Canadians settle into their local communities. These teachers had also had a wide range of other teaching experiences, including teaching ESL at both the primary and secondary levels, and teaching in undergraduate TESL training programs. Most had taught ESL in a variety of settings ranging from local community classes held in church basements to private schools in Japan, Indonesia, and Taiwan. Finally, the majority also spoke another language fluently; for one teacher, English was a second language, and at the time of the study she was learning a third language, Farsi.

Institutions

The three institutions involved in the study were selected because of their similarities. Each is a publicly funded, adult education institution in a metropolitan setting; each has a well-established ESL program; each offers courses designed to promote speaking and listening skills development. It should be noted here that while two of the institutions use an integrated skills approach (i.e., courses include all four skills of listening, speaking, reading, and writing), the third institution uses a skills-based approach with each course focusing on a particular skill. On paper, this indicates a significant difference in course content, but in reality this was not the case. Speaking and listening activities were the major components of the classes observed at all three sites; thus there was greater consistency in the actual implementation of these courses than is apparent in the institutional descriptions.

Data collection procedures

Observations

Each of the nine teachers was observed teaching four consecutive two-hour classes. These classes were videotaped, and notes were written during each observation. The researcher's notes included times, a running account of what was happening in the lessons, information regarding where students were sitting for various activities, and the movements of the teachers, particularly during small-group and pair work. In addition, reflective comments and questions were written concerning specific aspects of the lessons. These highlighted points to discuss with the teacher in the subsequent, post-observation conference.

During these observations, the researcher assumed the role of complete observer although at times was invited by the teacher to comment on a point being discussed in the lesson. The students in these classes did not seem to be at all concerned by the presence of the researcher or the video camera. The study was explained, and both the teachers and the students signed consent forms before the study began. Students were also invited to view the videotapes once the observations were completed, and a number exercised this option at the end of the study.

Postobservation conferences

Following each lesson, there was a postobservation conference about the lesson. During these videotaped conferences, teachers watched the videos of their lessons (stimulated recall technique) and were encouraged to comment on what happened in the lessons as well as the decisions (pre-active and interactive) leading up to those events. These comments revealed teacher beliefs about L2 teaching-learning and the role that beliefs, context factors, and theoretical knowledge played in their pedagogical decisions.

In addition, teachers were asked to analyze their lesson tasks in terms of participation structure and language focus on task grids developed for this research. In the postobservation conference, these task grids provided a stimulus for individual teacher comments on how tasks were conceptualized, designed, and implemented from the teacher's perspective. In turn, this allowed for a comparative analysis with the theoretical perspective of tasks presented in the L1 and L2 literature. In addition, the completed task grids for each lesson (and particularly the comments teachers made while completing them) provided a teacher perspective on how lessons were structured and the interrelationship of tasks within and across lessons (see Figure 2).

The task grid focused on two dimensions which emerged from the L2 literature review as central to an analysis of task implementation – participant structure and language focus (accuracy and fluency). The task grid required teachers to indicate two features of their lesson tasks: whether the task focused mainly on accuracy or fluency language learning objectives and whether the task was primarily teacher-centered or

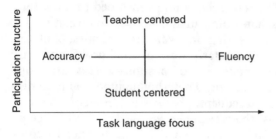

Figure 2. Task grid.

student-centered (the participation structure). These two task descriptors were considered significant for several reasons. First, both regular and L2 classroom-based studies have indicated that participation structure and tasks are interrelated features of classrooms (viz., Erickson 1986; Green and Harker 1982; Pica and Doughty 1985b; Pica et al. 1990). Second, research findings have shown that teacher-centered, whole-group instruction tends to dominate both L1 and L2 instruction (viz., Edwards and Furlong 1978; Long et al. 1976; Philips 1972). Third, L2 researchers examining classroom organization in relation to student language use have found that the type of student language use is influenced by the participation structure (e.g., Pica and Doughty 1985b). Studies have shown that while the use of unsupervised, student-centered, small-group organization is more likely to promote a communicative language use focus (defined in this study as fluency-focused), teacher-centered, whole-class organization tends to result in an emphasis on accuracy of language use. However, what L2 research has not investigated is whether *teachers* associate teacher-centered instruction with accuracy-focused language learning objectives and student-centered tasks with fluency-focused language learning objectives. That is, do teachers select a particular participation structure for a task according to the language learning focus they wish students to work on?

Interviews

After all the observations and postobservation conferences had been completed for the nine teachers in the study, each teacher was interviewed. The average length of each interview was approximately ninety minutes, although several lasted close to three hours. The interviews were structured so that set questions were asked of each instructor. This allowed for a comparative analysis of the data across all nine teachers. These questions were developed over the observation and conference data collection period so that these data as well as input from L2 theory informed the interview schedule. However, although there were set questions guiding the interview, these stimulated many secondary questions and lengthy elaborations of particular points. These enabled the researcher to probe for more in-depth information and to clarify certain points that had been noted in the observational and conference data.

The interview questions focused on five main topics: (1) teacher characteristics (teaching experience and TESL training background); (2) perceptions of the instructional context (administrative, collegial, student, and setting factors); (3) perceptions of the instructional task; (4) planning decisions; and (5) tasks and participation structure decisions. In addition to the set questions used for each interview, individual teachers were asked to clarify specific aspects in the data, which allowed for validation of researcher observations which had emerged from the preliminary analysis of the lesson and conference data.

Interviewing all nine teachers after completion of the collection and initial analysis of the observation and conference data allowed the researcher to probe issues emerging from both types of data, not only in relation to individual teachers but across the whole sample. This was particularly important in the latter case, since as the study progressed, patterns of behavior and themes common to all the participants became more evident and these could therefore be explored in the final interviews. Furthermore, propositions generated by the data from the last group of teachers could be checked with the first group in the final interviews. The interview stage also provided the opportunity to collect detailed information about the teachers' educational and teaching experience and, more significantly, teacher comments about the individual teaching approach and planning-instructional decisions in a context that was not linked specifically to a particular lesson observed. Although these types of data might have been collected in an initial interview, by waiting until the final stage of the study the researcher had a clearer understanding of the individual teacher's views and practices; as a result, a more purposeful exploration of the teachers' theoretical and practical knowledge was possible in the interviews. It was also felt that a full interview conducted at the beginning of the study might affect the observational and conference data collection in that teachers would be more cognizant of the particular constructs the study was examining.

Data analysis procedures

The analysis of the data began after the first observation had been completed and continued throughout the data collection period. In this way, data were concurrently collected and analyzed. This ongoing process enabled the researcher to identify themes and patterns of behavior emerging from both classroom practices and teacher comments. This concurrent collection and analysis process also served as a check that sufficient and appropriately focused information was being gathered before completion of the field work (Bodgan and Taylor 1975).

Initial analysis of the recorded observed lessons involved searching through the data to obtain an overall understanding of the lesson framework. Particular attention was paid to the tasks and participation structures that teachers implemented and the teacher roles that were adopted. During these first searches through the videos of the lessons, notes were made about specific points to pursue with the teacher in the conference about the lesson and in the subsequent, more in-depth analysis of the data.

After the initial process of becoming familiar with the data, a more thorough analysis was undertaken. This involved both transcribing the lesson videos and conference recordings as well as the use of a classification system. The classification system used was a modified version of the communicative orientation to language teaching (COLT) system developed by a group of researchers for a study investigating French instruction at the university level (Allen et al. 1984). This particular system was selected as an initial organizing framework because it provided a broader set of categories than other L2 observation systems, which were more concerned with classroom discourse. The COLT system includes categories for participation structures, materials used, and the content focus of a lesson. Since all of these aspects were important to code in the present study, this system provided a useful starting point for classifying the observation data. As the analysis proceeded, modifications to the system were made and categories added in order to reflect more appropriately the nature of the lessons observed and the focus of the research. In addition, the initial single classification scheme was reorganized into two separate charts: one for a detailed analysis of teacher-student interaction for each lesson task and one for a summary of tasks for each lesson activity. These charts were used in the initial in-depth analysis stage to classify the observational data. In the second stage of analysis, observational data were compared with information gathered through the postobservation conferences and final interviews.

In order to reduce threats to internal reliability of coding the data, several techniques were employed. First, the classification schemes used to analyze the lessons contained a number of low-inference descriptors (time, participation structure, language skills, input materials). The coding of the data into the other categories which were more open to researcher interpretation (language focus, accuracy focus, and task control) was validated with the teacher in the conferences following the observations. In addition, since each lesson was videotaped, there was a visual and verbatim account of what had occurred. By showing these tapes to the participant teacher, the researcher was able not only to corroborate what had been observed and recorded, but to validate researcher interpretations of what had occurred with the participants. This validation was provided both through teacher comments on the lesson as well as through the completion of the task grids by each teacher. The task grids focused directly on the teacher participant's analysis of the task structure of each lesson.

Findings

The major findings of the study have been organized into three areas: (1) the role of teacher beliefs and experiential knowledge in teacher decision making; (2) the influence of context factors on decision making; and (3) the nature of the decision-making process.

The role of L2 theory, teacher beliefs, and experiential knowledge

Teacher beliefs about language teaching and learning a second language emerged as the critical factor influencing the types of decisions these teachers made. These beliefs, while theoretically eclectic, were clearly articulated and consistent with individual teacher decisions. Although there were differences in how each of the nine teachers approached the instructional task, individual practices related not only to expressed beliefs about teaching ESL but also accumulated (successful) experience in using particular techniques and strategies in the classroom. This finding lends support to the views of practical knowledge researchers such as Clandinin (1986), who argue that experiential knowledge and beliefs are central to the types of instructional decisions that teachers make.

The central role that beliefs played was evident not only in how these teachers organized curricula and designed lesson tasks, but most significantly in their approach to instruction. Those teachers who considered grammar and accuracy to be a priority in instructional goals adopted a structural core for their curriculum design and developed lesson tasks which emphasized language code. On the other hand, the majority of teachers in the study were less concerned with structure and focused more on language for communicative purposes. They organized curricula with a functional or topical core and emphasized student interaction tasks in which emphasis was placed on the process of interaction and communicating meaningfully.

While teacher decisions were guided by a coherent set of personal beliefs, these teachers' use of theory was eclectic. This theoretical selection was particularly evident when relating teachers' decision making to the two central but opposing theoretical perspectives of L2 teaching-learning: the product view (teaching language as a product to be mastered) and the process view (teaching language as a communicative process). While these two perspectives are presented in the literature as quite distinct from each other (e.g., Long and Crookes 1989), such a differentiation was not evident in teacher practices; that is, individual teacher decisions did not wholly reflect one or the other but a combination of the two.

One obvious example of this process-product coexistence was the way in which different teachers implemented student-interaction tasks in their lessons. Theorists argue that these tasks should focus on communication of meaning, not accuracy of language use (e.g., Johnson 1981; Littlewood 1981). While all teachers in the study shared the view that these activities were beneficial for learner language development, their instructional goals for these activities differed. The more product-oriented teachers, consistent with their belief in the importance of structural mastery, developed student-interaction tasks with grammar-based objectives and were concerned primarily with the accurate completion of the task product. On the other hand, the more process-oriented teachers were concerned more with task process and communicative language use, although they frequently included language code components and products in the task design.

The findings in this study suggest therefore that experienced teachers first select from a range of theoretical ideas those aspects which correlate with their personal beliefs and use the surface features (the techniques) they have found to be effective from experience to meet their practical needs. In this way, the theoretical informs decision making but does not prescribe a particular approach or way of thinking.

A particular theme that emerged from the individual teacher data was the shared view that a positive social-affective climate was an essential element in the classroom. All the teachers in this group emphasized the need to build a positive and supportive learning environment. The word build is significant here because these teachers did not see such a climate as a given but as one that needed to be fostered by the use of student-centered, cooperative activities and appropriate materials. This belief in the importance of classroom climate was a central factor in the decisions these teachers made about tasks and materials.

In criticizing classroom-based research for its lack of attention to the social context of learning, Michael Breen (1987: 136) also points out that this is a central consideration for the teacher:

The teacher's priorities . . . are to build upon those inherent features of the classroom situation which may facilitate the learning of a new language. The teacher's question might be: 'In what way might I exploit the social reality of the classroom as a resource for the teaching of language?'

Breen suggests that while teachers consider the social conditions that impact on and enhance language learning in the formal setting, L2 researchers tend to overlook the role that social context plays and more often see the classroom as an experimental laboratory: "research has still to adopt a definition of the classroom which will encompass both cognitive and social variables so that their mutual influence can be understood" (Breen 1987: 141).

The findings from the study support Breen's contention that teachers view the social context for learning as central; however, the findings also indicate that teachers consciously work at fostering a particular social climate in a number of explicit ways rather than merely "exploiting" what is "inherent" in this context as Breen suggests. First, teachers talked about fostering a classroom "dynamic" which not only motivated students to come to class but to participate when they were there. They also referred to "building a supportive climate" in which students were encouraged to get to know one another and would ideally continue this social relationship outside the classroom. A number of teachers commented specifically that their most successful classes were those in which there was a "social gathering atmosphere" in which students were friends as well as classmates. For example, one teacher commented:

Self-image and all those affective domain issues are priority in L2 acquisition or any kind of learning because if it's not in place, I don't see any kind of potential. I think that's why building a supportive group environment so they can connect with people and make friends is so important.

Further, teachers did not consider this social rapport as necessarily an "inherent feature" of the social context, but one that needed encouraging through various means. They therefore made particular decisions about the types of activities and materials they used and the student-teacher roles adopted in order to promote group cohesiveness. For example, one teacher noted that she avoided topics that focused on negative topics such as stress, worry, or anxiety:

I want the topic to be positive because in the process of talking, people transfer positive feelings about an experience and pass those positive feelings onto the class as a whole.

Small-group or pair activities were seen as particularly beneficial for meeting students' affective needs. In addition, most teachers (but not all) stressed the use of affective feedback rather than corrective feedback to students. Many noted, for example, that in student-centered activities, they emphasized comments directed at *what* students said – e.g., "That's an interesting idea" – rather than how they said it.

The role of context factors in decision making

ADMINISTRATIVE FACTORS

All three institutions provided explicit course guidelines in terms of level and course objectives (structural, functional, and skill-based). Teachers felt that they had considerable freedom in the extent to which they were expected to use these for course planning. They did not view the institutional course objectives as prescriptions for planning but only as resource information for making decisions. Individual teachers varied in the extent to which they used these objectives for planning. Some stated that they were only "vaguely aware" of the institutional objectives; some referred to the objectives in the initial stage of course planning in order to get a "sense" of the course; only one teacher used the institutional list as the core for her curriculum plan.

COLLEGIAL FACTORS

A contextual factor that emerged as a significant setting difference was the extent of collegial collaboration in course level planning at the site. This collaboration involved both informal conferencing about courses as well as sharing of course materials. What was significant about this finding was that this collaborative planning approach seemed to exist only at the one site. Since this was a smaller department than the others (both in number of faculty and the size of the programme), it is speculated that this size factor had some influence on the increased level of collegial collaboration. Further research would need to be carried out to identify what contextual factors in particular contribute to this collegial planning approach.

STUDENT CHARACTERISTICS

Student characteristics were found to have the most impact on decision making, particularly at the lesson level. While knowledge of students' goals and interests, based on prior experience with students in this setting, informed initial course decisions, it was at the lesson level that student factors were of primary concern for these teachers. Student language learning goals and needs influenced preactive decisions about tasks and materials; student affective states had an impact on interactive decisions. Further, teachers stated that neither student expectations of teaching approach nor summative evaluation of students had much influence on their decision making. However, these teachers viewed for-

210

mative evaluation – not only teacher feedback to students on their progress but student feedback to teachers about the course – as critical.

The nature of the decision-making process

LEVELS OF PLANNING

The study data indicated that there are distinct levels of planning, with each one focused on a particular set of concerns. At the curriculum stage, these teachers were concerned with developing an overall course framework so that they had a global sense of the whole term's work. For lesson planning, teachers first developed a group of general lesson plans, usually for a week. This was a "mediating" stage of planning which linked the more abstract, content-focused curriculum plan with the more immediate, activity-based lesson focus. From these general plans, these teachers then determined specific activities for lessons on a daily basis. At this most immediate level of pre-active planning, the previous lesson events played a critical role in teacher decisions. However, even at this point, the teachers in this study did not consider the lesson plan to be finalized. All teachers commented on the importance of leaving final logistical decisions to the lesson itself, as interactive decisions, so that these could be made in response to immediate contextual conditions.

The study findings suggested that there are two types of interactive decisions: those decisions that teachers plan to make during the lesson, most often the timing of tasks, and those which are unanticipated. The latter type of interactive decision making was usually prompted by student factors (e.g., affective state of the students or unfinished homework) or teacher factors (e.g., forgetting to bring a key resource to class or a problem with a piece of equipment). Previous decision-making studies were mostly conducted in elementary school settings and have found that student misbehavior and student noncomprehension of subject matter are the two conditions that result in interactive changes to lesson plans (viz., Clark and Peterson 1986). This finding was not supported in this study, since student misbehavior was rarely an issue in these adult-level classes. Although difficulties with subject matter occurred, these were usually dealt with on a one-to-one basis during student-centered activities and did not involve a modification in lesson plans.

THE INTERRELATIONSHIP OF DECISIONS

Teachers connected curriculum-level, lesson-level and task-level decisions both sequentially and hierarchically. That is, they not only determined when certain course components and events would occur chronologically over the course and within lessons, they were also concerned with the developmental progression of the course toward meeting their overall objectives. This interrelationship of decisions was particularly evident at the task level. Although individual tasks had specific goals and processes, they were not planned or implemented as isolated learning events. The majority of tasks in the lessons observed were grouped into task units and linked thematically by a "content" core. In addition, in most lessons observed, the majority of task units consisted of a number of student-centered activities linked by teacher-centered transition segments, for example, explanations, instructions, task introductions, and closures. This finding suggests a more complex network of decision making than is implied by the single-task focus in current task-based research (e.g., Long 1989; Pica et al. 1990).

DECISIONS ABOUT TASKS

A finding from this study about teacher-designed tasks which is not captured by task-based research is the multifaceted nature of task goals. While the language learning goal of the researcher-designed task in current task-based studies is learner "negotiation of meaning" (viz., Long 1989; Pica et al. 1990), teachers in this study were concerned with a variety of short-term and long-term goals. Teachers referred to a number of goals for *each* lesson task. These included affective goals (e.g., building self-confidence), curriculum-based goals (e.g., using language of description and adjective clauses), communicative goals (e.g., practicing native-speaker gambits), content goals (e.g., learning about a particular topic), and critical thinking goals (e.g., evaluating opposite points of view on an issue). It was very evident from teacher comments that lesson tasks were purposeful events and not just "interaction for interaction's sake."

A surprising finding was how few information-gap tasks were implemented in the lessons observed. This type of task has played a central role in communicative language teaching methodology and is argued to be particularly effective for promoting communicative language use (e.g., Littlewood 1981; Rivers 1987; Savignon 1983). In addition, task-based researchers have found empirical support for information-gap tasks, particularly jigsaw and two-way information gaps, in their classroom-based studies (e.g., Pica and Doughty 1985a and b). However, in this study, only two jigsaw tasks – as defined in the literature – were implemented in the thirty-six lessons observed. Interestingly, teachers did consider that they used information-gap tasks; however, their view of what constituted an "information gap" was different from the theoretical notion presented in the L2 literature. They saw any task in which students were collaborating and sharing cultural, experiential, and/or linguistic knowledge as involving an information gap. In other words, for these teachers, the information gap was learner-centered and emerged during the task process; it was not necessarily built into the task design by controlling the amount of information each learner received.

DECISIONS ABOUT PARTICIPATION STRUCTURES

The study data did not support the prevalent view in the L2 literature that whole-class activities are focused on the transmission of information with an emphasis on language structure and accuracy (e.g., Kramsch 1985), while small-group or pair work provides opportunities for communicative language use with an emphasis on "message meaning" (Kramsch 1985; Littlewood 1981). In this study, participation structure was not the determinant of whether the language focus was structure and accuracy or communication and fluency; both of these foci were addressed in whole-class and small-group or pair activities. However, teachers did differ in the extent to which each emphasized one focus or another; the differences related to their underlying beliefs about how language should be taught. The majority, who approached L2 teaching from a process orientation, were concerned primarily with communicative language use; this was consistent in their approach to task design, task implementation, and feedback to students. On the other hand, a smaller group in the study viewed structure and accuracy as critical for language learning and emphasized this focus in their classroom instruction. The conclusion that can be drawn from these findings is that teacher beliefs about the nature of L2 learning are a critical factor in determining whether lesson activities and related participation structure have a structural or a communicative focus.

TEACHER ROLES

The implementation data indicated that teachers assume different roles in student-centered tasks. For tasks with specific, predetermined outcomes (e.g., completing a grammar exercise or a one-way description task), teachers tended to adopt a facilitative or monitoring role. This was consistent with the communicative language teaching view that teachers should "stay out of the limelight" (Rivers 1987) during student interaction activities. On the other hand, in tasks which were more open-ended discussions, teachers were more likely to become actively involved. Although most teachers indicated that they probably "shouldn't" be so involved in these activities, they also believed that their students enjoyed having teachers participate.

213

Conclusion

Theorists have argued that underlying any teaching approach there must be a consistent set of principles guiding activities and techniques and a correlative set of assumptions about the nature of language and the nature of teaching and learning a second language. This present research shows that such consistency exists but it is more teacher-based than theoretical. Teacher decisions revealed an eclectic use of theory but an internal consistency between individual beliefs and practices.

In ESL teaching theory, prescribed approaches to planning and implementation can be identified as predominantly product-oriented, in which language is a product to be learned, or process-oriented, in which language is a process of communication. However, teachers' actual planning and implementation practices reveal that both these views play a role in instructional decisions. On a macro level, teachers express beliefs that reflect a product or process bias in second language teaching and learning. However, their planning and teaching practices reveal a blending of these two theoretically dichotomous perspectives. The way in which teachers "blend" theoretical ideas for practical needs relates directly to their individual beliefs and what their experience tells them "works" to accomplish their instructional goals. The study concludes that teachers select and modify theoretical ideas in ways that are consistent with their personal beliefs about teaching and learning and their practical knowledge of the ESL instructional context.

References

Allen, J. P. B., M. Frohlich, and N. Spada. 1984. The communicative orientation of second language teaching. In J. Handscombe, R. Orem, and B. Taylor (eds.), *On TESOL '83*. Washington, D.C.: TESOL.

Allwright, R. L. 1983. Classroom-centered research in language teaching and learning. A brief historical overview. *TESOL Quarterly* 17(2): 191–204.

Bodgan, R. C., and S. K. Bilken. 1982. *Qualitative Research for Education: An Introduction to Theory and Methods*. Boston: Allyn & Bacon.

Bodgan, R. C., and S. J. Taylor. 1975. *Introduction to Qualitative Research Methods: A Phenomenological Approach to the Social Sciences*. New York: Wiley.

Breen, M. P. 1987. The social context for language learning – A neglected situation? *Studies in Second Language Acquisition* 7(2): 135–158.

Burgess, R. G. 1984. *In the Field: An Introduction to Field Research*. London: George Allen & Unwin.

Chaudron, C. 1988. *Second Language Classrooms. Research on Teaching and Learning*. Cambridge: Cambridge University Press.

Clandinin, D. J. 1986. *Classroom Practice: Teacher Images in Action*. London: Falmer.

Clark, C. M., and P. L. Peterson. 1986. Teachers' thought processes. In P. L. Peterson and H. J. Walberg (eds.), *Research on Teaching: Concepts, Findings and Implications*. Berkeley, Calif: McCutchan, pp. 11–28.

Connelly, F. M., and D. J. Clandinin. 1986. Rhythms in teaching: The narrative study of teachers' personal practical knowledge of classrooms. *Teaching and Teacher Education* 2(4): 377–387.

Cumming, A. 1989. Student teachers' conceptions of curriculum: Toward an understanding of language teacher development. *TESL Canada Journal* 7(1): 33–52.

1991. Teachers' curriculum planning for ESL instruction. Paper presented at TEAL Conference, Vancouver, B.C., Canada, March.

Doyle, W. 1983. Academic work. *Review of Educational Research* 53(2): 159–199.

Edwards, A. D., and V. Furlong. 1978. *The Language of Teaching: Meaning in Classroom Interaction*. London: Edward Arnold.

Elbaz, F. 1983. *Teacher Thinking: A Study of Practical Knowledge*. New York: Nichols.

Erickson, F. 1986. Qualitative methods in research on teaching. In M. C. Wittrock (ed.), *Handbook of Research on Teaching*, 3rd ed. New York: Macmillan, pp. 119–162.

Eskey, D. E. 1983. Meanwhile, back in the real world . . . : Accuracy and fluency in second language teaching. *TESOL Quarterly* 17(2): 315–323.

Green, J., and J. O. Harker. 1982. Gaining access to learning: Conversational, social and cognitive demands of group participation. In L. C. Wilkinson (ed.), *Communicating in Classrooms*. New York: Academic Press, pp. 183–202.

Kramsch, C. J. 1985. Classroom interaction and discourse options. *Studies in Second Language Acquistion* 7: 2169–2183.

1987. Interactive discourse and large groups. In W. M. Rivers (ed.), *Interactive Language Teaching*. Cambridge: Cambridge University Press, pp. 17–33.

Littlewood, W. 1981. *Communicative Language Teaching*. Cambridge: Cambridge University Press.

Long, M. H. 1983. Inside the black box: Methodological issues in classroom research. In H. W. Seliger and M. H. Long (eds.), *Classroom Oriented Research in Second Language Acquisition*. Rowley, Mass.: Newbury House, pp. 3–33.

1985. A role for instruction in second language acquisition: Task-based language teaching. In K. Hyltenstam and M. Pienemann (eds.), *Modelling and Assessing Second Language Acquisition*. Clevedon, U.K.: Multilingual Matters, pp. 79–99.

1989. Tasks, group and task-group interactions. University of Hawaii. *Working Papers in ESL* 8(2): 1–26.

Long, M. H., L. Adams, M. McLean, and F. Castanos. 1976. Doing things with words: Verbal interaction in lockstep and small group classroom situations. In R. Crymes and J. Fanselow (eds.), *On TESOL '76*. Washington, D.C.: TESOL.

Long, M. H., and G. Crookes. 1989. Units of analysis in syllabus design. Unpublished manuscript, University of Hawaii at Manoa.

Philips, S. 1972. Participant structures and communicative competence: Warm Springs children in community and classroom. In C. B. Cazden, V. P. John, and D. Hymes (eds.), *Functions in the Classroom*. New York: Teachers College Press, pp. 370–394.

Pica, T., and C. Doughty. 1985a. The role of group work in second language acquisition. *Studies in Second Language Acquisition* 7: 233–248.

1985b. Input and interaction in the communicative language classroom: A comparison of teacher-fronted and group activities. In S. M. Gass and C. G. Madden (eds.), *Input in Second Language Acquisition*. Rowley, Mass: Newbury House, pp. 115–137.

1986. Information gap tasks: Do they facilitate second language acquisition? *TESOL Quarterly* 20(2), 305–325.

Rivers, W. M. 1987. Interaction as the key to teaching language for communication. In W. M. Rivers (ed.), *Interactive Language Teaching*. Cambridge: Cambridge University Press, pp. 3–17.

Savignon, S. 1983. *Communicative Competence: Theory and Classroom Practice*. Reading, Mass.: Addison-Wesley.

Section III   Learning to teach: The role of language teacher education

The six chapters in this section address a central question in teacher learning, namely, the role and effect of formal teacher education as an intervention in learning to teach. As noted in the Prologue and expanded in the discussion in Chapter 16, the impact of teacher education on classroom teaching has generally remained unexamined in research. Language teacher education has been no different. The studies reported in this section, however, begin to probe how and to what extent formal preparation influences teachers' thinking and practice in the language classroom.

The first chapter in the section, by Donald Freeman, introduces a conceptual framework for teacher learning in teacher education. Based on a five-year longitudinal study of language teachers before, during, and after taking part in an in-service graduate program, Freeman's framework outlines the crucial role of professional language, or discourse, in exposing tacit thinking about teaching and thus stimulating learning and change. The study and its conceptual findings also raise the issue of the basic role of social constructivism in teacher learning.

Chapter 11, by Jack Richards, Belinda Ho, and Karen Giblin, looks at teachers' learning in a specific pre-service teacher education setting, the Royal Society of the Arts Certificate Program. This study is in many ways an exemplar of the kind of research that needs to be done in order to better understand the impact of pre-service training on entering teachers' conceptions and practice of language teaching. Read in conjunction with Johnson's and Gutiérrez Almarza's studies in Section I, these three chapters offer two perspectives on pre-service teacher education: examining trainees' first experiences of teaching on the one hand, and their preparation to enter the language classroom on the other.

The next three chapters focus on specific features in teacher education programs. The chapter by Francis Bailey is a finely drawn study of the social interaction among native and non-native English speakers in a graduate course on language teaching methods. Using techniques drawn from discourse analysis, Bailey draws attention to the particular ways in which knowledge is constructed through collaboration among the teacher-participants in one study group in the course. The study highlights the complex dynamics of language, social status, and expertise, and how these play out in developing new ideas about teaching. Bailey's research advances several themes in the preceding sections. Like Tsui's study in Section I and Ulichny's in Section II, Bailey takes us inside a particular teaching method. Although the particulars differ, these three chapters offer an invaluable composite of teachers as they learn and use classroom methods. Like Ulichny, Bailey demonstrates the strengths of careful analysis of classroom discourse as a frame for probing teachers' practices and their learning. And like Freeman's chapter in this section, his research shows evidence of the processes of social constructivism in teacher learning.

The chapter by Michael Wallace also examines a particular teacher education activity, in this case the final course project. In his study, Wallace investigates what teachers in one graduate program learn through a relatively common practice in language teacher education: a professional project using structured reflection to probe their classroom teaching. Wallace's study is a much-needed look at a widespread practice in language teacher education. It serves as an example of how useful research can be done when conventional wisdom is not simply assumed to be effective but rather is critically examined and assessed.

In Chapter 14, Ora Kwo expands the look at teacher education program design beyond the university to examine an integrated school-based project that emphasizes reflective teaching through action research. Kwo discusses the rationale for the program, drawing heavily on research in teacher thinking and learning to explicate its design. She then turns to a brief assessment of trainees' experiences in the program and identifies some key features that support more comprehensive learning of teaching in the school context. In its attention to place and impact of the classroom practicum in teacher education, Kwo's study is a good companion piece to Johnson's and Gutiérrez Almarza's chapters in Section I.

These three chapters, by Bailey, Wallace, and Kwo, each elaborate particular dimensions of language teacher education. The research moves from micro to macro levels of teacher learning, from Bailey's study of a methods course to Wallace's study of a professional project to Kwo's study of a comprehensive university school-based program design. Thus they offer insights into both specific issues and broader questions in language teacher education. Martha Pennington's chapter is a suitable finale to this progression. In her study, Pennington looks at the introduction of process writing in several Hong Kong schools. The study is about an in-service teacher education intervention that links university teacher educators and secondary school teachers through collaborative action research to promote this new model of teaching writing. Unique in the research reported in this book, Pennington organized a broad, multisite examination of this curriculum innovation and its impact on classroom teachers. Her study provides the wider frame for Tsui's chapter in Section I. Together these two chapters show the value of combining perspectives on a particular phenomenon in teacher learning, a broad survey-based study like Pennington's and a focused case study like Tsui's.

The chapters in this section all examine a core issue in teacher learning: the impact of formal education on what teachers know and what they do in their classrooms. The studies present examples of various types of work in this domain: conceptual frameworks, program studies, examinations of particular practices in teacher education, and research with pre- and in-service teachers. We are further fortunate to have three studies, by Tsui, Kwo, and Pennington, that draw from the same sociocultural milieu, the Hong Kong secondary school system. For readers interested in the interplay of the larger community setting with specific research questions and findings, these studies offer a useful set of diverse research all within the same broad sociocultural setting.

Suggestions for further reading

The following books and articles are suggested as further reading on topics in this section.

On social constructivism in teacher learning and teacher education
Fosnot, C. 1989. *Enquiring Teachers, Enquiring Learners*. New York: Teachers College Press.
Tharp, R., and R. Gallimore. 1988. *Rousing Young Minds to Life: Teaching, Learning, and Schooling in Social Context*. New York: Cambridge University Press.

On what is learned in teacher education and how it is used in classrooms
National Center for Research on Teacher Learning [NCRTL]. 1991. *Findings from the Teacher Education and Learning to Teach Study: A Final Report, National Center for Research on Teacher Education*. East Lansing, Mich.: NCRTL.
Findings on Learning to Teach. East Lansing, Mich.: NCRTL.

On uses of reflection in teacher education
Calderhead, J., and D. Gates (eds.). 1993. *Conceptualizing Reflection in Teacher Development*. London: Falmer.
Edge, J., and K. Richards (eds.). 1993. *Teachers Develop, Teachers Research*. Oxford: Heinemann.
Schön, D. 1987. *Educating the Reflective Practitioner*. San Francisco: Jossey-Bass.

Section III

On teacher education and social settings

Liston, D., and K. Zeichner. 1991. *Teacher Education and the Social Conditions of Schooling.* New York: Routledge.

On research design

Marton, F. 1981. Phenomenography: Describing conceptions of the world around us. *Instructional Science 10:* 177–200.

Miles, M., and A.M. Huberman. 1992. *Qualitative Data Analysis,* 2nd ed. Newbury Park, Calif.: Sage.

Yin, R. 1984. *Case Study Research: Design and Methods.* Newbury Park, Calif.: Sage.

On research in language teacher education

Flowerdew, J., M. Brock, and S. Hsia (eds.). 1992. *Perspectives on Second Language Teacher Education.* Hong Kong: City Polytechnic of Hong Kong.

Li, D. C. S., D. Mahoney, and J. C. Richards (eds.). 1994. *Exploring Second Language Teacher Development.* Hong Kong: City Polytechnic of Hong Kong.

10 Renaming experience/reconstructing practice: Developing new understandings of teaching

Donald Freeman

During the past fifteen years, examinations of how classroom teachers think about what they do have helped to demonstrate that teaching is more than behavior (Kagan 1988; Shulman 1986); it is indeed "thoughtful work" (Freeman 1990). This growing body of research and policy making has taken as its point of departure that teachers construct their understandings of classroom practice through various forms of experience (Kennedy 1992; NCRTE 1988). The 1975 report of the panel on "Teaching as Clinical Information Processing," convened by the National Institute of Education, put the principle quite succinctly:

The Panelists took seriously the value of the teacher's own description of *how he or she constructs the reality of his [sic] classroom*, of what is done and why, and of who the students are, and how he or she feels about them. (NIE 1975: 3; emphasis added)

The NIE panel's report inaugurated the area of inquiry that has come to be known as teacher thinking or teacher cognition (see Clandinin and Connelly 1987; Clark and Peterson 1986; Shavelson and Stern 1981 for major reviews of this literature). However, there continues to be some difference of opinion over both the ends and the means of such research (Pope 1993), as well as ambiguity about its applicability to teacher education (Floden and Klinzing 1990; Lampert and Clark 1990). Researchers have examined, among other areas, how teachers' subject matter knowledge evolves in teaching (Gudmundsdottir 1989; Wilson et al. 1987), how their understandings of classroom management and discipline shift with experience (Doyle 1977; McLaughlin 1991), and the various ways beginning and experienced teachers organize their knowledge and beliefs (Clandinin 1986; Elbaz 1983; Feiman-Nemser and Buchman 1985). However, the specific mechanisms by which teachers construct new understandings of classroom practice through the experience of teacher education have not been closely studied.

The practical side of this issue lies at the heart of teacher education as what Kennedy (1990: 3) has called "the improvement of practice problem": How do the activities of teacher education enable teachers to get

Reprinted from *Teaching and Teacher Education*, vol. 9, Donald Freeman, "Renaming experience/reconstructing practice: Developing new understandings of teaching," pp. 485–498, 1993, with kind permission from Elsevier Science Ltd., The Boulevard, Langford Lane, Kidlington 0X5 1GB, UK.

better at what they do? In this chapter, I examine one particular aspect of the problem, namely, how teachers-in-training move from using new professional terminology about their experience – renaming it – to thinking and acting in different ways – reconstructing their classroom teaching. The study (Freeman 1991) from which this analysis is drawn examines how teachers' classroom practices are influenced by participation in an in-service teacher education program. The findings suggest that *renaming* is a crucial feature of the process whereby the teachers renegotiate the meaning of their actions and thus construct different, more critical, ways of understanding what they are doing in their classrooms.

In research of this nature, it is difficult to show a direct relation among ways of talking, thinking, and behaving. If one looks at the behavioral side, teacher education seems to have minimal impact on classroom teaching (NCRTL 1992). If, however, one examines the participants' perceptions of what they are learning in such programs, a more complex view begins to emerge. To do so entails a shift in research perspective from examining actions to examining the perceptions on which those actions are based. Marton (1981: 171) defines the distinction as follows:

In the *first*, and by far most commonly adopted research perspective, we orient ourselves towards the world and make statements about it. In the *second* perspective, we orient ourselves towards people's ideas about the world (or their experiences of it.) Let us call the former a *first-order* and the latter a *second-order* perspective.

This study examined how teachers' ways of thinking about teaching, brought about through a teacher education program, might move into changes in action. The study adopted the second-order perspective described above to focus on the teachers' understandings of their practice as opposed to their behaviors and activities in the classroom. I have referred to this process by the double term *renaming experience/reconstructing practice*. To call it simply *renaming* reduces the process to a technical one of finding new words for familiar ways of doing things. To call it simply *reconstructing* overlooks the pivotal role which language plays in the development of new understandings in practice. I will return to this point in closing. The chapter introduces four concepts that emerged as findings and provides illustrations from the study. These concepts have implications both for research on teaching and teacher education and for the design and execution of teacher education programs.

The study

The longitudinal study (Freeman 1991a), designed in five phases, followed four high school French and Spanish teachers who were partic-

TABLE I. A SUMMARY OF THE PHASES, DATA, AND STRUCTURE OF THE STUDY (FREEMAN 1991)

Dates	Phase	Data	In-service program
Spring 1989	Pre-program	Interviews; observations	(Prior to matriculation, in home school)
Summer 1989	Summer #1	Interviews; document analysis of written work	First summer of coursework
School year 1989–1990	Interim year	Interviews; observations; document analysis	Interim-year on-the-job practicum teaching at home school
Summer 1990	Summer #2	Interviews; document analysis	Second summer of coursework
Fall 1990	Post-program	Interviews; observations	Coursework completed; thesis preparation

ipants in an in-service teacher education program leading to a master of arts in teaching (MAT) degree. The teachers were followed from just prior to their matriculation into the program (phase 1), through the two consecutive summers of coursework (phases 2 and 4), and the intervening school year in which they completed an on-the-job practicum at their home schools (phase 3). In the school year after the program (phase 5), the teachers returned to their home schools. In that all their teaching (phases 1, 3, and 5) was done in the same school setting over the course of the study, the influences of entering a new teaching environment were minimized in this design.

The data, which included interviews, observations, and documents written by the teachers during the program, showed the development of their thinking about their classroom practice through this eighteen-month period. In the data analysis, I developed intensive case studies (Yin 1984) of each of the teachers which detailed the shifts in their thinking, and gradually in their activity, in the classroom. The analysis also included a comparative examination of cross-case themes among the four teachers, from which the findings in this chapter are drawn. Table 1 summarizes the phases, data, and structure of the study.

Donald Freeman

Four concepts: Theoretical antecedents and findings

The findings of the study suggest that as these teachers learned to express their tacitly held ideas about teaching through the shared professional discourse of the in-service program, they gained greater control in shaping their classroom practice (Freeman 19921b). Four concepts which emerged as central in the study include the idea of teachers' *conception of practice* and of *tensions* in those conceptions, the process of *articulation,* and that of *local and professional languages* in which the articulation takes place. It should be emphasized that these concepts were not applied a priori but developed as grounded categories through the data analysis (Strauss 1987). They became key elements in the conceptual framework which came from the study (Miles and Huberman 1984). Only subsequently were they linked to related ideas from the professional literature which are presented here. I have chosen to present each of the concepts in reverse order, starting with its theoretical antecedents and moving to its definition and role within the study. I then show the concepts as they interact in the context of two illustrations from the study. The intent of this analysis is to provide insight into the means through which teachers construct new understandings of their teaching: how language works as they rename, and start to reconstruct, their experience in the classroom.

Conceptions of practice

The idea of a conception of practice in this study has antecedents in several areas of qualitative research. In education, the concept is found in the teacher socialization and the teacher cognition literatures, which share a concern for the actors' – in most instances teachers' – mental orientation toward their actions. The teacher socialization literature has examined how individual teachers are shaped by the institutions with which they have contact (Crow 1986; Etheridge 1988; Levine 1990; Ross 1987). Similarly, there is a major strand of the literature on teacher cognition which deals with teachers' views of practice, often labeled as their personal knowledge [see Clandinin and Connelly (1987) for a review].

As in these two literatures, the theoretical antecedents of a conception of teaching practice lie in the classic study of medical education by Becker et al. (1961), *The Boys in White,* which examined how medical students developed their perspectives on medical practice. Becker et al. (1961) defined the term *perspective* as "a coordinated set of ideas and actions [which] a person uses in dealing with some problematic situations. ... It is a person's ordinary way of thinking and feeling about and acting in such a situation" (p. 34). They referred to earlier work

224

by Shibutani (1955), who defined perspective as "an ordered view of one's world, what is taken for granted about . . . objects, events, and human nature" (p. 564). In the work of these researchers, the idea of perspective is used as a bridge between the person's internal "sense-making" and his or her actions in the world.

Becker et al. (1961) and Shibutani (1955), however, differ on the function of such perspectives. For Becker et al., they are triggered by "problematic situations": times when the individual is not constrained by the environment or habitual patterns to act in a particular way. For Shibutani (1955), on the other hand, the individual's perspective is constant and intrinsic:

It is an order of things remembered and expected as well as things actually perceived, an organized conception of what is plausible and what is possible; . . . The fact that men [sic] have such ordered perspectives enables them to conceive of their ever-changing world as relatively stable, orderly, and predictable. (p. 34)

Thus Becker et al. focused on the perspective as forged out of a situation that required the individual to take new or out-of-the-ordinary courses of action, whereas Shibutani saw it as an ongoing construct that guides the individual's actions.

The grounded category of conception of practice in this study echoes both views. Like Shibutani (1955), the teachers were found to have ways of thinking about what they do that are "organized conception(s) of what is plausible and what is possible" (p. 34), whether or not those ways are articulated or indeed seem coherent to observers. Like Becker et al., these ways of thinking were affected when the teachers entered new situations. Thus, in this study, the teachers organized what they knew to map out what was possible through their conceptions of practice; the conceptions also guided them in the face of new or problematic situations in their classrooms. In this sense, the findings revealed in a textured way the intersection of teacher socialization and the development of an individual teacher's knowledge.

Tensions

It is difficult, however, to uncover the teachers' conceptions of practice and to document them. In this study, much of what was routine in the teachers' thinking before they entered the teacher education program surfaced in tensions in their practice. These tensions are divergences among different forces or elements in the teacher's understanding of the school context, the subject matter, or the students. They are expressed as discomforts or confusions which interfere with the teacher's translating intention into action in the classroom.

Donald Freeman

This finding is not new. Other researchers have represented teachers' thinking in terms of the conflicts within their experience. Berlak and Berlak (1981) described sets of social and institutional dilemmas that are embedded in teachers' classroom actions; Lyons (1990), Lampert (1985), and Wagner (1987) narrowed the focus to the individual teacher. Lyons examined moral dilemmas embedded in instruction. For Lampert, a dilemma represents "an argument between opposing tendencies within oneself [as teacher] in which neither side can come out the winner" (1985: 110); for Wagner, knots come from the emotional and intellectual imperatives on which teachers believe they should act in their teaching.

In this study however, the teachers did not experience – nor did they express – tensions in their practice as oppositions; rather, these tensions were simply competing demands within their teaching. In one case, before entering the in-service program, Amy (a pseudonym), who was then a first-year Spanish teacher, talked about the content of her lessons. In explaining the tension she saw between Spanish as it is taught as content and as it is used in the world outside the classroom, she said:

Everything I liked and learned [about Spanish] was outside the classroom, and [I'm] trying to bring that into the classroom. It's not in the book, and it's tough to heighten students' awareness of the outside world and get them as excited about it as I was living it, but through the classroom.

This notion of tensions in the teacher's conception of practice helps to reframe the "improvement of practice problem" (Kennedy 1990). To develop their classroom practice, teachers need to recognize and redefine these tensions. In this process of renaming what they know through their experience, the teachers critically reflect on – and thus begin to renegotiate – their ideas about teaching and learning. The question remains, however: How does taking part in the teacher education program help them to do so? How does such participation enable them to reconstruct their conceptions of practice?

Articulation

In its dictionary definition, *articulation* refers to something being "made clear, distinct, and precise in relation to other parts [and] having parts or distinct areas organized into a coherent or meaningful whole, unified" (*Random House Dictionary*, 1982). As it emerged in the analysis of this study, articulation refers to clarifying tensions in the teacher's conception of practice that had previously been indistinguishable or had no clear connection to one another.

The concept of articulation describes the process through which the teachers gain access to their thinking about their classroom practice. It

226

must be emphasized that this finding does not imply that the teachers were somehow tongue-tied or inarticulate prior to their professional training. Rather, they lacked access to a unified means of conceptualizing their teaching, which was provided as they were introduced to, and started to use, the professional language of the teacher education program. Thus they developed two ways of talking about their teaching: the local language of their previous experience and the professional language of their training.

Local and professional languages

The fourth concept to come out of the study has theoretical antecedents in many areas of education (Lemke 1986), social theory (Foucault 1980; Habermas, 1972), and linguistics (Bakhtin 1981; Vygotsky 1962, 1987; Wertsch 1985) which have examined the complex interrelation of language, social definition, and power. Gee, in his work on the development of literacy (1989, 1990), introduces the concept of Discourses[1] which distills these discussions in a useful way. I start from his definition because it provides a framework for organizing many of the findings about local and professional languages from this study.

Gee (1989: 67) defines Discourses as "ways of being in the world, . . . forms of life which integrate words, acts, values, beliefs, attitudes, and social identities." Thus each Discourse is "a sort of 'identity kit' which comes complete with [ways] to act, talk, and often write, so as to take on a particular social role that others will recognize" (1990: 142). Gee argues that "each social institution commands and demands one or more Discourses and we acquire these fluently to the extent that we are given access to these institutions and are allowed apprenticeships within them" (1989: 8).

The concept of local and professional languages which emerged from this study echoes Gee's definitions of Discourse. *Local language* is the vehicle through which teachers explain what goes on in their teaching on a daily basis; it is the means of expressing – to themselves and to colleagues – the conceptions of practice which they bring to teaching as well as those into which they are socialized on the job. It provides the source of explanation for their teaching. Local language springs primarily from two sources. The first is the teachers' own experiences as students, their "apprenticeship of observation" (Lortie 1975); the second reflects the normative ways of talking and thinking about teaching and learning in their particular school environments (Rosenholtz 1989).

1 Gee capitalizes this Discourse to distinguish it from " 'discourse' with a little 'd' [which means] connected stretches of language that make sense." (1989: 6)

These two often overlapping sources of local language provide static and limited explanations of classroom practice.

The local language, which is the teachers' primary "identity kit" in Gee's terms (1990: 142), expresses their tacitly held, unanalyzed conceptions of practice. Because it is often not addressed directly in teacher education, the teachers' local language can create a barrier to reconceptualizing their teaching and to changing their classroom practices (see Roth 1987). In this study, local language voices the teachers' explanations of teaching prior to entering the in-service program. Upon matriculation, however, the teachers encounter the program's ways of conceiving of teaching and learning, which are expressed in its *professional language*. This language is itself a Discourse, built upon a set of socially constructed facts (Fleck 1935/1979) and procedures (Swales 1990: 24–27), out of which a different identity can be fashioned (see Freeman and Cazden 1991).

Articulation comes when the teachers combine the new professional language of the teacher education program with their local language explanations to reflect on and critique their practice. In a student paper written during the first summer, Amy showed the collision between three explanations for what happened when she began the year teaching a class entirely in Spanish. She voiced the first two explanations, (A) and (B), in her *local language*, and then critiqued them using the *professional language*, (C).

I began my first year of classes last year speaking [only] in Spanish. ᴬ"**This is a Spanish class und ve vill speak in Spanish! Von't dis be fun?**" Although not intentional, I scared four students out of the higher level course (seniors who didn't want a tough year). The only comment I got from my advisor (mentor) was ᴮ"**Good, you didn't want them anyway. They wouldn't have been there to work.**" Now I see it differently. ᶜ"**I want to create an environment where they will learn, but not by fear.**" I subsequently had an enjoyable year with the remaining students who decided to stick with it. Unfortunately though, I think my fear overtook my need to feel in control on that first day.

The first local language voice, (A), which echoes the stereotypical authoritarian Prussian from television comedy shows, appears to parody her own "apprenticeship of observation" as a student learning Spanish in school. The second voice, (B), in the local language of her school context, reports an explanation given by her mentor, a fellow teacher in her school assigned to work with her as part of the state certification process. The third voice, (C), which begins with "Now I see it differently," critiques the first two to offer a more complicated explanation. In this professional language, Amy weaves together issues of her fear as a first-year teacher, her need to be in control, and her intention to create a hospitable classroom environment. In the local language explanations, students are portrayed as an obstacle in instruction, (A) and (B). However, the professional-language critique, (C), reframes that view and provides an important step as Amy renegotiates her view of students.

Two illustrations of the concepts

As findings from the study, these four concepts were not a priori categories but developed through grounded data analysis. Together they provide a framework for what happens as teachers reconstruct their understanding of teaching. Two illustrations drawn from the study offer insight into the interaction of the concepts in the lives of these teachers. Although the concepts were derived from a grounded, cross-case analysis of the data from the four teachers in the study, they are more clearly seen within the coherence of individual cases. I have chosen illustrations which show a microanalysis of the renaming/reconstructing process. While these illustrations forecast change in teaching behavior, they focus on the reconstructing of ways of thinking about teaching.

Articulation in local and professional languages

CINDY DEFINES "COMFORT ZONE"

The first illustration shows the process of articulation by which an idea from local language is gradually transformed into the professional language of the teacher education program. Cindy is a high school Spanish teacher who entered the MAT program with five years of classroom experience. During her first summer of coursework, she began to articulate her thinking about the role which affective issues of classroom climate play in language learning. She first referred to these issues with a term drawn from her own local language, as developing a "comfort zone" in the class. Over a period of weeks, however, she constructed a new understanding of the idea using the professional language of the teacher education program. Through this process of articulation, her tacitly held ideas about teaching were given voice within the professional community of the in-service program.

In an interview during the first weeks of the program (See Table 1, phase 2), Cindy referred to her experience in the core course on second language teaching methodology that had helped her clarify her thinking about the "comfort zone". Designed to help participants "develop a personal approach to language teaching" (MAT Program 1989), the course examined five methodologies through an iterative series of experiences which began with being a language learner taught in the methodology, followed by discussion, peer teaching in the methodology, further discussion and analysis, and culminated in a brief first-person paper about what was significant in the methodology.

Through the study of different methodologies in successive cycles of the course, Cindy articulated her feeling about the role of what she called "comfort" in learning. She used the terms of the professional language to express, with increasing coherence and conviction, this aspect of her experience as a learner and its meaning for her as a teacher. In the following passage, her description of constructing the concept and an analysis of that process are laid out side by side.

Up until now, ^A*I keep talking about this strange thing called 'the comfort zone.' I didn't know what it was.* ^B*It was just a feeling that I was looking for. . . . I kept searching for something.*	Cindy starts with a feeling (B) that she explains in her own terms (A).

Up until now, ^A*I keep talking about this strange thing called 'the comfort zone.' I didn't know what it was.* ^B*It was just a feeling that I was looking for. . . . I kept searching for something.*

Cindy starts with a feeling (**B**) that she explains in her own terms (**A**).

^C*As we went through (two methodologies), I kept feeling more and more of it, but I just couldn't get a grasp . . . (on it). Papers would come back with a "Well, define it," and I couldn't. (Last night) I realized that the* ^D*security and* ^E*comfort for me as a student would mean the technique would allow for* ^F*student initiative.*

Over a period of two weeks (**C**), she begins to articulate the feeling (**B**) into a statement. She uses a concept from the summer Discourse (**D**), which she links to her own word (**E**), and defines with another term from the professional language (**F**), which comes from reading (Stevick 1980: 19ff).

For me, ^G*student initiative creates security if it's given slowly. I realized that's what I was talking about:* ^H*I was looking for 'initiative' and didn't know the word (for it).*

She concludes with a full statement in the new professional language (**G**), and then acknowledges the role of this language in enabling her to articulate the idea (**H**).

In a weekly paper written for the same course, Cindy referred to the same process of articulating her idea of comfort in the shared language of the program. Here she is more explicit in her use of the new professional language, rendered in bold type, to articulate her thinking about this aspect of her teaching.

As I move through each of these second language teaching techniques presented in Approaches class, I find my quest for a **comfort zone** becoming more well-defined. Looking back on the three – ALM, Silent Way, and Natural Approach[2] – I discover that **student initiative affects security**. In other words, I believe that the more likely an approach is to gradually develop **initiative,** the more inclined a student is to **become comfortable** with the second language learning. . . . The teacher through **careful control (class structure of time, objectives, techniques)** builds an atmosphere where students' individual learning needs may be realized. **"Careful control"** implies that the teacher is aware/sensitive to the moments when **initiative** is best utilized and by which students.

Cindy seems to recognize this process of articulation while it is happening, as she moves her ideas from their tacit form into the professional language shared by her peers in the in-service program. It is important to note that as she voices her ideas, she is developing and changing them. Articulation is not simply a matter of translating previously held feelings into a new professional language. It involves what McDonald (1992) calls creating texts out of teaching practice; existing explanations of classroom teaching are transformed as one learns to express them in terms which are shared by colleagues or, in this case, by the teacher education program.

Conception of practice: Amy rethinks a reading lesson

The second example is drawn from data from the second summer of the teacher education program, when participants have completed two thirds of their studies (see Table 1, phase 4); the first summer, from which Cindy's example is taken; and the interim year, during which they have returned to teach at their home schools and have corresponded with and been observed by a faculty member from the program. In the following passages, Amy, a first-year Spanish teacher, begins to rethink her teaching and her view of her students. The passages reveal the two dimensions of Amy's conception of practice. Something "problematic" in the teacher's conception, in this case from the previous school year, is articulated in a new way; this leads in turn to a shift in the conception itself.

THE PROBLEMATIC: "HOW COULD WE HAVE KNOWN THAT?" THE STUDENT DEMANDED.

During the second summer of her in-service coursework, Amy took a course on teaching second language reading and writing. In a paper for the course, she revisited an incident in a fourth-year Spanish class. Her

---

2   Three second language teaching methodologies studied in the course; see Larsen-Freeman (1986) and Richards and Rogers (1986).

description shows the process of renaming a previous experience which enables her to construct a different understanding of it: What she had seen as an issue of control and management came to provide her with insight into a student's learning.

I had a student who provided very informative feedback as I was explaining the background around some of the more difficult Spanish [in a reading text]: "How could we have known that?" [the student demanded]. I responded, "You couldn't have. But I didn't expect you to." To which she replied, "I didn't know I wasn't supposed to know that." In other words, her **schema for that reading level** didn't exist. She didn't know enough about the vocabulary, the form of writing, or the dialects of Spanish to distinguish the language as unique. Apart from that, she had been **reading at a Stage 1 level** with the text. She was **decoding words** so intensely that she had **missed all the meaning.** This **bottom-up approach** is characterized in the saying "she couldn't see the forest for the trees."

In using the technical language about reading – in bold type above – that she encountered in the course, Amy constructed a new explanation of her interaction with the student. Although she had previously thought of the incident as a breakdown in classroom discipline, she now wrote about it as illustrating the complexity of reading and what a student brings to the process.

In the same paper, Amy was also explicit about the process of articulation. She explained how the new professional language had helped her to define and express what had been shadowy feelings about her lessons:

I think now having ᴬthese stages will help me ᴮto visualize a more hierarchical progression. . . . As I read Chall's description of the stages (of reading) ᴮI see the logic whereas ᶜbefore I just had the feeling that something wasn't right. I didn't know how to back up or whether discipline would bring them [students] around. ᴰNow I can see that not being able to read doesn't mean they're not trying. It tells me I have to find what level they're reading at and work in that stage to develop the skills needed to move into the next stage.

Amy referred to Chall's (1983) stages of reading development, (A), which she had read in the course, as the new conceptual language out of which she was constructing a new understanding of reading. She described the process of articulation in visual terms: *"I see the logic"* (B') or "visualize" (B) what had been an intuition (C) about what was happening in the lesson. In a sense the new view of the reading process, and the language in which it is expressed, allowed Amy literally to see her feelings, and thus to begin to explain them to herself as she explains them to others (D).

THE ONGOING: "READ THE STORY AND
ASK COMPREHENSION QUESTIONS."

Working with a problem, as Amy had done in the preceding passages,
is important to change and development; however, understanding and
articulating the ongoing dimension of one's conception of practice is
equally critical in learning to teach. This dimension is similar to what
Shibutani (1955) called the individual's "organized conception of what
is plausible and what is possible" (p. 564).

The following passage shows this ongoing dimension of Amy's conception of classroom practice. In articulating her thinking about reading
and writing in a new conceptual vocabulary, Amy found that her understanding of teaching had changed. Using local language which echoed the abbreviated notes of a lesson plan, she talked about her previous
conception of practice as a linear one: "*My teaching style had been to
read the story and ask comprehension questions.*" In her usual reading
lessons, she wrote in a paper for the course:

I used to just work with unknown vocabulary as a pre-reading skill then give
reading assignments. I would then discuss anything the students didn't
understand. I knew this was ineffective but now I have a better idea why.
There had never been much time to interact with the text nor did I provide a
better purpose in my lesson objective other than to read.

In this conception of teaching, the content of the lessons was the new
vocabulary; the students were responsible for understanding the words
and through them, the text itself.

The local language is strong here. Amy used a number of voices
(Bakhtin 1981) – from the teacher's guide for the textbook to the instructions she had heard as a student and given as a teacher in such
lessons – to narrate this routine conception of teaching reading:

*Study a lot of vocabulary. Have the students go home and read the first part
[of the text]. Come back and talk in English about what they understood –
which is usually nothing or very little. Try to piece those pieces together in
English and then say, "OK, read along with me and stop me anytime you
don't understand," or "Let's try answering these questions. . . ." "OK, read
silently again." "Now, let's try to answer these questions. . . ." "a little bit
better?" "OK, read Part Two for tonight," and so on . . .*

Against this local language conception of practice, the language of the
teacher education program provided Amy with a means of reflection
and critique. As she expressed her emerging thinking in the new discourse, she articulated her conception of teaching. Amy now wrote
about the content of reading lessons as *skill building*, in contrast to the

233

local language view she expressed earlier, that reading is putting words together, through translation, into text.

I now believe that ^Astudents should be made aware of having **decoding skills, top-down and bottom-up strategies, skimming and scanning skills,** etc. so they can transfer them to other readings. . . . I'd like my students to see reading as an active process. If not, the written page will look like a pile of mere words which are meant to be decoded. Reading assignments would simply be completed for the sake of completion. I am sensing that ^Bit is the teacher who inspires a purpose and a sense of meaning to most reading until a student is trained to do so on his own.

In this new view of content in reading, Amy interwove two themes: that of student ability (A), and that of teacher responsibility (B). Together these themes created a more complex view of learning to read in a second language than the previous view of *"read the story and ask comprehension questions."*

The newly articulated view showed a central tension in Amy's emerging conception of practice, one she had grappled with throughout the past two years of teaching. When reading – and by extension teaching generally – was viewed as assembling the meaning of the text through vocabulary, the students' lack of knowledge became the teacher's strength and, by extension, the content of her lessons. When reading and teaching were viewed as "skill-building" however, the aim changed. The teacher's role was no longer to measure difference in their respective levels of knowledge, but rather to replicate her own skills as a reader, or language use generally, in her students. Of her new conception of teaching reading, Amy wrote:

I feel I truly know something when I can articulate it enough to teach it to someone else. Prior to this course, I wouldn't have been able to explain how I read, I only knew that I did. Now I feel empowered to improve my own skills as well as to open the door for my students to learn to read with greater feeling. There has been so much pleasure in my reading yet I have not known how to share the feeling with my students.

Amy sensed the tensions that this new way of acting as a teacher might bring in practice. She seemed aware that articulating a new conception of practice in words was one step in the process of change; articulating that same conception in action followed. She knew she would face conflicts with the demands of the school's curriculum and normative ways of teaching and learning. She said:

I've never taught reading and writing; I assigned reading and writing. Now if I want to teach [it] I just feel like I might get into some old patterns. . . . Wanting them to just produce – 'Go ahead read. . . . What'd you get out of it?' Quickening the pace too much.

Amy distinguished her emerging conception, which she called teaching, from her intuitive notion, which she expressed in local language as *"read the story and ask comprehension questions."* To assign reading and writing was a custodial process that focused on the issues of classroom control and management. To teach reading was to be responsive to learners; to do so, she believed she must use knowledge of her own processes as a reader and writer to guide her work with students.

Teacher education: Renaming experience/reconstructing practice

Two important questions are raised by the concepts presented from this study. The first question, which has implications primarily for research, has to do with the nature of teachers' conceptions of practice. The second question, which has implications for practice in teacher education as well, has to do with the durability of the changes which the articulation of teachers' conceptions in professional language seems to bring about. Together, these questions help to reframe what Kennedy (1990: 3) called the "improvement of practice problem" in teacher education: What in practice are we improving through teacher education, and how do we achieve those improvements in a lasting way?

Issues for research

In examining teachers' conceptions of practice from a research standpoint, it is important to consider whether they exist a priori, but on a tacit level, or whether they are created through the experiences of teacher education. Certainly the concept of local language as the original and primary expression of the teachers' thinking suggests that elements of the conception are present all along and that they find their way into expression in the new professional language, as with Cindy's idea of the "comfort zone." Another alternative is that the conceptions are formed directly through participation in the teacher education program, as with Amy's analysis of the reading lesson.

This study suggests that both processes are taking place simultaneously and interactively. Voiced in local language, the teachers' explanations that derive from their experiences as students and from working in their school environments become apparent to them only when they are contrasted with the new professional language of the in-service program. This professional language provides a different Discourse, in Gee's (1989) sense of the term. It provides an alternative "identity kit" that allows the teachers to recognize what they think, while reorganizing and critiquing it. So in this critical relation of local and professional language explanations as Discourses, the teachers' tacitly held explanations are both articulated and may be recast. Thus their conceptions of practice, or "identity kits" as teachers, are expanded and changed.

Cindy talked explicitly about the role of the new Discourse in the development of her thinking about teaching. In her final interview at the end of the two-summer in-service program, she referred to the professional Discourse as "jargon," although not in a pejorative sense:

At least if there's a word associated to what I'm thinking about. ᴬIt makes me feel good because I know it means I'm not the only one. It's not a unique situation; I'm not the only one experiencing it. It does exist. Other teachers are having the same problems with the same thing that's happening in their classroom or to them. ᴮIt helps organize things. . . . It helps with my thinking process.

Cindy's observation brings together the two main functions of participating in a Discourse: the social-referential function of becoming a member of a group, (A) above, and the cognitive function of organizing one's conceptual world according to the values and meanings of that group, (B), (see Freeman and Cazden 1991). Cindy points out that the two functions are, in fact, one and the same thing: Using the jargon makes you part of the group that thinks about and acts upon things in a particular way.

Implications for teacher education

The issue of how – and out of what – teachers make their understandings of classroom practice is a critical one if the aim of teacher education programs is not simply to transmit explanations of teaching but to support teachers-in-training in developing their own understandings. The concepts presented here reinforce and extend recent suggestions about the structure of teacher education programs (NCRTL 1992) that will enable teachers-in-training to build a viable sense of their own teaching. The following points present, as a summary, the implications of this study for teacher education.

1. To influence the reconstruction of practice, a teacher education program needs *a unified discourse*, a professional language which is in constant use among members of its community (see Wegener and Yinger 1991; Yinger 1987). On a concrete level, this involves more than speaking the same language; it means operating from a common view of teaching and learning – a shared set of socially constructed facts – which is made explicit in talk and action. Thus the teacher education faculty comes to share, to articulate, and to make

explicit a coherent approach to instruction, in both philosophy and in practice.

2. Instruction in the teacher education program should *demonstrate the professional Discourse in practice.* As Gee (1990) points out, a Discourse is more than a way of using language; it is a way of acting and being. When teachers-in-training are taught as they are expected to teach, they enter into the Discourse of the new professional language in different ways. They should also be encouraged to examine, through critical reflection, how the instruction they are receiving embodies what they are learning about teaching. It is a mistake to think that the value lies in modeling of classroom teaching per se; it allows the teachers-in-training to develop an understanding of the shared Discourse through their direct experience with it.

3. The teacher education program needs to involve the teachers-in-training in *different contexts of teaching.* Some contexts should be sheltered and involve limited risk, such as microteaching or guided practice, while others should be fully embedded in the world of schooling, such as mentored apprenticeships or team teaching (Fosnot 1989; Freeman 1989). It is important to provide for the continuation of the professional Discourse, although not exclusively, in all these settings, so that this Discourse can take hold within the escalating reality of teaching.

Renaming experience/reconstructing practice

NCRTL Director Mary Kennedy (1992: 2) points out in outlining the research agenda for learning teaching: "Teachers, like other learners, interpret new content through their existing understandings and modify and reinterpret new ideas on the basis of what they already know or believe." As teachers learn and change through teacher education programs, the process of articulating their conceptions of practice is not a linear one. It is not simply a technical substitution of terms in which teachers rename what they already know, through local-language explanations of practice, in professional language. The process is instead a dialectical one in which renaming allows for the attachment of new meanings to familiar perceptions so that tacit knowledge interacts with, and is reshaped by, newly explicit understandings from the professional discourse.

Given this interaction, the second question, of the durability of change vested in the teachers' newly articulated conceptions of practice, arises. Talking in a new way about teaching and learning is one thing; conducting one's classroom practice in new ways may or may not be a separate matter. In other words, does renaming experience lead inevitably to reconstructing practice? At the heart of this question is the complex interrelation of language use, thinking, and action. On this relation between cognitive and behavioral change, the study is inconclusive if one adopts only behavioral measures. Specific aspects of the four teachers' practice did change; however, some patterns or routines also endured.

The question of durability can also raise important issues about the nature of change. Here the study makes an interesting contribution. The "second-order perspective" (Marton 1981) of this research provides a window into the process of change in teaching for these four teachers. By viewing thought and activity as interrelated components, the findings offers a view of classroom teaching which highlights the development of teachers' thought as a major component of that practice. Within this view, the notion of change becomes more complicated because it is no longer possible to simply use behavior as the criterion by which to assess it.

When teacher education is conceived as a dialectical process of renaming experience and reconstructing practice, the question of how to achieve durable improvements becomes complex. Teacher education which is oriented toward how teachers understand what they do must enables them to remake the meanings associated with everyday actions – in short, to reconstruct their practice. If a teacher's practice is seen solely as behavior and activity, it is possible to miss the complex basis of understanding on which that activity is based. Likewise, if change in teaching means doing things differently, it overlooks how teachers' understandings may themselves be modified or amended, possibly without external evidence in behavioral change.

All of which leads to teacher education. When they are viewed exclusively as the inculcation of knowledge and skills, the potentially powerful effects of teacher education programs may remain unrecognized and unexamined. It may be that the role of teacher education lies less in influencing teachers' behavior than in enabling them to rename their experience, thus recasting their conceptions and reconstructing their classroom practice.

References

Bakhtin, M. 1981. *The Dialogic Imagination.* Austin, Tex.: University of Texas Press.
Becker, H., B. Geer, E. Hughes, and A. Strauss. 1961. *The Boys in White: Student Culture in Medical School.* Chicago: University of Chicago Press.
Berlak, A., and H. Berlak. 1981. *The Dilemmas of Schooling: Teaching and Social Change.* New York: Methuen.
Chall, J. 1983. *Stages of Reading Development.* New York: McGraw-Hill.

Clandinin, D. J. 1986. *Classroom Practice: Teacher Images in Action.* London: Falmer.

Clandinin, D. J., and M. Connelly. 1987. Teachers' personal knowledge: What counts as "personal" in studies of the personal. *Journal of Curriculum Studies 19:* 487–500.

Clark, C., and P. Peterson. 1986. Teachers' thought processes. In M. Wittrock (ed)., *Handbook of Research on Teaching*, 3rd, ed. New York: Macmillan, pp. 255–297.

Crow, N. 1986. The role of teacher education in teacher socialization: A case study. Paper presented at the meeting of the American Educational Research Association, San Francisco, Calif.

Doyle, W. 1977. Learning the classroom environment: An ecological analysis. *Journal of Teacher Education 28:* 51–55.

Elbaz, F. 1983. *Teacher Thinking: A Study of Practical Knowledge.* New York: Nichols.

Etheridge, C. P. 1988. Socialization on the job: How beginning teachers move from university learnings to school-based practices. Paper presented at the Mid-south Educational Research Association Annual Meeting, Louisville, Ky.

Fieman-Nemser, S., and M. Buchman. 1985. Pitfalls of experience in teacher preparation. *Teachers College Record 87:* 53–67.

Fleck, L. 1935/1979. *The Social Construction of Scientific Thought.* Chicago: University of Chicago Press.

Floden, R., and H. G. Klinzing. 1990. What can research on teacher thinking contribute to teacher preparation: A second opinion. *Educational Researcher 19:* 15–20.

Fosnot, C. 1989. *Enquiring Teachers, Enquiring Learners.* New York: Teachers College Press.

Foucault, M. 1980. *Power/Knowledge: Selected Interviews and Other Writings.* New York: Pantheon.

Freeman, D. 1989. Learning to teach: Four instructional patterns in language teacher education. *Prospect: The Journal of the Adult Migrant Education Program [Australia]* 4: 31–49.

1990. "Thoughtful work": A review of the literature on teacher thinking. Unpublished manuscript. Harvard University, Cambridge, Mass.

1991a. "The same things done differently": A study of the development of four foreign language teachers' conceptions of practice through an inservice teacher education program. Unpublished doctoral dissertation, Harvard University, Cambridge, Mass.

1991b. 'To make the tacit explicit': Teacher education, emerging discourse, and conceptions of teaching. *Teaching and Teacher Education* 7(5/6): 439–454.

Freeman, D., and C. Cazden. 1991. Learning to talk like a professional: Some pragmatics of foreign language teacher training. In L. Bouton and Y. Kachru (eds.), *Pragmatics and Language Learning*, Monograph Series Vol. 2. Champaign-Urbana: University of Illinois, pp. 225–245.

Gee, J. 1989. Literacy, discourse, and linguistics: Introduction. *Journal of Education* 17: 5–17.

1990. *Social Linguistics and Literacies: Ideology in Discourses.* Philadelphia: Falmer.

Gudmundsdottir, S. 1989. Knowledge use among experienced teachers: Four case studies of high school teaching. Unpublished doctoral dissertation, Stanford University, Stanford, Calif.

Habermas, J. 1972. *Knowledge and Human Interests*. London: Heineman.

Kagan, D. 1988. Teaching as clinical problem-solving: A critical examination of the analogy and its implications. *Review of Educational Research 58*: 482–505.

Kennedy, M. 1990. Policy issues in teacher education. East Lansing, Mich.: National Center for Research on Teacher Education.

1992. An agenda for research on teacher learning. East Lansing, Mich.: National Center for Research on Teacher Learning.

Lampert, M. 1985. How do teachers manage to teach? *Harvard Educational Review 55*: 178–194.

1986. Teachers' strategies for understanding and managing classroom dilemmas. In M. Ben-Peretz, R. Bromme, and R. Halkes (eds.), *Advances in Research in Teachers' Thinking*. Lisse, Netherlands: Swets & Zeitlinger, pp. 70–84.

Lampert, M., and C. Clark. 1990. Expert knowledge and expert thinking in teaching: A response to Floden and Klinzing. *Educational Researcher 19*: 21–23.

Larsen-Freeman, D. 1986. *Techniques and Principles of Language Teaching*. New York: Oxford University Press.

Lemke, J. 1986. *Using Language in Classroom*. Victoria, Australia: Deakin University Press.

Levine, S. 1990. *Promoting Adult Growth in Schools*. Boston: Allyn & Bacon.

Lortie. D. 1975. *Schoolteacher: A Sociological Study*. Chicago: University of Chicago Press.

Lyons, N. 1990. Dilemmas of knowing: Ethical and epistemological dimensions of teachers' work and development. *Harvard Educational Review 60*: 159–180.

Marton, F. 1981. Phenomenography: Describing conceptions of the world around us. *Instructional Science 10*: 177–200.

MAT Program. 1989. *Program Handbook*. Brattleboro, Vt.: MAT Program.

McDonald, J. 1992. *Teaching: Making Sense of an Uncertain Craft*. New York: Teachers College Press.

McLaughlin, H. J. 1991. Reconciling care and control: Authority in classroom relationships. *Journal of Teacher Education 42*: 82–195.

Miles, M., and A. M. Huberman. 1984. *Qualitative Data Analysis*. Newbury Park, Calif.: Sage.

National Center for Research on Teacher Education [NCRTE]. 1988. Teacher education and learning to teach: A research agenda. *Journal of Teacher Education 39*: 27–32.

National Center for Research on Teacher Learning [NCRTL]. 1992. *Findings on Learning to Teach*. East Lansing, Mich.: NCRTL.

National Institute of Education [NIE]. 1975. Teaching as clinical information processing. Report of Panel #6. National Conference on Studies in Teaching. Washington, D.C.: NIE.

Pope, M. 1993. Anticipating teacher thinking. In Day, C., J. Calderhead, and P. Denicolo (eds.), *Research on Teacher Thinking: Understanding Professional Development*. London: Falmer.

Richards, J., and T. Rodgers. 1986. *Approaches and Methods in Language Teaching*. New York: Cambridge University Press.

Rosenholtz, S. 1989. *Teachers' Workplace: The Social Organization of Schools*. New York: Longman.

Ross, W. 1987. Processes of perspective development among preservice social studies teachers. Paper presented at the meeting of the American Educational Research Association, Washington, D.C.

Roth, K. 1987. Helping science teachers change: The critical role of teachers' knowledge about science and science learning. Paper presented at the meeting of the American Educational Research Association, Washington, D.C.

Shavelson, R., and P. Stern. 1981. Research on teachers' pedagogical thoughts, judgements, decisions, and behavior. *Review of Educational Research 51*: 455–498.

Shibutani, T. 1955. Reference groups as perspectives. *American Journal of Sociology 60*: 562–569.

Shulman, L. 1986. Paradigms and research programs in the study of teaching. In M. Wittrock (ed.), *Handbook of Research on Teaching*, 3rd ed. New York: Macmillan, pp. 3–36.

Stevick, E. 1980. *Teaching Languages: A Way and Ways*. Rowley, Mass.: Newbury House.

Strauss, A. 1987. *Qualitative Analysis for Social Scientists*. New York: Cambridge University Press.

Swales, J. 1990. *Genre Analysis: English in Academic and Research Settings*. Cambridge: Cambridge University Press.

Vygotsky, L. 1962. *Language and Thought*. Cambridge, Mass.: MIT Press.
    1987. *Mind in Society*. Cambridge, Mass.: Harvard University Press.

Wagner, A. 1987. Knots in teachers' thinking. In J. Calderhead (ed.), *Exploring Teachers' Thinking*. London: Cassell, pp. 161–178.

Wegener, S., and R. Yinger. 1991. Developing a theoretical framework for faculty planning and collaboration. Paper presented at the meeting of the American Educational Research Association, Chicago.

Wertsch, J. 1985. The semiotic mediation of mental life: L. S. Vygotsky and M. M. Bakhtin. In E. Mertz and R. Parmentier (eds.), *Semiotic Mediation: Sociocultural and Psychological Perspectives*. New York: Academic Press, pp. 49–71.

Wilson, S., L. Shulman, and A. Richert. 1987. "150 different ways" of knowing: Representations of knowledge in teaching. In J. Calderhead (ed.), *Exploring Teachers' Thinking*. London: Cassell, pp. 104–124.

Yin, R. 1984. *Case Study Research: Design and Methods*. Newbury Park, Calif.: Sage.

Yinger, R. 1987. Learning the language of practice. *Curriculum Inquiry 17*: 292–318.

11 Learning how to teach in the RSA Cert

Jack C. Richards, Belinda Ho, and Karen Giblin

This chapter describes how five trainee teachers responded to a short introductory teacher training program, the UCLES/RSA Certificate in TEFLA,[1] a widely recognized TESL teacher training program which focuses on practical teaching skills. The study followed a group of five participants enrolled in the Cert course offered by the British Council in Hong Kong. The aim of the study was to examine how the trainees responded to the practice teaching experiences provided in the program, which aspects of teaching they found problematic, and how their ideas and beliefs about teaching developed during the program. Data for the study were based on the trainees' verbal and written accounts of their teaching experiences.

Background

An assumption underlying current approaches to the study of teaching is that teaching is a cognitive as well as a behavioral activity, and that teachers' theories and beliefs about teaching, teachers, and learners guide their practical classroom actions (Carter 1990, 1992; Halkes and Olson 1984; Richards and Nunan 1990). Teacher education is thus concerned with providing opportunities for trainees to develop their knowledge, awareness, beliefs, and skills, and finding ways of establishing connections among these dimensions of teaching through the experience of teaching itself and through reflecting on that experience. In TESOL teacher education, it has been argued that the field needs to

We are grateful to the British Council, Hong Kong, and to Tony O'Brien, Director of the English Language Centre, for supporting this project and allowing us to have access to the training program which formed the basis of the study. We are also indebted to the teachers who participated in the study, and who devoted a considerable amount of their personal time to completing the reflection sheets which provided primary data for the study: Celia Matthews, Diann Gaylord, Jacqueline Faker, Joseph Tashiro, and Susan Walker. Their cooperation, patience, and good humor were much appreciated. The course tutors were Karen Giblin and David Booth. David's support was also greatly appreciated. We would also like to thank Martha Pennington and Donald Freeman for helpful comments on an earlier version of this chapter.

1 University of Cambridge Local Examinations Syndicate/Royal Society of Arts Certificate in Teaching English as a Foreign Language to Adults, henceforth referred to as the Cert course.

move away from an "applied linguistics" orientation toward one which focuses on teaching in its own terms. As Freeman observes (1989: 29):

Although applied linguistics, research in second language acquisition, and methodology all contribute to the knowledge on which language teaching is based, they are not, and must not be confused with, language teaching itself. They are, in fact, ancillary to it, and thus they should not be the primary subject matter of language teacher education.

Elsewhere in the same article Freeman comments (p. 42):

We . . . need a theoretical and practical understanding of how people are taught and learn to teach, how they learn to implement that description of teaching in practice.

It was an interest in these issues that prompted the present study, which sought to clarify what happens when teachers-in-training reflect systematically on their teaching experiences, and how their thinking is shaped by the experience of reflective teaching. The study examined how teachers interpret and adapt information they receive in training and how it becomes part of the belief system and knowledge base which informs their classroom decision making. Pennington (see Chapter 15) points out that teachers-in-training, like any other learners, follow individual paths in the absorption and application of knowledge and, as in other learning, active involvement with the input received is required for it to become intake. How this process occurs was the focus of the study described here, which attempted to find answers to the following questions:

What aspects of teaching do trainees find problematic at different stages in their initial training?
How do they describe and evaluate teaching?
Are there individual differences in how trainees respond to practice teaching?
How does the content of the training program influence their approach to teaching?

The trainees and the course

The five trainees who formed the focus of the study, and who will be referred to as teachers A, B, C, D, and E, formed a cohort who were completing the course and working as a group. They had varied experiences of teaching before entering the program. Teacher A had been trained twenty-five years ago as a primary teacher in her home country, and had taught in both primary and secondary schools. She had had three years' experience as an EFL teacher and some experience with deaf students, but had no formal qualification in TEFL. Teacher B was a certified elementary teacher with a degree in counseling, who had had a variety of teaching experiences at the elementary and secondary levels. She had also had limited experience as a part-time EFL teacher. Teacher C had held a variety of jobs in business and had tutored private students in English. At the time of the study she was a sports teacher. Teacher D was a business woman with no previous teaching experience, but she had completed a thirty-hour introductory course in TEFL offered by the British Council. That course did not include practice teaching. Teacher E was a journalist who had one year's teaching experience at a private language school.

The UCLES/RSA certificate course is described as a pre-service/initial training scheme. It focuses on practical rather than academic or theoretical aspects of teaching and seeks to give trainees a broad perspective of current classroom practice. The approach to teaching which underlies the course could be described as "standard communicative language teaching," as this is interpreted in mainstream British English language teaching. The syllabus areas cover practical awareness of learners, language, and materials; practical ability in classroom management and lesson planning; presentation and practice of new language; developing the skills of reading, listening, speaking, and writing; and study of the nature of language, learner needs, and instructional materials. The teaching practice component of the course involves teaching lower-intermediate and intermediate level students. In a typical class, the lesson is taught by three of the trainees, while the other two complete assigned observation tasks. Following a practice teaching session, the trainees meet with the tutor to discuss the lesson.

Data sources

Two sources of data were used in the study: audio-recorded discussions between the tutors and the trainees and self-reports. Following each teaching practice session, the five trainees met with the course tutor to discuss the session. These sessions were recorded and transcribed, and this constituted the audio data. Throughout the course, the trainees completed self-report forms for each practice teaching session they taught. These took the form of a questionnaire in two parts. Part 1, which was completed after the trainees had completed their lesson plan, contained seven questions about the lesson plan. Part 2, which was completed after each trainee had taught a lesson, contained seven questions relating to both interactive and evaluative decisions concerning the lesson.

Data analysis

In analyzing the data, we attempted to identify concepts and categories which could be used to characterize recurring concerns and issues. To do this, the audio recordings and written reports were carefully examined in order to understand what was discussed, and notes were made of the main points on which the discussions or written descriptions focused. No attempt was made to try to match the data to preexisting concepts; rather, we tried to interpret what the teachers said and wrote in terms of more general concerns. From this analysis the following issues emerged: the trainees' view of their role in the classroom, the discourse the trainees used to describe teaching, the factors trainees considered important in achieving continuity in a lesson, the dimensions of teaching the trainees found problematic, and the trainees' evaluation of their teaching. These issues formed the focus of our analysis. In the remainder of the chapter, concerns and issues that were raised by the teachers in their oral and written accounts of their teaching sessions are discussed.

Results

How did the trainees describe their role as teacher?

A recurring concern in the initial teaching practice sessions was the image of teacher that the trainees presented to the students. This was seen in comments that individual trainees made about how they felt about their "performance" as teacher, and in comments from the observers on how the role of "teacher" was expressed. In early sessions, for example, observers commented on whether the trainee looked like a teacher, looked in control, communicated effectively, had good voice projection, could get students' attention, and looked confident and relaxed. For example, commenting on C's first practice teaching session, observers remarked:

She was confident and in great control. . . .
She just stood up and looked like a teacher.
She was relaxed.
She knew what she wanted to do and what was expected of the students.

After B's second practice teaching, observers commented:

The students liked her. She looks comfortable and as if she's enjoying it.
She has good voice projection.
Her instructions are good. Very clear.
She looks more confident than us. . . .

245

Jack C. Richards, Belinda Ho, and Karen Giblin

In the initial postteaching discussion of the earlier practice teaching sessions, the image the trainees communicated was a recurring concern.

As the course proceeded, the trainees commented on their improvement in areas such as classroom management, confidence, their ability to maintain students' interest and attention, and to give instructions.

C is very good at getting classroom control. The students know she is the teacher. She gives good directions.

C comes across as confident. Things are clear . . . You take time. You don't rush.

In my section, . . . I felt more in control today.

As they gained experience in teaching and could focus less on acting like a teacher and more on teaching itself, the trainees had to face the question of what teaching meant to them. Having developed a certain degree of confidence in working with the elementary level class, much of what they learned had to be relearned when they began working with the intermediate level class. Were they really teaching? What is the role of a teacher? These issues were the focus of a discussion which occurred early in their work with the intermediate class.

C: With all these games and props and things we use in the classroom, you feel like you're not really teaching but just having a good laugh.
B: It's because we're trying to get so much from them. . . . We need to find a balance between getting and giving and I'm very insecure about that.
A: I've been a teacher before but I feel that now I'm not teaching.
C: It depends on what you mean by teaching.
D: Now you're more of a guide.
E: You wonder why you don't just write [the things you want them to learn] on the board instead of trying to elicit it from them.
B: It's the teacher as facilitator.
E: I see the point of that with beginners, but not with intermediate students.

At this stage the tutor helps out and reassures them that they *are* teaching.

Tutor: It comes back to your perceptions of your role as the teacher. These students know things about language, but don't have much idea of appropriacy. They can talk about language but it's difficult for them to extend beyond that. . . . So your role is to give them confidence in using the language. It's different from a school teacher's role. Getting the balance is difficult and causes stress. But A *did* do some "teaching." When she presented "you'd better," she pulled out the "d" and pointed out it was "had," and not "would." So the teacher has to clarify meaning.

Gradually, the trainees became more comfortable with their role as a teacher and their attention turned to other aspects of teaching.

What discourse did the trainees use to describe teaching?

An important dimension of learning to teach is acquiring the discourse of teaching. Freeman and Cazden (1991: 244; see also Freeman, Chapter 10) point out that this professional discourse serves two important purposes:

One is a social/referential function which allows the teachers to make themselves part of the discourse community as they use it. The other is a cognitive function, which enables them to identify aspects of their experience and thus to organize and to develop their conceptions of teaching.

We saw two dimensions to this issue in the trainees' discussions of teaching: learning how to talk about teaching, and learning to talk like an EFL teacher.

LEARNING TO TALK ABOUT TEACHING

Learning to talk about teaching involves acquiring the terms used by EFL teachers to talk about teaching. The Cert course introduced students to a particular discourse for talking about teaching. Key terms in this kind of discourse are the following: *accuracy, concept, checking, drilling, eliciting, feedback, fluency, intonation, modeling, monitoring, orchestration, practice, presentation, production, sequencing, stress, structure, skills, syllable,* and *target language.* Terms like these belong to the metalanguage of the UCLES/RSA Cert approach to teaching and would most likely not be known to non-language teaching specialists.

Much of this terminology quickly passed into the trainees' vocabulary, and by their second or third teaching practice, much of their discussions of their own and their colleagues' teaching was shaped by this vocabulary (in italic below).

C's section was well organized. Good *sequencing* leading into the *drilling.*

B's *drilling* is very *concise.* The students know what to do.

I thought my *drilling* was still off. But it was better *orchestrated.* I liked my *elicitation* of the context for a story in the beginning. They didn't get the *responses* to the tape as quickly as I expected.

I was pleased with my lesson. For the *drilling,* the students produced the target language well. It was not difficult to *elicit* it from them. They had got the *structures* and understood them at the end of the *drill.*

247

By the end of the course the trainees had completely internalized the discourse and metalanguage of the course and were able to talk spontaneously and thoughtfully about their own and others' lessons, to compare and contrast performances, and to discuss causes and effects of teaching behavior using the appropriate technical terminology. At the same time, it can be seen that the metalanguage became a kind of filter directing the trainees' attention to aspects of teaching that can be described in these terms. Had the course been built around a different teaching approach, such as the "Natural Approach," or the "Silent Way," the teachers would have acquired a different metalanguage and a different set of focal points with which to discuss lessons.

DEVELOPING A DEEPER KNOWLEDGE OF THE SUBJECT

An issue which was of concern to each of the trainees was their limited understanding of English as the subject matter they were teaching. They all lacked any background in linguistics or English grammar and hence felt insecure about dealing with questions students might ask during the lesson. These concerns focused primarily on their understanding of the grammar of English, as the following comments illustrate.

The lesson went all right but one thing threw me. What's an infinitive? I guess it's the stem form of verbs, but I didn't know what to say.

It really threw me when a student asked me to explain what an auxiliary verb was!

I liked the way you talked about "infinitives" and "present tense" because I'm always afraid to name anything. It was really brave.

After a later lesson, the tutor offered a strategy for dealing with the problem of the teachers' knowledge base.

Tutor: A student said, "was blow." What's the problem?
D: Should be "was blown."
Tutor: What do we call that?
Trainees: (silence)
Tutor: It's the past participle. So if you don't know how to describe it, just give them the correct answer.

Developing a sense of what it means to be a teacher of English, that is, knowing something about the structure of English and being able to communicate this to students, was an important concern for each of the trainees.

What factors did the trainees consider most important in achieving continuity throughout a lesson?

A central focus of the course was being able to present an effective lesson according to the model of teaching which the students were trying to master, a modified version of communicative language teaching which also reflected the principles of situational language teaching (Richards and Rodgers 1986). A successful lesson moves through the stages of *presentation, practice,* and *production,* and has a sense of direction, movement, and dynamism. How this could be achieved was a focus of the course and a recurring concern of the trainees. While all of the trainees recognized the importance of coherence and development in dividing the lesson into the three stages of presentation, practice, and production, the major concerns of each teacher were different.

Teacher A, for example, was able to visualize relationships among the different sections of a lesson from the very beginning, and maintained a concern with continuity throughout the course. Perhaps this reflected her experience as a primary teacher. She also identified the need to arouse students' interest and participation as important features of a lesson. Teacher B felt that lessons should be well-structured, and that timing was essential in achieving this. In making timing decisions, she considered the responses anticipated from the students, the relative importance or difficulty of sections within the lesson, and the amount of material she had to cover. Experience with running short of time led her to take account of this possibility in subsequent lessons and to plan extra material for use if needed. In planning lessons, B kept timing in mind throughout the course, and developed more complex ways of dealing with timing as the course progressed. Teacher C's major concern was with the effectiveness of her portion of the lesson. As the course proceeded, she began to focus more on student concerns in her planning, such as whether she had allowed sufficient time for students to complete a task, whether she had allowed sufficient preparation for an activity, or variety in the choice of activities. Teachers D and E were very concerned with the step-by-step procedures they needed to follow in order to get through their segment of a lesson. They needed a recipe or format to help sequence the lesson. They felt they must make sure students had mastered one stage before moving on to the next. The different concerns of the teachers are shown in Table 1.

What dimensions of teaching did the trainees find problematic?

Since a primary focus of the course was on the use of such basic techniques as eliciting, drilling, concept checking (i.e., checking that students

TABLE 1. FACTORS NEEDED TO ACHIEVE CONTINUITY IN A LESSON

Teacher A	Part-to-whole relationship within the lesson
Teacher B	Good timing of each section of the lesson
Teacher C	Degree to which each section of the lesson prepared the students for what followed
Teacher D	Careful planning and well-thought-out procedures
Teacher E	Careful planning and well-thought-out procedures

understood new teaching points), monitoring (i.e., attending to student performance and giving feedback on errors), and how to use the overhead transparencies (OHT) and the white board, discussion of how to carry out these procedures effectively occupied a substantial portion of time in early group feedback sessions. Comments in early sessions, for example, focused on how to handle specific teaching techniques:

I'm still concerned about how much to elicit and when to give information. Sometimes elicitation didn't work and I wanted to give them [the language I was looking for]. So do you try several ways of eliciting it and then give it to them?

C did quite a lot of monitoring. And she got the correct responses she was looking for from another student, which was good, and she revised nicely.

After a month, the trainees felt that they had made progress in these areas.

Tutor: What basic skills have we dealt with and what can you cope with now? What basic teaching skills have you got now?
Trainees: Timing. We are handling timing much better.
A: Presentation. We know how to present and start off a lesson.
B: Our drilling is quite good.
C: Eliciting is getting quite good.

By the latter part of the course, a more holistic view of teaching was beginning to emerge, one in which the trainees were focusing less on the "mechanics" of the lesson, and more on such dimensions as structuring and cohesion, and student participation in lessons. However, the concerns of each of the five teachers were somewhat different, as shown in Table 2.

Teacher A felt that the final activities in her lessons or lesson segments were often the least effective because she did not manage to plan her timing, leading to a rush toward the end. She was conscious of her difficulties with drilling throughout, but felt some improvement through the course. Teacher B thought the least successful parts of her lessons

TABLE 2. PRIMARY CONCERNS OF EACH TEACHER

Teacher A	Timing; techniques for conducting drills
Teacher B	Timing; presentation phase of lessons; explanations
Teacher C	Eliciting desired level of student participation
Teacher D	Handling of materials, procedures, and techniques
Teacher E	Problems with explanations and clarifying intentions

were those where there was insufficient time to do things thoroughly. She found the presentation stage of lessons to be problematic for her, and commented on the difficulty of getting ideas across and giving instructions. When sections of lessons were judged to be unsuccessful, Teacher C attributed the causes to her own difficulties or inadequacies. For example, if a drill did not go well, it was because she was not concentrating enough. If an activity stopped, it was because she had not set it up properly. Although she was conscious of her role in the lesson, she used student performance and participation as the ultimate measures of how well she taught. Teacher D attributed reasons for unsuccessful lessons or lesson segments to the way the teacher handled materials and procedures. Either she had not prepared well enough, or she was unfamiliar with the basic mechanics of teaching. She saw room for improvement in such things as blackboard use, asking concept questions, drilling, and giving instructions, and these concerns continued throughout the course. Teacher E attributed problems to her own inadequacies in handling specific parts of lessons. If the students did not do well, it was because she had not explained clearly enough or made the activity clear.

The trainees differed in their concerns about the kinds of things that they would do differently next time. These concerns were related to the particular problems they thought were important. The strategies that they used to deal with these problems were also different. As the course proceeded, Teacher A identified specific strategies which would help her deal with problem areas, such as timing and drilling. Her view of how lessons could be improved moved from a focus on changes in procedures (e.g., how to use a tape more effectively during a listening exercise), to a broader view of how a lesson could be improved (e.g., by changing her approach to the segment or improving the link between her segment and other segments in the lesson). Things which Teacher B reported she would do differently related to timing and choice of activities. She described a variety of strategies she would use, including simplifying activities or using less material. This pattern was consistent throughout the course. Teacher C's strategies for improving lessons ranged from specific remedies for specific problems to things that went beyond the problems raised. Her strategy to remedy a problem was often to think of an entirely new way of carrying out an activity rather than fine-tuning a specific part of it, or even to design an entirely new activity. She always had specific solutions to propose, and was very flexible in her approach. Teacher D identified a variety of aspects of her own teaching as things she would handle differently from one lesson to the next, but did not identify particular strategies for making improvements. Her main focus was on improving the way she taught, through more preparation beforehand and better decisions during lessons. She thought preparation was the key to improving her performance as a teacher. The things Teacher E would change had to do with procedural aspects of lessons (e.g., using the OHT – overhead projector) or handling specific kinds of teaching techniques, such as drilling or asking concept questions.

How did the trainees' perspectives on successful lessons differ?

As we examined the audio and written data we had gathered during the study, we sought to identify how the teachers developed a workable theory of teaching from the experiences provided by the program. The individual differences in the way the five teachers planned, monitored, and described their own teaching suggested different ways in which the teachers approached their teaching. These differences are summarized in the following discussion.

A *teacher-centered perspective* sees the key features of a lesson primarily in terms of teacher factors, such as classroom management, teacher explanations, teacher questioning skills, teacher presence, voice quality, manner, and so on. This view of a lesson sees it as a performance by the teacher. A different view of a lesson, which can be termed the *curriculum-centered perspective*, sees a lesson in terms of a segment of instruction. Relevant foci include lesson goals, structuring, transitions, materials, task types, and content flow and development. A third perspective on a lesson can be called the *learner-centered perspective*. This views the lesson in terms of its effect on learners and refers to such factors as student participation, interest, and learning outcomes. These different perspectives on a lesson are summarized in Table 3.

Any lesson can be conceptualized in terms of any or all of these perspectives. In the present study, although the teachers referred to all three aspects of lessons in describing their teaching, Teacher A's focus of awareness was more consistently on teacher factors than other dimensions of her lessons. Teacher B included all three perspectives in her discussions of her lessons and moved easily from one perspective to

TABLE 3. DIFFERENT PERSPECTIVES ON LESSONS

Teacher-centered focus	The teacher is the primary focus, including teacher's role, classroom management skills, questioning skills, presence, voice quality, manner, quality of teacher's explanations and instructions.
Curriculum-centered focus	The lesson as an instructional unit is the primary focus, including lesson goals, opening, structuring, task types, flow, and development and pacing.
Learner-centered focus	The learners are the primary focus, including the extent to which the lesson engaged them, participation patterns, and extent of language use.

another, though the role of the teacher was a recurring focus. For Teacher C, the learner perspective has priority. For Teachers D and E, lessons were discussed more frequently from the teacher's point of view and in terms of the design of the lesson. In discussing each other's teaching in group sessions, these different perspectives often emerged. For example, Teacher B, commenting on one of A's lessons described it from the curriculum perspective:

You did a good job on building it up, starting with revision. You didn't waste any time on setting up the lesson. It flowed through beautifully.

Teacher A herself, however, commented on her lesson from the teacher perspective:

I thought the lesson deteriorated as it got to the end. I wasn't happy with the drilling. I didn't give myself enough time to do it properly.

Teacher C commented on the same lesson from the learner perspective:

I liked the way your lesson went at the end. The students were being expressive. They put feeling into it.

Differences in individual perspectives on the nature of successful lessons characterized the trainees' discussions of all aspects of the lesson, from planning, to presentation, to practice. For example, Teacher A felt that a successful lesson should provide plenty of opportunity for drilling and practice, with clear links between all the activities. Accuracy and thoroughness were also important dimensions of good teaching for her, as well as personalization, interest level, and relevance. All of these dimensions of teaching were seen to be the responsibility of the teacher,

253

and if a lesson failed to achieve them, it was the fault of the teacher. An effective lesson for Teacher B was one which interested the students, helped them to speak naturally and clearly, built confidence, challenged them, and so on, and the teacher's role was to bring these things about. As Teacher B remarked after one of her lessons:

Basically I wasn't happy with the way my lesson went today. My goal has been to shorten things and yet I think the activities went on too long. I didn't accomplish what I wanted. Looking back I could have made it shorter and done things differently, spending more time on getting the students to use the language.

Teacher C expressed the view that good language teaching creates a good context for practice, with plenty of opportunities for student participation and free production. Lessons should be relevant and useful to students, have variety, be interesting and fun, and follow a clear and structured presentation. For her, a lesson was successful to the extent that it engaged the students and generated useful practice of the language. Commenting on one of the teacher's lessons, C described it entirely in terms of its effect on the learners.

They were taught very well today. They got the concept well at the beginning, though it was lost a bit in the activities that followed. Too much was put into the lesson, too many activities. The students spent too much time working out what they were supposed to do in the activities.

And in her comments on another teacher's lesson, C noticed the effect on student performance.

I don't think you were monitoring your teaching very well. I don't think you moved around the class enough to hear what the students were saying. You didn't pick up that they didn't understand what they were supposed to do.

For Teacher D, good language teaching was dependent upon the design of the lesson, which must provide natural and useful language and provide plenty of time for practice. How well the students learned was very much dependent upon what the teacher provided for them, and classroom materials played a key role in this. For Teacher E, the teacher bore the responsibility for achieving a good lesson, not the students. This was done through attention to presentation, choice of materials, sequencing, instructions, and difficulty level. Teacher E tended to comment on her teaching largely in terms of the teacher, as is seen in the following comments:

I liked my performance. I got through the whole thing. I feel I was more animated. But I still need to work on timing and drilling.

Today's class didn't turn out as I expected. I had trouble with the OHT [overhead projector] and it threw me off. I worked hard to give clearer instructions. Also I rushed. I was afraid the students wouldn't finish the task.

The teachers' evaluations of their lessons also reflected these different perspectives on teaching. Teacher A, for example, described the success of her own teaching in terms of how she felt about her performance as a teacher. She felt more comfortable handling the presentation stage of lessons, because with these she was more in control and the lesson was more structured and predictable. She tended to evaluate her teaching in terms of herself as a teacher and how successfully she had brought about her intended goals, rather than on student outcomes. For Teacher B, however, no matter what part of the lesson she was teaching, her major concern was both her performance and the performance of the students. She focused on such things as whether they understood the concepts she presented, or whether they could do what she wanted them to do. Teacher C likewise consistently saw the success of her lessons in terms of student concerns and reactions. Activities were considered successful if students had fun, got useful practice, and understood clearly what was intended. She was pleased with her own performance to the extent that it achieved student-oriented goals. In discussing her stages of the lesson, Teacher D regarded the design of activities as an important criterion for determining whether a lesson was successful or not. She considered it important for the teacher to be confident, well prepared, and relaxed, and for the students to enjoy activities and be involved in them. Teacher E judged the success of her teaching according to how well she adapted the presentation, practice, or production phases of the lesson. For these to succeed, materials must be well designed and presented.

In Table 4 we have tried to depict the differences in the individual teachers' view of successful lessons by listing the three different perspectives according to the priority for each teacher.

So what did the trainees learn?

In trying to arrive at some generalizations from the information we gathered while following the five trainee teachers through the Cert program, a useful starting point is to examine the aims of the program and then to consider the issues which the trainees had to resolve both collectively and individually as they went through the program. The course aims are two types: awareness and practical abilities (i.e., skills). Within the domain of awareness, the course addresses issues relating to learners, language, and materials. Within the domain of skills, specifications are given relating to classroom management and lesson plan-

TABLE 4. PRIORITIES FOR EACH TEACHER ACCORDING TO PRIMARY FOCUS OF CONCERN

Teacher A	1. Teacher	2. Curriculum	3. Learners
Teacher B	1. Teacher and learners	2. Curriculum	
Teacher C	1. Learners	2. Curriculum	3. Teacher
Teacher D	1. Curriculum	2. Teacher	3. Learners
Teacher E	1. Teacher	2. Curriculum	3. Learners

ning, presentation and practice of new language, and developing the skills of reading, listening, speaking, and writing. Each trainee received the same input and had a similar range and number of practice teaching assignments. Each, however, came to the program with different expectations and beliefs about teaching, which might have been either explicit or implicit, based on what has been termed the "apprenticeship of observation." Kennedy (cited in Freeman 1992: 3) observes:

By the time we receive our bachelor's degree, we have observed teachers and participated in their work for up to 3060 days.

By contrast, the Cert program includes only a minimum of six hours' teaching experience. Practice teaching in the Cert thus provides experiences which are interpreted and reconstructed using knowledge, beliefs, and values which are partially given by the program but which presumably go much beyond the program itself. What the trainees learn from the program is not, then, simply a mirror image of the program content. And in the process of learning from the program, each trainee responds in a unique and individual way to the sometimes conflicting inputs in the learning process, those which are internal and personally driven and those which are external or program driven. We see these differences in perspective underlying the decisions teachers made and the ways they planned and evaluated their teaching.

In thinking about dividing the lesson into stages, the course had emphasized that each ninety-minute lesson, though initially taught by three different people, should be a coherent whole. Teacher A, as a trained teacher, had very little difficulty with this concept, and it formed a central theme of her planning decisions. Teacher B likewise had little difficulty with this notion but had to work harder than Teacher A to achieve it and saw her management of time as the key to achieving it. Trying to achieve a unified lesson was a major theme in her thinking, and she trusted her instincts much less than Teacher A. Teacher C tried to see lesson stages from the students' perspective, and felt that provision of sufficient time was a key factor in successful teaching. Teacher

D was concerned with how segments related to each other and how the lesson flowed, as was Teacher E.

The three basic phases of a lesson – presentation, practice, and production – which form the core teaching skills, are the key to a good lesson in the Cert program. The five trainees differed in the extent to which they mastered this framework. Teacher A felt more at home with presentation and practice (i.e., the more teacher-controlled sections). Teacher B found the presentation phase more problematic than the production phase, because of her problems with timing. Teacher C looked forward to the production phase (the student-focused section), where she felt real learning was going on. Teacher D likewise felt least comfortable with the presentation phase, and attributed this to inadequate preparation, unfamiliarity with teaching, and nervousness about teaching in front of others. Teacher E had most difficulties with the presentation phase of the lesson, and felt that this was due to her own inadequacies as a teacher.

The trainees' interactive decisions, as described in their written lesson reports of each practice teaching session, likewise reflected their current stage in understanding themselves as teachers, on the one hand, as well as the fact that they were each learning how to handle new kinds of teaching activities and classroom materials, on the other. Teacher A soon became confident of the kind of interactive decisions she made and saw the need for them in order to maintain the overall focus and direction of the class, i.e., in order to help her teach more effectively. Her decisions were teacher-oriented. Teacher B's decisions were linked to her overall concern for managing timing in the students' favor. Teacher C's interactive decisions were prompted by attention to student needs. Teacher D had to deal with her feelings of insecurity, and her monitoring of her teaching in her written lesson reports reveals a continuing concern that she was not doing things correctly or that the students were not understanding or responding well. Teacher E found it difficult to deal with interactive on-the-spot decisions which were required when things did not go as planned.

In evaluating their lessons and describing what they would do differently next time, some trainees suggested that they would merely fine-tune their lesson procedures, while others suggested more radical changes. Teacher A focused both on improving her timing and on making more substantive changes in her teaching approach. Teacher B focused on timing matters and improving her activities. Teacher C saw improvement as resulting from a complete change in the design or use of activities, and in the adoption of specific strategies to address particular problems. Teacher D saw many areas for improvement in her handling of specific teaching procedures. Teacher E's main concerns were to improve her presentation techniques and her teaching aids.

Conclusions

This study raises a number of issues that arise in any teacher preparation program. First, while a program such as the UCLES/RAS Cert is built around a well-articulated model of teaching, the model is interpreted in different ways by individual trainee teachers as they deconstruct it in the light of their teaching experiences and reconstruct it drawing on their own beliefs and assumptions about themselves, about teachers, about teaching, and about learners. As Colton and Sparks-Langer (1993: 45–46) observe:

In the constructivist view, the learner's direct actions, reactions, and interactions with objects, people, rules, norm and ideas result in the personal construction and reconstruction of knowledge and adaptive abilities. Thus, teachers learn from their experiences by constructing mental representations of their personal meanings which then are stored in memory to be revised as experience dictates.

Second, it is instructive for teacher educators to try to identify the questions each student teacher is asking and is struggling with as he or she completes a training program. Individual teachers ask different kinds of questions and take different routes in arriving at the answers. Identifying these questions by having teachers articulate their beliefs about teaching and describe their practices, through journal writing, self-reports, and other means, can help teacher educators see how the student teacher tries to relate the context and experiences of the program to a personal and workable theory of teaching. Borko et al. (1990) and Ellwein et al. (1990) have pointed out that student teachers hold multidimensional conceptions of teaching and different teachers emphasize different elements of success or failure in accounting for a lesson's outcome. The kinds of activities used in this study, which included the use of a structured reflection questionnaire, peer observation, and group conferencing, allowed the trainees to articulate their individual perceptions and interpretations of their practice. Third, the use of a well-established model of teaching, such as communicative language teaching, as the basis for a teacher preparation program, while serving as a useful starting point in learning how to teach, should be seen as only that. Although each of the five teachers had mastered the principles underlying the Cert program with varying degrees of success at the end of the program, the teachers were beginning to generate their own individual questions about teaching and learning, questions which went beyond the specifics of the method and which might, in time, as they enter real teaching situations, help guide their further understanding of teaching and their own development as teachers.

References

Borko, H., R. Lalik, and E. Tomchin. 1990. Student teachers' understanding of successful and unsuccessful teaching. *Teaching and Teacher Education* 41(5): 3–14.

Carter, K. 1990. Teachers' knowledge and learning to teach. In W. R. Houston (ed.), *Handbook of Research on Teacher Education*. New York: Macmillan.

1992. Towards a cognitive conception of classroom management: A case of teacher comprehension. In J. Shulman (ed.), *Case Methods in Teacher Education*. New York: Teachers College Press, pp. 111–130.

Colton, A., and G. Sparks-Langer. 1993. A conceptual framework to guide the development of teacher reflection and decision making. *Journal of Teacher Education* 44(1): 45–54.

Ellwein, M. C., E. Graue, and R. Comfort. 1990. Talking about instruction: Student teachers' reflection on success and failure in the classroom. *Journal of Teacher Education* 41(5): 3–14.

Freeman, D. 1989. Teacher training, development, and decision-making: A model of teaching and related strategies for language teacher education. *TESOL Quarterly* 23(1): 17–45.

1992. Language teacher education, emerging discourse, and change in classroom practice. In J. Flowerdew, M. Brock, and S. Hsia (eds.), *Perspectives on Second Language Teacher Education*. Hong Kong: City Polytechnic of Hong Kong, pp. 1–21.

Freeman, D., and C. Cazden. 1991. Learning to talk like a professional: Some pragmatics of foreign language teacher training. In L. Bouton and Y. Kachru (eds.), *Pragmatics and Language Learning, Monograph Series; Vol. 2.* Champaign-Urbana: University of Illinois, pp. 225–245.

Halkes, R., and J. Olson. 1984. *Teacher Thinking: A New Perspective on Persisting Problems in Education*. Lisse, Netherlands: Swets and Zeitlinger.

Richards, Jack C., and D. Nunan (eds.). 1990. *Second Language Teacher Education*. New York: Cambridge University Press.

Richards, Jack C., and T. Rodgers. 1986. *Approaches and Methods in Language Teaching*. New York: Cambridge University Press.

12 The role of collaborative dialogue in teacher education

Francis Bailey

> Adult education should have as one of
> its main tasks to invite people to believe
> in themselves. It should invite people to
> believe that they have knowledge.
> Paulo Freire (1973; cited in
> Wallerstein 1983: 11)

Introduction

This chapter reports on an ethnographic study of a methods course for ESL and bilingual teachers. The focus is on the role of collaborative peer dialogue in the learning process of a group of second language teachers. This research builds upon a body of educational research and thought that focuses upon the structure and function of instructional discourses used in classrooms (e.g., lecture, recitation, small group work) (Cazden 1988; Green 1983; Mehan 1979). Insights into teaching and learning can be gained by analyzing the types of communicative events that take place within classrooms. Here, I analyze the discourse of a multicultural group of second language teachers exploring Paulo Freire's problem-posing approach in the second language classroom (Wallerstein 1983). I demonstrate how issues of voice, knowledge, and task combine to play integral roles in the group's learning. By negotiating common understandings, discussing course texts, and drawing upon their own experiences, group members communally create a rich understanding of not only their topic of problem posing, but also the power of task-based, collaborative learning.

Collaborative peer learning is the central organizational feature of this course. It is in these groups – both small and whole class – that much of the course content is introduced, analyzed, questioned, and linked to students' own lives. The positive benefits of cooperative learning in the classroom have been extensively researched and reported in the educational literature (Cohen 1986; Johnson and Johnson 1990; Sharan 1990). However, much less is known about how cooperative learning benefits adult learning.

In this methods course the groups are expected to work collaboratively. A distinction is made between *cooperation* and *collaboration* which is not widely reflected in the research literature. *Cooperation* refers to a group working together on a task in which the members divide the work so that it can be completed individually. *Collaborative learning* is organized around learners working and learning together through face-to-face interaction (Damon and Phelps 1988).[1] In the methods course, members use their groups to explore fundamental ideas of language teaching.

The design

The project was grounded in the qualitative research tradition of ethnography (Goetz and LeCompte 1984; Moerman 1988; Peacock 1986), in which the researcher takes on a participant observer role within the social structure of the research site (Spradley 1980). I was a facilitator for one of the small groups in the methods course, which gave me access to both the whole class discussions as well as intimate knowledge of small group work. A major focus of my research was to better understand the discourse organization of collaborative dialogue and the social contexts which support the full participation of collaborative group members. I view the social structure of the classroom as a kind of "culture" which is created out of the communal interactions among course participants (Allwright 1984; Green et al. 1988). I collected data in field notes from my own observations of the class, interviews with course participants, audio- and videotaping of small group and whole class sessions, and materials written by group members. An important source of written materials was the dialogue journals that each group member wrote with her or his small group facilitator.

I conducted the study in a graduate-level methods and materials class for ESL and bilingual teachers (henceforth, methods class) at the University of Massachusetts in Amherst (Bailey 1993). The class, taught by Professor Jerri Willett, was composed of thirty-three students, with a third of the class international students predominantly from Asian countries. The class was largely female, with only six males. The students came with a diverse set of experiences in teaching and learning second languages, formal education in teaching, and career interests.

The course was organized around a task-based approach to the course content in which over half the topics are presented by students (Candlin 1987). Students were divided into six small groups of four to six students each and given the task of researching a particular topic in

---

1 I would like to thank Diane Sweet for bringing this distinction to my attention in a paper she co-authored at TESOL 1990 (Willett et al. 1990).

second language teaching[2] and then planning and executing a ninety-minute presentation in which they taught their classmates about their group's topic. The small groups met for the first hour of each class in order to discuss ideas and topic readings collaboratively and to plan for their presentations. Each small group was assigned a "facilitator" who supported the group in their efforts to work collaboratively.

The instructor's design focused on two interrelated goals: to create a rich learning environment in which a diverse set of students could communally explore central pedagogical issues in second language teaching within a whole-language perspective (Freeman and Freeman 1992; Goodman et al. 1991); and to create opportunities for students to experience authentic issues in teaching and learning by making students responsible for teaching and learning course content.

A crucial component of this course design was the creation of a class community in which peers could learn both with and from one another. This had not always happened in past years, and the professor was determined to structure a class in which collaboration would play an integral role and particularly to ensure the full participation of international students. In her opening remarks the first night of class, the professor asked students to act as "resources" for one another.

We find in fact that newcomers to the field are great resource people because you aren't jaded. You don't have all the answers and you come up with questions that are important to answer. . . . The whole idea is to begin seeing one another as resources and that's the key to success in the course . . . and so we have heterogeneous groupings as mixed up as possible so that we have lots of resources to draw on in the group and therefore you will have a stronger presentation.

The professor referred to students in the course as "resources" more than ten times during her introduction to the course. She stated that students who had taken courses with her previously were also "resources" based on their knowledge of collaborative learning and, further, that second language speakers are "extremely valuable" to the group because they could tell monolingual English speakers what it was like to learn English as a second language and to learn and teach English in other countries. Small group facilitators were also "resources" because they could provide "feedback on the collaborative process."

The effect of this course design on the small group interactions was evident in this study of the small collaborative group charged with researching and teaching Paulo Freire's problem-posing approach. The study focused on the nature of the collaborative dialogue within the group, and I used the voice framework outlined next to analyze the

2 Course topics included problem posing, simulations, reading and writing, content-based instruction, responding to writing, and literature for the ESL class.

group discourse. I also refer to the course structure, which was designed to support students' efforts to collaborate. Finally, through an analysis of dialogue journals and interviews with group members, these people's experiences with this form of education emerges.

The problem-posing group also provided access to data on the role of the task in group work. It is particularly intriguing the way the act of planning the lesson for their classmates played an integral role in their understanding of the subject matter. Tacking back and forth between their readings on problem posing, their own personal experiences, and planning for their presentation provided space for group members to create their own knowledge of this particular subject matter.

A framework for researching voice

The small collaborative groups were designed to provide a forum for all students to participate in the discussions of course readings on their topic and the planning of their presentations. However, ensuring the full participation of all the members of a diverse group of students was problematic. This study suggests that a key component was the co-construction of the *voice* of individual group members within the small group discourse. Voice is a communal product and cannot be reduced solely to the characteristics or performance of individuals. In order for group members to have a voice in their groups, there had to be a social system which supported their participation. Thus the current organization of the course was directly related to a history of marginalization of both international students and less experienced teachers in earlier versions. Crucially, there had to be a social setting in which members had an opportunity both to speak and to be heard (McDermott 1988). It appears that a discourse sequence for voice must include at a minimum the following three interactionally coordinated moves:

1. Gaining the floor
2. Speaking acceptably
3. Being heard by others

Gaining the floor

The first step in having a voice in a conversation is to gain the floor. While this step may often seem straightforward and unproblematic, researchers have demonstrated that turn-taking systems used in schools require a high degree of social coordination among participants (Mehan 1979; Sacks et al. 1974; Shultz et al. 1982). Further, these systems can be a barrier to student participation, particularly within cross-cultural educational contexts (Au 1980; Cazden 1988; Mohatt and Erickson 1981; Philips 1983; Scollon and Scollon 1981).

The work of Sacks et al. (1974) on the social organization of turn taking focuses the analysis of discourse not only on who gains the floor but also on how it is gained: through self-selection or by having a turn structured by another member. In the research presented in this chapter, I focus on both who talks and how he or she gains the floor.

Speaking acceptably

In order to have a voice in a social setting, the speaker must talk in a way that is both comprehensible and demonstrates that he or she has something worth saying. Differing types of speech events (Hymes 1974) in differing institutional settings constrain what are acceptable forms of speech both by topic and by what constitutes a warrant for voice: for example, personal experience, reason or logic, morals (Gergen 1989; Wertsch 1991). Hence, one of the factors that must be considered when investigating voice are the local criteria for warranting it. Here, I focus on the types of knowledge group members draw on, for instance, personal experience or text knowledge, in constructing collaborative dialogue.

Being heard by others

In order for a person to have a voice, others must be willing and able to hear what that person has to say (McDermott 1988). For a person to feel that his or her participation is valued in a conversation, there must be a system by which participants signal that they are attending to and valuing that person's talk or actions. In this framework, "hearing" is viewed as a social rather than a cognitive phenomenon. I am defining "hearing" as an *intertextual link* between a current speaker's turn of talk and the prior talk of a group member. *Intertextuality* refers to the juxtaposition of two texts, in this case, of two verbal turns (see Bloome and Bailey 1990; de Beaugrande and Dressler 1981). Thus a person is "heard" only if his or her speech is woven into the fabric of the ongoing discourse. "Hearing" can take various forms, such as evaluation (e.g., "That's a very good idea!"), personal reference (e.g., "Martha's idea is great . . ."), meaning negotiation (e.g., "What do you mean by 'code'?"), ideational reference (e.g., "code switching, like Bruno said, is . . . ").

Voice emerges out of the social interactions of participants engaged in an institutionally situated activity. In order for members in the methods course to have a voice in their small groups, they had to gain the floor and speak within the range of topics and warrants appropriate for their task. Furthermore, fellow group members had to signal publicly that they had heard and valued the participation. For educators, this framework provides a means of conceptualizing voice as a social outcome and directs our attention to specific barriers to participation in our own classrooms. The inability of international students to gain the floor or the unwillingness of some students or teachers to value the knowledge of other students are two examples.

Study of problem-posing group

The problem-posing group was particularly successful in creating a presentation through collaborative dialogue in which all group members had a voice. The two Chinese members of this group played a vital role in the group process. The norm introduced by the instructor that peers should be viewed as "resources" was clearly developed within this group's discourse. In other words, their discourse, rather than reflecting this norm, shows its actual creation within one group. Finally, the disturbing themes of loneliness and alienation which emerged from the stories of the two Chinese students provide a point for reflection for all of us who live near – but not with – the "aliens" in our midst.

A group of five students signed up for the task of researching and teaching the topic of problem posing. As the first student group to present, they had only five weeks in which to prepare. The group consisted of five group members: Xiaoli, from mainland China; Li Hwa, from Taiwan; Sarah and Martha, from the United States; and one group member who declined to be part of this research project. The names of the students have been changed to ensure anonymity. The group members worked well together, meeting both the first hour of each class and for several hours outside of class for more extended preparation. They did not choose this topic because they had experience with it. In fact, the two Chinese members of the group chose it as a result of misunderstanding. They thought that the topic would be on the problems of teaching in the ESL classroom.

Problem posing

Problem posing is a pedagogical approach to literacy instruction that was developed in the 1960s by Paulo Freire, a Brazilian educator (Freire 1970, 1973). The approach has been influential in the field of adult literacy and has been adapted for use in adult ESL classes. The course text, *Language and Culture in Conflict*, by Nina Wallerstein, describes Freire's approach this way:

Problem-posing is based on the premise that education starts with issues in people's lives and, through dialogue, encourages students to develop a *critical* view of their lives and the ways to *act* to enhance their self-esteem, and improve their lives. (Wallerstein 1983; original emphasis)

The *problem* in problem posing reflects an interest in education that confronts the societal problems which individuals and groups encounter in every day life, for example, racial discrimination, joblessness, substandard housing, lack of child care. Through dialogue about the problem, students are encouraged to connect their personal problems to greater social conditions. A teacher structures a specialized form of dialogue in which students are encouraged to (1) identify a problem in their personal lives; (2) understand that the problem is not limited to them but is shared by others, including classmates; (3) connect these personal problems to social conditions; and (4) act on these new-found connections by creating a plan in order to solve the problem. A fundamental premise of this approach is that society can be changed through ordinary people's collective analysis and actions, a concept known as *empowerment.*

In problem posing, educators must listen to their students in order to identify a shared problem or theme around which to structure the class lessons. Once a problem has been identified, the teacher creates a physical representation, called a *code*, which combines the group's problem(s) into one representation (Wallerstein 1983). Codes can be drawings, photographs, stories, role plays, movies, songs, and so on. "No matter what the form, a code is a projective device that is emotionally laden and identifiable to students" (Wallerstein 1983: 19).

Within the methods course, the topic of problem posing functions to alert students to the possibilities of learner-centered classes in which the curriculum is drawn directly from the students' own lives. It emphasizes the importance of teachers both structuring classes in which students' experiences can be heard and actively listening to and engaging in dialogue with their students. Over the years, this topic has generated some of the most dynamic and interesting presentations in the course, as students identify problems within their own lives and those of their classmates around which to center the presentation.

Problem-posing group meetings

In the short five weeks available to them, as is typical for the small groups in this course, the group focused much of its energy on planning a presentation. Their first idea was to organize their presentation around two types of ESL classes: a class which used problem-posing and a non-problem-posing class. They planned to develop role plays of students and teachers interacting in each of these settings in order to illustrate the basic techniques and philosophy of the problem-posing approach.

They decided to focus the role plays on the theme of a birthday party and to situate the "problem" in the fact that students from different cultures have various ways of celebrating birthdays. In the non-problem-posing class, this fact would go unnoticed. In the problem-posing class, led by the teacher, an exploration of the variety of ways in which cultures view birthdays would become an important part of the class curriculum.

A recurrent problem in this course over the years has been that international students are often silenced within both the whole class discussions and the small groups. Recently, the concept of creating a voice for all class members has become an important part of the course, with both the instructor and the facilitators actively scaffolding international students' participation in all phases of the course. During these first few weeks, group members reported that the students from the United States tended to dominate the group discussions. In the fourth group meeting, Li Hwa challenged the group to take another look at Wallerstein's text, as she felt that they had missed the main idea of problem posing, namely that problems and possible solutions must come from the students' own lives. With regard to the group's original plan to use contrasting classes for the presentation, Sarah noted in her dialogue journal:

The "problem" with our problem-posing class was that there really was no problem that the students were working out – the teacher had solved it for them. And this is where Li Hwa came in – she kept commenting on this – that what we were doing was not the same as her understanding of what she read in the book. We realized that we were trying to fit problem posing around our idea rather than vice versa, so we decided to start over and come up with a new "problem."

The international students played a crucial role in the direction the presentation took and the nature of what the group learned. Li Hwa's ability to get the group members to take a new look at the theory and critique their own presentation plans created the conditions for a new and richer understanding of problem posing and demonstrated the role that peers could play in the learning of group members. In the fourth group meeting, which the professor sat in on, Li Hwa persisted in bringing up her dissatisfaction with the direction they were taking in planning the presentation. Even though the presentation was only two weeks away, the group listened to her.

In an interview, Martha noted that one of the factors that allowed Li Hwa to be "heard" in this setting was the fact that the professor,

Jerri, was sitting in on that group session, as she often did before a group presented.

They [two Chinese students] had a much deeper understanding of what problem posing was. . . . I feel if she [Jerri] hadn't been there we wouldn't have heard it. You know I really do because I think that there would have been the "Oh we only have so many weeks to go . . . and you're changing the whole plan" and we really weren't listening to something important to hear.

While Li Hwa did not connect Jerri's presence with her own ability to talk and be heard in that session, clearly Jerri's participation in that meeting had an impact on Martha's perspective. After class that night she bumped into Jerri in the parking lot, and they discussed the participation of members in her small group. A few days later, in a Saturday meeting outside of class time, Martha brought up the importance of listening to one another in the group. In an interview, she recounted that conversation.

I just said I just wanted to bring something up before we went on and I felt that Li Hwa had something really important to contribute but that it wasn't easy to hear it . . . it was great because then I mean that session I don't know if any of this would have come up if we hadn't talked and that's when she started saying she volunteered the information about, uh, dorm life and alienation. . . .

Scaffolding voice

An important part of the small group experience was for group members to reflect on and discuss the value of ensuring everyone's participation in their collaborative learning. An examination of the dialogue journals between group members and the group facilitator showed many exchanges over issues of voice. The facilitator often encouraged and supported the two Chinese students in their efforts to speak up and participate in the group. Sarah had many entries which focused on issues of cross-cultural communication and its importance in the group process.

The group members did listen to Li Hwa in that fourth group meeting, and they continued to listen during the following Saturday session, which took place outside of class. That session proved to be pivotal for the group's presentation, as they decided to abandon the birthday party idea and draw instead upon the two Chinese students' experiences of being excluded from the lives of American students while living in the university dorms. The tacking back and forth – from personal experience to pedagogical theory to planning the presentation – allowed the group to construct a richer understanding of the nature of a "problem" in problem posing.

Personal stories: "They never invite you into their life."

The Saturday meeting began with the members of the group critiquing the current plan for the presentation.

Excerpt 1

Xiaoli: . . . but it's [birthday party] not kind of everyday life problem brought into the class so special an occasion it's very hard to say it's kind of

Sarah: But isn't it a problem if you say you don't enjoy your

Xiaoli: Yeah you can say you don't enjoy your birthday party and because of some cultural aspects that's okay. But if you say that's problem coming from cultural conflicts, I don't see any birthdays will have kind of cultural conflicts.

Xiaoli critiques the group's plan for the presentation because conflicts over birthday party rituals are "not kind of everyday life problem," which she believes is crucial for the problem-posing approach. As we shall see presently, she has had some personal experiences while living in the United States which provide a more suitable "problem." It also becomes clear that the concept of what a "problem" is in the problem-posing approach is under discussion and revision. The original "problem," a lack of awareness by a class of how different cultures celebrate birthdays, gives way to the idea that a problem emerges from students' own lives and should have the weight of real conflict or pain. As Xiaoli says, ". . . I don't see any birthdays having cultural conflicts."

After the group agrees that they are not bound to their original idea, Martha suggests focusing on the experiences of international students living in the United States.

Excerpt 2

Martha: . . . I was thinking what about the idea that somebody is new to this country living in a dormitory and they don't feel they are getting to know anybody.

Xiaoli: That's a very good idea.

Martha: And somehow that problem is being brought into the classroom. I remember them saying [Wallerstein text] that one of the reasons for a dialogue around the problem is to help the student realize that they are misunderstood. But they also are in a culture that they don't understand either

269

and that, you know, the misunderstanding comes from both sides and that, you know, to help that person better understand the situation so that they know how they can work in it and change it from their end. Do you know what I'm saying? Does that make sense?

This excerpt illustrates two crucial features of collaborative dialogue as enacted in this setting. First, this stretch of talk shows many of the features that I have identified with the co-construction of voice. The decision to change the group's plan provides a slot in the discourse for Martha to suggest a new problem amid which the group can build a lesson, namely, an international student living in a dormitory who is not "getting to know anybody." Martha's suggestion is immediately "heard" by Xiaoli through a positive evaluation: "That's a very good idea." Martha then connects her idea with the Wallerstein text and the importance of dialoguing with students about a problem in order to explore possible cross-cultural misunderstandings. Martha ends her turn by checking to see whether her ideas are understandable and reasonable. These questions also serve to structure the floor for another group member.

In this meeting, Martha clearly has a strong voice as group members weave her suggestion into the group discourse by positive evaluations and elaborations and, eventually, by accepting it as the core of the group's presentation. In this excerpt we see Martha moving between personal experience and textual knowledge to filter her suggestion through the language of the course text. This process plays a central role in the learning that takes place on this occasion. The idea of focusing on international students begins to come alive, as Xiaoli and Li Hwa begin to tell their own stories of not being included in the lives of their dorm mates. The suggestion by Martha structures the active participation of the two Chinese group members. By suggesting a topic that allows them to draw upon their own experiences, they are provided with a warrant to enter the conversation.

Excerpt 3

Xiaoli: . . . I've got an idea you know.
Sarah: Okay, tell us.
Xiaoli: It's like this, just based on your idea, say, ESL class trying to help people, help students, from different cultures to get (how to say) get into the dorm, get settled, not get settled (how to say), get around with people in the dorm.
Martha: Get acquainted, get to know them.

Xiaoli: Get acquainted, get into the culture actually. And each one maybe two or three of us will tell a story and demonstrate that story, and we'll change the theme and present it at the dorm. You see?

While Xiaoli's suggestion is ultimately not accepted by the group, we can see the ways in which Xiaoli's voice is co-constructed within the group. Xiaoli bids for the floor in order to make a suggestion, and that bid is acknowledged by Sarah, who then structures a turn for Xiaoli. Xiaoli signals that she has heard Martha's earlier suggestion, and she continues to build upon it. Martha signals that she is attending to Xiaoli's speech by supplying a vocabulary word, "acquainted," that Xiaoli is groping for. Xiaoli continues to explain her own idea to expand Martha's original suggestion.

The essence of collaborative dialogue is the ability of all members in a conversation to have their participation supported: turns structured, ideas attended to, evaluated, elaborated on, challenged, topics chosen that draw upon members' knowledge, and even providing a missing word for a second language speaker. In the group, the discussion then turns to issues closer to the hearts of Li Hwa and Xiaoli.

Excerpt 4

Li Hwa: . . . when I first came here, I had thought because, you know, I thought of being invited to parties every weekend. But no, no, never, even once. Never but had . . .
Martha: . . . You were never invited?
Li Hwa: But I have many American friends, we just say hello, sometimes talk a little bit, but
Xiaoli: They never invite you into their life.
Li Hwa: Yeah, that's true. . . .

Li Hwa's original expectations of the types of social relations she would have with American students have clearly not been met. Her frustration and pain are evident in this conversation, and Xiaoli's poignant comment that Americans "never let you into their life" is quickly heard by Li Hwa. It is clear that a real problem has emerged from this discussion: the loneliness and alienation felt by international students living in the United States. The voice of Li Hwa is supported by the social web of the group task, the collaborative norms of the course, and crucially, the multiple discursive moves among the members. Martha's question both acts as a type of hearing of Li Hwa and structures a turn for her to elaborate on her topic.

Li Hwa continues to talk about her own misconceptions of American parties and the rampant "sexual activities" which she believes took place there, based on American movies she has seen in Taiwan. Sarah then ties Li Hwa's story back to problem posing and Martha's earlier comments.

Excerpt 5

Sarah: That fits into what Martha was saying that in problem posing you want to have both sides. The other side to what you were saying is that a lot of your American friends might not have been going to parties every weekend. And you were. It was a two-way thing. Sometimes they. . . .

Martha: Yeah that's two way. . . .

Sarah: . . . inviting you, but other times you thought they were doing things they weren't doing. . . .

Martha: Yeah. Oh okay, I'm glad that we're all here because I don't think I would have understood that from what you said. I'm glad that we're all listening.

Sarah creates an intertextual link to Martha's earlier discussion of Wallerstein's idea that one of the functions of dialogue in problem-posing is to identify cross-cultural misunderstandings. Sarah's comments also function to "hear" Li Hwa's previous story about her dorm experiences. Martha then acknowledges the shared nature of understanding in this discussion. As the meeting rapidly progresses, Xiaoli tells her story of being excluded from the lives of dorm mates. In one instance, when her whole dorm floor went to see the *Rocky Horror Picture Show*, they assumed that Xiaoli could not possibly want to go. She was not sure that she did, but she was sure that she wanted to be invited.

This meeting provides an opportunity for the group members both to discuss something that is obviously important to the lives of two members and to connect it to the task of understanding problem posing and of planning a presentation. The collaborative nature of this discussion is also clearly evident. Group members listen to Li Hwa's critique of their earlier plan and are willing to alter it. They all participate in the group dialogue, listen to and build upon each others' ideas, and negotiate common understandings.

A crucial point to make is the role that personal knowledge plays in this discussion. One of the characteristics of many graduate programs is the lack of currency that personal experience has in graduate classes (Cazden 1988). Clearly, in this small group, personal experience provides a warrant for entering the conversation. Further, it is valued by other group members as they engage the stories of Li Hwa and Xiaoli. As Li Hwa noted in an interview:

We also have to integrate our own experience into that book or that concept and to present it to the whole class. That's why it's easier for me
to learn, because it's vivid. It's [how can I say] it's more practical than a
book. . . .

Li Hwa also reports that, for her, it is much easier to join the discussion
in her small group, something that she has felt unable to do in whole
class discussions.

Another important point to consider is the role of the task in structuring the group meetings. The need to clarify their own understanding
of what constitutes a "problem," and the imperative of creating a lesson
plan for the presentation, supplies the frame for this particular conversation. The creation of the necessary conditions for the voice of group
members to be heard becomes the vehicle that moves the conversation
along. The abilities of group members to be open to the critique of their
initial plan, consider Martha's suggestion, and then integrate Li Hwa
and Xiaoli's personal stories into their lesson plan are critical to the
development of their own understanding of the topic and to the planning of their presentation. In this discussion we see references to the
problem-posing text, personal experiences, and the presentation. Interestingly, each adds something essential to the mix. The texts provide
needed information about a new subject matter; the personal experiences of Xiaoli and Li Hwa make the abstract concept of a "problem"
come alive; and the planning of the presentation provides a framework
which united the two.

The group uses the combination of personal experiences and text
knowledge to construct richer concepts of "problem," "dialogue," and
"codes" within problem posing. Tharp and Gallimore (1988: 110) identify this process as central to learning.

Comprehension is established by the weaving of new, schooled concepts with
the concepts of everyday life. Textual material becomes meaningful because it
has gained a new attachment – it is now hooked by sense to everyday
concepts and hooked by system to the whole structure of meaning given in
schooling. . . . From kindergarten to graduate seminars, the small discussion
group in which text and personal understandings can be compared,
discussed, and related is the prime opportunity for this unique social
interaction.

The task requires that the students actually teach their classmates about
problem posing. The presentation not only provides a powerful social
motivator for the group to come to terms with their topic, but also
forces the group to address the complexities of teaching it. We turn
now to the presentation itself.

Francis Bailey

The problem-posing presentation: A ritual enactment

Field Notes/October 13: This is the first night of student presentations and the problem-posing group is up. After a brief question and answer session, Li Hwa stands up and reads some information about an upcoming role play with ESL students who live in dorms. The teacher of this group has overheard two students talking about their frustrations with never being invited to parties on campus. As the "class" begins, the teacher (Martha) passes around pictures of immigrants being processed through immigration – the "code." They talk a bit about the pictures and then the teacher writes on the board – "alienation," "parties," "rules – American rules," etc.

The presentation which this group produced centered around the issues raised in that Saturday meeting. The role play of the class followed the basic steps of problem posing as the class identified a "problem," explored it through various "codes," and discussed possible actions the students could take to resolve the problem. Following the role play, the group led a question-and-answer session with the entire methods class. Questions centered around the roles of students and teacher, choice of "codes," and dealing with some of the real challenges of using problem posing in ESL classes such as multiple levels of English, diverse problems among students and choice of codes. The session was intense and had a critical edge at times.

In the professor's written feedback to the group after their presentation, which was distributed to the entire class, Jerri noted that:

None of the presenters knew anything about the approach when they started, and yet they were able to put together a presentation that embodied problem posing, generated an excellent discussion and empowered them to respond confidently and thoughtfully to "tough questions." They went through a problem-posing experience – they used their own experiences (as international students, inexperienced teachers, second language learners, diverse learners) and listened to one another; they foreshadowed your "problems" (presenting to our class and teaching ESL); they found a code (their role play) that was projective, emotionally laden, and identifiable; they went through a critical dialogue to analyze their problem (Remember all the "debates" they had with one another and with you); and they acted. They did not seem intimidated by your questions but treated them as "critical dialogue." Were "consciousnesses raised"? I'll leave that for you to think about – but I "heard" in the discussion, the class thinking about teaching as "problem solving" not "recipe following."

In the professor's response we see clearly a kind of "positive spin," as she looks for what can be learned from student efforts. Several themes of the course were highlighted in this response. First, she noted that the problem-posing group was not experienced in the subject matter, and yet they produced a presentation which "embodied problem posing and generated an excellent discussion." She went on to note that the group used the problem-posing process to generate the presentation: They "used their own experiences," "listened to one another," "found a code," and "went through a critical dialogue to analyze their problem." Finally, she emphasized the value of viewing teaching as "problem solving."

Later on in this feedback, Jerri wrote about some of the mistakes which were made in the presentation, for example, forgetting to provide the large group with the "codes" so that they could follow along during the role play. She then turned to a central premise of her own approach to this type of education:

I bet that you will have learned as much from this group's mistakes as you have from their successes. And they will learn as much from your feedback as their learners have from reading Wallerstein or getting my feedback.

This statement embodied many of the fundamental elements of the course. First, the product, or presentation, was secondary to the learning process and the class could learn much from reflecting on the mistakes the presenters had made. The course was a kind of laboratory designed for exploration of teaching, and mistakes were an integral part of that learning. Second, learners together could use the experiences of the course to create their own knowledge, which would be superior to the knowledge of experts and which would not be limited to subject matter knowledge but would include the experience of the collaborative educational process.

Discussion with students in the class confirmed that some students felt that they had not gotten a clear demonstration of the full complexity and power of problem posing. The dialogue journal of one Japanese member of the class revealed that the presentation had had a strong effect on her and had touched more than just subject matter knowledge. She wrote:

The topic they chose was actually a very painful one for me. I, myself, experienced exactly the same problem. . . . When the teacher in the role play threw out the question, "What do you think is the problem?", I thought I was going to cry (of course, this is an exaggeration). . . . It was a question whether you want to pressure yourself to be accepted and somehow adapt to American culture or to stay with your own crowd.

For this Japanese student, as for the two Chinese students, the "problem" was real, complex, and deeply felt.

"Listen to different voices": Collaborative small group learning

Sarah wrote in her journal soon after the presentation:

I really found it to be quite a learning experience. We really did have to do a lot of collaboration, cooperation and compromise. . . . One aspect of group work that I found particularly comforting was the idea of shared responsibility.

An examination of the dialogue journals of group members and the group facilitator showed many exchanges on issues of collaboration and voice. The facilitator often encouraged and supported the two Chinese students in their efforts to speak up and participate in the group. Sarah had many entries which focused on issues of cross-cultural communication and its importance in the group process. In a journal entry discussing the presentation, Xiaoli discussed her views on being open to other points of view and critical questions and comments.

Listen to different voices is what I'd like to always do in my life. I believe it is very useful for a teacher. Moreover, this is also the first step suggested in "problem posing."

This group revealed that to "listen to different voices" is a complex and rewarding task. By listening to one another, group members were able to challenge their own conceptions of course content and connect it to their lives. Xiaoli noted in a later journal entry that she saw this as a course strength.

It [Jerri's class] is not at all like a traditional class. It makes the students explore the knowledge themselves, allows them to develop their independent researching ability. There is no pressure from the teacher but there is pressure from the students themselves.

It is clear that this group worked well together, and yet I do not believe that they are extraordinary. The task structure provided opportunities for students to "explore the [course] knowledge themselves," without constant pressure from the instructor but with the pressure of "shared responsibility."

Finally, I believe the opportunity this presentation afforded for students to "listen to different voices" of foreigners living in this country was particularly important. Despite a long history of immigration, with much lip service paid to heightened sensitivity to multicultural perspectives, international students and immigrants are still living in dorms with little opportunity to enter the lives of their American neighbors. In a course on second language teaching, this, too, is an important lesson for teachers to ponder.

276

Conclusion

This study of the problem-posing group highlights three fundamental points about the role of collaborative dialogue in teacher education. First, collaborative learning can provide a powerful mechanism for teachers to explore their own conceptions of teaching and learning. The process of interweaving knowledge gained from texts with the personal knowledge and experiences of group members is an effective way for teachers to acquire new conceptions of their own teaching practice. The group members enriched their conception of what constitutes a "problem" in problem posing not only by reading course texts, but also by going through the process of naming their own problem, negotiating a code, and planning a presentation for their classmates.

It is axiomatic in teaching that students can learn from interactions with their teachers. However, this research points to ways in which students can also benefit from interacting with their peers (cf. Cazden 1988). In the small groups of the methods course, group members explained their own understandings of course content, questioned and challenged one another, negotiated the meanings of words, and perhaps most important, listened to the ideas and experiences of a diverse group of classmates. It is through these rich dialogues that teachers can construct their own understandings of course content and acquire a new discourse for reconceiving their own teaching practices (Freeman 1992).

Second, this research highlights the situated nature of this form of discourse. Getting small groups of learners together does not guarantee learning. The methods course created a context in which group members were positioned as both capable and having knowledge. Members saw one another as resources for their opinions and experiences, as well as for understanding the course text. The ability of the group to create a voice for each group member was fundamental to this collaboration.

Third, the learning that took place in the small group was not limited to just the group's topic. Crucially, group members had the opportunity to experience for themselves the benefits and challenges of task-based, collaborative learning. For many group members, working in a collaborative group and being responsible for teaching their classmates provided a crucial experiential base to the course. However, this form of education also creates its own set of tensions. The structure of this class, while novel to many American students, was totally foreign to the international students. The pedagogical assumptions on which the class rested often did not make sense to many of these students. Further, small group work could be both accommodating to international students and, at times, overwhelming. The interactions in these groups were often very intense and emotional as deadlines approached. The discourse structure of collaborative dialogue could alienate some international students as they struggle to learn both new subject matter and how to participate in this new form of educational discourse.

The structure of this course also raises questions about what is missed when the instructor is removed from the central role in a class. While collaborative dialogue constructs voices for learners, it also mutes the voice of the instructor. This may play an essential role in positioning learners as resources for one another, but it can also cause tensions as students yearn for the familiar and authoritative voice of the teacher. In interesting ways, these tensions became part of the class discourse. In dialogue journals and in small and large group discussions, group members had opportunities to reflect upon their own experiences with this class and to confront the difficulties of collaborative learning. Students left the class with a sense that they had deeply engaged their own topic and also the whole-language principles on which the course was built. This engagement came not simply from studying these issues as in a typical methods course, but from the actual experience of participating in a task-based, collaborative classroom.

In conclusion, this study suggests that collaborative dialogue can be a powerful and effective form of instructional discourse in teacher education. It provides a viable means for exploring issues in teaching and learning, through both the process of peer dialogue and the experience of participating in a course designed around collaborative learning. Importantly, as suggested by the quote from Freire that began this chapter, collaborative dialogue can invite teachers to believe in themselves and their own knowledge.

References

Allwright, R. 1984. The importance of interaction in classroom language learning. *Applied Linguistics* 156–171.

Au, K. 1980. Participation structures in a reading lesson with Hawaiian children: Analysis of a culturally appropriate instructional event. *Anthropology and Education Quarterly* 11: 91–115.

Bailey, F. 1993. Voice in collaborative learning: An ethnographic study of a second language methods course. Doctoral dissertation, School of Education, University of Massachusetts, Amherst, Mass.

Bloome, D., and F. Bailey. 1992. Studying language and literacy through events, particularity, and intertextuality. In R. Beach et al. (eds.), *Multidisciplinary Perspectives on Literacy Research*. Urbana, Ill.: National Council of Teachers of English, pp. 181–210.

Candlin, C. 1987. Towards task-based language learning. In C. Candlin and D. Murphy (eds.), *Language Learning Tasks*. Englewood Cliffs, N.J.: Prentice-Hall.

Cazden, C. 1988. *Classroom Discourse*. Portsmouth, N.H.: Heinemann.

Cohen, E. 1986. *Designing Groupwork: Strategies for the Heterogeneous Classroom.* New York: Teachers College Press.

Damon, W., and E. Phelps. 1988. Critical distinctions between three methods of peer education. AERA Conference, New Orleans, La.

de Beaugrande, R., and W. Dressler. 1981. *Introduction to Text Linguistics.* London: Longman.

Freeman, D. 1992. Language teacher education, emerging discourse, and change in classroom practice. In J. Flowerdew, M. Brock, and S. Hsia (eds.), *Perspectives on Second Language Teacher Education.* Hong Kong: City Polytechnic of Hong Kong, pp. 1–21.

Freeman, Y., and D. Freeman. 1992. *Whole Language for Second Language Learners.* Portsmouth, N.H.: Heinemann.

Freire, P. 1970. *Pedagogy of the Oppressed.* New York: Seabury.

1973. By learning they can teach. *Convergence* 6(1).

Gergen, K. 1989. Warranting voice and the elaboration of the self. In J. Shotter and K. Gergen (eds.), *Texts of Identity.* London: Sage, pp. 70–81.

Goetz, J., and M. LeCompte. 1984. *Ethnography and Qualitative Design in Educational Research.* San Diego, Calif.: Academic Press.

Goodman, K., L. Bird, and Y. Goodman (eds.). 1991. *The Whole Language Catalog.* Santa Rosa, Calif.: American School.

Green, J. 1983. Research on teaching as a linguistic process: A state of the art. *Review of Research in Education* 10: 151–252.

Green, J., R. Weade, and K. Graham. 1988. Lesson construction and student participation: A sociolinguistic analysis. In J. J. Green and J. Harker (eds.), *Multiple Perspective Analyses of Classroom Discourse.* Norwood, N.J.: Ablex, pp. 11–47.

Hymes, D. 1974. *Foundations in Sociolinguistics: An Ethnographic Approach.* Philadelphia: University of Pennsylvania Press.

Johnson, D., and R. Johnson. 1990. Cooperative learning and achievement. In S. Sharan (ed.), *Cooperative Learning.* New York: Praeger, pp. 23–38.

McDermott, R. 1988. Inarticulateness. In D. Tannen (ed.), *Linguistics in Context: Connecting Observation and Understanding.* Norwood, N.J.: Ablex, pp. 37–68.

Mehan, H. 1979. *Learning Lessons: Social Organization in the Classroom.* Cambridge, Mass.: Harvard University Press.

Moerman, M. 1988. *Talking Culture: Ethnography and Conversation Analysis.* Philadelphia: University of Pennsylvania Press.

Mohatt, G., and F. Erickson. 1981. Cultural differences in teaching styles in an Odawa school: A sociolinguistic approach. In H. Trueba, G. Guthrie, and K. Au (eds.), *Culture and the Bilingual Classroom: Studies in Classroom Ethnography.* Rowley, Mass.: Newbury House, pp. 105–119.

Peacock, J. 1986. *The Anthropological Lens: Harsh Light, Soft Focus.* Cambridge: Cambridge University Press.

Philips, S. 1983. *The Invisible Culture.* New York: Longman.

Sacks, H., E. Schegloff, and G. Jefferson. 1974. A simplest systematics for the organization of turn-taking for conversation. *Language* 50: 696–735.

Scollon, R., and S. Scollon. 1981. *Narrative, Literacy, and Face in Interethnic Communication.* Norwood, N.J.: Ablex.

Sharan, A. 1990. *Cooperative Learning: Theory and Research.* New York: Praeger.

Shultz, J., S. Florio, and F. Erickson. 1982. Where's the floor? Aspects of the cultural organization of social relationships in communication at home and in school. In P. Gilmore and A. Glatthorn (eds.), *Children In and Out of School: Ethnography and Education*. Washington, D.C.: Center for Applied Linguistics, pp. 88–123.

Spradley, J. 1980. *Participant Observation*. New York: Holt, Rinehart and Winston.

Tharp, R., and R. Gallimore. 1988. *Rousing Minds to Life*. Cambridge: Cambridge University Press.

Wallerstein, N. 1983. *Language and Culture in Conflict: Problem-Posing in the ESL Classroom*. Reading, Mass.: Addison-Wesley.

Wertsch, J. 1991. *Voices of the Mind: A Sociocultural Approach to Mediated Action*. Cambridge, Mass.: Harvard University Press.

Willet, J., F. Bailey, T. Fuentes, M. Hawkins, M. Jeannot, M. Johnson, D. Sweet, and D. Zuccalo. 1990. Constructing a whole language teaching perspective. Paper presented at the TESOL Convention, San Francisco.

13 Structured reflection: The role of the professional project in training ESL teachers

Michael Wallace

Introduction

In language teaching today, the accelerating pace of change, increased public accountability and a growing awareness of the central role of education in social and economic development have all combined to place extremely heavy professional demands on the individual teacher, to an extent never before experienced. A passive or purely reactive teaching force will be ill prepared to meet these challenges and may even be demoralised by them. The teachers who will thrive in this new environment are those who are capable of generating their own professional dynamic, who are pro-active rather than reactive.

Schön (1983, 1987) and many others have argued that the most effective method of generating autonomous professional development is through the ability to reflect on one's own professional practice, with the correlative assumption that trainees can be "coached" in this ability. Such "reflective practitioners" will be able to continue to develop their professional expertise not *away* from classroom practice into academic theory, but by using theory mediated *within* their continuing practice. If this ambitious aim is adopted by an ESL trainer, what does it entail? This question is still very much an ongoing process, as will be made clear later in this chapter. It also involves many areas of ESL training, some of which are addressed elsewhere in the volume.

Many writers concerned with teacher education have gone further than Schön to suggest a model of the "teacher as researcher" and an orientation to "action research" [notably Stenhouse (1975); see also Hopkins (1993) and Walker (1985); for a view of action research in the language classroom, see Nunan (1990)]. The implication of this view is that trainees should be trained in research methods so that, as teachers, they can become their own researchers. Action research is distinguished from other kinds of research in that it is directly and immediately related to professional action in some way. However, as Cohen and Manion have pointed out (1989: 217), the words *action* and *research* "lie as uneasy bedfellows," as, indeed, one might add, do the words *reflective* and *practice*, albeit it to a lesser extent. This is a central issue, to which we will return later.

One way in which action research can be implemented is by means of an extended study of some aspect of the trainee teachers' own professional practice. This aspect is researched and subsequently written up in an extended essay or dissertation, often referred to as a *professional project*. I will use this label here for such kinds of exercises. What follows is a case study of the use of the professional project concept in a particular teacher education programme. I discuss some problems encountered in the implementation of the concept and draw some conclusions from this experience about the role of the professional project in developing reflective practice.

The case study

Background

The TESOL training in this case is a four-year honours bachelor of education course in TESOL [BEd (Hons) TESOL]. The students are young Malaysians who have been selected to come to the United Kingdom after creditable performance in the Malaysian school-leaving examinations. Those who successfully complete a two-year matriculation course are admitted directly into the degree course, which functions therefore as a pre-service training course. There are five periods of "school experience," or teaching practice. These periods are spread throughout the first three years of the course and are in the form of both serial placements of roughly one day per fortnight and block placements of a minimum of four continuous weeks. The placements occur in both the United Kingdom and Malaysia. The fifth and final period of placement is a block placement of three months which comes at the end of the third year and which occurs in Malaysia. There is no placement in the fourth year.

The professional project

The professional project is one of the major forms of assessment for the degree. It takes the form of a 10,000–word dissertation which is begun in the third year and submitted at the end of the fourth year. The professional project is intended to achieve several aims, three of which are particularly relevant to the present discussion.

1. It is intended to give students an opportunity to articulate their reflective practice, that is, their ability to reflect on their professional action and to report on that reflection in an appropriate way.
2. It should allow the student to synthesise the "received knowledge" acquired from reading and other inputs with the "experiential

knowledge" derived from their final period of school experience in Malaysia.

3. Finally, it is intended as a synoptic assessment of how well the students can integrate relevant elements from all areas of their course, including curricular areas, such as discourse analysis and phonology, and the pedagogical areas, notably TESOL methodology.

The process of writing the professional project was originally conceived of as taking place in the following way: First, the students would choose a spoken or written text, or a series of such texts, that they wished to exploit for teaching. They would subject that text to a linguistic analysis. They would then plan a programme to exploit the text in ways indicated by such received knowledge as they found appropriate and by their previous experience. During the final period of school experience, they would teach the texts, taking care to retain any hard data generated by this process, such as audio recordings of group work or examples of corrected exercises, and where appropriate, such data would be photocopied. They would then reflect on their professional action and the data, and evaluate it. If necessary or desirable, they could then modify their planned programme and start the cycle over again. During their fourth year, they would write up the whole process under the supervision of their tutor, deepening their reflection as necessary with further readings, and would finally submit the project.

The students are given various kinds of support for the successful completion of their project. They take a module on the analysis of spoken and written English, and they receive input on research methodology. During the period of school experience, supervisors monitor not only their teaching competence but also their progress on data collection for the professional project. In the final year, a module on the analysis of classroom practice is introduced which allows the students to reflect on their practice in group mode as well as individually. Each student is assigned a supervisor who monitors the writing up of the project and suggests further readings. The final honours examinations take place at the end of the second term, thus allowing most of third term to be devoted to the final stages of the presentation of the project.

Overall, the concept of the professional project has been successful in terms of its aims. Indeed, some of the best work produced has been adjudged by an external examiner to be "equivalent to master's level." However, certain problems have arisen, some of which raise general issues concerning the validity of this kind of exercise.

The first problem arose from combining the data collection for the project with the final period of teaching practice. The first cohort of students to do the course found that the data collection tended to be pushed aside because of the pressures of teaching. The data collection, when it was eventually done, tended to be rushed and consequently sometimes inadequate or incomplete. Steps were taken to obviate this problem. Students were given much more thorough preparation for the project before they went to their placement schools, and they drew up a detailed time schedule for data collection. Also, the process of the data collection was much more carefully monitored by the supervisor during the placement period. The supervisor was expected not only to evaluate the student's teaching formally, but also to report on how the student was coping with the data collection schedule.

A second problem was that the process of data collection sometimes caused perplexity among the students' colleagues at their placement schools. Why, for instance, did these students want to tape their classes and photocopy exercise books? Although the process had been described and justified in the briefing documents sent to the schools, these unusual procedures had to be much more fully explained before they were accepted. Fortunately, tutors from local training colleges who were familiar with the concept of action research were able to help in this respect. Further, the process of experimentation and data collection was often perceived to interfere with the overriding requirement to implement the syllabus. Students very often had to demonstrate how the procedures they wished to implement for the professional project were compatible with the fairly detailed national syllabus.

Another problem arose from the original specification of the project, which assumed that the data collection would be related to a spoken or written text. This text was to be fairly rigorously linguistically analysed. The idea was to form a clear link between the linguistic and pedagogic inputs in the course. The professional project was intended to mediate both inputs through reflection on the placement experience.

It is now clear that this tactic was ill conceived and fell into the trap of conceptualising language teaching as a direct application of linguistic theory. This concept had been consciously rejected by the course design team. In consequence, the students produced elaborate linguistic analyses of the target linguistic texts that were sometimes very impressive and insightful; but in many cases these analyses were largely irrelevant to the teaching plans that the students subsequently produced.

The fifth and final problem related to the nature of the mode of the professional enquiry embodied within the implementation of the professional project. In order to contextualise this problem, let us look at a brief account of two sample professional projects.

The sample projects

Both professional projects are by students within the middle range of ability and are therefore fairly typical of the trainees. However, they have also chosen two very different approaches to the design and implementation of the professional project. As a kind of helpful mnemonic for the reader, rather than the conventional A and B, they will be labeled as Student D (for developmental approach) and Student X (for experimental approach).

STUDENT D

The student chose as her pedagogical focus the teaching of reading. She had noted in her first period placement in Malaysian schools that the learners often seemed to lack global strategies for tackling reading texts. She therefore decided that, during her final period of placement, she would experiment with an approach to reading texts called the *standard exercise*. This approach was pioneered by a group of ESP tutors at the Federal University of Santa Catarina in Brazil (see Scott et al. 1984). One of the main thrusts of this approach is to provide learners with effective formulae for top-down processing of authentic texts.

In the standard exercise, students start by reading only the title of the text and then predict five key words which they expect to see in the text. They then skim the text quickly, looking for the key words. Next, they reread the text as many times as they like in order to do the next set of tasks. The first task is to decide what the writer's main intention is: to inform, to persuade and so on. Then they are asked to write down any apparently important words which are new to them and to guess their meanings. Next, they have to try to summarise each paragraph in one sentence. The reader has to try to divide the text into sections (e.g., introduction, conclusion). Then other tasks follow: writing one-sentence summaries of what was learnt from the text; giving a critical reaction to the text; indicating how interesting the text was on a scale of 1 to 5; saying how many times the dictionary was used; itemising any paragraphs not understood and the reasons for not understanding; and finally giving the reader's self-estimation of his or her understanding of the text (e.g. 50 per-cent, 80 per-cent). The thrust of all these exercises is to encourage top-down processing activities and to heighten self-awareness on the part of the reader.

This approach was attractive to Student D because it could be used with any text. It allowed her to use authentic material taken from a local newspaper (*The Malay Mail*). She then worked out the "new vocabulary density," which she estimated at 11 words for the 546–word passage and quoted Nuttall (1982) to the effect that 10 to 15 difficult words for a passage of roughly 520 words is acceptable provided that they are well spread. "I figured that the amount of new vocabulary was fairly reasonable," she concluded. She analysed each of the new vocab-

285

ulary items to see what might make it difficult or easy based on contextual clues and so on.

Student D described a number of constraints and limitations in implementing the procedures recommended in Scott et al. (1984). For example, according to the original scheme, learners were supposed to self-select texts from an extensive "menu"; however, this proved impossible for her to arrange. She also encountered unexpected problems in implementing the standard exercise procedures. Learners found the original questions impossible to understand; terms such as "key word" baffled them. In all, the instructions for five of the procedures had to be simplified. Other problems were caused by the material she had selected. When learners were asked to divide the text into sections, they encountered the problem that newspaper articles, unlike academic expository prose, do not usually have conclusions as such.

Upon reviewing the overall impact of the standard exercise, student D had some serious reservations:

The "standard exercise" was to be used in a flexible way. The students should be able to read and answer the exercise at their choice of place and time without the supervision of the teacher. This flexibility was not given to my students because I needed to monitor the students' work as well as to get the answer sheets back. Furthermore, the students were not used to the idea of carrying out a task in such a flexible way. If I were to follow what Scott et al. (1984) suggested, I might not be able to get many of the answer sheets back. The negative impact was that many of my students felt that completing the exercise was like sitting in an examination room which was obviously nerve-wracking for them!

When I carried out this project on the feasibility of using the standard exercise as a means of training the secondary school students to read efficiently, I assumed that they already had some background knowledge and experience of the different reading skills. It turned out that, to a great extent, I was wrong. Most of my students had very little experience of using the reading skills required in the standard exercise and therefore found it difficult to answer.

What I should have done first was to introduce the different reading skills in the standard exercise one by one to allow the students to have some practice with the different skills gradually before giving them the whole exercise. Even though I did explain to my students about the advantages of the procedure, the students did not feel that it was relevant to them. At the secondary level, they are not required to read extensively for their examination or for their language work. Thus, they did not see any immediate benefit to use the skills in the procedure.

What I could have done after the students have completed the standard exercise was to have them carry out a mini research project on a topic that they had read and present it to the classroom as a seminar, debate or even a role play. These activities would then give them a purpose for reading as well as providing them with some meaningful input. After the students had become more familiar with the reading skills, I might have been able to assign them a more difficult task such as writing on "The disintegration of the USSR and its impact on the world." This kind of writing demands a great deal of effective reading and thinking on the part of the students and would provide them the initial practice they greatly need before entering the tertiary level.

In summary, I should have taught the students all the skills involved in the standard exercise procedure before giving them the exercise itself. I should also have provided them with some meaningful activities to follow the exercise so that the students would have the chance to explore the topic in greater depth as well as to apply the skills to their assigned readings.

STUDENT X

Student X decided to investigate the problems that Malaysian fourth-year secondary learners have in understanding spoken spatial instructions. The student demonstrated in her report that she had read quite widely in the theory of listening comprehension and the teaching of listening skills, and could relate these issues to communicative methodology. She then described how she gave a "pre-test" of a listening text containing spatial directions, (how to find certain shops in a shopping area), to two fourth-year classes (4S and 4C). Over a period of some weeks, one of the classes (4C) was then given two further listening exercises. Then both classes were given a post-test. The student's hypothesis was that 4C would improve compared to the 4S class because of the extra work on spatial directions that they had been given. In the post-test, 4C scored higher and 4S scored lower than previously. Student X concluded her investigation as follows:

The achievement of the objectives

Objective 1 of my investigation was to identify the problems of listening to spatial instructions by giving the pupils a pre-test. The results show that I have achieved this objective and I have established that the pupils in Malaysian schools do have problems in listening to spatial instructions.

Objective 2 was to determine whether the two teaching sessions on spatial instructions had any effect on the listening proficiency of the students. The two teaching sessions do help pupils to improve their performance because the pupils got better results in the post-test than in the pre-test.

Objective 3 was to determine the effectiveness of the methods and techniques employed in the investigation and to come up with strategies to improve it. I have stated that the methods and techniques employed in the investigation are effective because the results of the post-test were better than the pre-test.

Improvements

To improve the investigation, I should have given more practice to both classes. For example, I think that it would have been better to include another piece of listening material taken from a real situation, such as a real conversation from the news or the radio so that I could see whether the pupils could understand real conversations. Nevertheless, the materials in the pre-test and in Lesson 1 were real situations which I think gave the pupils sufficient practice. My own general instructions and questioning techniques are worth mentioning. I think my instructions were not clear to the pupils especially when I was implementing Lesson 2. For example, my first sentence in the lesson was . . . 'First, draw a big square on a piece of paper.' The pupils were confused: 'How big?' 'Why should I draw it?' and so on. What I should have said to them was: 'We are going to do some drawing activities and I want you to draw a big square on a piece of paper. The square has to be big enough so that you can draw other things in it.' So, my investigation would have been better if my own questioning techniques and instructions had been better. To conclude, the investigation was not as easy as I thought it would be, but by looking at the results of the tests and exercises, I can say that my investigation was a successful one.

Discussion

Student X's project corresponded fairly closely to the paradigm of conventional experimental research. There was an "experimental group" (4C), which was given special treatment in the form of listening exercises, and there was a "control group" (4S), which was not given this treatment. There were pre-tests and post-tests. Finally, the experimental group was deemed to have made more progress than the control group, apparently vindicating the hypothesis that extra tuition in spatial directions leads to improved performance. Student D's project was quite different, however. Student D had a "bright idea" which she came across in her reading. She modified it as she thought appropriate to suit her teaching situation. She tried it out. Some things worked out as she expected; others did not. She made further modifications. Then she evaluated the whole procedure by getting feedback from the learners. She concluded by endorsing the new approach, with some additional suggestions for further modification. Thus her project was essentially developmental.

All projects were double-blind marked. There was provision for referral to a third marker, who would also mark blind, when the first and second markers could not agree. In such cases, the final mark is usually an average of all three markers. All referred cases are also read by the external examiner. In the case of the two sample projects, Student X's project was assessed to be seriously flawed, while Student D's project was assessed to be essentially sound. The flaws in Student X's project related partly to her inadequate research procedures. In fact, she had not "proved" anything. For example, the "research" and "control" groups had not been properly matched. It was in fact a "quasi-experiment" in Cohen and Manion's (1989) terms. There were also other flaws in the research design. Even if the experiment had been conducted more rigorously, it could be argued that the hypothesis was essentially trivial, as is often the case with such research. It is to be expected that, if learners get extra teaching in a particular area, they will consequently demonstrate greater proficiency in that area.

This might be taken as an argument for more rigorous training in research design, and probably the student should have been able to recognise faulty research procedures, especially in her own work. However, it could well be argued that more emphasis on the implementation of traditional empirical research methodology is not the complete answer, since this traditional experimentation mode of enquiry is not at all appropriate for the professional project in the first place.

The core of the problem relates to the tension between the words *action* and *research*, as noted previously in the quotation from Cohen and Manion (1989). The literature on action research and teacher education abounds in examples where this tension is unrecognised and unresolved. For example, talking about his proposals for "research-based teacher education," Tickle says (1987: 43):

The first need among teachers themselves is the recognition of the curriculum as problematic. Second is the disposition to seek understanding of specific curriculum events. Third is the need to master investigative skills to provide the data and means of analysing and testing hypotheses or theories (or in constructing hypotheses and generating theories upon which better-informed practice may be devised). Fourth is the capacity to effectively conduct that practice. These provide the essential characteristics of autonomous professional development.

This is clearly what Student X attempted to do: She had a hypothesis and she tested it, albeit ineffectively because she had not sufficiently mastered the necessary "investigative skills." This is also what Student D attempted to do. She had recognised the curriculum as "problematic," that teaching was not merely a matter of following unquestioningly the teacher's guide to the course book. She had honed in on "specific curriculum events" in the form of reading skills. From here on, however, we can continue to apply Tickle's statements to what Student D did, but only if we use his words in special senses. She did not "test" a "hypothesis" or "theory" in a way that would be recognisable or acceptable in a traditional research paradigm. The "testing" was uncontrolled, and the pedagogical decisions resulting from her trial were intuitive and selective, although they were well documented and clearly rationalised. So we cannot really apply Tickle's statement to

289

what Student X did in her project unless we use research terminology in a much looser, almost metaphorical sense.

So we have to address squarely the question: What sort of "research" do we want students to do in their professional projects? Do we aspire for them to do "proper research", or are they engaged in some other kind of exercise that can scarcely be called research at all?

ACTION RESEARCH[1]

In order to answer this question, we must return to the concept of action research and the inherent tensions in the term referred to previously. We must have a clear definition of exactly what we mean by action research, and this is not easy to come by. Cohen and Manion (1989: 217) quote Halsey's (1972) definition: "Action research is a small-scale intervention in the functioning of the real world and a close examination of the effects of such intervention". This definition is so broad, however, as to be practically useless, since it would seem to cover everything from a conventional empirical experiment, on the one hand, to an episode of *Candid Camera*, on the other!

Most other defining criteria usually given for action research are either partial or negative. Unlike the situation with other modes of research, there is no recommended methodology for implementing or reporting it. There is, instead, a large and open-ended variety of possible procedures (some of them described, for example, in Hopkins 1993). Indeed, action research findings need not be formally communicated at all, although Stenhouse (1975: 223) is keen that action research findings should be made available within each teaching community. "Communication is less effective than community in the utilisation of knowledge". Again, unlike conventional research, it need not be generalisable or even verifiable, although it can be. Some writers suggest that it is most effective when it is done on a collaborative basis, although again it need not be. Whenever one tries to grasp the essence of action research, it seems to slip away.

What, then, are the positive criteria for action research? I would like to suggest the following:

1. *Ownership*. Action research "belongs" to practitioners rather than to professional researchers or outside bodies, in the sense that it is controlled and implemented by the practitioner, or group of practitioners, concerned. It may or may not be initiated by outsiders, but normally one would expect it to be initiated by the practitioners themselves.
2. *Focus*. There is wide agreement that the focus of action research is

1 For an interesting comparison, see Chapter 14 in this book.

the improvement of the practice of the practitioner(s) engaged in implementing it. It has therefore, in the first place, a purely local and specific application.

3. *Structured reflection.* In terms of its methodology, action research is a means by which practitioners can structure reflection on their professional action. How complex this structure is will depend on the practitioners' aims, their resources, their freedom of action, and various other aspects of their professional and personal context. In the same way, what form the articulation of the results of the research takes will depend on similar considerations.

According to this definition, action research is therefore a form of structured reflection on professional action which is controlled and implemented by the practitioners themselves with the intention of improving some aspect of their own professional practice. This definition tilts the balance in favour of professional action at the expense of the research emphasis.

REFLECTIVE PRACTICE

If we now return to the issue of the professional project, one of the main issues in its rationale was to equip the trainees with the necessary skills to reflect constructively on their own professional action. Clearly there is no point in doing this in a way that is not going to be practical and meaningful in the trainees' actual professional practice, after their period of training is over. One would therefore see little benefit in encouraging experimental research of the type that Student X attempted for several reasons (among others). It is intrinsically difficult to conduct meaningful research of this type under actual classroom conditions without substantial disruption of normal class routine. There are constraints imposed by the need to follow a fairly tightly organised syllabus, and there is questionable morality in withholding pedagogic "treatments" that the teacher believes are appropriate from groups of learners simply to obtain differential data. Then, too, there is the difficulty of avoiding a "halo" effect while experimenting with new teaching procedures. Finally, much work of this nature is essentially trivial. It "proves" what would be usually expected as common sense, namely, that giving special emphasis to a particular area normally improves performance in that area.

The implications here are that the project work that is done should coincide as far as possible with the normal routines of teaching. It is quite normal for teachers to try out "bright ideas" and to see how they work with their classes. It is normal for teachers to monitor what actually goes on in group work in their classrooms. It is normal for them to think about the mistakes their students make and to think about remedial action. It is normal for teachers, from time to time, to informally evaluate various aspects of their professional expertise.

Thus what Student D did was to engage in normal development activity but in a more structured way than most teachers would have the time, or perhaps also the inclination, to do. Elements of this structure include, for example, the extra background reading done, the feedback obtained from the learners, and also, of course, the articulation of all this in the form of a 10,000-word report. On the other hand, what Student X was attempting to do with her experimental design was something that the vast majority of teachers would have neither the wish to do nor the capability to do because of the syllabus or other situational constraints. The practical difficulties which these two students encountered in data collection – attitudes of colleagues, time and syllabus constraints – are typical of those which any teacher would encounter. We have to recognise that highly structured action research is simply not part of the ethos of the vast majority of schools. This may change in the future, especially as schools take on a more active role in the teacher education process, as is happening in some national contexts. Until then, however, it is probably not helpful to our young teachers to encourage them to attempt forms of highly structured action research which are not going to be feasible within their normal teaching situation.

In the light of these comments, what then is the place of research methodology in undergraduate teacher training programmes? Richards (1987) has argued convincingly that the establishment of second language teaching as a profession has to be anchored in an adequate research agenda. It follows that undergraduates in EFL/ESL should be familiar enough with a variety of common types of research reports to comprehend them and to understand why the findings are reported in the ways they are. They should be aware of the distinction between pure and applied research and the requirements of both of these types of research in terms of the generalisability and verifiability of their findings.

Teacher trainees should be familiar also with the concept of action research and its distinguishing features, which are, as I have suggested, that it "belongs" to the practitioner rather than to an outside researcher, in the sense that the practitioner controls and implements it, that it is directed towards the improvement of practice, and that it need have only a purely local and specific application. They should be encouraged to see action research as a form of structured reflection, located within a continuing "reflective cycle" of reflection on practice which will form the basis of their ongoing professional development. They should be introduced to a variety of methods of structuring their reflection on professional action, some more rigorous, some less so. Finally, they should be invited to consider realistically which forms of action research will be desirable and feasible in their own teaching situations.

Conclusion

In this chapter I have examined the role of the professional project in training ESL teachers. The discussion has taken place within the context of the case study of a particular course. That discussion, however, has given rise to a number of far-reaching questions, such as the meaning of the term action research in training programmes and the function of research methodology inputs in those programmes. I have argued that there are much ambiguity and confusion in this area which could seriously distort the impact of our training programmes. I take the position that the professional project is a powerful training tool which has many positive features. However, the case study shows that it may foster forms of highly-structured research which are unlikely to be directly applicable to the future professional development of most practising teachers. Therefore, it may conceivably be counter-productive. I suggest that, for this important exercise, students should be encouraged to pursue a mode of enquiry which more closely complements the normal professional activity of classroom teachers. This more modest requirement, as the case study shows, can still allow trainees to produce work of high academic quality.

References

Cohen, L., and L. Manion. 1989. *Research Methods in Education,* 3rd ed. London: Routledge.

Halsey, A. H. (ed.). 1972. *Educational Priority: Volume 1: EPA Problems and Policies.* London: Her Majesty's Stationery Office.

Hopkins, D. 1993. *A Teacher's Guide to Classroom Research,* 2nd ed. Buckingham: Open University Press.

Nunan, D. 1990. Action research in the language classroom. In J. C. Richards and D. Nunan (eds.), *Second Language Teacher Education.* New York: Cambridge University Press, pp. 62–81.

Nuttall, C. 1982. *Teaching Reading Skills in a Foreign Language.* London: Heinemann.

Richards, J. 1987. The dilemma of teacher education in TESOL. *TESOL Quarterly* 21: 209–226.

Schön, D. A. 1983. *The Reflective Practitioner: How Professionals Think in Action.* London: Temple Smith.

    1987. *Educating the Reflective Practitioner: Toward a New Design for Teaching and Learning in the Professions.* San Francisco: Jossey-Bass.

Scott, M., L. Carioni, M. Zanatta, E. Bayer, and T. Quintanilha. 1984. Using a "standard exercise" in teaching reading comprehension. *ELT Journal 38:* 114–120.

Stenhouse, L. 1975. *An Introduction to Curriculum Research and Development.* London: Heinemann.

Tickle, L. 1987. *Learning Teaching, Teaching Teaching: A Study of Partnership in Teacher Education.* London and New York: Falmer.

Walker, R. 1985. *Doing Research: A Handbook for Teachers.* London: Methuen.

14 Learning to teach English in Hong Kong classrooms: Patterns of reflections

Ora Kwo

Introduction

This chapter addresses the nature of reflective teaching and reports on a study of student teachers' developmental patterns. By introducing a programme associated with a teacher education process defined by Doyle (1990) as the *reflective professional*, this study investigates student teachers' responses to innovations in the English methods course of the full-time Postgraduate Certificate of Education Programme of the University of Hong Kong. This chapter addresses two questions:

1. How do student teachers reflect on their learning at various points of an English methods course which is oriented towards reflective teaching?
2. How do student teachers develop in their classroom teaching over their teaching practice period?

The first question concerns the overall responses of student teachers to training in reflective teaching in terms of their own reflections, whereas the second question focuses on their teaching practice performance, which is an important dimension of the outcome of training.

The subjects were under the direct supervision of the researcher. Focussing on student teachers' ideas about their experience while learning to teach, the researcher collected data at six points in the year. Parallel to that, there was a natural generation of data from their assignments on action research. The results outline the patterns of student teachers' reflective teaching and illustrate the various levels of teaching competence in connection to their different concerns. The chapter concludes with a discussion on the conditions for reflective teaching. Implications are drawn for future development of this training paradigm.

Research literature

Stages of development in student teaching

Research has only recently begun to explore the developmental stages of student teachers. In his study of ten student primary teachers following a one-year postgraduate training course, Calderhead (1987) examined the quality of their reflections during the field experience. Although students differed in how they conceptualised and reflected on their own practice, they typically progressed through three stages: fitting in, passing the test, and exploring. In the early weeks of the field experience, students reported a high level of anxiety, particularly about classroom management. However, students' professional learning seemed quickly to reach a plateau as their daily work became routine, and most students developed a conception of the field experience as an assessment task. In the second stage, a series of "professional actions" considered worthy of credit in their assessment were identified, and their teaching behaviour was driven by their consciousness of assessment rather than by a concern for effective instruction. They were also remarkably resistant to much of the specific feedback that their college tutors provided. Instead, their class teachers were noted to have more influence in supervision of their teaching. Another impediment to learning to teach was the difficulty they experienced in carrying out detailed evaluations of their teaching. The third stage was identifiable towards the end of the field experience; when most of them knew that they could maintain control, they were willing to experiment, trying out different forms of classroom organisation. However, experimental lessons were rarely supervised, either by college tutors or class teachers, and the students were generally unable or unwilling to recognise and analyse the difficulties on their own.

On the basis of the study, Calderhead (1987) made some recommendations for the design of pre-service training. If teacher education is genuinely to pursue the objective in promoting reflection, he suggested, course organisation and support systems in schools should be carefully considered, especially in terms of supervision and assessment of teaching practice. The tutors and supervising teachers must develop a greater sensitivity to the complexity of professional learning. It may be only after a basic confidence and competence in teaching is achieved that student teachers' capacities to reflect on their teaching can be substantially developed. Ironically, appropriate supervision is missing there, even though it is at this stage that assistance in interpreting and evaluating teaching practice is required. The concern for readiness in reflection corresponded to Berliner's argument (1988) that the novice teacher may have too little experience to reflect on until extensive classroom experience has been acquired. Without suggesting that self-reflection is inappropriate for novice teachers, the studies carry criticism of the ambitious expectations of teacher preparation, and stress the need to consider the characteristic concerns of novices and their stages of development.

Concerns of novice teachers

Following twelve students of the first year of a B.Ed. course, Calderhead and Robson (1991) found that the principal images of teaching held by students were derived from their experiences in schools as pupils. These images were sometimes highly influential in their interpretation of the course and of classroom practice. Although the case studies cannot provide the basis for prescribing teacher education, the understanding of student teachers' knowledge about teaching urges the consideration of how best to design training activities in which students' existing knowledge is scrutinised and challenged (see Bailey et al., Chapter 1). In a study of nineteen student teachers at the end of their one-year preservice course, Alexander et al. (1992) reported that their orientations to the task of teaching were essentially pragmatic. There was a very strong concern to become competent as teachers within classrooms and with learners as they currently exist. Doing a practical job, and doing it well, emerged as the preprofessional disposition to teaching. As stable, competent, and responsible teachers are demanded in schools, it is natural that the novice teachers want to fit in at this stage of their professional career.

In a recent study, the author has noted that, at least in her sample, student teachers develop over time by engaging in more active reasoning and evaluation (Kwo 1994a). Despite the increased awareness of problems, generally no major decisions were reached to tackle the problems and alter directions of the lessons. Interestingly, this lack of problem-solving strategies can be related to the account of the pragmatic orientation of novice teachers (Alexander et al. 1992) and the "fitting-in" and "passing the test" stages described by Calderhead (1987). If the direction of professional development is to move towards pedagogical orientations to teaching, it is essential to facilitate further development in the "exploring" stage of student teachers with adequate support.

Constraints in teaching practice

Research continues to highlight the limited effect of teaching practice. Mistretta (1987) found that student teachers felt at risk while making decisions. They felt that the co-operating teachers were in charge, and student teachers conformed to the co-operating teachers' ideas. Owing to the limited skills in decision making while teaching, the student teachers failed to promote their autonomy despite their belief that autonomy was important.

The influence of the co-operating teacher has been well addressed in such studies as those conducted by Livingston (1990), Ben-Peretz and

Rumney (1991), and Woods (1991). Livingston (1990) pointed out that student teachers need integrated support from co-operating teachers and supervisors to engage in reflective practice. Teaching practice as currently structured in most programmes provides little time or encouragement for reflection. The shortage of opportunities to reflect was also highlighted in Bae's study (1990). The reasons for the lack of reflection in teaching practice is intriguing. It may be attributed to the shortage of opportunities as claimed by Livingston (1990) and Bae (1990). Alternatively, it may be a matter of student teachers' stages of development, as suggested by Calderhead (1987) and Berliner (1988). Future research has yet to clarify this dimension of teaching practice.

Research on the emotional aspect of student teachers provides another dimension from which to view their development. Szpiczka (1990) examined how pre-service teachers understood their teaching practice experience by describing their "display of self" (i.e., interpretation of their observable behaviour). Conflicting aspects of self-display suggested that becoming a teacher is a process of continual negotiation on the tensions between conflicting self-displays. By going beyond the observed behaviour and investigating pre-service teachers' intentions for behaving the way they do, research can enhance understanding how individuals become teachers. Along this line of enquiry, Woods (1991) examined the nature of teaching practice by investigating pre-service teachers' intentions for behaving the way they do. A critical point called "the wall" was identified and found to vary greatly among individuals. Woods asserted that student teachers need a support group during the period of teaching practice.

Prospects for innovations and action research

Current research studies appear to converge on several themes:

1. The pragmatic orientation of novice teachers corresponds to their lack of problem-solving strategies and the urge to conform with the school system.
2. The lack of reflection during teaching practice may be attributed to the structure of teaching practice, which provides little time or encouragement for reflection.
3. While novice teachers have potential for self-reflection, it is important to clarify its nature in relation to their training experiences and stages of development.

If teacher education is not simply meant to integrate student teachers into schools as they now exist, innovations are needed. As a corollary to that, if training is to have an impact on practice, the innovations should address the importance of listening to the voices of student teachers, and should examine their classroom practice with due emphasis on the support needed during the course of learning to teach. Arguably, student teachers' reflective teaching can be enhanced through curriculum development and action research (Kwo 1994b).

Through the use of video equipment and reflection exercises, the curriculum for a pre-service English methods course was developed to enhance self-reflections. The curriculum development through action research not only generated a new set of course material, it also led to a rich set of data about student teachers' learning processes. This chapter focuses on such data and draws implications for student teachers' developmental patterns.

Design and procedures

Participants and setting

This study aimed to investigate the developmental patterns of student teachers by adopting a "second-order" research perspective (Marton 1981). It followed a multiple case design (Yin 1984) that investigated student teachers in a specific context of training, under the direct supervision of the researcher. The researcher collected a full set of data on fifteen student teachers in the one-year, full-time, Postgraduate Certificate of Education Programme of the University of Hong Kong, majoring in English language teaching. Despite its pre-service nature, the programme attracted and accepted mature students who had been experienced teachers, as the Hong Kong system permits them to enter the teaching profession by virtue of their graduate status at a slightly lower salary scale. As shown in Table 1, the majority of students were female, and two thirds of them had Chinese as their native language. They were heterogeneous in their backgrounds in terms of origin, age, and teaching experience. For detailed descriptions in this chapter, only three of them were selected by variation in length of previous teaching experience and their common commitments to the professional training. For reporting, they are given the pseudonyms Anna, Bob, and Carol. They are considered to be a reasonable representation of members of the course. Anna was a mature student, and Carol a new graduate. Bob was a young male student with a little teaching experience.

TABLE I. PERSONAL DATA OF STUDENT TEACHERS

Student teacher		Gender	Native language	Origin	Age	Years of teaching experience
1		F	English	England	28	3+part-time
2		F	Chinese	Hong Kong	22	0
3		F	Chinese	Hong Kong	34	1
4		F	English	Pakistan	42	2+part-time
5		F	Tagalog	Philippines	26	4
6	Bob	M	English	Scotland	24	2+part-time
7		F	Japanese	Japan	37	part-time
8		M	Chinese	Hong Kong	22	part-time
9		F	Chinese	Hong Kong	40	part-time
10		M	Chinese	Hong Kong	27	2
11	Anna	F	Chinese	Hong Kong	42	8
12	Carol	F	Chinese	Taiwan	25	0
13		F	Chinese	Hong Kong	41	2
14		F	Chinese	Vietnam	30	5
15		F	Chinese	Hong Kong	22	part-time

Structure of the curriculum

TERM ONE

Term one was scheduled with three weeks of school experience between two periods of coursework on campus. The topics presented before the school experience gave student teachers some basic background for practical teaching. Pedagogical knowledge in the teaching of language skills was introduced, with attention to planning, teaching, and evaluation. Through the school experience, the student teachers gained acquaintance with a classroom reality in which they could expand learner knowledge and apply the pedagogical knowledge and skills to which they had been initially exposed in the course. In this way, they were prepared to pursue knowledge about teaching from practical experience. After the school experience, the pedagogical knowledge in the teaching of language skills was reviewed in relation to content knowledge in various aspects of applied linguistics. Skills in planning, teaching, and evaluation were built in as perspectives beyond lessons. Curriculum design was considered, with emphasis on critical use of textbooks and materials development.

TERM TWO

Coursework in Term Two focused mainly on preparation for the seven-week period of main teaching practice. The student teachers were prepared with skills in observation, analysis, and evaluation of video-recorded lessons. These skills were essential prerequisites for peer coaching during the main teaching practice, which demanded capability in problem solving and communication. The coursework before the main teaching practice concluded with an examination in which individuals had to independently analyse a video-recorded lesson after viewing it together in class. During the main teaching practice, alongside the further acquisition of learner knowledge and application of pedagogical knowledge and skills, each student teacher was engaged in the expansion of teaching repertoires and metacognition through conducting a classroom action research project as the final assignment. The supervisory school visits provided support on both action research and classroom teaching.

TERM THREE

Term three dealt with areas that supported the general progress of student teachers. Forums encouraged reflection on the main teaching practice, and the schedule also included student teachers' presentations of classroom action research, and teachers' general responsibilities and professional development.

Data sets

Data were collected throughout the year, both during coursework on the university campus and when the student teachers were in schools for teaching practice. To address the two research questions, the data were organised into two sets:

1. *Student teachers' reflections on learning experiences in the English methods course.* This set of review accounts was collected at six points during the course (see Appendix A at the end of this chapter). It focused on metacognition about the experiences of learning to teach. While this exercise engaged student teachers in reflecting on their learning experiences and provided feedback to the supervisor for the development of the curriculum, it also generated a substantial body of data for analysis of their reflections on their own progress during the course. In particular, their identification of problems and coping strategies contributed to knowledge about student teachers' emerging theories in action.

2. *Student teachers' development in classroom teaching over the teaching practice period.* In contrast to the first set, this data derived from the final assignment – classroom action research – which the student teachers conducted individually during the main teaching practice (see Appendix B). The assignment was designed to engage each student teacher in an investigation of one specific problematic area in his or her classroom teaching, to design strategies to overcome the problem, and to evaluate their effectiveness. As the requirements focused on the skills the student teachers should use during teaching practice, the assignment provided a database for the analysis of their development in classroom teaching.

Data analysis

The extensive qualitative data collected throughout the university course and teaching practice in schools were analysed in an interactive process of data reduction and verification (Miles and Huberman 1984: 21–23). Each set of data was reviewed and summarised according to identifiable themes, following which case descriptions were examined for patterns of similarity and difference. Finally, findings from the two sets of data were validated in the combined reviews of their case descriptions, and general patterns and variations of their development were drawn.

Results and discussion

This chapter presents a cross-case analysis of the subjects' reflections and development in the course of learning to teach. It is based on individual case descriptions, some of which are presented to illustrate patterns.

Student teachers' reflections on learning experiences in the English methods course

The results for this section are derived from the review accounts of student teachers at six points in the course. Findings are reported in temporal sequence, recounting their perceived learning, major concerns, problems, and coping strategies.

ON ENTERING THE COURSE

In order to develop relevance in the curriculum, and to understand the different routes through pre-service training that student teachers take, it is necessary to begin with this first review. It is expected that the state of motivation and values student teachers bring to teacher education can influence how they learn and develop themselves. The first review suggests that all three subjects were motivated learners on entry. After being a mother for fifteen years and a teacher for eight, Anna decided to pursue further education. Her goal was to pursue a further degree at the end of the course. In contrast, Bob had only two years of teaching experience, whereas Carol had none at all. Bob found teaching enjoyable, but was sometimes frustrated by inadequate skills. Carol had thought about becoming a teacher during secondary school but then worked for a computer company after graduating from university. This experience, however, prompted her to return to her original interest in teaching. Despite differences in past experience, all three students were committed to intensive training and saw the full-time programme as a solid ground for their career development.

At the outset, the students identified the specific teacher qualities they aimed to strive for. All three emphasised the love of learning, positive attitude, honesty, patience, care for students, enthusiasm, and dedication. Bob expressed some pedagogically-related qualities such as being fair, especially to mixed-ability students, and being friendly, but with leadership skills. Carol specifically mentioned communication skills and saw teaching as "lecturing" in an interesting manner. Given the open nature of the solicited reflections, the extent of agreement is noteworthy, and allowed the programme to be implemented in a congenial climate. If student teachers had been engaged in an "apprenticeship of observation" (Lortie 1975) in their previous schooling, the subjects in this study appear to have adopted some positive values in the apprenticeship. They brought such positive attitudes with them on entering the course which provided favorable conditions in which to engage in the pursuit of reflective teaching.

PERCEIVED LEARNING

Student teachers' perceived learning basically corresponds to the curriculum aims in promoting knowledge, skills, and a spirit of inquiry in teaching. However, different facets of emphasis were reported, which denote patterns of their responses to the curriculum. It is possible to identify Anna as "the comprehensive learner", Bob as "the integrated practitioner", and Carol as "the collaborator".

Anna's reviews of her learning experience before and after each period of teaching practice were rarely narrowly focused on content and pedagogy in English language as a subject. Alongside her experiences on campus and in schools, she characteristically engaged in some general reflections which related to her past and elevated her to an overview of herself as a learner. Initially she expressed satisfaction with her performance as a teacher in the past eight years, but was ready to acknowledge her mistakes and saw the programme as well timed to keep her from possible burnout. She completed the school experience with the realisation that many teaching principles did work when she tried them out. She guided herself with a maxim that "miracles happen to those who believe in them". The following extract from her review illustrates her receptiveness to learning:

I have begun to learn how to get rid of some rooted thinking from the past, and to replace it with some current ideas from educational studies and theories. It is not easy at all. In order to do so, I have to abandon something I have enjoyed doing so much (such as abundant teacher talk). . . . I have been challenged to excel myself. It is because the more I learn, the less I find I have known.

This philosophical view took Anna through the main teaching practice with concurrent senses of achievement and inadequacy in her knowledge and skills in teaching, as well as a willingness to learn from her students. She reported seeing herself as a student teacher for seven weeks, during which she had learnt a lot from her "teacher students".

Bob's perceptions, in contrast, follow closely the essence of the curriculum and are well related to content and pedagogy. Contrary to Anna's comprehensive overviews of her experiences in learning to teach, Bob was more identifiable as an integrated practitioner who drew immediate connections between the course and his field experiences. Initially he focused his learning on lesson planning. He related that aspect of the coursework to his past teaching, which he described as being muddled between objectives and means, thus attempting to create a link between concept and practice in lesson planning. He saw preparing lesson plans as particularly important to student teachers, since the plans would direct their attention from content to pedagogy. Seeing the range of student abilities and their varied pace in learning, Bob extended his concern for lesson planning to syllabus planning, and incorporated evaluation as an essential part of the teaching process.

At the end of the main teaching practice, he noted the inadequacy of textbook material in meeting the various demands and needs of students. His reflections were characterised by integration of concepts about teaching in different dimensions: lesson planning in the contexts of syllabus planning and evaluation, integrating language skills, and balancing teacher instructions with student-centred activities. In addition, there was an integration in the development of his personality and pedagogy:

I have developed my personality as a teacher. I have become more sensitive towards the students and when I identify any problem – academic or personal – I am willing to deal with them, thus increasing my confidence and understanding of the students. I now feel that I know what I am doing.

As one with no previous teaching experience at all, Carol pursued her coursework with apprehension about teaching. Initially she saw teaching as a job that demanded a lot of preparation and knowledge of the learning context, about which she was most ignorant. Her reflections often emphasised the importance of rapport with her students. Hence she developed her sense of collaboration initially out of a concern to work with students. She concluded her school experience with a sense of having achieved good relationships with students – "at least the students didn't hate me!" This value of collaboration later extended to a wider commitment in peer support:

Teachers' commitments in schools should not be limited to the teaching of their own students, but should include helping one another to improve their teaching skills and develop themselves. Their attention should go beyond their students to their peer colleagues through mutual observation and evaluation. . . . Being observed and given feedback by my peer helps to improve my teaching, and observing my peer gives me a chance to learn and develop my teaching skills.

While acknowledging peer supervision in teaching practice as a new concept not readily recognised in the conventional school reality, she was convinced of its significance and of her own competence in becoming a helpful partner to her peer student teachers. She concluded the main teaching practice neatly, with insights into student-oriented lessons and peer learning. Parallel to her emphasis on developing dynamic interactions among students was her perception of peers as "a resource of inspiration and encouragement". It appears that Carol's developmental process was centred on collaborative learning for both her students and herself.

MAJOR CONCERNS, PROBLEMS, AND COPING STRATEGIES

Regarding this theme, all three subjects shared major patterns, though they differed in the personal ways identified previously: Anna was "the comprehensive learner"; Bob, "the integrated practitioner", and Carol, "the collaborator". Their common patterns and variations are highlighted here according to the time sequence. Before the school experience, they all reported some self-doubts in their own knowledge and competence and in their relationships with students. Anna mentioned a concern about her lack of knowledge of her students. The dilemma for Bob was how to be friendly with students while also maintaining discipline, whereas Carol wondered how to keep smiling even if students did not respond.

During the school experience, all three reported problems of pacing in relation to time constraints and unexpected learning difficulties. In sharing a common awareness of the problems of handling student responses and their own teacher talk, they varied in their coping strategies. Anna decided to emphasise fewer and more focused objectives in a lesson, to improve and minimise teacher talk, and to communicate with students after class in order to understand them better. Bob emphasised the design of additional tasks for faster students, discipline in communicating purposes of activities to students, and refraining from repetition in teacher talk. Carol, in contrast, had little idea about coping strategies in her review, but extended her list of problems: She identified her inability to explain clearly as a crucial problem to tackle.

In their expression of concerns before the main teaching practice, all three subjects shifted attention from self-doubts to more sophisticated goals. Anna expressed relief from previous apprehensive feelings and a commitment to making the forthcoming seven weeks meaningful for her students and herself. Bob was keen to recognise problems during the flow of the lesson and to deal with extremes in good and poor student performance. Carol struggled to consider how to be efficient and effective and how to reach the students from the adult world. All of them adopted a serious attitude towards their learning during teaching practice, and they all related teaching to learning.

However, their reflections showed their concerns about a gap between targeted goals and the means to achieve them. In reflecting on the main teaching practice, all three subjects pursued higher goals in the context of higher-order problems through their self-generated coping strategies. In addressing passive learning amongst students, Anna saw herself as having an inadequate understanding of her students' culture. While reaching out for personal communications in and out of class, she realised that she also had to learn to accept students with a sense of humour. Bob perceived his major problem to be challenging students to higher goals of learning. He worried about both passive and dominant students. He strove to develop activities which demanded higher-order thinking, and allowed peer checking of answers instead of a teacher-centred mode of instruction. Seeing her own speech as problematic, Carol attempted to use cue cards and blackboard writing as support, and set for herself a rule to think before responding to unexpected student questions. In considering how to develop dynamic interaction among students, she brainstormed for a variety of activities from her own reading, as well as soliciting ideas in peer discussions. In all three cases, these developmental processes were contextualised in continual problem-solving attempts. Rather than arriving at any final solutions, each individual experienced teaching practice as having a momentum in which new problems were derived from the partial resolution of earlier ones.

REFLECTIONS AT THE END OF THE COURSE

The final reviews of all three subjects indicated their common perception that teaching was rational, required self-awareness, and made the teacher responsible for enhancing learning. The reviews also demonstrated positive attitudes about the development in students' pedagogical competence and in their personal maturation. Anna described herself as a weary and thirsty traveller on entering the programme. When given access to fresh water, she had to struggle to empty the vessel of old wine so that she could fill it with water in order to continue the journey. She felt that she had been challenged to give up her conventional practice before she could adopt a role as an effective teacher. Bob said that he had progressed in the direction he had decided to go. His initial apprehension had given way to a gradual increase in confidence when he learned to be better organised and more creative in materials development. Carol found it hard to identify her main track of development, for she felt that she had experienced too much to make a claim. Like Anna, she saw herself as having uprooted the concept of teaching planted in her since her own school days, and she had adopted a variety of new methods to motivate her students in learning.

Anticipating the coming year as a full-fledged teacher, Anna did not comment because she decided to continue with her studies in a master's programme, whereas Bob and Carol both reported expecting challenges in the increased workload. Carol found it particularly daunting to be in a staff room in which experienced and inexperienced teachers worked individually. While they were realistic about the new challenges, they were also positive about their readiness to cope. Bob looked forward to the opportunities. He was confident that he could organise his time efficiently and that his positive attitude would carry him through negative experiences. Carol was prepared to confront possible challenges to her ideology about teaching. She specifically mentioned her plan to make time for herself for language development and self-renewal. Generally, their overviews of their experiences in coursework and teaching practice were positive, despite the concerns and worries they reported over the different stages of the course.

Student teachers' development in classroom teaching over the teaching practice period

Findings of this section are based on each individual subject's final assignment on classroom action research.[1] Dimensions of analysis include focus, understanding of the problem, strategies in coping with the prob-

1 For an interesting comparison, see the chapter by Michael Wallace in this text.

lem, and insights derived from the action research. As the assignment established the knowledge and skills towards which student teachers should work, the data provided a legitimate way to observe their development during teaching practice. Video recording facilitated student teachers' critical reflections on their teaching. Accordingly, they developed teaching strategies on their own initiatives in response to their understanding of the nature of the identified problem. The cross-case analysis validated the previously identified patterns of learning to teach.

THE COMPREHENSIVE LEARNER

Anna identified the problem of pacing in her teaching, which she realized by contrasting her perceptions before and after a review of her video-recorded teaching:

On the third day of my teaching practice, I was aware of the inefficiency of my teaching, because I could only cover half of the materials. I promptly concluded that I must have had a bad PACING. I blamed the students for not paying attention to their work and they were lacking of motivation. In addition, I attributed the problem to external factors as well, such as the noise outside the classroom, the culture of the school, and the habitual practice of the regular teacher. . . . I then tried to control the students more strictly. I almost demanded from them 100 per cent silence, concentration and obedience. I put a lot of effort to detect any trace of unruly or disruptive behaviour, for I thought this would have helped me to control my pacing more properly. This lasted about one week but the situation remained unchanged, except I was more exhausted and frustrated. . . . A glimpse of light appeared when I reviewed my first video-recorded lesson – I realised the problem was the teacher, myself! I started to see that the "me today" was a product of my temperament and personality, my past experience, in particular my past teaching experience. To tackle the problem, I decided to humble myself.

Following her second perspective on the problem, Anna developed her strategies which emphasised good teacher-pupil relationships and the creation of a warm classroom atmosphere. Again, her traits as "a comprehensive learner" were apparent, as she emphasised pedagogical issues of macro level over subject-specific considerations by trying to modify learning materials and reducing irrelevant teacher talk. Her self-evaluation was both critical and positive: She was troubled by the gap between her expectations and the actual outcome of learning but was also able to rejoice in a "spark" of success when she conducted a lesson at what she considered an ideal pace. This positive experience convinced her that students could be motivated to learn at an ideal pace, despite unfavourable external factors. She adopted a long-term perspective, realising that appropriate pacing is a sophisticated technique demanding a lot of practice and requiring the teacher "to be humble, to renew herself, to serve, and to teach". Although she began the action research project with a focus on a specific problem, she concluded with a recognition that she had not overcome the problem. She evidently arrived at a theory on action which she could generalise to other problematic situations.

THE INTEGRATED PRACTITIONER

Bob focused on the problem of teacher talk when he gave instructions to set up student tasks. He saw redundant and ineffective teacher talk as detrimental to learning, because it was difficult to repair misunderstandings and caused frustration amongst students as well as loss of faith in the teacher. The analysis of his video-recorded lesson drew his attention to the nature of his weaknesses, particularly the sequence and timing of his instructions, confusing rhetorical questions which he did not want students to answer, mixing of the instructions for the task with those concerning classroom organisation, and numerous repetitions which caused him to run out of time. He developed a checklist of questions to consider in order to improve. The lesson that was video recorded at the end of the main teaching practice actually illustrated the strategies he had adopted from his list: "Stage directives and deal with one question at a time, check pacing of the instructions against students' responses, adapt language to students' level of understanding, use the blackboard whenever necessary to reduce teacher talk, and include an explanation of the purpose of each set task." Contrary to the style of "the comprehensive learner" in open and long-term pursuit of teaching improvement, Bob concluded his study by stating that:

It is vital when planning and delivering directives to keep teacher-talk to a minimum. . . . If a student clearly knows what to do and what is expected of him, then there is a better chance that he will do it and do it well.

Again, Bob's traits as "the integrated practitioner" can be seen in his action research project. He stayed close to pedagogical issues by analysing his teacher talk in depth and its effects on his students. Unlike Anna, who considered the context of learning at a macro level, Bob specifically defined and persistently pursued his research territory within the boundaries he set. His conclusion illuminated the integration of his concerns for both his and his students' performance.

THE COLLABORATOR

Carol's identification of a problem was consistent with her concerns for a positive relationship with students. She saw that questioning and soliciting answers from students was "a serious business in the class-room", and she was not satisfied with participation from only a few students. Her reflections on the first video-recorded lesson indicated her worry about a lack of effective strategies:

I planned to deliver the content of my lesson through questioning, but since the students were unwilling to respond to my questions, I just lectured and dropped all the questions I had prepared. . . . I always had to nominate students, or sometimes I simply jumped to the main task in order to avoid silent moments.

Her analysis led her to see the problem as originating with both the teacher and the students. She realised that she directed too many questions at the students when they were not ready, and she was too worried about her progress with the lesson plan to allow adequate time for her students to ponder the questions. From their facial expressions, she could detect that some students sensed her anxiety and were affected by it. They became too anxious about making mistakes to volunteer answers. She also speculated that some students might be scared of being laughed at by their peers. She identified another possible reason for students' passivity, namely, that they might be so used to one-way communication in the classroom that "they were physically or mentally not in the frame of mind to answer questions". Like Anna, Carol related these learning problems to her role as teacher: She believed that the students did not trust her and interpreted her questions as merely a means of identifying their weaknesses. Accordingly, her strategies included "creating an atmosphere of trust in the classroom", a list of reminders of "don'ts", self-directed training in improvement of her teacher talk, and fifteen suggestions for enhancing students' collaboration amongst themselves and with her as the teacher. She reported that these strategies showed some degree of success, noting:

Sometimes I gave myself thinking time by saying "That's a good idea!" or "Oh! I haven't thought about that". Alternatively, I asked the whole class to think about that answer, and then stopped talking to start thinking.

At the same time, she became aware of new problems. When students participated more actively she found herself without the language or spontaneity to handle unexpected responses. Carol consistently gave collaboration with learners and her peers a high priority. This also appeared to be her initial concern in learning to teach. She concluded her project by noting that she had just made a single step in "a journey of a thousand miles", but that she was confident that more practice would lead her to improvement.

General patterns and variations in development

When both sets of data – student teachers' reflections on their learning and their action research assignments – are reviewed, it is possible to trace agreement of the findings. These general patterns and variations of student teachers' development are discussed in this section.

As indicated in the first review, a common ground for all three teachers was their commitment to the teaching profession. However, it is also possible that the first review was useful in involving the student teachers in serious reflection for subsequent reviews. As an important component of their training, it also provided a window through which to look into their cognitive development. The data indicated that the student teachers commonly shared self-doubts at the beginning of the course. Their concerns for their knowledge and competence were also well related to their responses to pupils' learning. A common sense of care for pupils was obvious throughout the course, which was associated with their close attention to learning difficulties. Their willingness to tackle problems had moved them from self-doubts to the generation of coping strategies. Their development was well contextualised in the process of classroom action research. During the projects, higher goals were set in connection to their awareness of higher-order problems, and they strove increasingly to understand these problems from the perspective of pupils. A major positive pattern in all cases concerns their independent learning through self-reflection; this also indicates their potential for further development beyond the teaching practice experience. Overall, they became both self-critical in evaluation of their teaching and positive in their outlook towards their future development.

Apart from the general patterns, variations in their development were apparent. As mentioned earlier, Anna was "the comprehensive learner"; Bob, "the integrated practitioner"; and Carol, "the collaborator". Research on teachers' schemata helps to interpret these findings. A marked difference in the nature of and sophistication in understanding classroom events exists between novice and expert teachers, as described by Borko and Livingston (1989), Calderhead (1979, 1983), Carter et al. (1987), and Peterson and Comeaux (1987). Novices' cognitive schemata have been noted to be less elaborate, interconnected, and accessible than experts', and their pedagogical reasoning skills less well developed. Expert teachers appear to bring rich schemata to the interpretation of classroom events. Clark and Peterson (1986) suggest that these schemata might include (1) knowledge underlying their conception of what schoolchildren are like, and (2) knowledge underlying their awareness of what happens in the classroom. If experience counts as an important factor for the development of teaching expertise, the subjects' variation in previous teaching experience may indicate their different points of development on entry to the course. Hence the three subjects' styles in learning to teach may suggest different stages in the maturation of these schemata.

Since she was already experienced in teaching, Anna might have acquired a developed schema which allowed her to weigh information in the complex, dynamic world of the classroom and to determine its salience quite quickly. Accordingly, this sophisticated style characterised her reflections and classroom action research. Her initial description of "getting rid of some rooted thinking from the past" and her final metaphorical review, about having to become empty in order to be refilled for the continuation of a teaching journey, demonstrated that she had existing schema to reconstruct and that she was open to the training experience and willing to transform the schema. In contrast to Anna, Bob appeared to be in the process of developing his schema. Since he had had a little teaching experience, he might have had some simple framework on which to begin his teaching practice, but it did not weigh him down with preconceptions or demand an active reconstruction of his conception. During the course, he seemed to have confidently developed his schema in an integrated manner. Being totally inexperienced, Carol had to construct her schema from the fundamental level. She emphasised collaboration with learners and colleagues while exploring the complex classroom reality with originality. Carol appeared to especially value peer coaching. Towards the end, she reported struggling with "multidimensional" problems. It was evident that, despite her increased sophistication in reflection, she was still in the process of constructing her schema and had not arrived at a clear integration of concept and practice, as had Bob. Nevertheless, her reviews provided a vivid illustration of a possible route of novices' progression towards schema construction. Overall, the tracks in learning to teach followed by Anna, Bob, and Carol add to existing knowledge about student teachers' emerging theories in action.

Conclusions and implications

This chapter reports on the effects of training for reflective teaching. If an innovative curriculum is implemented, the empirical data indicate how student teachers will respond to this particular training, which is, in essence, the philosophy associated with the reflective teacher paradigm (Doyle 1990). I have argued that the different backgrounds of individuals should be considered on entering pre-service training. Parallel to this concern, it is important to observe that teaching competence needs to be developed through inquiry skills that proceed at an individual pace from where the trainees are. All three cases reported here show a consistency between the student teachers' perceived learning and their actual development through action research. The findings illuminate their different learning tracks, which demonstrate their self-directed initiatives. Their common attention to learning problems and their active pursuit of strategies to tackle these problems contrast with the literature on constraints in teaching practice discussed in the first part of this chapter. This raises important issues about conditions for reflective teaching and their implications for teacher education and future studies.

Dewey (1933) suggested three conditions for reflective teaching: open mindedness, responsibility, and wholeheartedness. Findings of this study agree that these conditions are necessary but argue that, in addition to personal qualities, social conditions are vital. As Chen (1993) observes, reflective teachers are culturally and socially nurtured by significant others, such as co-operating teachers, peers, pupils, supervisors, and principals, and the total formal and informal schooling context. Although co-operating teachers and school principals were not part of this study, the findings strongly support the view that individual practitioners, together with these other people in the school setting, construct reflective practice.

The open curriculum of the course provided the framework in which to build a context of reflective teaching. However, it could not, by itself, sustain continued development of these student teachers. Rather than being simply a matter of rational planning, the curriculum required contributions from the participating student teachers and their supervisors. This study shows positive effects of collegiality amongst student teachers and the benefits in learning they gained from one another. Peer help was especially significant for an inexperienced teacher like Carol. Personality differences amongst the student teachers may be useful in peer coaching, but they can also cause difficulties when there are clashes. Parallel to the school context, teaching at the university requires the supervisor to be actively involved in reflection on teaching – learning processes in the same ways that the student teachers had to be. The self-education of the supervisor-researcher is an implied but essential part of this curriculum that builds a desirable context in training for reflective teaching. This is illustrated by an extract from my own journal, which I shared with the student teachers at the end of the course:

To me, it has been a special experience, too! It has been a period of breakthrough to a new stage of maturity in my role as a teacher – I can see evidence of the possibility for experienced teachers to change and develop, as well as for novice teachers to overcome the different hurdles. As much as you, I am also aware of the uncertainty we have to live through in order to attain further enlightenment in teaching. I echo some of your feelings, as cited in your reviews. . . .

There is indeed an intimate connection between teaching and learning. Learning to teach and teaching to learn are simultaneous activities for student teachers as well as for reflective practitioners who seek to improve themselves. Conditions for reflective teaching include the entire environment and the persons associated with it.

While echoing Chen's argument (1993) that reflection is cultural and social, this study suggests the need to involve schools, where professional life in teaching takes place. The contribution of co-operating teachers and school principals is vital to strengthening the social and cultural context for this program, and future developments of the program will be shown in school realities. Another reason to call for extended work in schools concerns the continued development of novice teachers. Carol's call for collaborative learning and her apprehension about life in school as a full-fledged professional where teachers work in isolation illustrate the possible gap between the training context and the school reality. This gap may be detrimental to the continual development of student teachers, and it is necessary to explore ways to support novice professionals beyond their initial training. Thus, while a case of curriculum innovation may have positive effects on student teachers, I conclude by stressing the need to face the new challenge of partnership for implementing reflective teaching in schools.

Appendix A: Review of progress

At six points in the course, you are asked to submit responses to questions which aim to engage you in reflection about your progress. A file is set up for each of you to accommodate these data, which are related to your performance in the course and in school, thus enabling the supervisor to facilitate your development as individuals. Therefore it is important for you to convey frankly and accurately what you have in mind.

1. Orientation:
   - Why have you chosen to do the full-time P.C.Ed programme? (In considering your career, what are your options?)
   - What do you see as essential qualities of a teacher which you are striving to develop? (List them and describe role models, if any)
   - What do you expect from the English Major Methods course? (What would you like to be the objectives of the course?)
2. Before the School Experience:
   - From the course, what do you see as *new* learning experiences for you? i.e. something (you think) will change your conception about and practice in teaching.

- What are your major concerns and worries about the School Experience?
- Given the time constraints, what would you like to have as further support from the course?
3. After the School Experience:
   - What insights about teaching have you gained from the teaching practice (what principles of teaching have you put into practice), and in what ways have you developed as a teacher?
   - What are the major difficulties you have encountered and what are the strategies you have adopted to cope with these problems?
   - Given the time constraint, what would you like to have as further support from the course?
4. Before the Main Teaching Practice (same questions as "Before the School Experience")
5. After the Main Teaching Practice (same questions as "After the School Experience")
6. End of the Course:
   - From your perspective, how far have you developed yourself over the year in the essential qualities of a teacher which you have been striving to develop? (If necessary, elaborate or modify your views about the essential qualities of a teacher.) How do you anticipate your experience as a full-fledged teacher in the coming year?

Appendix B: Assessment – classroom action research

The purpose of this assignment is to engage you in an experience to investigate one specific problematic area in your classroom teaching, design strategies to overcome the problem, and evaluate the effectiveness of the strategies.

By reviewing your School Experience and the first video-recorded lesson, identify major problems in your teaching and select one from the list that you wish to work on. Describe your selected problem with an episode of recorded data in transcriptions. Design strategies to overcome the problem and carry them out during the Main Teaching Practice. Keep notes in the Teaching Practice Log File (which can be used as a framework for data collection).

The notes should help you to trace:

1. the identification of the problem in various contexts, that is, how you deepen your understanding about the nature of the problem;
2. your developing strategies to overcome the problem (refer to the notes in the course, guided reading, various material sources, and advice from tutors and peer coach);

3. your actual attempts to tackle the problem; and
4. your evaluation of the attempts.

Despite its linear outlook, your ideas related to these four aspects naturally develop in a cyclical process of planning-teaching-evaluation. A cumulative record in these four aspects is essential for the subsequent report.

During supervisory visits over the Main Teaching Practice period, you can discuss any insights and queries with your supervisor. By the end of the Main Teaching Practice, review the Teaching Practice Log File and write up the report of your investigation, focusing on the four aspects above. For illustrations, you can retrieve relevant data on teaching material, classroom anecdotes or critical incidents, transcriptions of section(s) of the second video-recorded lesson of less than 15 minutes, and include them in the Appendix. The main report should not exceed 2,000 words.

Teaching Practice Log File

Purpose

The Log File helps to structure your experience in teaching practice and to keep a record of your progress in learning how to teach. While promoting a balanced concern for planning, teaching, and evaluation, the accumulated data offer a substantial basis for completion of the final assignment. Your progress as reflected in the Log File also contributes towards the assessment of teaching practice.

Content

1. **Programme Plan:** to be organised at the beginning of the practical teaching period.
   a. Date
   b. Focus
   c. Teaching material/assignments
   d. Schedule of observations and peer coaching sessions

2. **Programme:** to be accumulated during the practical teaching period. It is important to maintain a balance between planning and evaluation.

   A. *Lesson Plan*
      a. Date
      b. Class
      c. Goals
      d. Teaching materials and aids:
         Specify the type and source; include in the file if revised or teacher-made.
      e. Previous learning
      f. Teaching procedure:
         Activities / Purposes / Classroom organisation / Pacing
      g. Follow-up (and assignments, if applicable)

   B. *Lesson Evaluation*
      a. A general framework of evaluation:
         Strengths and problems
         Issues deserving further attention
         Alternatives (consider pedagogical principles)
      b. Self-evaluation:
         Sample of pupils' assignments;

Anecdotes or critical incidents, if any. (Note this during the lesson, or as soon as possible afterwards. Formative evaluation followed by prompt action or immediate adjustment is more demanding of your decision-making capacity, but deserves to be incorporated into your evaluation mechanism.)

c. External evaluation:

Peer (Refer to documents on peer coaching.)

* There should be one video-recorded lesson followed by a proper report derived from discussion with your peer-coach.

Teacher tutor; University tutor

3. **Programme Summary:** to be completed by the end of the practical teaching period. Refer to the Programme Plan and summarise the actual progress you have made in the implementation of the plan. Briefly comment on how adequately your pace is related to learner responses and the demand of the school syllabus.

References

Alexander, D., D. Muir, and D. Chant. 1992. Interrogating stories: How teachers think they learned to teach. *Teaching and Teacher Education* 8(1): 59–68.

Bae, S. T. 1990. The evolution of two student teachers' professional beliefs during their student teaching period. Doctoral dissertation. Urbana-Champaign: University of Illinois.

Ben-Peretz, M., and S. Rumney. 1991. Professional thinking in guided practice. *Teaching and Teacher Education* 7(5/6): 517–530.

Berliner, D. C. 1988. Implications of studies on expertise in pedagogy for teacher education and evaluation. In *New Directions for Teacher Assessment* (Proceedings of the 1988 ETS Invitational Conference). Princeton, N.J.: Educational Testing Service, pp. 39–68.

Borko, H., and C. Livingston. 1989. Cognition and improvisation: Differences in mathematics instruction by expert and novice teachers. *American Educational Research Journal* 25(4): 473–498.

Calderhead, J. 1979. Teachers' classroom decision-making: Its relationship to teachers' perceptions of pupils and to classroom interaction. Doctoral dissertation. Stirling UK: University of Stirling.

——— 1983. Research into teachers' and student teachers' cognitions: Exploring the nature of classroom practice. Paper presented at the American Educational Research Association, Montreal, Canada.

——— 1987. The quality of reflection in student teachers' professional learning. *European Journal of Teacher Education* 10(3): 269–278.

Calderhead, J., and M. Robson. 1991. Images of teaching: Student teachers' early conceptions of classroom practice. *Teaching and Teacher Education* 7(1): 1–8.

Carter, K., D. Sabers, K. Cushing, S. Pinnegar, and D. C. Berliner. 1987. Processing and using information about students: A study of expert, novice, and postulant teachers. *Teaching and Teacher Education* 3(2): 147–157.

Chen, A. Y. 1993. Experienced and student teachers' reflection on classroom practice. *Education Research and Perspectives* 20(1): 46–63.

Clark, C. M., and P. L. Peterson. 1986. Teachers' thought processes. In M. Wittrock (ed.), *Handbook of Research on Teaching*. New York: Macmillan, pp. 255–297.

Dewey, J. 1933. *How We Think: A Restatement of the Relation of Reflective Thinking to the Educative Process*. Chicago: Heath.

Doyle, W. 1990. Themes in teacher education research. In W. R. Houston (ed.), *Handbook of Research on Teacher Education*. New York: Macmillan.

Kwo, O. W. Y. 1994a. The relationship between instructional behaviour and information processing of student teachers: A Hong Kong study. *Singapore Journal of Education* 14(1): 13–30.

1994b. Enhancing reflective teaching in teacher education: Curriculum development and action research. In D. C. S. Li, D. Mahoney, and J. C. Richards (eds.), *Exploring Second Language Teacher Education*. Hong Kong: City Polytechnic of Hong Kong, pp. 113–130.

Livingston, C. C. 1990. Student teacher thinking and the student teaching curriculum. Doctoral dissertation. College Park: University of Maryland.

Lortie, D. C. 1975. *Schoolteacher*. Chicago: University of Chicago Press.

Marton, F. 1981. Phenomenography: Describing conceptions of the world around us. *Instructional Science* 10: 177–200.

Miles, M. B., and A. M. Huberman. 1984. *Qualitative Data-Analysis: A Sourcebook of New Methods*. Newbury Park, Calif.: Sage.

Mistretta, A. M. T. 1987. Decision-making in student teaching: An ethnographic study examining autonomy in the elementary school student teacher's relationship with the cooperating teacher. Doctoral dissertation. Storrs: University of Connecticut.

Peterson, P. L., and M. A. Comeaux. 1987. Teachers' schemata for classroom events: The mental scaffolding of teachers' thinking during classroom instruction. *Teaching and Teacher Education* 3(4): 319–331.

Szpiczka, N. A. 1990. Preservice teachers' perspectives on student teaching. Doctoral dissertation. Syracuse, N.Y.: Syracuse University.

Woods, H. E. 1991. The student teaching experience: A qualitative examination. Doctoral dissertation. Corvallis: Oregon State University.

Yin, R. K. 1984. *Case Study Research: Design and Methods*. Beverly Hills, Calif.: Sage.

15 When input becomes intake: Tracing the sources of teachers' attitude change

Martha C. Pennington

Introduction

In recent years, attempts to introduce change in education have often focused on the long-range development of teachers as reflective practitioners (Cruickshank and Applegate 1981). As pointed out by Pennington (1993: 47):

> In recent literature on teacher education, two major themes recur. These are the themes of *reflection* and *development*. The terms *reflection* and *development*, in their multiply ambiguous richness of denotation and connotation, are useful for describing the nature of a general orientation to language teaching and learning which is intended not merely to change learners and teachers, but to transform them from their traditionally limited roles of implementing a curriculum into active agents shaping the future in their mutual contexts.

In the view of Schön (1983), reflective practitioners are those who continually develop their professional expertise by interacting with situations of practice to try to solve problems, thereby gaining an increasingly deep understanding of their subject matter, of themselves as teachers, and of the nature of teaching.

There are many ways to approach reflective practice and to seek to develop a reflective orientation in teachers [see Clift et al. (1990a) for an overview of programs]. One approach to developing reflectivity among pre-service and in-service teachers is that of *collaborative action research* (Clift et al. 1990b), in which teachers work together – often in co-operation with a teacher preparation unit at the tertiary level – to address common problems. Through collaborative action research, it is expected that teachers will become more reflective about their individual and collective practice, as they share experiences and develop their individual and collective resources for dealing with specific problems in their school and classroom environment and, more generally, for managing the complex work that is teaching.

This chapter is an abridged and revised version of an internal research report, "Assessing training inputs in collaborative action research to introduce process writing in Hong Kong secondary schools", Research Report No. 27, Department of English, City Polytechnic of Hong Kong, June 1993, funded by the Hong Kong University and Polytechnic Grants Council.

Action research which aims to develop individual and collective responses to the challenges of education can be viewed "as a model for professional growth and the ongoing examination of school problems and issues" (Clift et al. 1990b: 53) and for the long-range development of teachers (Whitford et al. 1987). In the best case, "collaborative action research [goes] beyond a search for solutions to immediate problems [and] toward the creation of a professional learning culture in schools that emphasizes inquiry and reflection as the norm" (Clift et al. 1990b: 54).

Learning to be reflective through collaborative action research, and reflection itself, is a time-consuming, intensive process as "teachers struggle to learn to work with other adults" (Clift et al. 1990b: 59) and to create personal understandings of their teaching contexts which situate them within a larger context of theory and practical reality as determined by individual and collective knowledge and experience. To the extent that teachers in a common context interact well and are congruent in their beliefs and needs, to that extent they will develop a synergistic relationship through the collaborative project in which the quality of the experience of the group as a whole will be greater than the sum of the individual experiences of its members. Thus, collaborative action research adds the extra dimensions of group development and teamwork which may enrich the experience of the individual. In the case of collaborative action research between secondary and tertiary institutions, it also adds the possibility for "vertical" and abstract learning through mentoring by someone at a higher academic level.

This chapter assesses a project involving the adoption of a process approach for teaching English composition by eight experienced secondary-level English teachers in collaborative action research with a tertiary institution in Hong Kong as part of their M.A. thesis work. In describing and evaluating the project, which implements a particular collaborative model for school-based action research and reflective practice, the chapter is an attempt to heed the call of Zeichner (1987) for more research on the preparation of reflective teachers. Based on an assumption of the crucial importance of awareness and attitude change as underlying all other types of teacher change (Freeman 1989), the chapter focuses on the teachers' awareness of and attitudes towards the different types of input and support they were offered in the project, seeking to understand the success or lack of success of different forms of input in changing their awareness and attitudes in relation to the innovative practice of process writing. It is found that the forms of training and support which have the greatest impact on the individual teachers' awareness and attitudes are those which represent the most accessible part of the input, and a concept of *accessible input* as the condition for *intake* is developed, by analogy to the *input–intake* distinction introduced by Corder (1967, 1971) for second language acquisition and elaborated in Krashen's (1981, 1982) monitor model.

Background to the project

The project aims to provide the necessary background and support for native Cantonese-speaking English teachers working in Hong Kong secondary schools to apply a process approach to writing (Pennington, 1993). Although all of the participating teachers had at least six years of prior teaching experience and some prior knowledge of process writing, all felt that they did not know how to apply the approach effectively in their teaching contexts, nor were they certain that the approach could be applied in the examination-centred, transmission-based teaching culture of the Hong Kong schools (Pennington and Cheung, 1995). Given the product-oriented nature of the Hong Kong educational system and the limited initial state of the teachers' knowledge of and attitudes towards process writing, the approach can be considered a type of innovative practice in the context of investigation.

The training and support offered to participants [see Cheung and Pennington (1994) for details] and the interpretation of findings of the research follow the Rogers (1983) model of how innovations diffuse in new contexts, as "an individual (or other decision-making unit) passes from first knowledge of an innovation, to forming an attitude toward the innovation, to a decision to adopt or reject, to implementation of the new idea, and to confirmation of this decision" (p. 163). The project aims to provide a knowledge of process writing, skill training for applying a process approach, and reflective input and training so that the participating teachers can make a decision whether or not to make an initial adoption of the new teaching approach by trying it out in their individual classrooms. At an early stage of implementation, adopters usually apply an innovation on a limited basis, modifying it as needed to fit the conditions of their individual situations. After some period of implementation, the adopter will either confirm or reverse the earlier decision made to adopt the innovation. Some adopters will in this process gradually come to implement the innovation on a wider scale and to consolidate their new behavior into their own personal adaptation and application of the innovation over the longer term.

The research traces the teachers' starting state, before being exposed to the organized input provided in the project, and then their reactions and ongoing process of adoption over a period of one and a half years. The present chapter reports on the participating teachers' adjustment in the "intensive" initial phase of the project, a six-month training and try-out period in which they prepared and executed three process writing units in one of their English classes and completed a series of written evaluations and reflections on their experience as part of their M.A. thesis work. The discussion concentrates on participants' written assessment of the training program by means of an evaluation questionnaire completed at the end of the training and try-out phase and reproduced here in the appendix at the end of this chapter.

Input to teachers

The preparation for participating teachers was part of a funded research project investigating the adoption of process writing by practicing bilingual secondary teachers in Hong Kong. The participants included eight secondary teacher volunteers attending a part-time evening master of arts in teaching English as a second language (MATESL) course in the English Department at City Polytechnic of Hong Kong and working full time during the day at a variety of types and levels of secondary schools. The organizers of the project include the project head, or principal investigator who is a researcher and faculty member in the department (the author); the project trainer-research assistant who is a former secondary teacher from Hong Kong now pursuing a doctorate in the same department (Marie Cheung); and the project's associate investigator who is a faculty member in the department (Mark Brock).

A variety of types of input were provided beginning in August 1992 in four-hour programs of two initial training sessions and five monthly follow-up meetings. At a general level, the different kinds of input were designed to help participating teachers try out a process-oriented teaching approach for writing instruction and evaluate its appropriateness for their own classroom environments. More specifically, the project goals were to:

- Build up participating teachers' knowledge base of principles and practices for implementing process writing in the Hong Kong secondary school environment
- Encourage and assist teachers to adapt and "re-invent" process writing to fit it comfortably into their own teaching situation
- Establish good communications channels for participating teachers to learn about process writing, to share information, and to express their concerns, their problems, and their successes in adopting the approach for their individual teaching contexts
- Develop a common language and common understandings for dis-

cussing the nature of process writing, the problems surrounding its adoption, and potential solutions to those problems
- Develop attitudes and skills for reflection and problem solving so that teachers can effectively address the difficulties they experience in relation to process writing during the time frame of the project and beyond.

Informational presentations and handouts

The training included two types of informational presentations by the project head (Pennington) and trainer (Cheung) during the training sessions. One of these presented content information on process writing and how it might be implemented in the Hong Kong context, based on the relevant literature in the field and the project organizers' previous experiences teaching writing from a process approach and preparing teachers for the teaching of writing in Hong Kong and elsewhere. The other type presented comparative information on the participating teachers as individuals and as a group, based on the ongoing analysis of the data of the research project and fed back to them at the monthly meetings as it became available.

In conjunction with these presentations, participants were given handouts describing process writing in the form of a teacher's manual, worksheets to help them in their initial decision process in relation to adoption, and summaries of the information fed back to them in the ongoing analysis of findings, such as their responses and those of their students to several questionnaires [see Pennington and Cheung (1995) for further information on the questionnaires].

Guided sharing by participants

Closely tied to the informational presentations and handouts was planned time for guided discussions to elicit information and reactions from participants of their relevant background to the project, their worries and problems related to process writing, and the teaching techniques which they had found to be successful in applying aspects of process writing.

Lesson materials

Early in the project, participants were provided with three sample process approach lessons developed by the trainer, and considerable time was spent going through these and discussing how they could be used or adopted in the participating teachers' classes. In particular, time was spent working on the areas of peer work and feedback, offering concrete teaching guidelines as well as discussion of how process-oriented feedback might differ from product-oriented feedback. Later, participating teachers brought in their own materials and described these to each other in one of the project sessions. At their request, copies of all these shared lesson materials were made and distributed to other participants.

Lesson reflections and observations

Teachers made written reflections on their process writing lessons and turned these into the associate investigator (Brock) for oral and written feedback at the next training session. A preliminary analysis of this data is given in Brock (1994). They were also observed once by the project head or the trainer in each of the three process writing units taught in late 1992 and early 1993. A meeting was held following the observation to discuss what had been observed, and a detailed written report of the observation was prepared afterwards and then given to the observed teacher.

Pre- and postquestionnaires

The participating teachers filled out a number of self-assessment questionnaires at the beginning and the end of the training to describe their experience and attitudes in relation to writing, the teaching of writing, and the process approach. A summary of the changes in perceptions of the teachers as a group is reported in Cheung and Pennington (1994).

One-on-one contact with project members

The teachers met monthly on an individual basis with the project head and were also encouraged to be in telephone contact with the trainer, the project head, and each other between training sessions.

General profile of assessment of training input

In February 1993, a questionnaire was given to participating teachers to assess the value of the forms of input they were exposed to during the training and try-out phase of the project (see the appendix). By means of this questionnaire, the teachers rated each form of input in terms of a "helpfulness" scale ranging from 1 = "very helpful" to 4 = "not at all helpful". Respondents then provided comments on what they thought they had learned from the input in each category and what use they had made or would make of that information. Table 1 presents

325

Martha C. Pennington

TABLE 1. MEAN ASSESSMENT OF HELPFULNESS OF EACH FORM OF INPUT BY
THE EIGHT TEACHERS

	Mean[a]
1. Informational presentations	1.75
2. Informational handouts	1.75
3. Guided sharing by participants	1.94
4. Sample process-approach lesson materials	1.63
5. Shared materials from other participating teachers	1.75
6. Reflection sheets on process-approach lessons	1.88
7. Feedback on reflection sheets	2.25
8. Observation feedback	1.63
9. Initial teacher questionaires	2.25
10. Final teacher questionnaires	1.88
11. Individual meetings with project head	1.25
12. Telephone access to trainer	1.75
13. Telephone access to other participating teachers	3.00

[a]1 = Very helpful, 4 = Not at all helpful.

the group means for the various types of input according to the "help-fulness" scale.

On the whole, participating teachers rated the project favorably, with only three items receiving less than a 2 ("helpful") rating and with an overall mean rating of 1.90. As a group, the teachers found the individual meetings with the project head (item 11) to be the most useful form of input (mean 1.25), indicating in their written comments that these meetings helped them to clarify their project-related problems and learn research skills. The next most useful forms of input (mean 1.63) were judged to be the feedback given on observations (item 8), which teachers commented helped them to learn about and improve their teaching, and the sample process approach lesson materials (item 4), which all of the participating teachers found they could make direct use of in teaching their own classes or indirect use of in designing their own lessons.

The least valuable type of input (mean 3.0) was judged to be the telephone access to other participating teachers (item 13), which the teachers in fact hardly made use of. Also judged somewhat lower in value (mean 2.25) than other categories of input were the feedback on the reflection sheets (item 7), which some participants commented would have been of greater value if given individually and with less time having elapsed from the time the reflections were written, and the information which teachers wrote on the initial questionnaires (item 9). Though the initial questionnaires were the same ones filled out for comparison at the end of the training phase of the project, about six months into the research, some of the participating teachers objected to how long it had taken them to fill these out and could hardly see the purpose of filling these out twice.

As the responses in Table 1 indicate, in general, the project teachers as a group found the information given to them in the form of (1) presentations and handouts on process writing prepared by the project head and the trainer and (2) lesson materials provided by the project trainer and shared from other participants more valuable than the attempts to develop reflectivity in the group and a deeper understanding of the innovation represented by process writing through (3) guided sharing by participants, guided written reflections on their own process approach lessons, feedback on those reflection sheets from the project associate investigator, and information on the teacher questionnaires. The teachers also generally preferred individual activities such as meeting with the project head or receiving one-on-one feedback after observation of their classes to group activities such as guided sharing of experiences by participants and feedback on reflection sheets, also done in a group. This response pattern is perhaps the one that would be most expected from teachers trained in a heavily product-oriented, transmission-oriented teaching culture, with its emphasis on content of materials, individual achievement, and learning from authority.

The eight teachers as a group had low awareness of the value of the telephone contact with each other, the grouped and individual feedback given on their reflection sheets, and the initial questionnaires. The final questionnaires, the observation feedback, the sample process-approach lessons, and the one-on-one meetings with the project head had higher credibility and utility for them, as they understood their purpose and could use this information readily. Thus, forms of input which were of an unfamiliar type, and which had a less obvious and less immediate utility for them, had less of an impact on participants than those which could immediately be interpreted and added to their repertoire without major changes in behaviour or shifts in point of view. It can be concluded that for the project as a whole, the most successful types of input were those which were most accessible, that is, those with which participants were most familiar and those which they could apply at an individual, additive level, without much self-investment or investment in the group.

To be able to interpret this response to the project input by the group members and what it means in terms of the impact of the project on the teachers' adoption of the innovation, it is necessary to look more deeply into the available information about the eight teachers as a group and as individuals. For this purpose, participants' overall response to the project as judged by this assessment instrument can be contrasted with their starting state of mind, as interpreted from their responses to

TABLE 2. INITIAL IMPLEMENTATION ATTITUDES OF PROJECT TEACHERS

Implementation attitude		Teacher
Enthusiastic	Very positive, with some concerns about feasibility	A B
Favourable	Positive, with some concerns about feasibility	C D
Highly conflicted	Very interested but very doubtful about feasibility	E
Conflicted	Interested but very doubtful about feasibility	F G
Unenthusiastic	Mildly interested but very doubtful about feasibility	H

Source: Pennington and Cheung 1995.

the initial teacher questionnaires filled out six months previously (Pennington and Cheung, 1995). By contrasting these response patterns, one can make a global evaluation of (1) how positive or negative the individual teachers' perceptions are and (2) the degree of change in their perceptions since the beginning of the project, thereby judging their degree and manner of adoption of the innovation while also assessing any other changes which occurred in their outlook towards the project. This contrastive information on the earlier and later profile of the teachers' general attitudes can also be supplemented by their individual responses to the open-ended questions. The contrastive information on the teachers' earlier and later attitudes and the individual response patterns for the open-ended, summative questions of the project assessment instrument make it possible to evolve a coherent picture of the changing profile of the eight teachers in this research.

Comparison with teachers' initial profile

Table 2 shows the starting implementation attitudes of the eight project teachers, as judged from their initial questionnaire responses, characterized in terms of a scale of descriptors from "enthusiastic" to "unenthusiastic". The individual teachers are represented by the letters A to H, arranged alphabetically according to how positive their perceptions were of the implementability of the innovation in their specific educational contexts.

As can be seen from Table 2, at the beginning of the project, all participants expressed some concerns about the feasibility of implementing a process approach in their teaching situations, with Teachers E, F, G, and H expressing deep misgivings and doubts about implementing process writing even on a very limited basis. Teachers A, B, C, and D expressed mainly positive implementation attitudes, though tempered with some concerns about feasibility. From these profiles of participants, some logical inferences or predictions can be made, and these can then be tested against the data of the project assessment questionnaire.

From the profiles of the teachers reported in Table 2, it can first of all be logically inferred that teachers with the most internally consistent implementation attitudes – that is, those at the top and the bottom of the implementation attitudes scale – will show the least change in attitudes during adoption. In the case of Teachers A and B, who were at the top of the implementation attitudes scale at the start of the project, there is less room for positive change than in the case of other participants. Moreover, since they do not have major concerns about feasibility, there is little reason for them to question their favourable view of process writing and to develop more negative attitudes than those they held at the outset of the project. In the case of Teacher H, the lack of both enthusiasm and strong interest in process writing, coupled with strong doubts about feasibility, predict a low level of involvement with the project and with the innovation. This low level of involvement in turn predicts minimal change in attitude as well as in behaviour. However, since Teacher H's implementation attitude is in the lowest category, any attitudinal change is likely to be in a positive direction, that is, in the direction of the higher group norm.

In contrast to these relatively stable attitudes of the teachers in the highest and lowest categories – i.e., Teachers A, B, and H – those in the middle categories – i.e., Teachers C, D, E, F, and G – would appear to have more mixed and therefore more mutable attitudes towards the project. In addition, the highly conflicted position of Teacher E suggests the likelihood of a change in attitude, as this teacher tries to adjust her point of view to make her attitudes more internally consistent. As before, the most logical prediction is that Teacher E's attitudes will become more favourable under the positive modelling of the project investigators and the positive group norm set by other participating teachers with profiles at a higher level on the implementation attitudes scale. However, because of the serious doubts which she entertained at the beginning of the project about the possibility of implementing a process approach in her own classroom – and indeed in Hong Kong in general – Teacher E could exhibit a "rollercoaster" pattern of attitudes in the project, shifting up and down the scale depending on contextual and/or personal factors. Thus, while the attitudes of Teachers A, B, and

H appear to be the most stable and therefore the least amenable to change, the attitudes of Teacher E appear to be the most unstable and therefore the most mutable of all the teachers in this particular group.

TABLE 3. INDIVIDUAL PROJECT TEACHERS' OVERALL ASSESSMENT OF TRAINING (MEAN FOR ALL QUESTIONS)

Training assessment		Teacher
Very helpful		
	1.46	D
	1.77	E
	1.85	A/C
	1.92	F
Helpful	2.00	G
	2.04	B
	2.29	H
Not very helpful		

Note: The vertical dimension in the table represents the numerical or conceptual distance between items.

Table 3 depicts the differences in overall mean assessments of training by each of the eight teachers. By considering the relative position, or rank, on the "helpfulness" scale and the relative order of the alphabetic letters, one can see the relative differences in six-month assessments among the eight teachers in comparison to their original implementation attitudes. For example, the table shows that Teacher H, who was at the lowest position (eighth rank) in the original evaluation of implementation attitudes by the project investigators, is also at the lowest relative position in his attitudes to the training (eighth rank), while both Teacher D's and Teacher E's attitudes in relation to the training are, relatively speaking, more positive than were their original implementation attitudes, having assumed the first and second ranks, respectively.

TABLE 4. COMPARISON OF PRE- AND POSTTRAINING ATTITUDES OF INDIVIDUAL PROJECT TEACHERS

	Pretraining attitude	Posttraining attitude
Very positive		
		D
		E
	A	A/C
	B	F
Positive		G
	C	B
	D	
	E	H
	F	
	G	
	H	
Negative		

Note: The vertical dimension in the table represents the numerical or conceptual distance between items.

The relationships between the earlier (pretraining) and the later (posttraining) attitudes of the teachers are more explicitly compared in terms of their relative positions on a scale of "negative" to "very positive" perceptions in Table 4. As can be interpreted from this graphic comparison, all of the participants except Teachers A and B could be said to have shifted their point of view in a positive direction in relation to the project. Teachers A and B, as predicted, show the least difference in the level of their pretraining and posttraining attitudes. Teacher A's posttraining position in third rank suggests a still positive attitude at more or less the same level as at the beginning of the project but with no strong attitudinal effect of training, while Teacher B's pretraining enthusiasm appears to have dropped off a bit, as she slips to a slightly unfavourable position below the midpoint of the rating scale, which places her lower in the postassessment attitudes than all of the others except Teacher H. Teacher H, though still the most negative of the participants, has become more positive in his attitudes. Also in line with prediction, Teacher E has shifted her position among the participants substantially, to the second most positive rank, while the most positive rank is reserved for Teacher D, who appears to have made the biggest jump in general attitude of all the participanting teachers. Teacher C's attitude appears to have shifted only moderately in a positive direction, retaining third rank, but with Teachers F and G narrowing the gap in the next two ranks.

The big positive jump in attitudes of Teachers D and E and the apparently negative reaction to the training of Teacher B, who was one of the two most favourable teachers at the beginning of the project, can only be explained with reference to additional information about these teachers. The big shift in attitude of Teacher D and the comparatively slight shift in attitude of Teacher C, coupled with the greater positive attitudinal change in Teachers F and G, must be due to some differences in their pre-existing characteristics or in the amount or type of learning which they had during the project. Such individual differences in fact emerge from the teachers' comments on the two summative questionnaire items (15 and 16), asking which forms of input from the project had the greatest impact for them. Differential adaptation to the project is also revealed in the teachers' suggestions for improvements in response to item 17, as these responses point out weaknesses in the training program that may have caused some of the teachers to react less favourably to certain types of input than they would have otherwise.

Response pattern in individual comments

The group profile presented in Table 1, and the summary of individuals presented in the other tables, while valuable as an overall picture of the teachers' reaction to the intensive training and try-out phase of the project, obscure individual differences in participants' responses. For example, while the majority did not rate the feedback on their reflection sheets as very helpful, one participant (Teacher D) rated it as having the greatest long-term impact on her teaching (question 16), "as it's a written response to the reflection I have done". The fact that the feedback on the reflection sheets was personalized and given in relation to her own reflections apparently made it of great value to Teacher D, though other participating teachers did not comment on this feature of that form of input.

In what follows, the similarities and differences in individual awareness and attitudes are examined through a look at the teachers' responses to the summative questions 15 and 16, where participants were asked to evaluate which input had been of the greatest value or impact to them, both immediately (question 15) and in the long range (question 16), and to give reasons for their answers.

Individual teachers

Teacher A

In response to question 15, Teacher A mentioned the most sources (five) of influential input, an indication perhaps of her basically positive reaction to process writing and to the project as a whole. Her responses included three kinds of input mentioned by others – observation feedback ("obtain insights"), individual meetings with the project head ("could clarify uncertainties"), and reflection sheets on process-approach lessons ("self-evaluation") – and two not cited by others – the initial and final teacher questionnaires ("organize our own thoughts"). In all cases, the reasons given by Teacher A for her choices (as indicated in parentheses) are summarized from her comments in earlier sections of the questionnaire. In response to question 16, Teacher A stated that the informational handouts had been the most valuable form of input, as they provided useful information about process writing.

Teacher B

Teacher B mentioned only observation feedback in her responses to questions 15 and 16. With reference to question 15, Teacher B remarked that observation feedback had the greatest immediate impact and value for her as a teacher,

... since it is the direct contact from the third person with my students. The observer can make use of her own subjective sense to give an overview of the lesson.

In response to question 16, she observed:

Observation feedback gives me a long-term impact as I can see my development in teaching from an observer which gives objective and whole lesson

333

reflection as feedback. Sometimes, I think something which is not so valuable can have great potential for development from others' viewpoint. I find my own identity and accept both my strengths and weaknesses.

These comments demonstrate a desire on the part of Teacher B to improve her teaching and to learn from the experience and reflections of others. At the same time, they indicate a focus away from the training sessions and towards her own classroom and students.

Teacher C

Teacher C's response to question 15 centered on sharing, as she mentioned the two input types of guided sharing by participants and sharing of materials from other participating teachers, commenting that these were most important for her "because they are real experience and the effectiveness of implementation is reflected in a real authentic situation". Teacher C went on to comment in answer to question 15, "I've learnt a lot from the other participating teachers". Teacher C stated that the most useful long-term impact was the concepts and theory provided to support a belief in the workability of process writing, suggesting that the concepts and theory covered in the training gave her the confidence to apply process writing in her own context.

Teacher D

Teacher D is the only teacher, other than Teacher C, who cited the guided sharing in the training sessions as having the most immediate impact or value for her as a teacher, "as I can see myself in some of the issues raised". Teacher D goes on to state that, as a result of this sharing:

I don't feel that I am working towards an impossible task nor are my students really hopeless. Learning takes time and patience. My job is to share what I know with them and support them.

In contrast to all of the other participants, Teacher D focused on the feedback received on the reflection sheets as having the greatest long-term impact or value for her as a teacher. She viewed these responses as

. . . a summary of how my teaching of writing has evolved. I'm going to take them out in a year or so and see if there has been any changes.

Thus, Teacher D's responses to questions 15 and 16 show a strongly reflective orientation, coupled with a long-range orientation to her own development and change.

334

Teacher E

With regard to question 15, Teacher E stated that the sample process-approach materials had the most immediate impact or value, as "the basis for me to design my own materials". In terms of long-range impact or value, Teacher E commented:

The reflection sheets written by myself gave me a long-term impact. That is the way I should learn how to review/evaluate myself in my teaching. This will help me to develop a continuous and personalized self-supporting life-cycle.

Like Teacher D, Teacher E took a long-term career or whole-life view of her experiences in relation to the project.

Teacher F

Teacher F focused on the sample process-approach teaching materials and the shared materials from other participants as having the most immediate impact or value for her as a teacher: "They could be ready for adaptation and use". In terms of long-range impact or value, she listed the informational presentations and handouts ("strengthen my background knowledge"), the observation feedback ("helps my reflection in teaching, gain insights and confidence"), and the individual meetings with the project head ("better understanding").

Teacher G

Teacher G mentioned articles, handouts, and direct contact with the project head as forms of input that had the most impact on him, both immediate and long-range. Teacher G focused as well on other forms of input that helped him to assess his performance, including the reflection sheets in his answer to question 15:

From my personal point of view, I think the individual meetings with the PI, the reading material and reference materials and the reflection sheets had the greatest immediate impact to me as a teacher. I tried to remedy my weakness every time I received the above inputs. The research is not only a teaching process. It is also a learning process that I learn about myself and my teaching career.

Teacher G's answer to question 16, in terms of long-range impact, included only the informative source materials and handouts:

The informational presentations and the informational handouts have the greatest long-term impact to me as it provides me with the latest information about the process writing as well as the basic understanding about how to teach the process and its methods and approaches.

Teacher H

Even more than Teacher G, Teacher H focused on information transmitted through articles, handouts, and direct contact with the project head as the kinds of input that had the most immediate and long-range impact. In relation to the individual meetings with the project head, Teacher H remarked:

She could often answer my questions and help me solve the problems worrying me. For example, once when I got very upset for not knowing whether I should cut the number of drafts my students had to write (because of the students' low motivation), she gave me advice that helped me make a prompt and wise decision.

Teacher H focused on the intellectual and research aspects of the project in his response to question 16, commenting that the articles given out at the beginning of the project were the most valuable for him for the long-term:

Not only did they help me understand process writing and its related issues, but I think they will also go on inspiring me with ideas about possible areas about process writing to explore.

Thus, Teacher H's view of his long-range benefit from the project is in providing him with potential ideas for future research.

Comparison across teachers

The responses to the open-ended questions reinforce the differential profile of teachers' attitudes obtained in the initial assessment of teacher attitudes and experience at the beginning of the project, as reported in Pennington and Cheung (1995), and in the phase one project evaluation. Those teachers who showed the most reflective orientation in their responses to question 15, about the input having the strongest immediate value or impact – i.e., Teachers A, B, C, and D – were also those with the most positive implementation attitudes at the beginning of the project. These were presumably the teachers who were most ready to accept the types of input that allowed them to consider their own response to process writing and to adopt the innovation on a deeper level, beyond simply applying new materials.

Those teachers who focused on the sample process-approach materials, the informational handouts, the reference materials (articles), and/or the meetings with the project head as having the greatest immediate impact or value – Teachers E, F, G, and H – are those who had the most negative feelings at the start of the project. Of these, Teacher E, who said that she was affected in the long term by the reflection sheets, and Teacher F, who said that the observation feedback had a long-term influence on her, began the training with a more positive outlook than Teachers G and H, who focused on the long-term impact of the intellectual and research-focused aspects of the project. At the same time, Teacher G, who was also focused on the teaching aspect of the project, started out with a more positive outlook than Teacher H.

Looking across these eight teachers' summative responses on the evaluation questionnaire, one can also gain some insights about the attitudes and awareness that predict major changes. Although both Teacher A and Teacher C show positive and reflective attitudes in their responses to question 15, their general response to the questionnaire and to question 16 indicates a less deep level of participation in the adoption process, predicting Teacher A's lack of change and Teacher C's modest change in overall attitude during the course of the project, as illustrated in Table 4. Unlike Teacher A, who mentioned a wide range of types of input on the project as being valuable to her, or Teacher C, whose response centred on sharing with other teachers during the training sessions, Teacher B focused only on the impact of observation feedback, a form of input gained outside the training sessions. This focus may be indicative of a not entirely positive response to those sessions, which may in turn account for her comparatively low position in the ranking on the evaluation questionnaire.

Teacher D had a strong focus on her own reflectivity in promoting change. Like Teacher D and unlike Teacher F, who said that the informational handouts and meetings as well as the teacher-shared materials and observation feedback had value for her, Teacher E also discussed the value of the reflection sheets in promoting her long-range development. Their comparatively greater focus on reflection may account for the comparatively greater change in attitude of Teachers D and E as contrasted with Teacher F, who nevertheless showed positive movement from her earlier to her later implementation attitudes.

Teacher G, like Teacher H, was strongly focused on the research aspects of the project. Unlike Teacher H, however, he attempted to make use of other project input and specifically mentioned the reflection sheets and observations as being of value to him. This is perhaps one reason why his attitudes seem to have improved somewhat more than that of some of the other teachers in the group. Teacher H, who had the most negative initial implementation attitudes of all the teachers in the group and who remained at the bottom of the ranking in the later assessment of attitudes, showed the greatest tendency to an intellectual, nonparticipatory approach to learning of all the members of the group.

He was also the most focused on research and the least focused on teaching and self-reflection.

To highlight the main finding of this comparative analysis, the two teachers who most explicitly articulated a long-range view, Teachers D and E, gave the highest evaluation overall to the project, which may be taken as an indirect indication of their comparatively greater positive change in attitude from the start of the research and/or their greater benefit from the project. This long-range, whole-career, or whole-life outlook was the most notable difference between Teachers D and E and the other teachers in their responses to the postproject assessment questionnaire and may represent a major reason for their higher project assessment and/or greater positive movement in attitude. In the case of Teacher E, the positive movement in attitude may have resulted from her dilemma of having such conflicting views about process writing and its implementability in her teaching context. In the case of Teacher D, it seems to stem from her experience with the reflection sheets and the feedback received on these, which appeared to influence her to become increasingly reflective over the three lesson cycles (Brock 1994). It is also possible that Teacher D's attention to reflection stems in part from a basically analytical personality and a pre-existing reflectivity vis-à-vis herself and other people, as she appears from her questionnaire responses to be particularly receptive to and interested in input from others in relation to her own reflections.

In constructing a picture of the teachers' response to the process writing project, one final element to be considered is the suggestions they made for improvement of the training – information which reinforces and supplements other aspects of their response. In particular, this information points to areas of resistance which may have impeded intake, both for the group as a whole and for some of the individual teachers, particularly Teacher B.

Suggestions for improvements in future training

The participating teachers all made one or more suggestions in response to question 17 about maximizing the effectiveness of future training. Their comments were mainly to suggest adding something to the training and involved issues of additional materials, structure, training in specific areas, and time in relation to the project. Teacher D, for example, suggested more prestructuring and follow-up to project sessions, for example, by giving out an extensive outline and the teacher's manual in advance, and adding the element of individualized sessions with the associate investigator to follow up the whole-group feedback sessions on the reflection sheets. Teacher B felt that there could have been more interaction with participants, suggesting that a "workshop or group work (role-play) on giving oral feedback" would have been useful. She also made the following suggestions:

In sharing materials design, each participant can highlight the success or failure in using their materials during the teaching process. They can raise the problems and the problems to be solved by the others through discussion.

A session on sharing feelings, problems encountered which are not included in the writing lessons can be a source of emotional support. Sometimes, a mutual support not only focusing on the project can also be very essential.

Teacher B included other suggestions, often in conjunction with criticisms of the project, in her responses to other questionnaire items. A major suggestion was given in her answer to item 1, right at the beginning of the questionnaire: "It would be much better if the training session was not mainly on Saturday morning, more time was needed." In responding to the question about what was learned from the guided sharing by participants, Teacher B wrote:

I appreciate the sharing very much but it took me some time for warm-up before I could concentrate on the issue discussed. Having training on Saturday morning is a factor.

In her response to the question in item 7 asking what had been learned from the feedback on the reflection sheets, she wrote: "The feedback would have been more useful if we could get immediate feedback as there was a time gap in between". As these comments illustrate, Teacher B made the most suggestions for improvement and was critical of the schedule of the training and the way some activities were handled.

Teacher E commented on the need for more time "to help participants to digest what we have learnt in each session", and Teacher F made a similar point:

The informational presentation should take more time. Teachers need more time to go through the handouts and discuss about them.

From these comments, it seems that several teachers felt that they could have benefited from more time for sharing and reflection during the whole-group training sessions. Also, in Teacher H's view, the number and length of the questionnaires should be reduced if possible: "To complete all the questionnaires given at the beginning of the training is an exhausting task".

The suggestions made for improving the program in future training make it clear that some of the participating teachers had criticisms of the way in which the sharing by participants and the feedback given on their reflections were carried out, while others felt there had not been enough time for adequate absorption of the training input. Hence, in addition to any reasons related to the nature of the individuals involved, it may be that the way in which participation was solicited from group members and the lack of time for thorough sharing were at least partially responsible for the teachers' lack of strong support for these aspects of the program. Some participants' negative attitudes in relation to the structure or content of certain types of project input may therefore hold the key to understanding why some forms of input did not become intake in general and in particular cases. Moreover, the fact that Teacher B had so many suggestions and criticisms in relation to the training suggests that she may have developed attitudes of resistance that impeded intake of some kinds of input. In addition, Teacher H's lack of intention to use much of the input made available to him in the future, as stated in his open-ended responses to some of the earlier questions, is reinforced by his comment in question 17 about the time it took to fill out project questionnaires.

Discussion

Teachers change in areas they are already primed to change, and this priming depends on their individual characteristics and prior experiences, which shape their view of their classroom, their students, and themselves as teachers. Freeman (1989) stressed that teacher change is predicated on the attitudes and awareness of individual teachers towards their teaching contexts. Accordingly, attempts to influence teachers' behaviour will have an impact only in areas where the input is valued and salient to the individual, and where it is congruent with, and interpretable within, the teacher's own world of thought and action.

Drawing on the distinction between *input* and *intake* first proposed by Corder (1967, 1971) and later developed by Krashen (1981, 1982), it can be said that in teacher change, input does not equal intake. Rather, teachers take in only those aspects of the available input which are accessible to them. *Accessible input* refers to those types of information which teachers are prepared to attend to because of a high awareness and understanding of the input, coupled with favourable attitudes such as a pre-existing interest in or positive attitudes towards the form of input or the person giving the input, a strong recognition of a need for input or change, or a strong feeling of discomfort at a pre-existing clash of values. In contrast, input for which teachers have low awareness, low understanding, or unfavorable attitudes is *inaccessible input* in whole or in part and will consequently have little or no impact in the way of teacher change.

In the present project, the group as a whole were most primed for direct, one-on-one input from the project head, who acted as a mentor modelling skills, giving directions for solving problems, and motivating abstract learning in relation to process writing and the conduct of research. The group perceived the teaching materials to be highly accessible forms of input and were able immediately to notice and appreciate their application in their own teaching contexts. Of the different forms of reflective input provided, the feedback via classroom observations was for them most accessible, probably because it was the most familiar, the most immediately relevant, and the most directly interpretable.

In contrast, the group as a whole found the access to other participants and the training mode of learning through reflection, particularly in the case of the baseline questionnaires and the written feedback on their reflection sheets, of relatively low accessibility. This reaction may have been in part a consequence of the inherent nature of these kinds of input, or it might have been a result of the way in which the teachers were introduced to this input. It seems likely that in some cases, certain types of input were low in accessibility to some participants because of the way in which the input was presented in the training sessions. Individual differences in response were also apparent in cases where a certain person found a specific form of input valuable in fulfilling an interest or in meeting a need which was particularly salient for that individual.

High-intake components of the training program included those types of input which represented the least change in the teachers' established patterns of thinking and of learning. Thus, they had high intake in relation to the role of being a student of and an apprentice to the project head, who had been their teacher previously in other M.A. courses and whose authority and knowledge they accepted with little question. For some of the teachers, the trainer did not have as high credibility, being herself a graduate student and former secondary teacher. Similarly, the associate investigator, who was not involved in the early project training sessions and who was less well known to the participants than the project head, may have been an unfavorable influence for some of the participants in determining the intake of the feedback on the reflection sheets. For others, however, the trainer was an important resource person and facilitator, who mediated between them and the project head and helped to interpret project input and make it more accessible, and the associate investigator also provided useful input that significantly influenced their responses to the project.

Much of the input within the project was presented in a group format, with many opportunities to learn from each other's experiences built into the training. Although some of this input may not have been developed as successfully as it might have been, it is nevertheless the

341

case that the accessibility of many of the forms of input on the project were mediated by the group. In such cases, the nature of the group and of the norms which it develops act as favouring or disfavouring influences in how input is received and whether it becomes intake. In the particular case at hand, it seemed that little group synergy developed within the training sessions. Only Teachers D and E spoke up frequently or at length in many of these group sessions, thus exhibiting a greater commitment to and acceptance of the project aims and the format of the sessions. Certainly, individual differences played a role, as Teachers D and E were more likely to volunteer answers in their previous coursework as well. But it also seems likely that the particular dynamic of the group was not a favouring one, possibly based on pre-existing negative feelings in some group members.

The lack of synergy in this particular group was due partly to the fact that the participating teachers were all working at different schools and mainly at different grade levels. It is also possible that the lack of group dynamics and the lower accessibility of group-oriented input in this project was a result of prior expectations or cultural norms. Some lack of understanding about working with each other to get ideas and to solve problems comes out, for example, in a comment by Teacher C to the question about what was learned from telephone access to other participants: "I had not called any of the other participating teachers because I thought the guidance and instructions from PI and trainer were adequate".

The pattern of high- and low-intake forms of input may be due in part to the larger cultural context, which favours individualized, non-participatory, no-risk learning – for example, from a master or from tried-and-true methods and materials. Thus, the subjects as a group were most favourably disposed to those aspects of the project which put them into direct contact with the project head or which gave them ready-made materials. Cultural norms may also help to explain the lack of strong response to the reflective aspects of the project. In general, the collaborative aspect of the research was helpful to participants only in so far as it made resources available. Participants hardly exploited the collaborative possibilities for sharing and co-developing insights, commiserating, or working jointly on solutions to problems – functions which might come more naturally to a group of Western teachers more familiar and comfortable with interpretation-oriented teaching and learning. Because they were not greatly exploited, the opportunities for collaboration which had been built into the training were not entirely successful in fulfilling the intended purposes of promoting group communications channels, teamwork, joint development, and a more reflective outlook in all of the participating teachers.

The reaction of these teachers to the different kinds of input to which they were exposed in the process writing project may be a result of the strong cultural tradition of transmission-oriented teaching and learning in Asian education. Such an orientation predicts that input in the way of materials, structured presentations, and information provided by an authority or "expert" would be received more readily than input developed through collaboration and reflection, that is, through interpretation-oriented teaching and learning. Nevertheless, in the responses on the phase one evaluation of some of the participating teachers, there is evidence of receptivity to collaborative and reflective input, indicating some possible impact of the training in developing more process-oriented and interpretation-oriented values for teaching and learning.

Reflective outcomes are most apparent in one teacher, Teacher D, who might have been the most reflective of the teachers to begin with, adding weight to findings that efforts to develop reflective approaches to teaching are most effective in those who already have reflective attitudes (Korthagen 1985: 14) or who show some predisposition to reflectivity in their attitudes of curiosity and interest in exploring knowledge (Goodman 1986: 121). Interestingly, in Goodman's (1986) study, one student teacher who did not react positively to the reflective aspect of the training showed a strong orientation to presentation of information in materials, expressing the view that time would have been better spent showing the trainees the best way to use textbooks. It might be that a strong orientation to concrete input from sources such as teaching materials is generally associated with a lack of reflectivity, perhaps as a consequence of underlying transmission-based values.

While accessibility appears to be a necessary condition for input to become intake, reflection may be a precondition for intake to enter the *teacher change cycle* (Pennington 1995), through which it will be processed at an increasingly deep and personal level to become part of the teacher's system of values and classroom behaviours. In this way, the intake to the teacher change cycle becomes *uptake* which is eventually represented in teaching outcomes.

Conclusion

On the whole, the phase one project assessment shows a positive response to an action research collaboration between a group of bilingual secondary teacher M.A. students and a tertiary institution in Hong Kong to introduce process writing as an innovation in their classrooms. In particular, their response seems to indicate some positive momentum on the part of every individual in the initial six-month "intensive" period of the project, which may carry over into the one-year "extensive" period of individual adoption that follows. The examination of the

343

characteristics of the individual teachers, the group as a whole, the different types of input provided in the project, and the ways in which these were delivered accounts for differences in individual assessments of the project. This same examination also helps to elucidate differences in the accessibility and the intake of the various forms of input offered to participants in the course of the training, and in the way those forms of input might have been interpreted in relation to pre-existing transmission-based values or the promotion of greater reflectivity and interpretation-based, process-oriented values.

It would seem to be desirable in a project aiming for innovation and teacher change to have different options for input to become intake, in order to meet the differing profiles of individual participants. It would also seem desirable to organize such a project in conjunction with the teachers' own research projects – e.g., M.A. theses or action research requirements in other courses – to sustain the effort and attention needed to persevere throughout the implementation period. However, at the same time as it ensures their continuing motivation, cooperation, and communication with investigators, tying in a project such as the one described here with graduate research runs the risk that some participants will become more involved in the research than in the teaching aspects of the project and so will be less likely to be changed by it as teachers.

Realistically, one can probably not prevent individuals from focusing on those aspects of a project which are for them most accessible – i.e., most relevant, interesting, or important. Moreover, it is possible that a focus on research may help to reinvigorate experienced teachers, giving them new ways of approaching practice that may affect their teaching in major ways in the future. Finally, by allowing different teachers to focus on whichever aspect of a project attracts them, each individual follows his or her own path of professional development, which for a not insignificant number of teachers means that they will eventually exit from their jobs in the classroom to become supervisors of other teachers or tertiary-level educators themselves.

Appendix: Evaluation questionnaire

City Polytechnic of Hong Kong Process Writing Project –
Dr. Martha C. Pennington

Assessment of training input

The different kinds of training input that you have received in the project are listed in the following questionnaire. Please rate them in terms of how helpful you found them by assigning a ranking number according to this scale: 1 = very helpful; 2 = helpful; 3 = not very helpful; 4 = not at all helpful. Then comment on what you think you learned from each type of input and what use you made or will make of each of these inputs. Before beginning, please look over items 1–17 to become acquainted with what you will be asked to comment on.

1. Informational presentations by Private Investigator and Trainer in training sessions

   What do you think you learned from this input?
   What use did you or will you make of this information?

2. Informational handouts given by Trainer and Private Investigator in training sessions

   What do you think you learned from this input?
   What use did you or will you make of this information?

3. Guided sharing by participants in training sessions

   What do you think you learned from this input?
   What use did you or will you make of this information?

4. Sample process approach lesson materials given by Trainer and Principal Investigator

   What do you think you learned from this input?
   What use did you or will you make of this information?

5. Shared materials from other participating teachers

   What do you think you learned from this input?
   What use did you or will you make of this information?

6. Reflection sheets on process approach lessons

   What do you think you learned from this input?
   What use did you or will you make of this information?

7. Feedback on reflection sheets from Assistant Investigator

What do you think you learned from this input?
What use did you or will you make of this information?

8. Observation feedback from Trainer and Principal Investigator

What do you think you learned from this input?
What use did you or will you make of this information?

9. Information on initial teacher questionnaires

What do you think you learned from this input?
What use did you or will you make of this information?

10. Information on final teacher questionnaires

What do you think you learned from this input?
What use did you or will you make of this information?

11. Individual meetings with Principal Investigator

What do you think you learned from this input?
What use did you or will you make of this information?

12. Telephone access to trainer

What do you think you learned from this input?
What use did you or will you make of this information?

13. Telephone access to other participating teachers

What do you think you learned from this input?
What use did you or will you make of this information?

14. Other input

What do you think you learned from this input?
What use did you or will you make of this information?

15. Of all of these project inputs, which one(s) had the greatest immediate impact or value for you as a teacher, and why?

16. Which project input(s) do you think will have the greatest long-term impact or value for you as a teacher, and why?

17. If we were to run a project like this again, what suggestion(s) could you make for maximizing effectiveness of the training?

Thank you for assisting us with the project and its evaluation.

References

Brock, M. N. 1994. Reflections on change: Implementing the process approach in Hong Kong. *RELC Journal* 25(2): 51–70.

Cheung, M., and M. C. Pennington. 1994. Cultivating product-oriented teachers to adopt process writing: An example of an innovation-related inservice programme. In D. C. S. Li, D. Mahoney, and J. C. Richards (eds.), *Exploring Second Language Teacher Development*. English Department, City Polytechnic of Hong Kong.

Clift, R., W. R. Houston, and M. C. Pugach. 1990a. *Encouraging Reflective Practice in Education: An Analysis of Issues and Programs*. New York: Teachers College Press.

Clift, R., M. L. Veal, M. Johnson, and P. Holland. 1990b. Restructuring teacher education through collaborative action research. *Journal of Teacher Education* 41(2): 52–62.

Corder, S. P. 1967. The significance of learners' errors. *International Review of Applied Linguistics* 5(4): 161–170.

1971. Idiosyncratic dialects and error analysis. *International Review of Applied Linguistics* 9(2): 147–160.

Cruickshank, D. R., and J. H. Applegate. 1981. Reflective teaching as a strategy for teacher growth. *Educational Leadership* 38: 553–554.

Freeman, D. 1989. Teacher training, development, and decision making: A model of teaching and related strategies for language teacher education. *TESOL Quarterly* 23(1): 27–45.

Goodman, J. 1986. Making early field experience meaningful: A critical approach. *Journal of Education for Teaching* 12(2): 109–125.

Korthagen, F. 1985. Reflective teaching and preservice teacher education in the Netherlands. *Journal of Teacher Education* 36(5): 11–15.

Krashen, S. D. 1981. *Second Language Acquisition and Second Language Learning*. Oxford: Pergamon.

1982. *Principles and Practice in Second Language Acquisition*. Oxford: Pergamon.

Pennington. M. C. 1995. The teacher change cycle. *TESOL Quarterly* 29(4): 705–731.

1993. Implementing process writing in Hong Kong secondary schools: Towards a context-sensitive model of educational innovation. Earmarked Research Grant No. 904051, Hong Kong University and Polytechnic Grants Council.

Pennington, M. C., and M. Cheung. 1995. Factors shaping the introduction of process writing in Hong Kong secondary schools. *Language, Culture and Curriculum* 8(1): 1–20.

Rogers, S. M. (1983). *Diffusion of Innovations*, 3rd ed. New York: Free Press.

Schön, D. A. 1983. *The Reflective Practitioner: How Professionals Think in Action*. Aldershot Hants, England: Avebury.

Whitford, B. L., P. C. Schlechty, and L. G. Shelor. 1987. Sustaining action research through collaboration: Inquiries for invention. *Peabody Journal of Education* 64(3): 151–169.

Zeichner, K. M. 1987. Preparing reflective teachers: An overview of instructional strategies which have been employed in preservice teacher education. *International Journal of Educational Research* 11(5): 565–575.

Section IV   Epilogue

16 The "unstudied problem": Research on teacher learning in language teaching

Donald Freeman

Revisiting the introductory metaphor of stories

In the first chapter we noted that, in the field of teacher education, scant attention has been paid to understanding how people learn to teach. Referring to the field of language teaching, we introduced the metaphor of stories, arguing that we have had enjoyable and entertaining accounts of classroom language teaching – proposals for teaching methods, classroom activities, materials, and the like – with little examination of the characters, plots, and settings in which those stories transpire, or even careful examination of how the stories themselves are assembled. We pointed out that although people have been learning to teach languages for a long time, few in our field have paid much attention to understanding how the processes of teacher learning actually unfold or the knowledge and experience that underlie those processes. Thus most conventional practices in language teacher education have operated like hand-me-down stories, folk wisdom shared as "truths" of the profession with little other than habit and convention on which to base them.

We in language teaching are not alone in this oversight, however. In an article titled, "Teacher education and learning to teach: A research agenda," researchers at the National Center for Research on Teacher Education noted (NCTRE 1988: 27):

Despite the plethora of suggestions, teacher education is still an "unstudied problem." We know relatively little about what goes on in different teacher education programs and how teachers are affected. The fact that friends and foes of teacher education hold different conceptions of what teaching is like, and what teachers need to know, and how they can be helped to learn makes it difficult to compare and evaluate the various proposals for reform.

Since 1975, however, teacher learning and thinking have become established as core concepts in educational research, which has led to a re-examination of the stories and common assumptions by which teaching and teacher education are done (Clark and Peterson 1986).

Preparation of this chapter was supported in part by a grant from the Spencer Foundation.

Until very recently, language teacher education has been slow to engage these core concepts or to pursue similar research that could inform its practices. Most conventional practices have been based on academic tradition and the need to define a professional identity for language teachers, and not on any solid, inquiry-derived understanding of what individuals need to know in order to teach or to learn to do what they do in classrooms (Freeman 1994a). The research reported in this volume is a departure from this norm, however. It is fair to say that it marks the first step in establishing a formal research base for language teacher education.

Calls to establish a research base for language teacher education started in earnest in the late 1980s (Freeman 1989; Richards and Nunan 1990;), but progress was hampered by lack of a common conceptual framework through which to organize such work (Freeman and Richards 1993). Drawing again on our introductory metaphor, there has been no shared view of the basic elements of plot, setting, and character by which to assess the accuracy or veracity of the various stories about language teaching that are told in teacher education, curriculum design, methodology, and so on. We have not had a common way to analyze what we take for granted in the practices of language education – the folk wisdom on which we operate – and therefore to establish a useful and critical conversation about those practices.

In order to develop such a framework, three basic questions need to be addressed:

- What are the *antecedents* in general educational research on teacher learning and thinking that relate to teacher learning in language teaching?
- What *conceptual issues* need to be addressed in teacher learning in language teaching to establish a framework for research?
- Which *research methodologies* are most useful and productive in studying how teachers learn to teach languages?

These questions, taken together, form the organizational structure of this chapter. In the following analysis, I consider each question separately and then jointly to outline a conceptual framework for research on teacher learning in language teaching. Because the work reported in this volume is critical to this endeavor, I refer to various chapters as exemplars of both the conceptual issues and the research methodologies I discuss. The chapter may thus be read as a summary of the research reported in the book or as a conceptual overview and introduction. My aim is to outline how the "unstudied question" of teacher learning in language teaching can be fruitfully approached and productively studied.

Antecedents

As a field, language teaching has not been unique in paying little attention to how people come to know what they know and do what they
do as teachers. In educational research and policy making generally, it
has been only since the mid-1970s that teaching has been fully viewed
as a cognitive undertaking. In the symbiotic way that is typical of good
research and theory building, this development has both led to and been
fueled by new conceptual understandings and diversification of research
methodologies. The movement has also been a critical step in the study
of teacher education. In order to establish a basis on which to research
the practices of teacher education, teaching has to be approached as a
complex cognitive activity (Floden and Klinzing 1990). Similarly, teachers have to be viewed as individuals who learn, shape, and are shaped
by the activity of teaching (Freedman et al. 1983). In language teaching,
as I noted at the beginning of this chapter, these questions have just
begun to surface. Thus, to discuss productively the conceptual frameworks and research methodologies employed in the study of language
teacher education, it is useful to have some understanding of their antecedents in general educational research.

Throughout its development in this century, educational research has
generally focused on student learning and achievement. Thus teaching
has been examined almost exclusively through that lens (Suppes 1978).
The evolution of the accompanying process-product research paradigm
casts teaching in terms of behaviors and activities that could be studied,
quantified, and assessed via learning outcomes. In summarizing such
process-product models of teaching, Shulman (1986: 5) cites Gage to
identify four common elements:

These are (A) the perceptual and cognitive processes of the teacher, which
eventuate in (B) action elements on the teacher's part. The teacher's actions
are followed by (C) perceptual and cognitive processes on the pupil's part,
which in turn lead to (D) actions on the part of pupils.

In this paradigm, teachers' thoughts lead to their actions, (A) to (B),
which in turn trigger students' thoughts (C), which lead to their actions
(D); see Figure 1. Reading from left to right, we see the individual
teacher and student, who meet in a social domain of classroom and
school. The teacher's thinking and actions, (A) to (B), are her individual
world, while the student's thinking and actions, (C) to (D), are his own
world. Between these two domains lies the social landscape of their
interaction. The second perspective, however, is a horizontal one that
contrasts the invisible mental world with the publicly accessible behavioral one. This distinction alerts us to the private cognitive worlds of
teacher and student, (A) and (C), as contrasted to the public world of

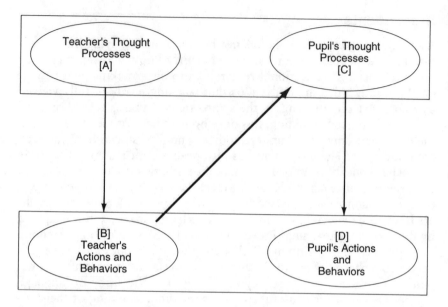

Figure 1. The process-product research paradigm.

their actions and behaviors, (B) and (D). Research in the process-product paradigm has focused on the public behavioral domain and taken it as an indicator of the underlying individual cognitive processes. Thus public teaching could be linked to private learning.

In what has become a classic statement of this research architecture, Dunkin and Biddle (1974) outlined four types of variables in process-product research: *presage* or *background variables* (about students' backgrounds, gender, ethnicity, and so on), *context variables* (about the community, school, and classroom), *process variables* (behaviors and changes in the classroom), and *product variables* (short- and longer-term effects on student learning and achievement).[1] The argument was made that, through examination of the effects of these variables on one another, teaching could be related to learning:

A major goal [of process-product research] was to estimate the effects of teachers' actions or teaching performances on pupil learning. The assumption was made that differences among teachers in how they organize instruction, in the methods and materials they use, and in how they interact with pupils would have different effects on how much children learned (McDonald and Elias, quoted in Shulman 1986: 10)

1 Chaudron (1988), discussed later, gives an overview of these variables in terms of research on the second language classroom. See Nunan (1991b) for a critical review of work, specifically research methods, in classroom-based research.

This same goal has generally permeated the conceptual and practical development of research in language teaching and learning (Long 1980). In introducing his major survey of such research, titled *Second Language Classrooms*, for example, Chaudron (1988: xv) writes:

This book reviews classroom-based research and attempts to provide confirming or disconfirming evidence for claims about the influence of language instruction and classroom interaction on language learning. *This is achieved by comparing studies that describe teachers' and learners' behaviors in classrooms and synthesizing them into generalizations about the processes that take place in second language classrooms* [emphasis added].

Thus Chaudron identifies the process-product paradigm and its accompanying view of teaching as behavior, as the predominant structure of research in language teaching (see Freeman 1995b; also Nunan 1992a: 1–20). Although qualitative studies have begun to appear in studies of second language learning, teaching continues to be viewed generally as a means of delivery of subject matter, rather than as an activity unto itself.[2]

In part, the study of teaching per se has been hampered by the lack of a clear aim. Within the process-product paradigm, the purpose was quite clear: Teaching was understood in terms of the learning outcomes it produced. Referring to Figure 1, it was the link, often assumed to be almost causal, between the teacher's actions (B) and the student's mental processes (C) that counted. In this framework, however, the teacher's thinking and mental processes (A) were of little or concern. To consider teaching independently, and to examine fully the connections between the teacher's mental processes (A) and her actions (B), required a newly articulated research aim. This challenge was in part sociopolitical and in part conceptual and methodological. Several events in educational research in the mid-1970s marked the advent of this new research aim which combined the sociopolitical and epistemological agenda of advancing teaching and teachers with the conceptual and research agenda of how to do so.

Clear articulations of this agenda appeared in several areas, most particularly in high-profile research reports in the United States and in England and in the publication of two books that became highly influential: Philip Jackson's (1968) *Life in Classrooms*, and Dan Lortie's (1975) *Schoolteacher: A Sociological Study*. These books argued for

2 A notable exception has been the work of Allwright (1984, 1988; also Allwright and Bailey 1991), which has examined the relationship – or lack thereof – between what teachers teach in lessons and what learners learn from those lessons. See also Prabhu (1992), as discussed in the next section. See also Bailey and Nunan (1995) for the first major collection of qualitative research in second language education.

recentering educational research on the classroom, as Lortie stated in his Preface (p. vii):

It is widely conceded that the core transactions of formal education take place where teachers and students meet. Almost every school practitioner is or was a classroom teacher; teaching is the root status of educational practice. . . . *But although books and articles instructing teachers on how they should behave are legion, empirical studies of teaching work – and the outlook of those who staff school – are rare.* [emphasis added]

Lortie's view of the primacy of teachers drew upon Jackson's study of elementary schools, *Life in Classrooms,* written seven years earlier (Jackson 1968). Jackson had focused attention on schools and classrooms as contexts through which to examine and understand teaching. However, he extended to classroom life certain assumptions of stability, regularity, and predictability that derived from process-product research. Jackson observed (1968: 7): "Not only is the classroom a relatively stable physical environment, it also provides a fairly constant social context. Behind the same old desks sit the same old students, in front of the familiar blackboard stands the familiar teacher."

From this etic – or outsider's – perspective, there appeared to be great regularity in the external world of classroom teaching. Perhaps for that reason, the teacher's internal mental world was perceived to be minimally sophisticated as well. Noting the "absence of technical terms in teachers' talk," Jackson (1968: 144) commented: "Not only do teachers avoid elaborate words, they also seem to shun elaborate ideas." In a sense, Jackson's views captured the consensus of the period, one that was challenged in the mid-1970s at a [U.S.] National Institute of Education meeting outlining directions in research on teaching. In a report titled, "Teaching as clinical decision-making," a panel of distinguished educational researchers chaired by Professor Lee Shulman[3] took issue with this view. They noted:

The Panelists took seriously the value of the teacher's own description of how he or she constructs the reality of his [sic] classroom, of what was done and why, and of how the students are, and how he or she feels about them. (NIE 1975: 3)

In 1976–1977, a separate report by the Working Group on Classroom Decision-Making of the Social Science Research Council in England made a similar argument for focusing on teachers' decisions in the process of teaching (Eggleston 1979; Sutcliffe 1977). Thus two influences converged to establish a new conceptual framework focused on

---

3 Shulman's role here is worth noting, as he introduced decision making (see Shulman and Elstein 1975) as the first major conceptual framework for examining teachers' thought processes (see Kagan 1988 for a review).

the teacher: the educational research community's increasing interest in the contexts of teaching and in the person and life experiences of teachers, as reflected in Jackson's and Lortie's work, and the highly visible reports from these two panels. Together this influence helped to delineate the area of inquiry that came to be known variously as *teacher thinking, teacher cognition, teacher learning,* or *teacher knowledge* [see Clark and Peterson (1986), and Shavelson and Stern (1981) for the first reviews of this literature].

The aim of this new direction in research was relatively clear from the outset, perhaps because its locus was easily identifiable. Writing in the proceedings of the first meeting of the International Study Association of Teacher Thinking, held in 1983, Halkes and Olson (1984: 1) stated:

Looking from a teacher-thinking perspective at teaching and learning, one is not so much striving for the disclosure of *the* effective teacher, but for the explanation and understanding of teaching processes as they are. After all, it is the teacher's subjective school-related knowledge which determines for the most part what happens in the classroom; whether the teacher can articulate her/his knowledge or not. [emphasis in original]

Comparing teacher cognition to its antecedents in process-product research, Halkes and Olson concluded: "Instead of reducing the complexities of teaching-learning situations into a few manageable research variables, one tries to find out how teachers cope with these complexities" (1984: 1).

Although the locus was established, the field of work had yet to be fully articulated. In her seminal article, "Research on teacher's knowledge: the evolution of a discourse," Elbaz (1991: 1) outlines the conceptual categories into which this area of inquiry evolved. She suggests that the areas of "teacher thinking, the culture of teaching, and the personal, practical knowledge of teachers" now comprise research on teacher knowledge. However, although the field has become differentiated, the aim continues to be much the same: to provide, within the research process, a means and forum for the expression and examination of teachers' views and experiences of their worlds. Elbaz (1991: 10) explains this aim in terms of "voice":[4]

Students of teacher thinking have all been concerned to redress an imbalance which had in the past given us knowledge of teaching from the outside only; many have been committed to return to teachers the right to speak for and about teaching.

4 Carter (1993) gives an extended discussion of the notion of story and voice in the study of teachers' knowledge.

The orientation toward how teachers think and what they know about teaching inaugurated by the panels and the books mentioned earlier and articulated by Elbaz, permanently altered the terrain of educational research. Under the rubric of teachers' knowledge, these inquiries have made a clear and convincing case for the need to include the perspective and knowledge of teachers in understanding teaching. They have thus helped to broaden and to refocus the ends and the means of understanding education. These sociopolitical changes in the status of teachers and teaching, and the accompanying diversification in research methodologies, have been useful, however; teacher education continues to be relatively untouched and unstudied by them. The natural connection that one might expect between such research and deepening the understanding of teacher education and teaching practice has been less clear or forthcoming. Floden and Klinzing (1990: 15) comment on the shifting nature of those expectations:

A decade ago [i.e., 1980], researchers were optimistic about the contributions they could make to the improvement of teacher education; practitioners seemed hopeful, even if skeptical, about the prospect of practical applications. Now the tables seemed to have turned. Although research-based descriptions of effective teaching actions are used in teacher education and form the basis for state-prescribed teacher competencies, some prominent researchers are skeptical.

Teacher education endures as a domain in which opinion and tradition hold sway, while little is understood empirically about how or to what extent it actually works. A recent set of major research studies of teacher education conducted by the [U.S.] National Center for Research on Teacher Education[5] has made important inroads in challenging basic myths about teacher education and in documenting the processes of teacher learning involved (NCRTL 1992). Nonetheless, as cited in introducing this chapter, teacher education and teacher learning continue to be an "unstudied problem" (NCRTE 1988), particularly in the domain of language teaching (Freeman 1994a). While lack of knowledge and understanding are part of the issue, they are not the entire problem. Rather, the basic issues have been conceptual. It has been unclear what kinds of teaching will be the focus of research, how teaching derives from particular understandings of subject matter, student ages, and

---

5 These studies, known under the rubric of "Teacher Education and Learning to Teach," were part of large, multisite program funded by the U.S. Office of Educational Research and Improvement and conducted by the National Center for Research on Teacher Education at Michigan State University to examine pre- and in-service teacher education in a variety of subject matters (NCRTE 1988; NCRTL 1992). In its second five-year funding cycle, the Center was renamed to the National Center for Research on Teacher Learning, in part to focus on the more fundamental questions of teacher learning on which teacher education needs to be based (Kennedy 1991).

teaching contexts, or teachers' experience and background. Further, we do not know on what basis these understandings are developed and thus the role that teacher education plays – or can play – in the process. Therefore it remains difficult to forecast the relationship between research on teacher thinking and knowledge on the one hand, and learning to teach – through teacher education or other means – on the other. Lampert and Clark (1990: 21), in responding to Floden and Klinzing's discussion, couch this problem in terms of three critical questions:

> We would not disagree that teacher education would be improved if it were informed by research on practicing teachers' expertise. Yet this argument points to additional questions which need to be addressed if such reforms are to be effective: *What is expertise in teaching? How is expertise communicated from experts to novices? How do we decide who is an expert?* [emphasis added]

Although these questions have yet to be resolved, they are being addressed by interesting work in three areas: studies of teacher expertise and how it evolves, studies of the development of teachers' understanding of their subject matters, sometimes referred to as their "pedagogical content knowledge" (Shulman 1987), and studies of mentoring. All three strands of research focus on context, though each in a different sense of the word. In expertise research, the premise is that contexts of time, which we normally call experience, guide teachers' actions. Thus novice teachers are said to interpret their classroom worlds differently than their more experienced colleagues (Berliner 1988; Genburg 1992). In studies of subject-matter knowledge, researchers contend that contexts of place – the classroom in particular – profoundly shape what teachers know, so that knowledge derived from academic disciplines and knowledge from classroom experience are distinct (Grossman et al. 1989; Kennedy 1990). In studies of the mentoring process, researchers examine how teachers can learn in and through mentoring as an interpersonal context which brings novice and experienced teachers together for classroom-based professional education (Feiman-Nemser and Parker 1992).

The changes in perspective on teaching and teachers that have affected educational research since the mid-1970s have only recently begun to affect thinking and research in language education. Discussions of exploratory teaching (Allwright and Bailey 1991: 194–220), action research (Nunan 1991a), and teachers as researchers (Edge and Richards 1993) have begun to focus attention on language teaching in its own right and on the power of teachers to study it. While the development of this epistemological and sociopolitical agenda is a critical step, it has left uncharted the domains of teacher education and learning to teach. Here, although theoretical discussions about the nature and practice of language teacher education intensified during the 1980s, empirical inquiries lagged behind (Alatis et al. 1983; Clark 1984; Freeman 1989; Pennycook 1989; Prabhu 1990; Richards and Nunan 1990).

In language education, work has been hampered by the same dual challenge faced in general educational research. There has been the need to study, to understand, and in a sense to define, *teaching* independent of its outcomes; this includes coming to understand the role and person of the teacher, the place of language as subject matter, and the role of diverse contexts and learners. There has been a parallel need to study *teacher education* as the means of developing in teachers the capacity to teach. Since teaching is the subject matter of teacher education, and teachers are its learners in that context,[6] the two challenges are intertwined both conceptually and methodologically. This brings us to the second area of discussion, namely, the conceptual framework of such research.

The conceptual framework

In the task of understanding teacher learning in language teaching, research and theorizing in general education have provided a useful initial frame for the issues and an overall context in which to understand them. To recap: The development of the domain of teacher learning and teacher thinking since the early 1980s has raised sociopolitical questions about teachers and their role. It has also raised epistemological questions about the nature of what teachers know and how they learn it (Elbaz 1991). Throughout this period, there has been a concomitant methodological shift away from strict dependence on the process-product paradigm. The latter, which casts teaching as externally assessable behavior, is largely unproductive in understanding the inner, mental life of the teacher as well as the complex socio-cognitive environment of classrooms, schools, and communities in which learning to teach takes place. Thus the movement in research methodology toward a hermeneutic paradigm, which focuses on the perspectives of participants (often as contrasted with those outsiders), offers a means to examine the purposes, meanings, and interpretations of teaching (Shulman 1986).

The principal focus of the hermeneutic paradigm is on what people think and how they understand the worlds in which they live and act. Thus researchers endeavor to understand and interpret actions from the perspective of participants. Researchers examine teachers' mental processes (A), teachers' interpretations of their own actions (B), of students'

6 Freeman (1994a) presents a fuller discussion of this point, proposing a framework for the knowledge base of language teacher education.

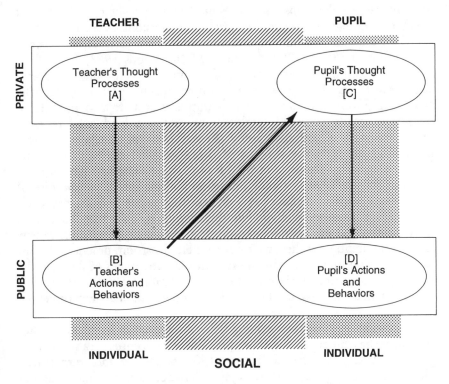

Figure 2. The hermeneutic research paradigm.

behaviors (D), and even what teachers think students think or believe (C)[7] as these intersect within the social world of the classroom. However, there are substantial conceptual and methodological issues to be grappled with in this research paradigm. Leaving aside the question of how to do such research, to which we will return in the final section of the chapter, the conceptual issues are themselves quite complex.

A central challenge has been to identify the form in which the teacher's thought processes will be represented. Recent research on language teaching has drawn on decision making as a framework to offer a cognitive map of the teacher's mental world and intentions while teaching, and to provide a means for the researcher to gain access to that world. The decision-making framework divides teachers' thinking into two broad categories: preactive decisions, or those made prior to teaching;

7   For example, the major work in U.S. curriculum reform in the teaching of mathematics and in science has focused on teachers' understanding of how students think about mathematical and scientific concepts and therefore where the sources of their misunderstandings in these subjects may lie (see, e.g., McDiarmid 1989).

and interactive decisions, or those made while teaching.[8] Studies of teacher planning have focused on preactive decisions, while those studies which examine teaching itself have tried to chart interactive decisions (e.g., Johnson 1992a, 1992b; Nunan 1992b; Woods 1993).

As a conceptual framework, decision making accomplishes several important things. It focuses research on the teacher and recognizes the central importance of his or her cognitive world. It also provides a methodologically accessible architecture that can lend itself to both qualitative and quantitative study. Researchers can categorize, document, and interpret the content of decisions, and they can compute frequencies, correlations, and the like for those decisions (see, for example, Johnson 1992b). Finally, decision making offers the promise of a potential point of contact between teaching per se and the processes of teacher education. Perhaps, the thinking goes, once they have been documented and understood, certain decision-making strategies can be taught to potential teachers to improve their classroom practices. In this sense, decision making seems to skirt problematic issues of defining the "best" or most appropriate methodology (Prabhu 1990), by offering instead a neutral view of the cognitive activity of teaching (Freeman 1989).

In decision making, the fledgling field of research in language teacher education has inherited the most prominent conceptual framework in teacher thinking (Clark and Peterson 1986; Shavelson and Stern 1981). However, it is important to recognize that decision making is neither the only, nor now the most prevalent, research construct for examining teacher thinking, teacher learning, or teacher education. While the clarity and neutrality of decision making as a construct is very useful, it is worth noting its limitations. These fall into three principal areas: the fixed nature of decision making as an a priori construct, the lack of attention to the socio-cognitive contexts of decisions, and the potential to overlook language as both the substance and the research vehicle for decision making. Even as we review these limitations, however, it is crucial to acknowledge the useful and productive nature of research in teachers' decision making and what it has, and can, bring to understanding teacher learning in general and language teaching in particular.

The first potential limitation has to do with the a priori nature of the construct. It must be noted that this concern holds for any construct that is brought to the research process, whether it is formally adopted beforehand or provides the conceptual backdrop for the study. It is, however, a concern that may be compounded when working within the

---

8 It is interesting to note that the distinction between the preactive and interactive phases in teaching was originally proposed by Jackson in his work, *Life in Classrooms* (1968: 151–152), discussed earlier.

hermeneutic paradigm, since such research focuses on how participants interpret their actions and their worlds. As an a priori construct, decision making proposes a highly structured view of teachers' mental lives, one which needs to be questioned from time to time. For instance, does all thinking take the form of decisions? What about the relation of the teacher's past experience to his or her present practices? Can the "storied" or narrative nature of thinking and understanding (Bruner 1990; Carter 1993) be adequately distilled in the binary world of pre- and interactive decisions? Lowyck, an early researcher in teacher thinking, voiced similar concerns as decision making took hold in that research domain (1986:184):

We divide complex teaching activity into a chronological dissection without attention to more meaningful categories. We emphasize isolated variables within the preactive, interactive, and post-interactive phases without great concern for the interaction between phases.

The second, and related, concern is how contexts of place and time shape what teachers think and do in their teaching, as well as how they learn to teach. Here it is possible that decision making may obscure the mutual influence of these areas. The issue of what is meant by context is a complex one, as we saw in the discussion of teacher expertise in the preceding section. Context, in the sense of place, can include classroom, school, community, and national levels that influence policies, expectations, and the technical cultures of teaching (Kleinsasser and Sauvignon 1992). Arguing the importance of such social contexts of place in understanding teachers and their work, Rosenholtz (1989: 2 – 3) notes:

Teachers, like members of most organizations, shape their beliefs and actions largely in conformance with the structures, policies, and traditions of the workaday world around them. . . . The ultimate social organizational variable [then] is the meaning that organization has for those who work within it. To understand schools, we must understand them as teachers do, that is, we must attempt to construe how schools appear to teachers who inhabit them.

Context, in its temporal sense, can include the longitudinal contexts of teachers' life histories and professional life spans (Kelchtermans 1993; Levine 1990) and how these influence the teacher's thinking about, and learning of, teaching. Together these contexts of place and time provide macro frames in which the defined processes of decision making operate. To fully understand teaching as decision making, one must grapple with and account for these frames of context.

The third area of concern has to do with the role of language itself, both substantively in teacher education and as a vehicle for research. The two issues are interrelated; they connect the development of teachers' views of teaching with how those views are studied. We know that language is a central socializing force and plays a key role in any learning, so we may ask about teachers' professional development: How does language work to shape teachers' learning in pre- and in-service contexts as well as in the contexts of their classrooms and schools? This raises the connected question of how to research the role of language in teacher learning and, likewise, what role language plays in such research. Decision making as a construct does not address either the role of language per se in teacher learning or the fact that, in the research process, teachers' decisions are documented in language; they are usually narrated verbally, recorded on audiotape, and written down.

In researching teacher learning, there is the question of what can be understood about the complex internal cognitive processes involved in teacher thinking and learning through close examination of linguistic data. This point turns on the complicated role of language as data, as the vehicle through which researchers gather teachers' thinking about their work (see Freeman 1994b). While decision making offers one important use of language to render teachers' thinking, there are clearly other avenues as well. Narrative studies, self-reflection and journal studies, and discourse-based studies, among others, provide alternative ways of construing teachers' mental worlds and of gathering, through the research process, language data about those worlds.

In this volume, decision making as a construct is represented effectively in the chapters by Burns (Chapter 7) and by Richards, Ho, and Giblin (Chapter 11). These two studies contribute in useful ways to our growing understanding of language teachers' learning and their thinking in practice. There is also work that represents alternative conceptual constructs in understanding teachers' mental worlds and their relationship to teaching practice. The chapters by Knesevic and Scholl (Chapter 4) and by Moran (Chapter 6) use narrative and biography as their central research constructs. The studies by Johnson (Chapter 2) and by Wallace (Chapter 13) are based in the ethnographic tradition of interviews and observations, focusing on understanding the teacher's experience and activities from his or her perspective. And the study by K. Bailey et al. (Chapter 1) uses reflective journals to examine a key concept in teacher learning – what teachers learn from their experiences as students.

There are also studies that examine social contexts in relation to teaching practices. Three chapters share the Hong Kong educational system as the venue and context of their research. Pennington (Chapter 15), Tsui (Chapter 5), and Kwo (Chapter 14) all look at interventions – in the form of specific training or more general teacher education programs – in the context of place. For Tsui the context is a specific Hong Kong classroom, while for Pennington and for Kwo it is the broader context of several schools within the Hong Kong community. Three studies examine how the context of time and experience relates to learning to teach. K. Bailey et al. (Chapter 1) and Gutiérrez Almarza (Chapter 3) consider, in very different settings and using distinctive research methodologies, how the experience of a being a student shapes one's teaching. Moran (Chapter 6) looks at time from the standpoint of experience and how one teacher transforms what she knows about teaching in one subject area into learning to teach in another.

The relationship between language and cognitive change in teacher development is the focus of three studies. Using classroom discourse combined with interviews and observational data, Ulichny (Chapter 8) presents a finely grained analysis of the teaching methodology in one classroom. F. Bailey (Chapter 12) and Freeman (Chapter 10) make use of similar research procedures to examine how teaching methodologies are learned, in the context of a course (F. Bailey) and a teacher education program (Freeman).

This pluralism in conceptual frameworks is not only useful and intellectually healthy, it is also critically important to evolving an understanding of the relationship between language teaching and language teacher education. Clearly, variety in conceptual frameworks and constructs lies at the heart of productive research within the larger hermeneutic paradigm. However, these differences, useful as they are, highlight certain fundamental methodological questions with which research on teacher education, and on teacher knowledge more broadly, is grappling. This leads to research methodology as the third and final area of discussion.

Appropriate research methodologies

It has become fairly commonplace in educational research to point out that how one observes and collects data shapes what one sees; however, this caveat is particularly apt in research on teacher knowledge. Indeed, because it deals with a cognitive world that is unseen, unheard, and only indirectly knowable, research on how teachers think and what they know is critically dependent on the conceptual frameworks it uses and the research methodologies it employs to gather data within those frameworks. To lay out this terrain, the distinction between first- and second-order research is very useful (Marton 1981). First-order research examines phenomena in the world with the assumption that accurate objective accounts can be established through carefully assembling and triangulating data from multiple sources. Thus, in first-order educational research, when teaching is studied as behavior or activity, the phenomena themselves – such as turn taking, classroom language, oral or written forms of discourse, or gender and participation, to name a few examples – are relatively clear. Likewise, the data documenting these phenomena are straightforward: audio- or videotapes can capture classroom participation, student classroom work captures written discourse, and so on.

Second-order research, on the other hand, shifts the focus to examine participants' perceptions of phenomena in the world. The aim is to uncover and to document these understandings, and not the phenomena themselves. Swedish researcher Ference Marton (1981: 178), who pioneered a form of second-order research known as "phenomenography," or phenomenological ethnography, makes the distinction as follows:

In the first, and by far most commonly adopted perspective, we orient ourselves towards the world and make statements about it. In the second perspective, we orient ourselves towards people's ideas about the world (or their experiences of it.) Let us call the former a *first-order* and the latter a *second-order* perspective. [emphasis in original]

Thus the existence and veracity of the data are clear in first-order research and therefore the focus is on competing forms of analysis to produce and corroborate different insights. Second-order research, however, must be explicit on two levels. It must define its data, whether they be teachers' decisions, narratives, reflections, or whatever, as well as how that data is gathered, analyzed, and interpreted. Because neither the data nor its analysis is self-evident in second-order research, these two levels – what the data are and how they are worked with – are interlocking and mutually contingent.

In the second-order study of teacher knowledge and thinking, any data are by nature indirect evidence of the internal mental processes and states that the researchers are seeking to document. For example, a first-order examination of turn taking might use tape recordings to capture the phenomenon in the world of the classroom. However, a corresponding second-order study of how teachers think about turn taking, how they perceive who talks in a language class, when, and why, might use data from interviews or stimulated recall based on videotapes of the class to capture the teachers' perceptions of the phenomenon. The direct connection between the data and the phenomenon in first-order research becomes an indirect and assumed connection in second-order work. Therefore the nature of the data itself and how they are gathered, analyzed, and interpreted are inescapably central concerns in the second-order research process (Freeman 1994b).

In establishing learning to teach languages as an area of inquiry, we are forced to grapple with each of these areas. The studies in this volume present a variety of positions on what constitutes external data for internal mental processes, as well as several different approaches to gathering, analyzing, and interpreting that data. But simply to observe that there are a variety of ways in which language teacher learning and thinking can be studied would be misleading. There are important commonalities in this research, commonalities that are captured in three fundamental methodological questions:

- What are the data, and how are they linked to the purposes of the study?
- How are the data gathered?
- How are the data analyzed and interpreted, and by whom?

Together these questions provide a framework for determining the general appropriacy of the research methodology in the study of language teacher thinking and learning. Table 1 summarizes the studies in this volume and may be a useful guide while reading the following sections.

What are the data and how are they linked to the purposes of the study?

The studies in this volume draw on a wide and conventional variety of qualitative data that include observation and field notes, both open-ended and structured interviews, documentary evidence, stimulated recall using videotape, audiotaped classroom language, and survey questionnaires. However, this variety of data-gathering techniques may obscure a basic commonality discussed in the preceding section, namely, that all the data are rendered in language. This is, in fact, a broader truth about educational research generally, and indeed most qualitative research in the social sciences. As teacher-cognition researcher Freema Elbaz (1987: 501) has observed: "What we know of [a teacher's] practice is actually researcher assertion: *We have access to practice only through the language we use to formulate what we have seen*" [emphasis added]. Language provides the pivotal link in data collection between the unseen mental worlds of the participants and the public world of the research process. In the study of teacher knowledge and the cognitive processes that are part of teaching, this issue is a central one since language is always used to express – and to represent – thought. Thus the ways in which language data comes about in a particular study are intimately connected to the purposes of the study; there is a crucial link between means and ends.

In the Knesevic and Scholl study (Chapter 4), for example, the authors report on their own learning of teaching through the experience of team teaching an intermediate Spanish class. Their data are the study itself, which documents their collaborative process. It reveals the public development of their private ideas about teaching and learning in order to expose what they come to understand about teaching through their

TABLE I. SUMMARY OF RESEARCH METHODOLOGY IN THE STUDY OF TEACHER LEARNING

How are data gathered?		How are data analyzed?		
Data source	Gathering	Analysis: stance	Analysis: process	Analysis: categories
Observation/ field notes	Time: "real" versus ex post facto collection	What is the researcher's relationship to the study?	How are data linked to analysis?	How is the interpretation of the data arrived at, and by whom? (see Figure 4)
Interviews				
Documentary analysis	Relation of researcher to data: (see Figure 3)	Participatory	Linear/ Iterative	Emic
Stimulated recall (videotape)	Emic	|		|
	|	|		Grounded
		|		|
Classroom discourse/ language data (audiotape)	Self-generated	Collaborative		Negotiated
	|	|		|
	Collaborative	|		|
	|	|		Guided
	Documentary	|		|
Survey data/ questionnaire	|	Declaratory		A priori
	Etic			|
				Etic

collaboration. Thus the study gives an account of their perceptions of their work together, one that depends entirely on the two participants, Knesevic and Scholl, as both the researchers and the researched. Richards, Ho, and Giblin (Chapter 11) is a very different study, one that uses interviews, observational data, and documentary evidence to examine what a group of student teachers learn in a particular form of pre-service teacher education, the Royal Society of the Arts Certificate course. Here the data are gathered externally to provide evidence of the participants' views of the course and what they learn from it, in order to offer insight into learning to teach in one form of preservice teacher education. An interesting middle ground between these two poles of self-reported data and analysis on the one hand and externally gathered data and analysis on the other is provided by Moran's study (Chapter 6) of how Katherine Russell educates herself to become a high school Spanish teacher. In this study, Moran develops a co-constructed narrative in which his data become the story of the interactions that he shares with Katherine Russell about her personal history as a language

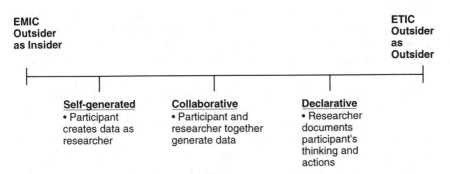

Figure 3. Sources of data and how they are gathered.

teacher. Unlike Knesevic and Scholl, these interactions would never have happened in the usual course of Katherine Russell's life as a teacher, had Moran not engaged her in the study. Unlike Richards, Ho, and Giblin, however, Moran's data show his hand as a researcher as he exposes the negotiated nature of the researcher-teacher interaction.

Figure 3 shows how the sources of data for second-order studies of teacher learning and knowledge and the methods of data gathering form a loose continuum which runs from *self-generated* data, as in the self-reported accounts and analysis in the study by Knesevic and Scholl, to *collaborative* data, as in the co-constructed narrative in Moran's study, to *declarative* data, as with the externally observed and assembled data in the study by Richards, Ho, and Giblin. These broad categories, each of which outlines a relationship between the source of the data and how it is assembled, give more explicit definition to the basic *emic-etic* distinction in qualitative research which lays out the relationship between participant and observer. Since, as we have said, all data in second-order research provide indirect evidence of the phenomenon under investigation, the central issue is how those data are made public. At its core, the choice of *self-generated, collaborative,* or *declarative* data concerns how private, internal information becomes publicly accessible through the research process. This choice is closely tied to the researchers' particular purposes in the study; it also provides a bridge to the second question.

How are the data gathered?

The question of how the data are gathered is a deceiving one. On one level, it encompasses mechanical or procedural issues which, in documenting the cognitive dimensions of teaching, are linked to the critical question of time. First-order information, such as classroom language, field notes, or videotapes, might be called *real-time data* because they capture external evidence of teaching and learning. These data do not, as we have said, provide access to the perceptions, thinking, or decision making that underlie the particular act of teaching. Therefore, *ex post facto data*, such as stimulated recall, journaling, or interviews, and procedures that are usually gathered immediately after the lesson, are used to reconstruct the teacher's thought processes about his or her teaching from a retrospective viewpoint. Given the unavoidable lapse between the actual teaching and the data collection, these data are by nature always incomplete because they are collected after the act of teaching is finished. However, since this factor is common to any study that relates thought to action, one can reasonably argue that the issue of time lies in the structure of the research process and is not intrinsic to the data themselves.

Further, certain research designs can mitigate the role of time in gathering second-order data. Longitudinally designed studies that gather data repeatedly over an extended period can help to build an ongoing, and thus potentially more coherent, second-order picture. Thus time can serve as an important way to triangulate data. Researchers can also draw on data that are not time sensitive, such as documentary evidence – lesson plans, curricula, or materials written for purposes outside the research process – or general data, such as background interviews. These sources are less susceptible to the relation between time and action and thus can provide a broader background and context for the teacher's cognitive activity. Further, they can also serve as an important means of triangulation.

Studies in this book exemplify these various types of data collection. F. Bailey's study (Chapter 12) uses *real-time* classroom language data as a way to document what student teachers are learning from one another about teaching through the group work in a methodology course. Ex post facto data figures in the study of a trainee, Maja (Chapter 2), in which Johnson uses stimulated recall to gather data about what Maja is learning from her practicum experience. Similarly, in Chapter 7, Burns uses interviews to query the understandings of teachers who are learning to work with beginning language students. Several studies use data that are not time sensitive to develop a richer view of teachers' learning and thinking. In Chapter 3, Gutiérrez Almarza uses interviews to probe the various experiences that contribute to how student teachers learn to teach Spanish in British secondary schools. Similarly, in Chapter 5, Tsui uses interviews and documentary evidence to examine the experience of a teacher who is learning to use process writing in her classes. Like the research reported in this book, data gathering in studies of teachers' learning and thinking hinges on a fundamental distinctionbetween *real time* and *reflected time*. On a procedural level, the distinction focuses on when the data are gathered; on a methodological level, however, it captures the central issue of the relation between thought and action, and how language depicts that relationship.

How are the data analyzed and interpreted, and by whom?

To a certain degree, data analysis in research on teacher thinking and learning reflects the issues of what the data are and how the data are gathered. In data analysis and interpretation I include three elements: *stance, process,* and *categories.* By *stance* I mean the attitude the researcher adopts toward participants in the study in analyzing the data; by *process* I refer to the way in which the data analysis unfolds throughout the research process. Both stance and process are binary choices. The researcher can adopt a *participatory* stance or a *declarative* one. In the former, the researcher includes the teacher as a participant and co-analyst of the data; in the latter, the researcher handles the analysis with little or no further input from the teacher. The *process* of data analysis can be *linear,* in which the researcher progressively breaks down the data, analyzes them, and arrives at findings. Or the researcher can work with the data in an *iterative* fashion, breaking them down, assembling meanings, and then returning to the data to verify and extend those meanings, and so forth.

Both stance and process in data analysis are shaped by the choice of *categories* which the researcher uses. The literature on data analysis in qualitative research (Miles and Huberman 1994; Strauss 1987) commonly distinguishes between grounded and a priori categories of analysis. *Grounded categories* are developed from, and hence are "grounded" in, the data themselves, with the researcher trying to limit as much as possible prior assumptions about what may be significant. A *priori categories,* on the other hand, are used as a framework to organize and classify the data so that findings emerge as responses in these previously determined areas. Thus an open-ended interview produces data that can be analyzed into grounded categories, while a questionnaire or survey usually generates data according to the a priori categories by which it is designed.

In actuality, the concepts of grounded and a priori form the two poles of a continuum of data analysis that includes at least two other significant types of categorization, which I call *negotiated* and *guided* (see Figure 4). *Negotiated categories* are those which the researcher and the teacher develop through a participatory, and usual iterative, analysis of the data. These may begin as grounded categories, but they ultimately need to be confirmed by both parties, thus creating a process in which meanings are negotiated. Similarly, *guided categories* are shaped by interaction with the data. While they spring from a priori categories that

Donald Freeman

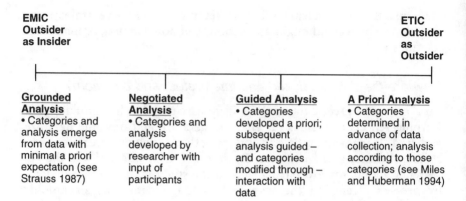

Figure 4. Data analysis and interpretation.

previous knowledge and experience might suggest about the topic, they respond to what the researcher actually finds in the data. Thus negotiated and guided categories each represent modified versions of their pure counterparts at either end of the continuum.

In the actual practice of research, however, nothing is this clear or straightforward. The binary distinctions between participatory and declaratory stances, and between iterative and linear processes of analysis, are often interwoven in the service of good research. Guided by their purposes, by the complexity of the cognitive phenomena that they set out to study, and by the strengths and limitations of the human settings in which these phenomena are found, researchers make choices. The studies in the book display the full range of such choices. In the study of their "apprenticeship of observation" as language learners, K. Bailey and her colleagues (Chapter 1) take a clearly participatory stance as they study their own experience collaboratively. The analysis in their study is highly iterative, as they return to their data repeatedly to develop and test the grounded categories that structure their findings. In contrast, Pennington's study of the innovation of process writing in Hong Kong secondary schools (Chapter 15) assumes a declaratory stance and a linear process of data analysis that uses a framework of very useful a priori categories. The difference in these two studies is entirely appropriate and illustrates how data analysis must match the means of a study with its ends. K. Bailey and her colleagues mean to probe their own experiences and practices as teachers, thus leading to the grounded, iterative, and highly participatory approach to their data. Pennington, on the other hand, sets out to understand how a particular innovation plays out within a specific educational community and setting. Thus she uses a more linear, a priori, declarative form of data analysis. Table 1, earlier, summarizes this discussion of research methodology in the study of teacher learning. It can provide a framework through which to approach and to read critically the studies in this book.

Towards new issues in validity

The research on teacher learning examines a complex human phenomenon: what teachers know about teaching and how they learn it. This phenomenon is to degrees both individual and social, intrapersonal and interpersonal; likewise, it is both immediate and longitudinal, as well as idiosyncratic and normative. Thus it is critical to recognize that no single research formula will suit its study. To argue otherwise would be reductionist and simplistic. It would place the rigidity of the research process over the complexity of the human phenomenon under study. However, there are criteria against which we can scrutinize such research in order to establish its validity. These criteria are proposed in the three questions outlined in the preceding section: What are the data? How are the data gathered? How are the data analyzed and interpreted, and by whom? Each of these questions must be understood within the context of an overarching question: How are these choices of data and procedure linked to the purposes of the study?

These criteria are clearly broader that those invoked in more traditional treatments of validity, but it should be noted that such traditional treatments, which usually include apparent (or face) validity, instrumental (or criterion) validity, and theoretical (or construct) validity, derive from the enduring influence of the process-product paradigm (Kirk and Miller 1986: 22ff; also Maxwell 1992). While they may be suited to studies of behavior and action in classrooms, they can become problematic when research enters the realms of thought, meaning, and subjective understandings of public actions.

Arguments are sometimes raised against this broader definition of validity primarily because it is based on what some consider subjective forms of data. However, the crucial issue may center on the notion of validity itself. When research enters the domain of meaning, hermeneutic analysis, and interpretation, the alignment of traditional categories may no longer serve. There is a need to view validity in such research as a judgment that links the participants, the researchers, and the wider community that uses the research. Educational researchers who make use of narrative have proposed the test of trustworthiness as a means of assessing such linkages (Mishler 1990: 419).

The essential criterion for such judgments is the degree to which we can rely on the concepts, methods, and inferences, of a study, or a tradition of inquiry, as the basis of our own theorizing and empirical research. *If our overall assessment of a study's trustworthiness is high enough for us to act on it, we are granting the findings a sufficient degree of validity to invest our own time and energy.* [emphasis added]

In this view, validity is linked to action rather than to the creation of a canon of what are sometimes termed "objectively truthful findings." Assessments of validity are based on what one does about what one knows. This view is especially apt in teaching and teacher education, where interpretations must connect to action in classrooms and with students. However, these judgments share the standard that they continue to reflect the particular inquiry, the trustworthiness of what has been understood, how it has been studied, and by whom.

Studying "the unstudied problem"

The proposals in this chapter are intended to frame both the fifteen specific studies in this book and, more broadly, the emerging field of research in teacher learning to the field of language teaching of which they are a part. The framework addresses three areas: the antecedents for such work in general educational research and in research in language teaching, the central conceptual issues facing such work, and the research methodologies that are appropriate to its study. As such, the chapter provides both a map of some of the specifics in the studies reported in the preceding chapters as well as a framework for this new area of research.

The research in this book is intended to further our understanding of what language teachers know and how they learn to teach. It should also help to establish these topics as an important field of inquiry and study. Language teaching and language teacher education have long been an "unstudied problem" in which traditional practices, conventional wisdom, and disciplinary knowledge have dominated. These practices and assumptions have been subject to little critical scrutiny and less organized study. The research reported in this volume is an important step in addressing this situation. More important perhaps, the fact of such research in learning to teach languages, as well as the methodologies by which it is carried out, serve to open an important area of inquiry and to begin the study of an "unstudied problem."

References

Alatis, J., P. Strevens, and H. H. Stern (eds.). 1983. *Applied Linguistics and the Preparation of Second Language Teachers: Toward a Rationale.* Washington, D.C.: Georgetown University Press.

Allwright, D. 1988. *Observation in the Language Classroom*. London: Longman.

Allwright, R. L. 1984. Why don't learners learn what teachers teach? – the interaction hypothesis. In D. M. Singleton and D. G. Little (eds.), *Language Learning in Formal and Informal Contexts*. Dublin: IRAAL, pp. 3–18.

Allwright, R., and K. Bailey. 1991. *Focus on the Language Classroom*. New York: Cambridge University Press.

Bailey, K., and D. Nunan (eds.). 1996. *Voices and Viewpoints: Qualitative Research in Second Language Education*. New York: Cambridge University Press.

Berliner, D. 1988. *The Development of Expertise in Pedagogy*. Washington, D.C.: American Association of Colleges for Teacher Education.

Bruner, J. 1990. *Acts of Meaning*. Cambridge, Mass.: Harvard University Press.

Carter, K. 1993. The place of story in the study of teaching and teacher education. *Educational Researcher* 22(1): 5–12, 18.

Chaudron, C. 1988. *Second Language Classrooms*. New York: Cambridge University Press.

Clark, C., and P. Peterson. 1986. Teachers' thought processes. In M. Wittrock (ed.), *Handbook of Research on Teaching*, 3rd ed. New York: Macmillan, pp. 255–297.

Clarke, M. 1984. On the nature of technique: What do we owe the gurus? *TESOL Quarterly* 18(4): 577–594.

Dunkin, M., and B. Biddle. 1974. *The Study of Teaching*. New York: Holt, Rinehart & Winston.

Edge, J., and Richards, K. (eds.). 1993. *Teachers Develop, Teachers Research*. Oxford: Heinemann.

Elbaz, F. 1991. Research on teacher's knowledge: The evolution of a discourse. *Journal of Curriculum Studies* 23(1): 1–19.

Eggleston. J. 1979. Editorial introduction: Making decisions in the classroom. In J. Eggleston (ed.), *Teacher Decision-Making in the Classroom: A Collection of Papers*. London: Routledge and Kegan Paul, pp. 1–7.

Feiman-Nemser, S., and M. Parker. 1992. Mentoring in context: A comparison of two U.S. programs for beginning teachers. East Lansing, Mich.: National Center for Research on Teacher Learning.

Floden, R., and H. G. Klinzing. 1990. What can research on teacher thinking contribute to teacher preparation: A second opinion. *Educational Researcher* 19(5): 15–20.

Freedman, S., J. Jackson, and K. Boles. 1983. Teaching: An imperilled "profession." In L. Shulman and G. Sykes (eds.), *Handbook of Teaching and Policy*. New York: Longman, pp. 261–299.

Freeman, D. 1989. Teacher training, development, and decision-making: A model of teaching and related strategies for language teacher education. *TESOL Quarterly* 23(1): 27–45.

1994a. Educational linguistics and the education of second language teachers. In J. Alatis (ed.), *Proceedings of the 1994 Georgetown University Roundtable on Languages and Linguistics*. Washington, D.C.: Georgetown University Press, pp. 180–196.

1994b. The use of language data in the study of teachers' knowledge. In G. Handal, I. Carlgren, and S. Vaage (eds.), *Teachers' Minds and Actions*. London: Falmer, pp. 77–92.

1995. Redefining the relationship between research and what teachers know. In K. Bailey and D. Nunan (eds.), *Voices and Viewpoints: Qualitative Research in Second Language Education.* New York: Cambridge University Press.

Freeman, D., and J. C. Richards. 1993. Conceptions of teaching and the education of second language teachers. *TESOL Quarterly* 27(2): 193–216.

Genburg, V. 1992. Patterns and organizing perspectives: A view of expertise. *Teaching and Teacher Education* 8(5/6): 485–496.

Grossman, P., S. Wilson, and L. Shulman. 1989. Teachers of substance: Subject-matter knowledge in teaching. In M. Reynolds (ed.), *Knowledge-Base for the Beginning Teacher.* New York: Pergamon Press and the American Association of Colleges of Teacher Education, pp. 23–36.

Halkes, R., and J. Olson. 1984. *Teacher Thinking: A New Perspective on Persisting Problems in Education.* Lisse, Netherlands: Swets and Zeitlinger.

Jackson, P. 1968. *Life in Classrooms.* New York: Holt, Rinehart & Winston.

Johnson, K. 1992a. Instructional decisions of preservice ESOL teachers: New directions for teacher preparation programs. In J. Flowerdew, M. Brock, and S. Hsia (eds.), *Perspectives in Second Language Teacher Education.* Hong Kong: City Polytechnic of Hong Kong, pp. 115–134.

1992b. Learning to teach: Instructional actions and decisions of preservice ESOL teachers. *TESOL Quarterly* 26(3): 507–536.

Kagan, D. 1988. Teaching as clinical problem-solving: A critical examination of the analogy and its implications. *Review of Educational Research* 58(4): 482–505.

Kelchtermans, G. 1993. Getting the story, understanding the lives: From career stories to teachers' professional development. *Teaching and Teacher Education* 9(5/6): 443–456.

Kennedy, M. 1990. *A Survey of Recent Literature on Teachers' Subject Matter Knowledge.* East Lansing, Mich.: National Center for Research on Teacher Learning.

1991. *An Agenda for Research on Teacher Learning.* East Lansing, Mich.: National Center for Research on Teacher Learning.

Kirk, J., and M. Miller. 1986. *Reliability and Validity in Qualitative Research.* Newbury Park, Calif.: Sage.

Kleinsasser, R., and S. Sauvignon. 1992. Linguistics, language pedagogy, and teachers' technical cultures. In J. Alatis (ed), *Linguistics and Language Pedagogy: The State of the Art.* Washington, D.C.: Gerogetown University Press, pp. 289–301.

Lampert, M., and C. Clark. 1990. Expert knowledge and expert thinking in teaching: A response to Floden and Klinzing. *Educational Researcher* 19(5): 21–23, 42.

Levine, S. 1990. *Promoting Adult Growth in Schools.* Boston: Allyn & Bacon.

Long, M. 1980. Inside the "black box": Methodological issues in research on language teaching and learning. *Language Learning* 30: 1–42.

Lortie. D. 1975. *Schoolteacher: A Sociological Study.* Chicago: University of Chicago Press.

Lowyck, J. 1986. Post-interactive reflections of teachers: A critical appraisal. In Ben-Peretz, M., R. Bromme, and R. Halkes (eds.), *Advances in Research in Teacher Thinking.* Lisse, Netherlands: Swetz & Zeitlinger, pp. 172–185.

Marton, F. 1981. Phenomenography: Describing conceptions of the world around us. *Instructional Science 10*: 177–200.

Maxwell, J. 1992. Understanding and validity in qualitative research. *Harvard Educational Review 62*(3): 279–300.

McDiarmid, G. W., D. Ball, and C. W. Anderson. 1989. Why staying one chapter ahead doesn't really work: Subject specific pedagogy. In M. Reynolds (ed.), *The Knowledge-Base for Beginning Teachers.* Elmsford, N.Y.: Pergamon, pp. 193–206.

Miles, M., and A. M. Huberman. 1994. *Qualitative Data Analysis*, 2nd ed. Thousand Oaks, Calif.: Sage.

Mishler, E. 1990. Validation in inquiry-guided research: The role of exemplars in narrative studies. *Harvard Educational Review 60*: 415–442.

National Center for Research on Teacher Education [NCRTE]. 1988. Teacher education and learning to teach: A research agenda. *Journal of Teacher Education 39*(6): 27–32.

National Center for Research on Teacher Learning [NCRTL]. 1992. *Findings on Learning to Teach.* East Lansing, Mich.: NCRTL.

National Institute of Education [NIE]. 1975. Teaching as clinical problem-solving. *Report of Panel #6; National Conference on Studies in Teaching.* Washington, D.C.: NIE.

Nunan, D. 1991a. *Understanding Second Language Classrooms.* Englewood Cliffs, N.J.: Prentice-Hall International.

1991b. Methods in second language classroom-oriented research: A critical review. *Studies in Second Language Acquisition 13*(2).

1992a. *Research Methods in Language Learning.* New York: Cambridge University Press.

1992b. The teacher as decision-maker. In J. Flowerdew, M. Brock, and S. Hsia (eds.), *Perspectives in Second Language Teacher Education.* Hong Kong: City Polytechnic of Hong Kong; pp. 135–165.

Pennycook, A. 1989. The concept of method, interested knowledge, and the politics of language teaching. *TESOL Quarterly 23*(4): 589–618.

Prabhu, N. S. 1990. There is no best method – Why? *TESOL Quarterly 24*(2): 161–176.

1992. The dynamics of the language lesson. *TESOL Quarterly 26*(2): 225–241.

Richards, J. C., and D. Nunan (eds.). 1990. *Second Language Teacher Education.* New York: Cambridge University Press.

Rosenholtz, S. 1989. *Teachers' Workplace: The Social Organization of Schools.* New York: Longman.

Shavelson, R., and P. Stern. 1981. Research on teachers' pedagogical thoughts, judgments, decisions, and behaviors. *Review of Educational Research 51*: 455–498.

Shulman, L. 1986. Paradigms and research programs in the study of teaching. In M. Wittrock (ed.), *Handbook of Research on Teaching*, 3rd ed. New York: Macmillan, 3–36.

(1987). Knowledge-base and teaching: Foundations of the new reform. *Harvard Educational Review 57*(1): 1–22.

Shulman, L., and A. Elstein. 1975. Studies in problem-solving, judgment, and decision-making: Implications for educational research. *Review of Educational Research (3)*: 3–42.

Strauss, A. 1987. *Qualitative Analysis for Social Scientists*. New York: Cambridge University Press.

Suppes, P. (ed.). 1978. *Impact of Research on Education*. Washington, D.C.: National Academy of Education.

Sutcliffe, J. 1977. Introduction to the volume on classroom decision-making. *Cambridge Journal of Education* 7(1): 2–3.

Woods, D. 1993. *Processes in ESL Teaching: A Study of the Role of Planning and Interpretative Processes in the Practice of Teaching English as a Second Language (Occasional Papers #3, 1993)*. Ottawa: Centre for Applied Language Studies, Carleton University.

Author index

Subject index

Research index

a priori construct, 362

case study format, 53, 154, 159, 174, 178, 219, 223, 229, 282
cross-case analysis, 223, 229, 302, 311–312
further readings on, 220
multiple case studies, 299
collaborative research, 8, 12, 26–27, 156, 169, 175, 179–180
collaborative data, 369
teaching as, 79ff., 94–95
writing in, 13, 23–25

data analysis
a priori categories, 51, 206, 224, 373
categories in, 53, 157, 245
COLT system in, 206
concurrent analysis and collection, 205
content-analysis procedure, 157
cross-case analysis, 53, 223, 302
deductive, 53
discourse analysis, 184ff., 217–218, 227, 260ff.
further readings on, 220
grounded categories, 371
inductive, "grounded," 32, 53, 224, 225, 229
internal reliability in, 206
processes of, 371
questionnaire, 326
schema of, 54
data gathering and collection, 52, 126, 130, 156, 199–200, 223, 242, 244, 261, 301–302
alternative constructs in, 364

assessment questionnaire in, 344–346
classroom language as, 180
documents in, 203
ex post facto data, 370
judgment sampling, 201
in professional projects, 284
researcher notes in, 203
self-reports in, 244–245, 314–315
sources, 99, 369
stimulus recall, 32, 52, 156–157, 203
task grid in, 203

ethnography, participant-observation procedure, 32, 130, 261
etic perspective, 356

"first-order" versus "second-order" research, 222, 238, 299, 365–366

hermeneutic paradigm, 360–361

interviews, 75, 126, 148, 156–157, 180, 204–205, 229–230

language in data collection, 367
language learning autobiography, 12, 14, 22, 23, 25

narrative research, 121, 126
analysis of, 125
further references on, 123
stories, 80, 81, 93, 94, 125, 130, 153

observation, data gathered in, 126, 156, 202